Alaa
Atan

Diversity and Difference in Childhood

Diversity and Difference in Childhood

Issues for Theory and Practice

Second edition

Kerry H. Robinson and Criss Jones Díaz

Open University Press

Open University Press
McGraw-Hill Education
8th Floor
338 Euston Road
London
NW1 3BH

email: enquiries@openup.co.uk
world wide web: www.openup.co.uk

and Two Penn Plaza, New York, NY 10121-2289, USA

First published 2005
First published in this second edition 2016

A catalogue record of this book is available from the British Library

ISBN-13: 978-0-33-526364-6
ISBN-10: 0-33-526364-X
eISBN: 978-0-33-526365-3

Library of Congress Cataloging-in-Publication Data
CIP data applied for

Typeset by SPi-Global

Fictitious names of companies, products, people, characters and/or data
that may be used herein (in case studies or in examples) are not intended
to represent any real individual, company, product or event.

Printed and bound by CPI Group (UK) Ltd, Croydon, CR0 4YY

Praise for this book

"This thoughtful, topical book addresses a considerable range of diversity issues relevant to teacher educators, their students, and other professionals who work with children and their families within and beyond Australia. Indigenous issues including language maintenance and revival have particular relevance within postcolonial nation states. Other issues of international relevance include: identities and retention of community languages, gender equity, childhood and sexuality, poverty and inequalities, and related policies. The writing is critical, scholarly, and engaging. This timely second edition draws on the authors' longstanding teacher education experiences, and their most recent research, to revisit the challenges of diversity and difference in children's lives".

Dr Valerie N. Podmore, former associate professor,
Faculty of Education and Social Work, the University
of Auckland, New Zealand

"The second edition of Robinson and Jones Díaz's Diversity and Difference in Childhood *is a thoroughly welcome addition to my list of key texts for students of early childhood and childhood studies. It provides a means from the outset for educating undergraduate students from within critical postmodern and post structural perspectives – thus orienting their views of and actions within their future professions towards critical and equitable practices that value difference rather than treat is as a problem to be solved.*

Furthermore, for practitioners who find themselves questioning modernist constructions of children, development, difference, diversity and their work, the book provides a thorough grounding in frameworks and tools that will help them re-theorise what they are doing whilst simultaneously supporting them towards positive change."

Alexandra C. Gunn, Associate Dean (Teacher Education),
University of Otago College of Education, New Zealand

"This is the 21ˢᵗ century early childhood education text. **Diversity and Difference in Childhood** *provides early childhood educators and scholars a powerful space for asking social justice questions in a profoundly innovative way. Diversity and difference in childhood is not a 'traditional' early childhood conversation. As the authors appropriately suggest, this book is for educators to challenge taken for granted knowledges/practices and to take "personal and professional risks for social justice".*

Veronica Pacini-Ketchabaw, Ph.D., Professor,
School of Child and Youth Care, University of Victoria, Canada

"This new edition of **Diversity and Difference** *is both important and timely. There is a new urgency to some emerging childhood issues, including those associated with childhood sexuality, and a distinct lack of critical resources to inform the debate. This book helps fill this gap. Undertaking a major revision and incorporating new material, the authors have ensured the book's continued relevance and renewed significance in the very dynamic context of childhood studies. The book makes an important contribution to resourcing explorations of the many difficult and complex issues associated with childhood in a globalised yet differentiated world. Readers will find the new theoretical resources and additional chapters that have been included give the book a sense of enhanced rigour and its depth and breadth of coverage make it an ideal resource for a wide variety of interests and perspectives."*

Christine Woodrow, Associate Professor and
Senior Researcher, the Centre for Educational
Research, Western Sydney University, Australia

Dedication

Kerry would like to dedicate this book to four very special wonder kids: Elliot James Hansen-Burns, Charlie Patrick Carlsen, Aliana Cristyn Minassian, and Matthew and Tan Davies' baby daughter arriving imminently . . . the future is yours.

Criss would like to dedicate this book to her two children, Dominic and Miguel Jones Díaz and her partner Ramon Díaz Gomez. Their creative, imaginative and inventive approach to life is a true inspiration for me in my work.

Contents

Acknowledgements

Kerry and Criss would like to thank the following people who have contributed in many different ways to this second edition. We very much appreciate the many hours of support and direction offered by Rosemary Noble in initially getting this second edition off the ground. We thank the anonymous reviewers who provided very thoughtful feedback on the proposal for this second edition – their academic and collegial generosity and time, are very much valued. We also thank Fiona Richmond from Open University Press, for her editorial leadership across both the first and second editions of *Diversity and Difference*; and thanks to the many other Open University Press personnel who have supported the production of this book – it has been a long and fruitful partnership.

We would like to thank Professor Jayne Osgood for her willingness to write the foreword for this second edition. It is a privilege to have this professional endorsement from Jayne. We are equally honoured and thankful for the endorsements from Dr Valerie Podmore and Associate Professor Christine Woodrow.

The writing of books is often supported by a number of excellent research assistants. Thanks and appreciation for many hours of hard work goes to Lesley Wright, Dan Perell, Jawed Gebrael and Georgia Ovenden for their literature searches, reading of drafts, editing skills, meeting our deadlines, formatting and perseverance with 'the log' – you are all outstanding early career academics.

We believe that book covers are an integral component of the overall intellectual project, making important artistic statements reflective of ideas and feelings captured within. The picture on the first edition, called 'Mardi Gras', a reflection of diversity from a child's perspective, was designed and drawn by Criss's son Dominic Jones Díaz, when he was (6 years old). We have continued this familial trend on the cover of this second edition with a drawing titled 'Fire' by Ramon Díaz Gomez, Dominic's father and Criss's partner. We thank Dominic and Ramon for sharing these very special images with us.

As always Criss and Kerry would like to acknowledge the educators, parents and children who have participated in their various individual and collaborative research projects over the years that have informed this book. Their perspectives and voices are always respected and appreciated in our work.

Finally, we are also forever indebted to those we live with on a daily basis, who keep us going, who care and nurture us through those "I'm never going to get there" moments, who contribute hours of reading and commenting on drafts, and who share in the thrills of a completed project – Kerry would like to especially thank Cristyn Davies; Criss would especially like to thank Ramon Díaz Gomez.

Foreword

The theoretically rich but practically informed approach taken by Kerry Robinson and Criss Jones Díaz in the second edition of Diversity and Difference in Childhood: Issues for Theory and Practice, makes it a must-read for everyone involved in work with young children. In the intervening ten years since the first edition early childhood classrooms have become spaces where neoliberal demands for accountability, measurability and standardization have increased exponentially and act to divert attention from what might be learnt from children about the complexity of childhoods lived in the twenty-first century. Despite policy and curricular reform (e.g. DEEWR, 2009) which claims to have improved the 'quality' of provision and the 'professionalism' of the workforce (both hotly contested and internationally debated issues, see for example, Cannella et al., 2015; Jones et al., 2016) childhood educators find themselves with ever increasing demands for performativity and less space for criticality and creativity (see Osgood, 2012). Meanwhile, for many children their understandings of themselves and their place within the world is ever more expansive and experimental. There is an urgent need for adults working with children to understand childhood as a space where borders can be crossed and a place where multiple ways of being, seeing, doing and becoming are routinely occurring (for a discussion of this see Osgood, 2015).

The ways in which early childhood teachers come to understand themselves, the children that they work with, and the nature of work with young children are constantly being fabricated through policy, curricular and media discourses. In this text, Robinson and Jones Díaz expose these discourses and how they work on subjectivities to limit and contain; they offer the reader the means to identify and critically reflect on how such discourses play out in their everyday practices and relationships with(-in) communities, with families and with young children. It is imperative that early years educators make space within and through their daily negotiations, with children and families, to grapple with diversity and difference and this book offers a robust and accessible means to embrace that task.

The authors recognize the political situatedness of contemporary global childhoods and attend to issues that are unlikely to find space in other books on early childhood because they are considered too risqué; taboo or irrelevant. The authors make a persuasive case for the reasons issues such as indigeneity, racism, immigration, refugees; bi/multilingualism, neoliberalism, social class and poverty; gender, sexuality and homophobia should be fundamental concerns to early years teachers. Children are of the world, their engagements with diversity and difference are everywhere and are constantly being reworked from routine daily entanglements with people, places, events and matter. For example, something as routine as a bus journey can expose a child to diversity and difference in terms of 'race', social class, age, (dis)ability, gender and sexuality in ways that adults cannot know but crucially, that they must not dismiss as unimportant or irrelevant. Anyone working with children has a responsibility to take them seriously and recognize their interconnectedness to the worlds of which they form part. Childhood educators are arguably amongst the most important adults in children's lives – as the authors stress, they are in a position to make a positive difference to the lives of children and their families but crucially, through exercising critical reflexivity, they are afforded opportunities to challenge and disrupt normalizing discourses – through the ways in which the curriculum is delivered, policies implemented, and the pedagogies used – and through the routine conversations and events that occur every day in the in-between spaces. Robinson and Jones Díaz offer the means to watch, hear and listen to what children say and so engage in halting conversations; conversations that might stop educators from re-inscribing taken-for-granted ideas that children neither understand nor need to be concerned about diversity and difference. This book opens up possibilities and provides the resources adults need to work with children in respectful ways on issues that they shape and in turn, are shaped by.

This book provides a comprehensive introduction to key issues and theories which can facilitate a socially just approach to working with children. It is intended to support early years and education professionals to develop capacities to become critically aware of the taken-for-granted ideas about children and childhood that are so prevalent in Australia, but which are also relevant in many other international contexts. The chapters underscore the important need to engage with policies, perceptions and practices in ways that expose diversity and difference and its relevance to contemporary childhoods. Each chapter benefits from practical scenarios, informed by examples from the authors' research, and theorized through a range of critical frameworks.

The passion and commitment to social justice sings from every page of this book – the authors push for a broad and deep appreciation of diversity and difference so that early childhood educators can develop broad and deep critical dispositions towards working with children and their families in ways that can make a worldly difference (Haraway, 2008). By providing carefully theorized accounts of practical examples of ways to exercise social justice practices in work with young children, the authors have crafted a book that has the potential to make real and lasting differences to the thoughts and practices of early childhood professionals, students and researchers.

Professor Jayne Osgood

Middlesex University, London, UK

References

G.S.Cannella., M. Salazar Perez & I, Lee. (2016) (Eds). *Critical Examinations of Quality in Early Education and Care.* New York: Peter Lang.

Department of Education, Employment and Workplace Relations (DEEWR) for the Council of Australian Governments (2009). *Belonging, Being, Becoming: The Early Years Learning Framework for Australia.* ISBN 978-0-642-77873-4.

Haraway, D.J. (2008).*When species meet.* Minneapolis: University of Minnesota Press.

Jones, L., Osgood, J., Holmes, R. & Urban, M. (2016). 'Reimaging Quality in Early Childhood', in *Contemporary Issues in Early Childhood.* March 2016 17(1) pp3-7, first published on February 3, 2016, doi:10.1177/1463949115627912

Osgood, J. (2012). *Narratives from the Nursery: negotiating professional identities in early childhood.* Maidenhead: Routledge.

Osgood, J. (2015). 'Reimagining gender and play' in J. Moyles (Ed). *The Excellence of Play (4th Edition).* pp.49-60. Milton Keynes: Open University Press.

1

Changing paradigms and theory in childhood education: critical perspectives on diversity and difference in childhood

Writing this book

This book is based primarily on the research we have conducted together and separately around issues of equity and social justice in childhood education in Australia over the past 20 years. It is also based on our experiences as pre-service teacher educators working with early childhood students for the past two decades in a metropolitan university in Sydney, in one of the most culturally and linguistically diverse communities in Australia. Over the past three years, Kerry Robinson has continued her work in the field of childhood studies and gender and sexuality studies, but has shifted her employment focus with pre-service teachers to working with students in the School of Social Sciences and Psychology. Many of these students take up employment as social welfare workers, child psychologists, and government and community-based professionals working in children and family services. Criss Jones Díaz has retained her focus working with pre-service early childhood and primary teachers in the School of Education. Her research interests have expanded beyond the field of languages education to diverse literacies, cultural studies, critical 'race' theory and postcolonial studies. Despite the fact that it is Australia-based research we undertake, we feel that the issues we are dealing with are equally relevant to childhood educators and community-based professionals elsewhere in the world. The social, political and economic factors that are impacting on children and their families, as well as the social inequalities that continue to plague the lives of many of these families, are operating on both global and local scales.

Our joint research has focused on exploring early childhood educators' perceptions of diversity and difference, and the impact these have on pedagogy, policies and practices. Through the utilization of surveys and individual interviews we have focused on early childhood educators' perceptions and practices around issues of gender, multiculturalism, bilingualism, sexuality, Aboriginality, family and social class issues, as well as how early childhood institutions incorporate these equity issues into their policies and organizational practices. Unfortunately, a book of this scope, which critically examines difference and diversity within a social justice agenda in education, cannot deal adequately with all the relevant social, political and economic issues facing children and their families. Consequently, the different foci of the chapters are a representation of our combined and separate areas of research expertise, particularly in the areas of bilingualism, diverse literacies, multiculturalism, racism, gender, sexuality, family, childhood, social class issues, asylum seeker and refugee issues, globalization and neoliberalism. It is these areas that we feel that have particular international relevance and significance.

It is also important to highlight that childhood educators and community-based professionals are heterogeneous groups from a variety of backgrounds, with a multiplicity of perspectives and voices based on their different locations within social discourses that operate around diversity and difference. Consequently, the perspectives and voices presented in this book do not speak for all childhood educators and community-based professionals, but rather represent the dominant discourses prevailing among those educators, other staff, resource workers, children and their families, and pre-service teachers with whom we have worked in Australia over the past decade or so.

The state of play

The international fields of childhood education and community service provision are currently experiencing a major challenge to the authority of many of the long-standing traditional theories and practices that have been utilized in approaches to children and children's learning. This challenge has stemmed largely from the new sociology of childhood, critical psychology, historical anthropology and cultural historical psychology, critical theory, critical 'race' theory, cultural and postcolonial studies, new materialism, and the utilization of queer and feminist postmodernist/poststructuralist frameworks, which call for educators, researchers and others working with children to begin to reconceptualize their understandings of childhood and their work with young children. Consequently, many of the universalized 'truths' about 'the child' established in modernist perspectives and underpinning taken-for-granted or common-sense assumptions about childhood and what it means to be a child, are being seriously critiqued and disrupted by these new and different ways of understanding children as subjects.

This book has been written in the light of these significant and exciting social and educational changes, and is a contribution to the growing body of work that aims to reconceptualize childhood, childhood education, and the delivery of child and family-based services. These perspectives have particular significance for understandings of diversity and difference, social inequalities, and for doing social justice education with children and their families. Utilizing a feminist poststructuralist approach, informed by other social theories, including queer, critical, cultural and **postcolonial** theories, we explore the possibilities these perspectives have for extending understandings of childhood, constructions of **identity**, and the negotiation of power that underpin social relationships and perpetuate social inequalities, as well as for personal, institutional and social transformations.

Since the late 1980s there has been a significant increase in awareness of the importance of childhood education policies, practices and curriculum positively reflecting the diverse cultural identities of children and their families. Today, this embracing of the diversity that exists in children's lives is a central feature of the different philosophies that broadly underpin childhood education in Western countries – for example, those encompassed within the *anti-bias curriculum* that emerged from the United States (Derman-Sparks and the ABC Task Force 1989) and in the perspectives of Reggio Emilia, stemming from Europe (Dahlberg, Moss and Pence 1999). Recently, in Australia, the first national curriculum, the Early Years Learning Framework Australia (EYLFA) (DEEWR 2009), has had an important impact in providing a set of principles, practices and learning outcomes that are informed by a variety of theoretical perspectives including critical theories, socio-cultural theory and poststructural theories to emphasize the notion of being, belonging and becoming in children's lives.

Such philosophies that enhance and foster diversity and difference are critical in a world that is encountering broad social, cultural, economic, political and technological shifts that are continually challenging and changing the lives of children, their families and communities at both global and local levels. In this book we are particularly concerned with how and to what extent these philosophies, founded on concepts of pluralism, inclusion and democracy, are put into practice on a daily basis in early childhood institutions. How diversity and difference are perceived and taken up by individual childhood educators and community-based professionals, and are included and articulated into everyday policies and practices with children and their families is critical. It is important to address social justice and equity issues. To date, there is a growing body of research on how childhood educators' perspectives of diversity and difference impact on their pedagogy, and how institutional policies and practices either disrupt or perpetuate the social inequalities that exist broadly in society.

This book is also a reflection of our growing concern with the potential impact that the global movements of neoliberalism, neoconservatism, and the marketization and corporatization of childhood can have on children, families, and childhood education and child/family community services. Of particular concern is the growing homogenization of social, cultural and linguistic identities of children and their families. Discourses of neoliberalism and neoconservatism have the potential to seriously impact on what knowledge is included in programmes, how it is to be taught, the recognition and inclusion of cultural diversity and difference, and the abilities of families, particularly from low socio-economic backgrounds, to meet the financial commitments of their children's early education. The marketization of childhood and early education is about shareholder profits, rather than the quality of service provision.

Hence, within the discourse of neoconservatism, which operates in tandem with neoliberalism, diversity and difference become problematic, as they are perceived to undermine Western values and traditions regarded as essential to the prevention of the social decay that is seen to be operating in society. Consequently, within this discourse, founded on the cultural **binary** opposition of us/them, a fear of the **Other** is maintained and perpetuated. The impact of these discourses is already being felt in childhood education throughout the world – for example, the vigour with which standardized testing has been taken up in the early years, and the economic spin-offs that have been captured by corporate bodies in preparing children to meet the requirements of such testing (Cannella and Viruru 2004). Further, parental anxiety fuelled by the impact of parenting literature heavily informed by child development theory, has led to a preoccupation with ensuring that children meet all the necessary 'milestones of development' at the 'right time'. Moreover, the recent censorship and moral panic in Australia of the showing of the documentary *Gayby Baby*, directed by Maya Newell, depicting the lives of four children growing up in same-sex families, highlights the need for further critical work on sexualities in childhood education in Australia. In Chile, the scandal caused by the publication of *Nicolas has two Daddies* [*Nicolas tiene dos Papás*], which resulted in an attempt by evangelicals to have the book banned from distribution, highlights entrenched homophobia apparent in right-wing Christian groups in Chile.

Children's perceptions of difference

The childhood years (from birth to age 12) are formidable in terms of the growth and development of cognition, language, social, emotional and physical competence. This development takes place within different social contexts, where issues related to human diversity and difference impact significantly on children's learning and understandings of and ways of being in the world (Kontopodis, Wulf and Fichtner 2011). Over the past 20 years, research has increased educators' awareness of the discrimination that can be experienced by young children for being different, and of the discrimination that children can hold and perpetuate towards those who are perceived as different from themselves and the dominant culture. This research highlights that, by the time children enter primary schooling, their perceptions of difference largely reflect and perpetuate the dominant racialized, linguicized, gendered, sexualized, classed and (dis)ableized body **stereotypes** and prejudices that prevail in the broader society (Blaise 2010; Jones Díaz 2011; Buchori and Dobinson 2012; Gunn 2015).

Children do not enter early childhood programmes as empty slates, but rather bring with them a myriad of perceptions of difference that they have taken up from their families, peers, the media and other social sources, and negotiated in the representations of their own identities. Robinson (2013) found that 3 and 4 year olds can have strong opinions on what is appropriate gender behaviour for males and females. This behaviour was linked to heteronormative understandings of gender. For example, a 4-year-old girl challenged a 3-year-old boy who was initially adamant that two boys could get married. The battle continued between the two about who was right or wrong, until the girl stood up declaring that she was right because she had never seen it before and that she was bigger than the boy. In the early 1990s Glover (1991) found that, as 2- and 3-year-old children become aware of differences, they simultaneously develop positive or negative feelings about the differences they observe. For example, racial awareness is developed early in young children, impacting on their perceptions of skin colour, and on their preferences in the social relationships they initiate and foster with other children (Palmer 1990) (see also Chapter 6). Glover (1991) reports that children frequently exhibited negative behaviours towards children from different racial backgrounds: refusing to hold their hands, never choosing to play with dolls from different racial backgrounds and always picking same-'race' pictures for collages. An Australian study by Palmer (1990) clearly illustrated how preschool children were able to make negative evaluative judgements based on racial characteristics. In Palmer's study, the non-Aboriginal children made negative comments such as 'Blackfellas dirty', and children were reported as saying 'You're the colour of poo . . . Did your Mum drop you in the poo?' and 'Rack off wog. We don't want to play with you' (cited in Glover 1991: 5). Kutner (1958) found that racial prejudice in young children affects their ability to make sound judgements, and often their perception of reality is distorted. By age 3–4 years they are becoming more aware of ability and other differences, and are developing critical understandings of their own identities, as well as the diversity and differences of others. Bredekamp and Rosegrant (1991) pointed out that 2 year olds are already aware of and curious about differences and similarities among people, and they construct 'theories' about diversity congruent with their cognitive stages of development and life experiences.

As children grow older, other differences, such as language variation and linguistic diversity, become obvious. Children become aware that speakers use different language codes and literacy practices in different contexts, and bilingual children are highly aware of contextual differences in their use of languages (Genesee 1989; Lanza 1992; Falchi, Axelrod and Genishi 2014). Lanza (1992) investigated the language use of her bilingual 2 year old, and found that the child was able to separate the two languages or mix them according to the social expectations and context of the language used. Non-bilingual children also demonstrate an awareness of language differences, and comments such as 'He speaks funny' or 'I don't understand her' are not uncommon.

Early childhood educators in our combined research largely perceive children's prejudice more as the passive reflections and expressions of adults' values towards difference, rather than as representations of the narratives and perceptions of the world that children, as individual agents, own themselves. This perspective is reflected in the following remarks: 'Children aren't aware of these things unless it is pointed out to them by adults'; 'Children's prejudices are just a reflection or a mimicking of what they directly pick up from adults' behaviour'; 'They don't really understand what it means, they just say it.' Dominant discourses of childhood that constitute children as too young to engage in or understand discriminatory practices or power, as naturally blind to differences, and as passive recipients who soak up adults' perceptions and values, are still highly influential in children's education.

However, in recent years, primarily with the influence of poststructural perspectives shifting understandings of childhood and constructions of identity, research has highlighted how children play a critical and active role in the constitution and perpetuation of social inequalities through their perceptions of the world and everyday interactions with one another and with adults (Alloway 1995; Devine, Kenny and Macneela 2008; MacNaughton 2009; Blaise 2010; Ringrose and Renold 2010; Robinson 2013; Priest et al. 2014; Jones Díaz 2015, 2016).

Walkerdine (1990) found that 4-year-old boys were capable of yielding power, based on the way they repositioned their female teacher within the discourse of 'woman as sex object'. They utilized derogatory sexual language and explicit sexual references to undermine her power as an adult and a teacher. Research conducted by Alloway (1995), which studied the construction of gender from preschool to grade 3, consistently reported incidences in which boys employed subtle forms of manipulation to constitute themselves as the dominant gender. Such examples include preschool boys throwing objects at girls as they played on outdoor equipment, and harassing them by lifting up their skirts and commenting on their underwear. In MacNaughton and Davis's (2001) study of non-Indigenous children's understandings of Indigenous Australians, their findings revealed how non-Indigenous children drew on processes of colonial 'othering' to position Indigenous Australians as exotic, creating the binary of 'us' and 'them'.

Hierarchies of difference: childhood educators, diversity and social justice

Childhood educators and community-based professionals are in an ideal position to make a positive difference in the lives of children and their families. This is possible not only on the broader level of advocating for their rights, but also challenging and disrupting normalizing discourses through the curriculum that we teach, the policies that inform our practice and the pedagogies that we utilize in teaching children. However, the location of childhood educators and community-based professionals within the various discourses of diversity and difference that are available to them will impact on how they perceive these issues and approach them with children and their families. Educational institutions, government organizations and community-based services are microcosms of the broader society; many constitute and perpetuate the normalizing discourses that underpin social inequalities through professionals' practices, educational programmes, educators' pedagogies, the hidden curriculum and everyday interactions. There is often great ambivalence and contradiction surrounding various forms of diversity and difference that exist in society, resulting in what we have called a hierarchy of differences (or comforts). The existence of this hierarchy is a reflection of the different degrees of commitment given by individuals and institutions to the provision of equity across the spectrum of civil risks or social justice issues that exist (Robinson and Jones Díaz 2000; Robinson and Ferfolja 2001; Robinson 2013). It is also a reflection of the varying levels of comfort experienced by individuals and institutions, associated with different equity issues in society. Contradictory practices around diversity and difference are often based on normative assumptions about people, their social behaviours and their entitlements to justice, especially if they choose to step outside what are widely considered socially acceptable conventions in society. For example, gay and lesbian equity issues are often located at the bottom of the hierarchy of differences. The research of Kobayashi and Ray (2000: 402) echoes the findings in our research: they talk about a 'hierarchy of rights', highlighting that institutions responsible for setting public policy and providing public services, such as health care, social services benefits and education, 'represent a network that also functions ideologically to determine what kinds of risk are more or less acceptable and what levels of risk will be publicly tolerated'. Similarly, these researchers point out that many rights are controversial and not all receive the same support, recognition or priority, acknowledging that a 'spectrum of political ideologies' results in 'varying degrees of commitment to equity provision' (Kobayashi and Ray 2000: 406).

Some childhood educators and community-based professionals, who have strong commitments to social justice and equity issues such as 'race', languages, ethnicity, gender or (dis)ability, for example, can ironically uphold homophobic and heteronormative values and practices when it comes to dealing with sexuality (Robinson and Jones Díaz 2000). This slippage or contradiction around doing social justice work is not surprising when individuals are viewed as shifting subjects. Within the feminist poststructural context, subjects are viewed as irrational, contradictory and complex beings that change and shift discursively according to different contexts across periods of time (Weedon 1997; Blaise 2009; Osgood 2012; Ferfolja, Jones Díaz and Ullman 2015). Individual subjects are constantly negotiating the power relations operating through the different discourses available to them; therefore their locations can change according to the context in which they are operating. Locations within discourses are primarily influenced by the personal investments that individual subjects have in being positioned in one discourse over another. As Robinson (2013) has previously pointed out, the variation in comfort around diversity issues may be related to a number of factors, including an individual's own identity, their experiences or lack of experiences with difference, their knowledge about difference, their religious and cultural values, their positioning in sexist, heterosexist, homophobic and racist discourses, and so on.

The notion of a hierarchy of differences, or of rights, poses some critical questions for childhood education and community-based professionals in terms of how the field approaches social justice issues. There is still a lot of reflexive work that needs to be done in terms of addressing minority rights. This is especially so when some social justice issues – for example, sexuality – continue to be excluded from programmes and considered, in some contexts, unworthy of the same respect and democratic principles privileged to other equity issues. With regards to Aboriginality, the preoccupation is still focused on deficit discourses and superficial approaches, deflecting from critical contemporary issues such as Indigenous languages education and constitutional recognition. There is still a long way to go from 'tolerance' to respect. Further, the perception of children as critical thinking active citizens in their own right, with valuable contributions to make to families, communities and society more generally, is often over-shadowed by traditional and normative understandings and constructions of childhood as a period of innocence, powerlessness and incompetence (Steinberg 2011; Robinson 2013). For many educators and community-based professionals in our research, broad social, political and economic factors contributing to social inequalities, and significantly impacting on the lives of children and their families, are considered marginal to the 'world of children'. Rather, they are perceived to be adults' issues from which children, in the name of prolonging their 'innocence', need to be protected.

Childhood educators and community-based professionals are tradi-tionally taught to value families as an important resource and, in order to do this, they must recognize that their perceptions, values and beliefs about family diversity will directly impact on their work with children. Relationships developed between staff and families will depend on how the educator interacts with diverse and different religious practices, sexual preferences of families, child-rearing practices, language differ-ences, gendered practices, ability levels and socio-economic backgrounds of families. Jones Díaz (2003) argues that it is crucial that early childhood educators acknowledge the **intersections** between identity and difference in understanding the multiple ways in which children and families negoti-ate everyday lived realities through which they experience their identity.

For professionals working with children and families there is a need to recognize the various power dimensions that operate between them-selves, children and the different families using their services. Families placing their children in the care of educators do so in the trust that their children's needs and interests will be met. Families can often feel alien-ated, silenced and marginalized when their experiences and perceptions of the world are not included and represented in their children's education.

Shifting paradigms in early childhood education: a historical overview

The following discussion provides an introductory historical overview of the paradigmatic shifts that are currently impacting on early childhood education that we have alluded to so far in this chapter. We have found that many early childhood educators have limited knowledge and experience with social theories, despite a major focus of their roles involving working with and advocating for the rights of families from diverse socio-cultural backgrounds. This discussion identifies the main issues and the critical points of difference between **postmodern** and modernist thinking relevant to our various discussions in this book.

The Enlightenment, humanism and scientific 'truth'

To understand the paradigmatic shift that is impacting on early childhood education in the twenty-first century we have to go back as far as the Enlightenment period, which began in Europe in the eighteenth century. The Enlightenment, as the word suggests, was considered to be an awakening from a bleak period of human existence, known as the Dark Ages, which began in medieval times. The Dark Ages represented a time when brutality reigned and dominant knowledge was founded on ancient superstitions and medieval Christianity. The Enlightenment, in contrast, is represented as a period of intellectual awakening sparked by geographical discovery and the scientific revolution in which new knowledge associated with mathematics, astrology, physics, biology and anthropology emerged. Based on scientific 'fact' or 'truths', this new knowledge revolutionized the way in which the world was viewed, including the position of 'man' within the universe and the role of God. This period also saw the emergence of Western philosophy, which extended the Enlightenment from greater understandings of the natural world into the social realm of human relationships and interactions. It was perceived that not only could science discover the natural order of the world and the laws that governed it, but also such knowledge and laws could also be discovered about human beings and what it meant to be human. The Enlightenment gave way to the notion of a universal human history united by the common ideals of human reason and rationality, progress and perfection, all reinforced by and founded on scientific 'truths' (Erickson and Murphy 2003). It was within this context that positivism emerged, which is an outlook that promoted detached, 'value-free' science as the model for social scientific inquiry – that is, scientific objective truth. The insistence that human beings have the capacity to engage in reason and rationality, leading to moral and intellectual progress and ultimately perfection, became the ideal behind what is known as humanism, as well as the foundation stone of modernist thought. Erickson and Murphy (2003: 40) aptly define these concepts:

> Reason referred to the exercise of human intellect unfettered by authoritarian faith, including faith in religion. Progress referred to the resulting positive direction of historical change, opposite to the direction presupposed by medieval Christianity, which considered humanity degenerate and fallen from the grace of God. Perfectibility referred to the final outcome of reason and progress, which, according to Enlightenment thinkers, would lead to steady improvement of human conditions on Earth.

Many different intellectuals and social and political groups have taken up these humanist principles since the late eighteenth century. They were the rallying cries of the French Revolution and often the slogans of social reform, even today.

Marxism, social class and ideology

The failure of the French Revolution to deliver a new egalitarian world, based on the values of humanism, plunged Europe into a period of conservatism that lasted for many decades. It was a period in which the middle and upper classes of Europe and Britain continued to prosper at the expense of the working classes, who grew more unsettled as a result of their exploitation. The Industrial Revolution of the nineteenth century entrenched **capitalism** as an economic and social system throughout the world – a system in which the consequences of the inequitable distribution of wealth and access to resources, including land, which excludes and exploits the majority of the world's people, continue to be seen today. It was within this context of the social and political unrest in nineteenth-century industrial Britain and Europe that Marxism as a political movement found its roots. Marxism, in its various forms, has had a profound impact on the world's politics, particularly in terms of theorizing social inequalities and social change.

Karl Marx (1818–83) and Friedrich Engels (1820–95) were the cofounders of Marxism, which basically upheld that true social equality was possible through a workers' revolution in which the capitalist state system would be overthrown and replaced by a communist social and economic system run by the people, for the people. Marxism, an economically based social theory, is considered a grand narrative or a universal theory in which a particular perspective provides a totalizing and universalizing explanation of the events at its focus. For Marx and Engels the structure of reality was embedded in the material base of economics. They considered human thoughts, actions and institutions to be determined by their relationship to the means of production – that is, how one makes a living in the material world (Erickson and Murphy 2003).

Social class was viewed as the organizing principle in modern societies and the primary context in which inequality and relations of power operated. Social class distinction was based on a binary relationship between those who own the means of production (that is, those who own and control the land, factories, businesses, multinational corporations and so on), the ruling class or bourgeoisie, and those who work for them (the ruled workers or proletariat). This relationship is perceived to be one constituted within conflict and exploitation, where the owners of the means of production exploit workers to gain the greatest profit from the resources and/or the goods they produce. Social power is linked to those who have access to and control of the means of production in a capitalist society – that is, the ruling class.

Marxist theorists view power as primarily being repressive, negative, and universally and monolithically yielded by the state, which ultimately operates to keep the ruling class in power. State institutions such as schooling (including early childhood education) perpetuate ruling-class ideologies that reproduce the values and practices that keep them in power. Marxist theory continued to be a major political movement well into the mid-twentieth century, spreading its influence beyond the borders of Britain and Europe into other parts of the world, including North America, South America and Australia. Neo-Marxist perspectives (new versions of Marxist thought) are utilized today by some social theorists, to theorize social inequalities in globalizing capitalist economies throughout the world.

Feminisms, patriarchy, women's subordination

There are several strands of feminist theory (for example, **liberal**, radical, socialist, **poststructuralist**) and each provides a different explanation of how gender operates in society to structure broad social power relations between men and women. Most, except for feminist poststructuralism, tend to view power as primarily operating through a patriarchal social system where men exploit women, children and some men; thus gendered inequalities need to be addressed through major structural changes in society. Socialist feminists take the perspective that this patriarchal social system works jointly with the economic system of capitalism to exploit women, particularly in the workforce, but also more generally in society. Thus, gender tends to be viewed as the main organizing principle behind power and inequality in society, with other sites of inequality, 'race', ethnicity, social class, sexuality, and so on, intersecting with gender.

The women's movement in the 1960s began to question the taken-for-granted gender relations in society in which women tended to be viewed as being generally oppressed by a patriarchal system. The workforce was one sphere where women tended to be restricted to low-paid, low-status service positions, did not receive equal pay for the same work, and experienced a glass ceiling in the way of promotion into management positions. The division of society into the feminized private sphere of the family and the masculinized public sphere of the economy and politics was upheld as an artificially constructed division of power between men and women. The private patriarchal nature of the family was challenged as a particular source of women's inequality and **oppression**, especially in terms of widespread domestic violence. Feminisms challenged the view that men's power over women was the natural order of things and that women's lot in life was determined by their biology – that is, that women were naturally mothers and carers of children and family.

The emergence of postmodernism and poststructuralism, anti-humanism and challenges to scientific 'truths'

The social theories outlined above are considered grand narratives – that is, they tend to provide monolithic universal explanations of social relationships and of power. For example, in many feminist perspectives, the oppression of women by men was considered the primary form of power and inequality that women experienced in their lives, and this tended to be universalized to all women. Such universalized macro-explanations of power have provided valuable foundations on which to view social inequalities, but they are limited in that they do not provide an adequate means through which to understand micro-relations of power, or power as multifaceted, shifting and contextually changing, and as constitutive of performances of identity. They tend to view power negatively, and individuals as its 'victims', rather than looking at the positive and productive exercise of power in people's lives.

Consequently, there was a need for an explanation of power that theorizes not only how power operates in broader social structures, but also on the complex micro levels in individuals' lives; that provides insights into how individuals negotiate power every day in different contexts. Individuals are not always powerless; indeed, power can change across contexts, where one may have more power in one instance, but less in another. Thus, power is contextually located, shifting and fluid. Intellectuals began to seek out different ways of theorizing social power and inequalities within new social movements.

Social unrest in Europe, epitomized in the student riots in Paris in the late 1960s, marked the emergence of new social movements in Europe, the United States and other parts of the world. These new political movements included feminism, gay and lesbian liberation, and black civil rights, which 'emerged in response to the oppressive effects on social and personal life of capitalism, the state, and the pernicious ideologies such as sexism, racism, and **homophobia**' (Best and Kellner 1991: 24). One of the major theoretical shifts to find support among these new political movements at this time was postmodernism, which reflected a growing dissatisfaction with the ability of humanism and universal social theories such as Marxism to adequately explain contemporary society and its diverse modes of power (Best and Kellner 1991).

Many intellectuals and political groups associated with the new social movements rejected Marxism as being 'too dogmatic and narrow a framework' to theorize the diverse modes of power that operated in contemporary society (Best and Kellner 1991: 24). As a social theory, Marxism did not adequately deal with the multiple sources of oppression and relations of power associated with other sites of identity (for example, gender, sexuality and 'race') that were not irreducible to the exploitation of labour; nor did it adequately deal with the micro-politics of everyday interactions, which was considered the essential focus of the success of political struggles by postmodern theorists. Thus, postmodern theorists were drawn to these new social movements, proposing that there needed to be a decentring of political alliances, replaced by a focus on 'difference' and recognition of the various perspectives and experiences among and within social groups; as well as focusing on the micro-political struggles of everyday life. For example, postmodernists were critical of the women's movement's universalized perspective that women's oppression was the sole result of patriarchal oppression, which led to their powerlessness – that is, women's oppression and subordination were the result of a patriarchal social structure or system, in which men had supreme power, as well as controlling access to resources and opportunities, keeping women subordinated and powerless.

Hence, postmodernists challenged the very concept of 'woman' as a universal and unifying term, pointing out that it failed to recognize the differences among women in terms of their 'race', ethnicity, sexuality, social class, and so on, that impacted on their diverse experiences of inequality or oppression, as well as their power or powerlessness. Thus, postmodernists presented important new avenues for politicizing social and cultural relations, based on what Best and Kellner (1991: 25) identify as 'radical democracy'.

What is postmodernism?

The text uses movement instead of theory

Postmodernism is an intellectual and cultural movement that has gained prominence since the mid-twentieth century, significantly reconceptualizing how identity, the subject (the self), power and difference are theorized. Postmodernism primarily provides a critique of modernist perspectives, which have dominated since the Enlightenment, producing new models of thought. However, postmodernism is not a homogeneous mode of thought; it incorporates a range of perspectives, with some extreme versions totally severing any intersections with modernism. Some others view the prefix 'post' as misleading as some versions have relationships with modernist views, but operate to disrupt and radicalize what they see as the difficulties and barriers of modernist thinking. According to Best and Kellner (1991: 181), 'The discourse of the postmodern is a borderline discourse between the modern and the postmodern that allows a creative restructuring of modern theory and politics.'

What is poststructuralism?

Poststructuralism is part of the matrix of postmodernism; it is a 'subset of the broad range of theoretical, cultural, and social tendencies, which constitute postmodern discourses' (Best and Kellner 1991: 25). The German philosopher Friedrich Nietzsche (1844–1900) provided the theoretical premises of many postmodern and poststructuralist critiques. Nietzsche, critical of the modernist humanist and positivist principles that emerged during the Enlightenment, 'attacked philosophical conceptions of the subject, representation, causality, truth, value, and system, replacing Western philosophy with a perspectivist orientation for which there are no facts, only interpretations, and no objective truths, only the constructs of various individuals and groups' (Best and Kellner 1991: 22). In poststructuralist theory (as in postmodernism more generally) primacy is given to discourse theory, which we discuss in depth in Chapter 2. Discourse theorists, such as the French philosopher and historian Michel Foucault (1926–84), argue that meaning is not simply given but is socially constructed across a number of institutional sites and practices. Discourse theorists emphasize the material and heterogeneous nature of discourse, and analyse the institutional bases of discourse, the viewpoints and positions from which people speak, and the power relations these allow and presuppose. Discourse theory also interprets discourse as a site and object of struggle where different groups strive for **hegemony** and the production of meaning and **ideology** (Best and Kellner 1991: 26). Sawicki (1991: 20) points out that the focus of poststructuralism is on the 'myriad of power relations at the micro level of society'. Poststructuralism is primarily concerned with language, signs, images, codes and signifying systems, which organize the psyche, society and everyday social life but, as Sawicki points out above, this perspective is linked to broader social, political and economic institutions that also make up the social body. This point is also reinforced by Foucault, who views the social body as 'a thoroughly heterogeneous ensemble consisting of discourses, institutions, architectural forms, regulatory decisions, laws, administrative measures, scientific statements, philosophical, moral and philanthropic propositions – in short, the said as much as the unsaid' (Foucault 1980: 184).

A feminist poststructural approach

The emergence of postmodern and poststructuralist perspectives, reflected in the new sociology of childhood and the reconceptualization of the early childhood education movement, has created different spaces and lenses through which the production of new knowledge about children as subjects is made possible. Feminist poststructuralism is the main theoretical framework that is utilized in this book and is outlined in depth in the following chapter. This perspective provides an invaluable approach to dealing with diversity and difference with both adults and children, and allows for an understanding of how inequalities are played out differently in different situations. In terms of understanding the social inequities that exist in society, feminist poststructuralist perspectives allow for the following critical analyses and understandings:

- knowledge as being partial and constituted within discourses
- identities and individual subjectivities as constituted within social discourses, and as negotiated, shifting, complex and contradictory
- power as a process, operating through social discourse that is practised and negotiated by individual subjects at both the macro (institutional) and micro (everyday life) levels in society
- individual subjects having **agency** in their lives, rather than being passive and powerless 'victims'
- social inequalities as constituted within and perpetuated through the social discourses historically and culturally available to individual subjects
- childhood as a socially constructed concept that is constituted in the social discourses historically and culturally available to individual subjects
- how individual subjects perpetuate social inequalities through their everyday interactions and practices
- how change is possible through the processes of altering citational practices, **deconstruction** and reflexivity.

Consequently, feminist poststructuralist perspectives provide a different critical lens through which to theorize contemporary society, to understand the constructions of individual subjects, to negotiate the politics associated with identity differences, to explore the diverse modes of power that operate in society at both the macro (broad societal and institutional context) and micro (everyday personal interactions) levels that underpin the vast inequalities that exist, and to explore possibilities for individual and social transformations. Further, feminist poststructuralism allows us to effectively develop understandings of the way that individual subjects negotiate and construct their own identities, to challenge normalizing discourses that operate on micro and macro levels in their lives, and to demonstrate how individual subjects are instrumental in the perpetuation of social inequalities.

Critical to feminist poststructuralist perspectives is the process of the construction of **subjectivity** – that is, the 'self'. This process of subjec-tification is crucial to an understanding of the different perspectives, or 'truths', that we take up as our own ways of looking at the world; these 'truths' become the foundations of our judgements of and interactions with others in the world. For educators, an awareness of this process is paramount to a reflexive understanding of the way their perspectives are constructed, and impact on the way they interact in the world and, more specifically, interact with other educators, children and their families. As Davies (1994: 3) aptly points out:

> An individual's subjectivity is made possible through the discourse s/ he has access to, through a life history of being in the world. It is possible for each of us as teachers and students to research the process of subjectification in order to see its effect on us and on the learning environments we collaboratively produce.

Feminist poststructural perspectives have provided a means through which to move beyond the limitations of modernist perspectives in order to view the complexities, contradictions, contextuality, and shifting nature of power and subjectivity, critical to an understanding of difference, political struggle and inequality.

Other social theories influencing this book

Apart from our work being primarily influenced by feminist poststructur-alist perspectives, other social theories, and particular social theorists, have also been utilized to inform our various analyses of identity, rela-tions of power and social inequalities. For example, the works of Michel Foucault, Pierre Bourdieu, Judith Butler, Stuart Hall and Michael Apple have been critical to the development of our perspectives and approaches to diversity and difference, and doing social justice education. Foucault's concepts of 'regimes of truth', the knowledge/power nexus and discourse are outlined in depth in Chapter 2. Bourdieu's concepts of **cultural capital**, **habitus**, **field** and symbolic violence are also important and useful theoretical concepts that inform our discussions of social inequal-ity and have been incorporated across the chapters (see Chapters 4 and 8). Overall, we take an eclectic approach to social theory, supporting the perspective that 'a combination of micro- and macro-theory and politics provides the best framework to explore contemporary society with a view to radical social transformation' (Best and Kellner 1991: 298). The following social theories are particularly relevant to our work.

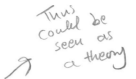

This could be seen as a theory

Cultural studies

Cultural studies comes from theoretical tenets of neo-Marxism, emphasizing the significance of class and capitalist relations within cultural analysis (Davis 2004). The works of Stuart Hall (1996) and Homi Bhabha (1994, 1998) have contributed significantly to our understandings about how knowledge and representation work to define and construct identities. Cultural studies provides an analysis of representation, examining how knowledge is situated in and applicable to specific immediate political and historical circumstances, particularly in relation to issues of representation. Hall's critical examination of representation through media, texts, imagery, language, discourse and ideology as an instrument of social power is an important principle in cultural studies.

Three important concepts emerge within cultural studies that examine issues of identity and representation. They are **diaspora**, **hybridity** and **'third space'**, which articulate our contemporary cultural reality of blended or mixed cultural and racial identities in our society. The term 'diaspora' denotes dispersal and scattering of cultural groups. In our contemporary world, diaspora and the identities through which it is produced are a result of globalization and migration that are embedded in contexts and constructs of identity (Vertovec and Cohen 1999; Bloomaert 2013). The term 'hybridity' signifies a two-way borrowing and lending between cultures. It involves fusion and the creation of a new form, set against the old form of which it is partially made up (Young 1995). Hybridity comes into existence at the moment of cultural, linguistic and social practice, in which meaning is articulated both from within past and present cultural histories and trajectories. Bhabha (1994, 1998) builds on ideas of hybridity and diaspora through his notion of the 'third space' to articulate new possibilities created out of difference that 'initiates new signs of identity, and innovative sites of collaboration and contestation' (1994: 1).

Consequently, in many nation states with super-diverse populations, the diasporic and hybrid reality of blended cultural, racial and linguistic identities remains a significant contribution to the increased diversity in many local and global communities. Hence, hybridity and diaspora inform our work in helping us understand the complexities in how identity is articulated and represented across a terrain of intersecting and often contradictory points of self and group expression.

Postcolonial theory

Since all postcolonial societies, including Australia, have experienced the full impact of neocolonial domination, this theoretical framework influences our social justice research and equity work in relation to constructions of childhood, identity, diversity and difference. It is part of a growing body of literature in childhood education that aims to reconceptualize

childhood, primarily through the disruption of Western hegemonic modernist assumptions constituted within dominant colonizing discourses.
These colonizing discourses continue to perpetuate oppositional thinking
associated with 'common sense' knowledge around cultural binaries such
as Western/non-Western, white/black, civilized/primitive, adult/child.

Postcolonial studies critiques the cultural hegemony of European
knowledges and centres on the historical fact and consequence of
European colonialism (Ashcroft, Griffiths and Tiffin 2013). Postcolonial
theory is useful for directing attention to the impact and embodiment
of Western neocolonialism throughout the world; this includes political, cultural and economic domination and marginalization, as well as
power over identity and intellect (Ashcroft *et al.* 2013). Hence, postcolonial perspectives provide a vantage point that challenges the centre of
Western thought that produces oppression, objectification and othering,
particularly in relation to the meanings and consequences of the colonial
encounter as a result of invasion and colonization (Cannella and Viruru
2004; Viruru and Cannella 2006).

Central to a postcolonial perspective is the concept of power, and
how it is utilized to define and control the lives and silence the voices of
the Other, from which colonization has rendered unequal power relations
between Indigenous and non-Indigenous people, and between children
and adults. In terms of social justice education, Cannella and Viruru (2004:
123) point out that 'decolonial possibilities can offer knowledges from the
margin, unthought-of perspectives/life experiences, hidden histories, and
disqualified voices as positions from which to reconceptualize discourses,
individual values, and actions'.

Not only does this perspective provide a framework for understanding the impact of Western imperialism in terms of racialized and
ethnicized social inequalities, it is also relevant and useful to childhood
education with the insights that it can offer in relation to the socio-cultural
construction of discourses of childhood and the adult/child dualism that
undergird Western relationships between adults and children. Postcolonial
perspectives can broaden current understandings of children from diverse
socio-cultural backgrounds, challenge the colonizing practices and philosophies of modernist universalized 'truths' that construct children as different from adults and the powerless and less worthy Other, as well as create
new and different possibilities and avenues for children.

Critical 'race' theory

Critical 'race' theory (CRT) is a critical framework that interrogates
whiteness as a historical and social construction that is unnamed and
invisible. CRT draws on postcolonial theory and cultural studies to
unravel its evasion as a racial marker. Its focus on 'race' as a construct

(similar to gender, sexuality, ethnicity, and so on) is used to challenge normative white privilege that constructs racism and inequality. CRT provides a useful toolkit for educators in understanding education as a racialized landscape (Ladson-Billings and Tate 2006; Vass 2010; Leonardo 2012). Vass extends this by arguing that education is where 'relationships occur, understandings are shared and developed, and power is expressed and deployed founded on race-based assumptions' (2010: 178).

Queer theory

Queer theory, which stems from poststructuralist theoretical perspectives, reinforces the notion that identities are not fixed or stable, but rather are shifting, contradictory, dynamic and constructed. This perspective holds that all identities are performances and challenges normalizing practices, particularly in terms of sexuality and the heteronormative constructions of gender. Queer theory challenges the unquestionable, natural and normal positioning of heterosexuality as the superior sexuality and the othering of non-heterosexual identities, which is constituted within the cultural binary heterosexual us/homosexual them. The term 'queer' encompasses those who feel 'marginalized by mainstream sexuality' (Morris 2000: 20), including those who see themselves as heterosexual but challenge the conformity constituted and enforced in hegemonic discourses of heterosexuality. Ultimately, queer theory disrupts the notion that one's gender and sexuality are inherently fixed in one's biological sexed body, upholding the pluralities of sexuality and the multiplicity of gender. Thus, this perspective provides a critical theoretical lens through which one can begin to see the everyday processes of **heteronormativity** operating within everyday contexts.

Critical theory

Perspectives of critical theory utilized in this book draw principally from Bourdieu's theory of social practice. Bourdieu (1930–2002), a French sociologist and cultural theorist, examined human potential and interaction using a metaphorical lens of economic systems. He proposed three significant concepts of social practice, which included capital, field and habitus. In education, his work has been applied to the analysis of cultural reproduction of inequality through educational practices that reproduce power and privilege for children whose home and cultural practices are congruent with the pedagogical practices of the school (including early childhood education), at the expense of children whose home and cultural practices differ from mainstream educational pedagogy. Hence, those children from middle-class, heterosexual, monolingual and urban families are likely to experience academic success through the pedagogically congruent experiences between home and the educational setting.

Bourdieu argues that different forms of capital, such as cultural, social, economic and symbolic capital, operate together to accumulate various forms of social power in different social contexts or fields. However, he also argues that capital and field do not exist in isolation. Ways in which individuals take up and make use of the various forms of capital in social contexts are fundamental to his theory. Further, Bourdieu's concept of habitus focuses on the dispositions, perceptions and attitudes generated throughout one's cultural history that can enable or prohibit effective exchange or accumulation of one's capital. Bourdieu has informed our work through his analysis of social practice and inequality, particularly in relation to how social practices are informed by power, politics and self-interest that are constrained by and developed through the rules and conventions of culture (Schirato and Yell 2000).

New material feminisms and posthumanism

Although new material feminism and posthumanism do not feature as central concepts in the various chapter discussions in this book, it is important to acknowledge these theoretical perspectives and the increasing influence they are currently having in the field of education and elsewhere. New material feminist and posthumanist theories are extending feminist poststructuralist understandings of constructions of knowledge through a focus on the affects or material consequences of discourse or knowledge production on the constitution of subjects (Lenz-Taguchi and Palmer 2013). Barad (2007: 149–150) calls this the material-discursive apparatus of knowing. Central to these theories is a decentring of the human subject to include new ways of understanding the production of knowledge and of subjects through human intra-active entanglements with the non-human (animal, material agents, e.g. school buildings, objects) and more-than-human (computers) (Osgood and Robinson in press). Davies (2014) points out that intra-active moments are more than interactions but rather multiple encounters where each participant affects and is open to being affected by the other. In the early childhood context, feminist researchers are engaging in these theories to provide new liberatory ways of looking at gender in childhood, which is viewed as a relational process of entanglements with the material, semiotic and affective (Blaise 2013; Davies 2014; Huuki and Renold 2015; Osgood and Giugni 2015).

Chapter overviews

The following chapters in this book cover a wide cross-section of issues relevant to the diverse lives of educators, children and their families. The main issues of the chapters are outlined below.

Chapter 2 provides an in-depth overview of the critical theoretical concepts and tools utilized within a feminist poststructuralist theoretical framework. This includes defining what is meant by: feminist poststructuralism, subjectification, Foucauldian concepts such as discourse, knowledge and power, agency, reflexivity and deconstruction. How these theoretical concepts are useful to policy and practice is also discussed in this chapter.

Chapter 3 provides an in-depth discussion of the social construction of childhood and the significant changes that are impacting the lives of children, challenging current dominant understandings of childhood. Within this discussion it highlights the challenges to mainstream development theory that continue to underpin discourses of childhood in the West. The impact of 'childhood innocence' is explored in regards to children's access to knowledge and the implications this has for increasing children's vulnerabilities. The chapter also addresses the increasingly complex role that social media, technology and popular culture play in constructions of childhood, and in children's and young people's lives. The increased 'regulation' of childhood and its impact is also discussed in terms of children's citizenship. The implications of these issues for educators and other professionals working with children and families are outlined. This chapter draws on Robinson's research on the regulation of children's knowledge, especially associated with sexuality (2013).

Chapter 4 argues that there is an obvious need to begin to reconceptualize the family as performative social space in the twenty-first century, in order to include the different family practices and structures that exist. The dominant discourse of the Western nuclear family, which is predominantly white, heterosexual and middle class, continues to powerfully inform the curriculum and practices in many education and community services settings, to the exclusion of other families. However, the traditional nuclear family in reality is not reflective of the experiences of many children. The chapter explores the social, political and economic issues challenging the normalizing discourses of family, and how these have been perpetuated in society, as well as the various social theories that have extended understandings of the role of family in society. Pertinent issues that impact on families, such as sexual, domestic and family violence, globalization, and migration and asylum, are also examined and implications for educators and community service professionals provided.

Chapter 5 addresses the historical and social constructions of Indigeneity both in Australia and internationally, with a critical focus on racialization processes for Indigenous children, families and communities. As non-Aboriginal authors, we are cognizant of the risk we take in writing about Indigenous issues, given the historical misrepresentations of Aboriginality and the tendency for non-Aboriginal people to 'do' research 'on' and write 'about' Aboriginal people. In acknowledging that the story of invasion, colonization, the dispossession of land and the destruction of languages and cultures is an issue for all people, both colonized and non-colonized, we have endeavoured to raise pertinent issues of racialization and inequality relevant to all postcolonial nation states. However, this chapter specifically highlights the significance of Indigenous languages, identities and cultural practices in postcolonial Australia. It also examines issues of assumed absences and visible identities, health and education issues as they impact on Aboriginal children and their families in education and community services. In addition, this chapter draws on data from a case study site from a larger study (Pennycook, Morgan Cruickshank and Jones Díaz 2010–2011) investigating the language and literacy practices of children from culturally and linguistically diverse communities in informal settings. The data examined highlights the significance of making safe spaces for Indigenous families and children in a supported playgroup setting in marginalized community in Greater Western Sydney, NSW. Implications for educators and community service staff working with Indigenous children, families and communities are discussed.

Chapter 6 examines multiculturalism as policy and practice, with a critique on the limits of pluralism, extending the discussion to critical multiculturalism and whiteness. A critical focus on multiculturalism in contemporary contexts of post multiculturalism and globalization is offered. Political agendas and media debates that construct refugees and asylum seekers in the context of global moral panic and Islamophobia are explored. This chapter draws on frameworks of cultural studies to examine 'whiteness' that operates in the pedagogies and practices of childhood education. It draws on data from two research studies to highlight educators' perceptions of children's understanding of 'race', ethnicity, power, racism and marginalization. Implications for educators and community service professionals are offered.

Chapter 7 offers a conceptual reframing of bilingualism, language retention and identity construction in children. The significance of bi/multilingualism in view of its relationship to identity and English as a global language is examined. This chapter provides a critical focus on the politics of languages, and the structural and discursive power relations that exist between global languages, community languages and Indigenous languages. The chapter highlights the benefits of growing up with more than one language, extending the focus to the significance of multilingual and hybrid language practices evident in diverse families and communities. Issues associated with learning English at the expense of the home language in childhood are also examined. This chapter also draws on data from our study and recent research from Jones Díaz (2007) to highlight practitioner perceptions towards home language retention and additional language learning, to demonstrate the impact of broader socio-political forces and power relationships, which regularly operate and position young bilingual children, families and educators into marginalized situations in everyday relations and social practices. Implications for educators and community service staff working with bi/multilingual and/or bi/multidialectal children and families are considered.

Chapter 8 provides an overview of critical perspectives of class and inequality within local and social relations, but extends this analysis to cultural reproduction in a globalized world deconstructing discourses of poverty and disadvantage in education and community services, policy and practice. A critical analysis of disadvantage in terms of how children and families experience poverty not only within the family, but also externally due to the lack of health and education services, poor infrastructure and isolation, is provided. Concepts of neoliberalism are examined and linked explicitly to the implications of neoliberalism in terms of the implications for disadvantage and inequality. Contemporary discourses of 'vulnerable and at risk' children and communities are reframed, and implications for educators and staff working with disadvantaged and marginalized children, families and communities are provided.

Chapter 9 begins by asking the question of whether gender has fallen off the educational policy and equity agenda, particularly in childhood education. The chapter provides an overview of the major theories of gender that have influenced understandings of gender formation and gender differences. It is argued that Butler's (1990) concepts of performativity and the heterosexual matrix provide critical insights to extend understandings of gender construction in early childhood. The discussion points out that the process of gender formation cannot be fully understood without acknowledging how gender is heteronormalized in the process – that is, without examining how normalizing discourses of masculinity and femininity are heterosexualized. A focus is also given to gender diverse and transgender children, and the issues they can encounter. Based on our combined research with early childhood educators, a glimpse of educators' perspectives on gender, and how these impact on their practices with young children, is also provided. The chapter also explores how early childhood education contributes to the process of heteronormativity in young children's lives through educators' everyday practices and policies.

Chapter 10 provides an overview of some of the main issues relevant to childhood and sexuality, and to children's sexual citizenship (see Robinson 2013). The chapter examines theoretical understandings of sexuality and considers the relationship between sexuality and gender. The theoretical discussion is extended to provide an overview of the dominant discourses about childhood and sexuality that impact contemporary perspectives of children as sexual subjects. How these discourses influence the regulation of children's access to knowledge of sexuality, and the implications this has for children's health and well-being is also explored. Drawing on Robinson's research with children, parents and educators, the chapter also looks at the construction of children's sexual subjectivities and how children are active agents in this process, as well as the role children, parents and educators play in the constitution of children as heteronormative subjects. The chapter also explores the pervasiveness of the discourse of compulsory heterosexuality, and the assumed absence of gay and lesbian families in settings; and how homophobia and **heterosexism** operate in early childhood education. The chapter concludes with a discussion of the implications that all of these major issues have for policy and practice, pedagogy, working with families, and for building respectful and ethical relationships early in children's lives.

Chapter 11 is a concluding chapter that reiterates the importance of **reflexivity**, and building ethical relationships and community responsibilities in doing equity and social justice work when working with children, families and their communities. It is argued that it is critical for educators and community-based professionals to reflexively analyse how their own perceptions and practices can perpetuate social inequalities through their interactions with children and their families. Consequently, there can be an element of risk taking, personally and professionally, when it comes to challenging normalizing discourses that operate to construct powerful points of privilege for some individual subjects and groups in society, while excluding others. This chapter also highlights the importance of drawing on feminist poststructural, cultural and critical theoretical perspectives of childhood, diversity and inequality that informs a pedagogy of social justice, deconstructs deficit thinking about children and families, and challenges normative assumptions about the world. Communicating with families, encouraging critical thinking in children and developing policies that promote equity, diversity and difference in all aspects of the programme or curriculum are essential. This chapter has also highlighted the importance of professional development in keeping staff up to date and the need for further research in diversity and difference in education and community-based services.

The book also includes a glossary of critical terms that are used throughout the chapters as a quick reference point for readers.

Recommended reading

Ferfolja, T., Jones Díaz, C. and Ullman, J. (2015) The unseen half: theories for educational practice, in T. Ferfolja, C. Jones Díaz and J. Ullman (eds) *Understanding Sociological Theory and Pedagogical Practices*. Sydney: Cambridge University Press.

Grenfell, M. (ed.) (2012) *Pierre Bourdieu: Key Concepts*, 2nd edn. London: Routledge.

2

Doing feminist poststructuralist theory with early childhood educators

Introduction

Doing social justice education primarily aims to disrupt the normalizing discourses that constitute and perpetuate social inequalities in society, and operate to privilege certain identities and marginalize and silence others. As part of this process, social justice education also endeavours to improve the experiences of those who are othered in some way by the mainstream society. 'Other' is defined as those groups that have been marginalized, silenced, denigrated or violated, in opposition to the privileged and powerful groups that are identified as representing the idealized, mythical norm in society (Kumashiro 2002). For example, groups that have been othered include people of colour, Indigenous people, gays and lesbians (or those perceived to be gay or lesbian), people who are gender diverse and transgender, women, single parents, people with disabilities, the unemployed, religious minorities and those from minority language backgrounds.

Doing social justice and equity education with children and their families is not easy work. It often involves negotiating a range of different perceptions and values around 'difficult knowledge' (Britzman 1998) or controversial issues. It involves challenging understandings of 'normal' and can involve interfering with individual (adult or child) subjects' 'truths', belief systems or common-sense ways of looking at the world. Primarily, social justice education is work that disrupts individual subjects' locations within social discourses that constitute their understandings of difference. Critical to doing social justice education with children and their families is awareness of how educators themselves perceive difference, and in which social discourses they are located when it comes to issues of equity associated with different sites of identities, such as 'race', ethnicity, gender, sexuality, social class and disability. As pointed out in Chapter 1, educators' perceptions of difference can significantly impact on their practices with children and their families, despite the claims often made that 'We treat everybody the same' (Lundeberg 1997; Robinson and Jones Díaz 1999). Thus, a major premise from which we operate in relation to doing social justice education is that educators need to be willing to do the same difficult and reflexive work around *change* in terms of the way they view the world as they are attempting to undertake with the children and families with whom they work. It is important that educators are willing to take up the issues they find personally confronting, uncomfortable or even somewhat risky.

The main aim of this chapter is to provide educators and community-based professionals with an understanding of doing social justice education that is informed primarily from feminist poststructuralist perspectives (Hollway 1984; Davies 1989, 1993, 1994, 1996; Walkerdine 1990; Weedon 1997), as well as by social theorists, such as Foucault (1977, 1978, 1980), Bourdieu (1990, 1991a, 1991b, 1993), Britzman (1998, 2003) and Butler (1990). An overview is provided of the main theoretical concepts that are critical to an understanding of the processes involved in the construction of identity, difference, power and inequality. These concepts include knowledge/'truth', discourse, power, subjectivity, agency, reflexivity, deconstruction and performativity. However, of particular importance to a feminist poststructuralist perspective is the process of subjectification (that is, the construction of self – who you are), in terms of not only how one comes to view the world, but also understanding potential sites for individual and social change or transformation.

What is feminist poststructuralism?

Feminist poststructuralism, as the name suggests, is a perspective that incorporates aspects of feminism with poststructural understandings, in order to produce a richer version of social theory and cultural analysis that moves beyond some of the limitations found in the original theories of feminism and poststructuralism. Feminism provides important insights into the construction of gendered and sexualized subjects, while poststructuralism (like postmodernism) highlights the need to acknowledge the differences and heterogeneity that exist between individuals, groups and subject positions (Best and Kellner 1991). For example, feminism has been criticized for the way it universalized women's oppression and powerlessness as being solely the result of patriarchy – that is, women's oppression and subordination were perceived to be the result of a patriarchal social structure or system, in which men had supreme power over women, controlling their access to resources and opportunities. Poststructuralists challenged the very concept of 'woman' as a universal and unifying term, pointing out that it failed to recognize the differences among women – in terms of their 'race', ethnicity, sexuality, social class, and so on – which impacted on their diverse experiences of inequality or oppression, as well as their power. This critique echoed the concerns of many women of colour, lesbians and women from working-class backgrounds, who had become dissatisfied with the movement and critical of the way the term 'woman' had become synonymous with a middle-class, white, heterosexual perspective of women's experiences in the world. Some women were feeling as oppressed by their white, middle-class heterosexual 'sisters' as by male power. Many women of colour were acknowledging that it was not their gender, but their colour or 'race', that was the main cause of their oppression, and that they often had powerful positions within their families and communities (Collins 1990). Consequently, feminists who were critical of the universalizing tendencies of feminism looked to postmodernism and poststructuralism to develop different understandings of the way that women's oppression is experienced differently and changes across intersections of identity, within different contexts and over time. Consequently, feminist poststructuralists criticize the reductive, essentialist and problematic universalizing tendencies of feminism and other such grand narrative theories.

Poststructuralism takes on a feminist perspective when issues associated with gendered and sexualized identities and power relations are central to the analysis at hand. However, the centrality of gender and sexuality are always framed within an analysis of the way that they intersect with other sites of identity such as 'race', ethnicity, social class and disability. As MacNaughton (2001: 122) aptly points out:

> In redefining identity as multiple, contradictory, and dynamic, feminist poststructuralists have politicized identity formation. They have argued that identity is constituted in and by social relations of gender, sexuality, class, and race, and that each of us lives our gendered, sexualized, 'classed', and 'raced' identities in and through the power relations that constitute our daily lives. Their beginning point is that individuals are inseparable from social institutions; they do not simply interact but are interdependent and mutually constituting. Individuals are born into already-existing social worlds consisting of social structures, social processes, and social meanings. The individual does not and cannot exist outside of the social, nor can the social exist over and above the individual.

MacNaughton's comments highlight how individual identities and the meanings that are attached to these (gender, sexuality, class, ethnicity, 'race', and so on) are not fixed in biology, but rather are constituted in and through our everyday social interactions and the relations of power operating in our daily lives. Consequently, identities are negotiated, managed and reinvented across the different social contexts in which we operate. The formation of identities is constituted within the process of subjectification, which is the focus of the following sections.

Understanding the 'self': the feminist poststructuralist subject

Feminist poststructuralist understandings of the subject (or the self – who you are) and how it is formed are different from those held in modernist perspectives that have tended to dominate the knowledge in this area. In modernist humanist perspectives (as briefly outlined in Chapter 1) the individual subject is one that is fixed in biology and incorporates an essence of 'humanness' that is shared across all human beings. That is, all human beings are considered to share particular characteristics that are inherent in their humanness; these shared and unchanging characteristics are reason, rationality and coherency, which universalize the human experience and set it apart from that of other species. It is upheld that, through the explorations of 'objective' science, the human essence is both discoverable and knowable. Within this framework, the human subject is viewed as sharing a universalized human history that is united by the common ideals of the possibility, through human reason, of progress and ultimately human perfection. The humanist subject is considered to be in control and the author of his or her own experience and meaning. Consequently, individuals are perceived to have an 'essential nature' – that is, where the meanings of experiences originate from within the individual. In other words, each person is perceived to have a unique essence or personality that comes from within them, and emerges and develops over the person's lifetime.

In contrast, feminist poststructuralists, like other poststructural theorists, perceive the subject as being socially constructed, and define subjectivity as encompassing the unconscious and conscious thoughts and emotions of the individual – or their sense of self and how they relate to the world (Weedon 1997). Subjectivity originates not inherently from inside the person, but from the social realm; consequently, it is not fixed, but rather is fluid and dynamic. In this perspective, the subject does not share a discoverable or knowable human essence or human history, and the possibility, through scientific progress, of reaching human perfection is rejected. Feminist poststructuralists are anti-humanist in that they are critical of essentialist notions that there is a 'knowable essence' of individuals. In other words, they believe that individuals do not have an innate unique, rational, coherent and fixed personality that emerges from within them over their lifetime. This perspective is quite difficult for some to comprehend, as it has been upheld as a very powerful 'truth' in society, so powerful that it has rarely been questioned, until the introduction of postmodern and poststructuralist perspectives in recent times. It is easier to understand this view when we take the time to look closely at ourselves and notice that we are complex beings, who are, more often than not, irrational and contradictory in the way we look at the world and in the way we behave. How often have you done something knowing full well that it was not really the most logical thing to do, but you did it anyway, for whatever reason(s) at the time? Do you constantly change your mind about a particular issue and feel unsure about what you really believe? Feminist poststructuralists consider that it is more useful to view individual subjects as changing, contradictory, unstable, irrational and shifting across different contexts. Individual subjects are constantly reinventing themselves as they negotiate the various power relationships that exist in their lives.

The process of subjectification

How do we each come to be the people we are? Why do we look at the world the way we do? In terms of social justice education these are critical questions, especially since much of this work involves negotiating the differing values and belief systems that people have in the world. According to feminist poststructuralist perspectives, individual subjects are constantly in a process of subjectification in which their subjectivity (or self) is formed through the *discourses* that they locate themselves in throughout their lifetime. The following discussions explain the critical concepts involved in this process of the construction of self.

Knowledge and discourse

Feminist poststructuralists, like other theorists that fall into poststructuralist paradigms, reject modernist humanist beliefs that human perfection and enlightenment are possible through the discovery of knowable objective scientific 'truths' about the world. They uphold that knowledge is only partial and that 'truths' are only ever interpretations or perspectives held by various groups or individuals, rather than objective facts or truths. According to Burr (1995: 64), knowledge refers 'to the particular construction or version of a phenomenon that has received the stamp of "truth" in our society'. The knowledge that we take up in our lives is generally upheld as our 'truths' about how we see the world; and, as Fuss (1989) points out, truth becomes the authority of experience. We gain knowledge from our everyday social interactions with people and institutions – for example, interactions with family, schools, the church, the government or the law. Our everyday discussions with our friends can contribute to the knowledge that we take up as our own.

However, this knowledge is often based on limited insights into the world, on stereotypes and on 'common sense' beliefs, which work to construct, define and 'essentialize' our understandings about the world and the different groups that live within it. **Essentialism** means that certain characteristics become naturalized and normalized representations of groups, defining and fixing who and what they are; it is also the tendency to see one aspect of a subject's identity (often the visible parts) and make that representative of the whole individual. For example, a lesbian mother is typically reduced to her lesbianism and generally read within the context of the stereotypes that abound about what it means to be lesbian; or an Asian child is similarly reduced to a defining characteristic of 'Asianness'.

This knowledge is largely constituted within cultural binaries that result in oppositional or dualistic thinking, and it is commonly perceived to represent 'common-sense logic'. For example, boy/girl, men/women, white/black, heterosexual/homosexual, Western/non-Western, adult/child are a few of the vast number of binaries that exist; they are perceived to be natural opposites, and are thus constructed and defined in opposition to each other. What it means to be a boy or a man is generally considered to be opposite to what it means to be a girl or a woman. These cultural binaries, which have tended to underpin modernist knowledge, are very powerful in the way that they influence how people look at the world. Boys who are perceived to behave in feminine ways often experience harassment from peers or others, who are making it clear that there has been a serious breach of the social regulations that operate around appropriate gender behaviour; thus their behaviour is considered 'abnormal' and they are punished for the slippage in their performance of masculinity.

Cultural power relations are constituted in and maintained through these binary relationships, based on hierarchies of power, in which one side of the binary has the power to define and subordinate the Other – for example, whites have had the power to largely define, officially and unofficially, what it means to be non-white in society, and whiteness has had the privileged position of not being viewed as a racialized colour. Another very powerful example of this process is the stud/slut binary – constituted within these two words is a powerful hierarchical relationship (one epitomized by double standards) around gender and (hetero)sexuality.

Michel Foucault developed a theory of discourse, which provided a theoretical framework for understanding how the world operated in terms of identity and power. For Foucault (1974), knowledge is constituted within *discourses* operating in society, which are historically and culturally formulated. Foucault (1974: 49) defines discourse as 'practices that systematically form the objects of which they speak'. Others have also defined Foucault's concept of discourse in the following ways – the definitions below combined give a comprehensive overview of what this term encompasses.

> [Discourses are] about what can be said and thought, but also about who can speak, when, and with what authority. Discourses embody meaning and social relationships, they constitute both subjectivity and power. (Ball 1990: 2)
>
> A system of statements, which constructs an object. (Parker 1992: 5)
>
> A set of meanings, metaphors, representations, images, stories, statements and so on that in some way together produce a particular version of events. (Burr 1995: 48)

According to Foucault (1974), discourses operate through language, and constitute the different knowledge we have available to us about the world and those in it; but they are generally invisible or not part of our everyday conscious awareness. The various discourses (or knowledge) that we take up as our own ways of looking at the world are both constituted in and perpetuated through the language that we use in our daily interactions; when we talk to one another the world gets constructed, objects take on the meanings we attach to them, and certain knowledge becomes powerful. They are often perpetuated through the common-sense cultural binaries that we rarely critically review or challenge. However, discourses are not only constituted through our verbal language, but, as Burr (1995) highlights above, also operate through representations in images – for example, images in posters or on television can represent very powerful ideas about people or objects; these images can be taken up as a true representation of that group or object, regardless of how 'real' these images are. Discourses are not about what is 'real' – remember that knowledge is only ever partial and we can never know the 'truth' about something. They are only ever perspectives or interpretations of the world. However, the knowledge we take up is often perceived as 'truth' and we can hold on to these perspectives very strongly as the only 'true' and 'correct' way to look at the world or version of events. Through our everyday interactions we speak and perform discourses into existence. There are numerous ways of looking at the world and sometimes there are many versions of a single event or phenomenon, reflecting the point that there are different discourses operating simultaneously that are constructing different understandings about objects and of the world and how it operates.

The following are examples of discourses that operate in society. These statements contribute to the constitution of the different knowledge that prevails around the various issues, groups, events or phenomena that they address.

- Families are safe, loving environments in which to raise children.
- Families are microcosms of society and are oppressive institutions that perpetuate inequalities between men and women, adults and children.
- Abortion is a woman's right to choose.
- Abortion is the taking of life.
- Women have natural instincts to nurture and care for others; mothering is instinctual.
- Mothering is learned, so there is no reason why men cannot mother.
- Heterosexuality is normal, non-heterosexual relations are deviant and abnormal.
- Heterosexuality is only one example of natural and normal sexual relationships in society; homosexuality and lesbianism are other examples.
- Masculinity is naturally aggressive; men are tough and make better leaders.
- There are many ways to do masculinities and not all men are aggressive, and there are different ways in which to manage people without aggression.
- Immunization is crucial for healthy children.
- Immunization compromises children's immune systems, making them even more vulnerable to diseases.
- Domestic violence is a private family matter.
- Domestic violence is a public issue that requires social interventions.
- People with disabilities are helpless and vulnerable.
- People with disabilities are capable and productive.
- All Arabs are Muslims.
- All Muslims are Arabs.
- Children should be seen and not heard.
- Children are critical thinkers who can make valuable contributions to conversations.

Individual subjects will experience a range of different and precarious subject positions within these discourses – for example, they might be taken up as 'truths' that constitute their knowledge and perceptions of the world; or as misconceptions or false statements that do not represent their knowledge or perceptions; or they may shift in and out of them in a contradictory manner, depending on the context in which they are operating.

Why is it that one version of events or certain knowledge is considered more truthful than others? Various discourses coexist, competing to be recognized and accepted as the officially sanctioned knowledge or 'truth'. Discourses govern the way we live our lives but do so in ways that are most often not visible or tangible. The invisibility of discourse works to strengthen the relationships of power operating within discourses. As Foucault (1974: 49) comments, 'For those who speak it, a discourse is a given – it operates "behind their backs", it is an "unthought".' Discourses become powerful only when they are taken up by social institutions, such as those related to religion, education, the law, the government, and individual subjects, who live and speak them as their 'truth' or official version of events about the world. People can have different 'truths', and this is where conflicts can arise. For example, the discourse that children need to be immunized against diseases is given more credibility and power when governments and medical associations officially sanction it as the 'truth'. In the process of this discourse being socially sanctioned, other discourses that constitute different perspectives – for example, that immunization compromises children's immune systems, making them more vulnerable to other diseases – find less credibility and support from individual subjects because they do not receive the official stamp of 'truth'. If the government and medical associations took up the second perspective, the credibility and power of this discourse could change.

It is important to point out that the discourses that constitute our knowledge of the world are historically and culturally specific; they change across and within cultures and over time. For example, understandings and beliefs about women have changed over time and are different in various cultural contexts. In some Western cultures it was historically upheld that women should not be educated, therefore they were excluded from universities. This perspective was based largely on the discourse that if women spent their energies on learning, rather than on having children, their reproductive capabilities would eventually be compromised or could become defunct (Spender 1983). Obviously this discourse was challenged by women and today finds little support; it has been replaced by different and new knowledge about women – for example, that women are capable of balancing career and family life. Discourses are also culturally specific. For example, understandings of masculinities and representations of what it means to be a man or boy in Anglo-Celtic Australia today may be very different from understandings and representations of masculinities within Balinese cultures or within Brazilian cultures. Discourses are also contextually changing within cultures. Therefore, discourses of masculinities can change across class, 'race', ethnicities, sexual identities, and so on.

Subjectivity, discourse and power

Foucault's discourse theory is critical to an understanding of the process of subjectification within a feminist poststructuralist perspective. According to Foucault, our self or subjectivity is constituted within the discourses that are culturally available to us, which we draw upon in our communications with other people. That is, our unconscious and conscious thoughts and emotions, our sense of self and how we relate to the world, as well as the ways that we become individual subjects, who are gendered, classed, racialized, ethnicized, sexualized, and so on, are constituted within the discourses that we locate ourselves in and take up as our own ways of being in the world (Weedon 1997). Foucault (1974) points out that discourses live themselves out through people. Our subjectivity and identity originate not inherently from inside us, but from the social realm in which discourses are constituted and perpetuated, constructing and determining the possibilities of who we can be and what we can think. Consequently, our subjectivity is not fixed, but dynamic and fluid.

Subjectivity is therefore made up of a range of shifting and precarious subject positions as a result of its constitution within the contextual, changing, contradictory discourses that are culturally available. Consequently, the subject is no longer in total control, and this is in stark contrast with the modernist perspective. The discourses that form our subjectivity and identity have implications for what we perceive we can and cannot do, and what we should and should not do – for example, how we represent ourselves as sexualized subjects will be constituted within the discourses of sexuality that we have available to us. Once we take up a subject position in discourse, we have available to us a particular limited set of concepts, images, metaphors, ways of speaking, self-narratives, and so on, that we take on as our own. Individuals make an emotional commitment to the category of person constituted within the discourses they have chosen to take up as their own, as well as to the appropriate system of morals (rules of right and wrong) encompassed within these discourses. However, individuals are confronted with a variety of discourses, each with a different version of what it means to be a sexualized being. As pointed out previously, some of these discourses are socially sanctioned over others, thus they are given more credibility and power. The dominant discourse that heterosexuality is natural and normal, and all other sexualities abnormal and deviant, is very powerful, and is socially sanctioned by particular religious faiths, governments and legal and medical institutions. Thus, heterosexuality becomes the normalizing discourse that operates in that society. Those who locate themselves in another alternative or counter-discourse that constitutes heterosexuality as only one choice among many natural, normal and acceptable sexualities, and choose to be gay or lesbian, will find this discursive position more difficult to negotiate as it does not carry the same privileges as are offered to those who take up heterosexuality. Feminist poststructuralists uphold that to understand the person, you need to look to the social realm, within the linguistic space in which people move and interact, rather than within the individual.

Discourses are constituted in language, and if discourses constitute subjectivity, it follows that language is a critical site in terms of the construction of subjectivity. The person you are, your experience, your identity, your perceptions and knowledge, your ways of being in the world, are all the effects of language and our interactions with the material world. As Burr (1995) points out, we represent our experiences to ourselves and to others by using concepts embedded in language. Language is fundamentally a social phenomenon, occurring between people. The construction of the person or one's subjectivity takes place in these exchanges. There are many different ways we exchange language, including conversation, reading, writing, visually, and so on. Language in this sense is not just spoken and written, but a meaning system in which ideas, thoughts, values, and so on, are shared. Language is perceived not as a system of signs with fixed meanings upon which everyone agrees, but as a site of variation and potentially conflicting meanings. Conversations, writing and social encounters become sites of political struggle and power. For example, the word 'queer' is contested by different meanings. In recent times it has been reclaimed as a positive signifier of non-conformism, particularly in terms of sexuality (both heterosexuality and non-heterosexuality), but also in relation to other aspects of identity. Consequently, our subjectivity is never fixed, but is changeable, contradictory, contextual, and in a state of flux and instability. This is reflected in the way that individual subjects can be located within different and contradictory subject positions in discourses. Some early childhood educators indicate that, personally, they would never choose to put their own children in care, believing that it is more appropriate for mothers to look after their children in the early years. Educators who espouse strong social justice and human rights principles, but are also homophobic and heterosexist, provide another example of contradictory subject positions.

Individual subjects do not just locate themselves in discourses, but will also read others from their own discursive positions. For example, the father who is positioned in the discourse that normalizes representations of masculinity as heterosexual, a discourse that primarily perpetuates the oppositional thinking that masculinity is everything that femininity is not, will read his son's interest in playing with dolls and women's clothes in 'home corner' as unhealthy, unnatural and abnormal. The father will not only question his son's masculinity, but will also fear his son's potential slippage in terms of his heterosexuality. From a feminist poststructuralist perspective, the son's playing with women's clothing is not problematic, but represents a range of possible experiences open to the child in play. The child will understand such play in shifting and contradictory ways – possibly a feeling of power and exhilaration in challenging the perceived limitations of his gender, or a sense of freedom in being able to do his gender differently, or fear and embarrassment if reprimanded or excluded from such play by adults. The discursive location from which educators read the boy's behaviour will be critical in influencing the boy's perceptions of his own behaviour and feelings, and his experiences of power in this context, as well as the possibilities he sees for doing his masculinity in multiple and different ways. We are constantly reading other people from the discourses that we take up, often making judgements about who we perceive them to be. For example, the young woman who performs her femininity in a challenging way, seeing herself as a strong, independent, sexy, outgoing individual, who primarily represents the difference through her dress codes – black, short dresses, tight clothing, make-up – can either be read as powerful and independent or as 'sluttish' and provocative.

Power is a critical concept in understanding the process of subjectification. According to Foucault, power operates through discourses that prevail in society. Consequently, our power as individual subjects is bound up in the discourses in which we position ourselves, as well as how we are read by others from their discursive locations, as in the above example. We have discussed how particular discourses have more power than others through the way that individuals and social institutions take them up as their own 'truths' and ways of looking at the world. Where individual subjects locate themselves in discourse will be a matter of negotiation around power relations, as well as what personal investments they see themselves as having in locating in one discourse rather than the other (Hollway 1984).

As discussed previously, subjectivity is complex, changing, contradictory and often irrational. This shifting is primarily a result of the way that we negotiate power relations in our daily interactions. For example, a pre-service teacher might be willing to engage in racist or homophobic harassment when out socializing with peers, but express anti-racist and anti-homophobic sentiments in their compulsory social justice class. In this context, the pre-service teacher has to negotiate the various power relations at hand, such as the degree of importance they place on remaining popular with peers, or the fear that they might also be a target of peer harassment if they do not participate, or a concern that they might be failed by the diversity lecturer if they appear to be racist or homophobic. Their decisions will be based on negotiating the power relationships and their own investments in different contexts. This is similar to the way that young children negotiate the discursive power relations in their daily lives.

An awareness of this process becomes critical for educators. For example, educators who try to positively intervene in a young boy's bullying behaviour will not necessarily succeed if their strategy is primarily to make the boy feel bad about his behaviour and to feel sympathy for the victim, which is more often than not the pedagogical case. For many young boys who are positioned in the discourse of hegemonic masculinity, aggressive physical behaviour is part of the performance of their gendered identities. This performance is often about getting their gender performance correct in front of other boys, who are positioned in a similar discourse of masculinity (Butler 1990). Consequently, the boy will continue to engage in this aggressive behaviour, despite the educator's intervention, if his male peers are positively acknowledging his gender performance and his position of power remains intact. The young boy will have to negotiate the existing power relations at hand, such as being in trouble with the educator, or with parents, or not getting his gender performance correct in front of his peers. Thus, his behaviour may be contradictory; he may respond to his teacher's reprimands, only to continue the bullying when the teacher is not around.

Ultimately, individual subjects can change their subjectivity only through their relocation in another discourse, but there has to be more investment in the shifting than is offered through remaining in their current discursive location. As contradictory subjects we are constantly negotiating power relations in our everyday lives, shifting contextually according to how we read and negotiate our daily interactions with others. If we consider that it will be more beneficial and desirable to locate in one discourse rather than another, then we can shift our discursive position in order to gain more power and reap the perceived benefits.

As alluded to previously, a discourse gains a position of power over others in the way it is supported and 'activated' by individuals and institutions in society. Consequently, if powerful institutions in society, such as governments, religious bodies, and the legal and education systems, take up a discourse, its power is reinforced and its ability to persuade individuals that it is the most appropriate view of the world is increased. Those who position themselves in this discourse will share in the privilege, advantage and power that are culturally sanctioned through the dominant culture's support for this 'truth'. Those who locate outside this dominant discourse will frequently experience inequities, diminished power, and little or no support from the dominant culture for their perspective. For example, 'abortion is a woman's right to choose' is a discourse about a controversial issue that often divides people. This may be a dominant discourse taken up by feminists and reinforced in some cases through legislation that makes abortion legal. However, it will be a discourse that gets little support in religious and pro-life contexts, or in countries where governments support anti-abortion legislation. In the latter contexts, the discourse around abortion that is more powerful and considered more truthful is that abortion is the taking of life. Consequently, if you are a feminist who believes in a woman's right to choose, your individual and group power may be compromised if you reside in Ireland, but not necessarily if you live in the United Kingdom. Thus, the power constituted within the particular discourses that you take up as your own perceptions of the world will contextually shift and change. As can be seen from this example, discourses are not simply abstract ideas; they are intimately linked with the way society is organized and run. To take another example, the discourse of capitalism results in the formation of different subject positions – workers, unemployed, employers – which all have different access to power in this context. Further, access to power in these various subject positions is also linked to gender, class, sexuality, 'race', ethnicity, and so on.

According to Foucault, power is knowledge, but it is much more than just gaining more understanding or 'knowing' about the world; it is about which particular discourse one takes up as one's way of looking at the world. The discourses that are officially sanctioned in society are about perpetuating particular social relationships that reaffirm the power and privilege of particular groups over others. For example, officially sanctioning the discourse that defines marriage as being between men and women operates primarily to normalize heterosexuality, and to exclude and socially marginalize non-heterosexual relationships. Consequently, our positioning in particular discourses, depending on their status in society, is about the everyday politics of either reaffirming or disrupting social inequalities. As we are well aware, there can be dire consequences for not taking up the socially sanctioned discourses that operate in society. However, as Foucault reminds us, where there is power there is always resistance. How people make sense of their lives is an important starting point for understanding how power relations structure society (Weedon 1997). New modes of subjectivity can become available to individuals, resulting in individual changes in perspectives and different choices, which open up new possibilities for political change and social transformation.

Foucault's definition of power

Living and working as an academic in Paris during the students' and workers' uprisings in the 1960s, Foucault developed a reading of power that challenged the Marxist perspectives on power that were influential during the early to mid-twentieth century in Europe. In contrast to the Marxist approach, Foucault does not see the state/economic structures as the primary and sole locus of power; they are important, but he sees relations of power extending beyond the limits of the state. Foucault argues that power is everywhere and ultimately nowhere in particular. What this means is that power is not located in one central body. Rather, he views power as operating through discourses, as pointed out above. Foucault views the relationship between economics, social structures and discourses as a complex relationship, with none being more dominant than the other. Economic relations of power are only one of a range of power relations. This perspective on power challenges not only Marxist perspectives but also those espoused by other grand narratives. It challenges some feminisms, which centralize power within patriarchy, viewing men as the primary owners/holders of power, which they use to dominate women in society.

In Foucault's perspective, power can be visualized as a network of capillaries, starting at the bottom and moving slowly upwards, sideways and back down; rather than operating from the top down, as it tends to be visualized in more traditional perspectives. Power is primarily a relation rather than a simple imposition; power circulates throughout society, rather than being owned by one individual or group (Mills 2004). Foucault (1978: 86) makes the point that 'Power is tolerable only on condition that it masks a substantial part of itself. Its success is proportional to its ability to hide its own mechanisms.' Of particular importance to Foucault's understanding of power is the critical perspective that where there is power there is always resistance. No power relation is simply one of total domination. He acknowledges that power is not always negative, coercive or repressive, but can be positive and productive. Thus, power produces as well as represses. For example, Foucault explores children's sexuality in his *History of Sexuality Vol. 1* (1978). He argues that the regulation and surveillance of male children's masturbation foregrounded this sexuality, producing a pleasure based on secrecy and guilt that resulted from the enforced need to hide the behaviour. Thus, the repression of acts by those in power does not simply result in the erasure of the behaviour. This is a rather simplistic model of actions and power relations. Rather, power incorporates a negotiation of power relations; for example, parents do not generally have unconditional power to get children to do things, and they often have to negotiate power with children. Forms of subjectivity are produced in negotiation with existing power relations.

Foucault's concept of 'regimes of truth' is useful in terms of understanding how certain discourses gain dominance and power over others. 'Regimes of truth' are depicted by a range of discourses that are sanctioned within particular contexts (or discursive fields, such as the family, the church, education, the law, medicine) that are mutually reinforcing, and operate to maintain particular 'truths' and current power relations. The discourses that form our identity are intimately tied to the structures and practices that we live out in society from day to day. It is in the interest of relatively powerful groups that some discourses and not others receive the stamp of 'truth' – for example, dominant discourses of femininity serve to uphold gender power inequalities and the gender binary male/female; education and capitalism as systems of social control and exploitation are less likely to enjoy widespread acceptance as common-sense truths. In terms of social justice, individuals can contribute to producing, sustaining, but also undermining and transforming relations involving domination and subordination. Subject positions in discourse often work on behalf of different social interests; for example, the discourse that 'men are born to lead and women are born to breed' has been powerful in perpetuating a particular social system based on gender inequalities.

Foucault provided a perspective on power that shifted from explanations of monolithic sovereign power to one that focused on disciplinary power, based on surveillance and normalization. Within this perspective, populations were not just normalized through the way they were subjected to the daily surveillance and the scrutiny of other people and official institutions, but individuals also became self-surveillant and self-scrutinizing, thus normalizing their own behaviours. With increases in population numbers it became untenable for one sovereign power to watch over or control large numbers of people. Foucault upheld that the need to control large populations of people resulted in the utilization of surveillance processes in order to regulate and normalize people's behaviours. Foucault theorized disciplinary power particularly in the context of schools and prisons. He argued that power does not always use force or aggression, and that it can be self-regulating through its potentiality. That is, the threat of power or the perception that one is being watched can result in individuals regulating or normalizing their own behaviour. In schools the prefect system operates as a surveillance process to regulate and normalize students' behaviours.

Foucault utilized the notion of panopticism to explain how disciplinary power operates. The panopticon was an architectural design developed in the nineteenth century, where prison cells were located around a central watchtower that could view all the cells from that one vantage point. Prisoners tended to regulate their own behaviours under this constant process of surveillance. People could be controlled through self-surveillance and therefore start to regulate their own behaviours through self-discipline. It is interesting to point out that in some early childhood settings in Australia the panopticon design is incorporated into the baby change area and/or toilets. This baby change area is often located within a centralized room made of glass, so that individual workers can be viewed by other workers while changing babies' or young children's nappies or clothes; this surveillance has intensified in recent years with increased concerns around potential sexual abuse of children in child-care institutions. The process of disciplinary power can also be seen in terms of the way that perpetrators of child sexual abuse can regulate young children's behaviours through potential threats of power. Perpetrators do not have to be with children all the time to make them do what they want or to make them remain silent about their abuse; the threat of power (for example, hurting someone dear to the child) is often enough for children to self-regulate their behaviours. Thus, disciplinary power operates as a form of social control.

Foucault's perspective is a major shift away from the oppressor–victim models of power encapsulated in Marxist and feminist perspectives. However, Foucault's perspective on power has been criticized by some for not dealing adequately with questions of individual agency, or for not fully theorizing resistance – that is, locating, describing and accounting for subjects who resist power (McNay 2000). Consequently, some feminist and postcolonialist theorists have modified Foucault's work to incorporate a more in-depth theorization of resistance and agency (Sawicki 1991; McNay 2000).

Agency

Foucault's process of subjectification, in which subjects are constituted within the discourses available to them, has been criticized for being somewhat deterministic. What this means is that individual subjects do not seem to have any active participatory role in the construction of self. Rather, they are considered to be reduced to 'docile bodies' (to use a Foucauldian term), with control residing totally in the powerful devices of cultural discourses through the process of subjectification (McNay 2000). However, in his later work around 'technologies of self', Foucault provides a more substantive understanding of subjectivity. 'Technologies of self' are understood 'as the practices and techniques through which individuals actively fashion their own identities' (McNay 2000: 8). Through this process of self-formation, individuals can consciously resist the 'technologies of domination' that operate in society.

To what extent individual subjects have agency in the construction of self and social relationships has been debated throughout history, but it is a significant component of feminist poststructuralist perspectives (Davies 1994; Robinson and Jones Díaz 1999; MacNaughton 2000). Agency is about our ability to act with intent and awareness, and this raises important questions about individual and collective responsibility and culpability (Hall 2004). Burr (1995) points out that individuals are capable of critical historical reflection, and able to exercise some choice with respect to the discourses and practices they take up for their use. That is, individual subjects are active *agents* in the construction of their subjectivity. In critically analysing the discourses that constitute their lives, individuals can claim or resist them according to the effects they want to establish, and can be creative in this process (Sawicki 1991). Sawicki (1991: 103) highlights that the subject is 'able to reflect upon implications of its choices as they are taken up and transformed in a hierarchical network of power relations'. Hall (2004: 127) points out that 'We are subject to discourse, not simply subjects through discourse with the ability to turn around, contemplate, and rework our subjectivity at will.' Ultimately, and critically, individual subjects have to take responsibility for their position in discourse and its implications for the perpetuation of social inequalities and injustices. Consequently, agency is a critical concept in terms of social justice education, and Hall (2004: 124–125) makes the pertinent point that:

> 'Agency', its possibility and practicality, brings us face to face with the political question of how we can motivate ourselves and others to work for social change and economic justice . . . Do we respond to injustice and the Machiavellian moves of politicians and business leaders with cynicism or with a belief that human beings, individually and collectively, can change for the better, if they revisit some fundamental decisions about their own priorities and values?

Reflexivity

The theoretical concepts and processes outlined above provide a framework from which educators can start to increase their understandings of the formation of individual subjects (both adults and children). It also provides a critical context in which to analyse the construction of the social order, which is steeped in hierarchies of power that perpetuate social, political and economic social inequalities on both the micro and macro levels of society. As pointed out above, our positions in discourse are paramount to the perpetuation or disruption of these social injustices that operate in society. Consequently, it is important that educators take up a *reflexive* approach to their daily practices and pedagogy.

Reflexivity is the 'critical awareness that arises from a self-conscious relation with the other' (McNay 2000: 5). We started this chapter with a discussion of the Other and the process of othering, which are important to an understanding of social justice education. It is imperative that all educators critically review their perspectives, practices, policies and pedagogies in terms of the way that they may be consciously or unconsciously implicated in the process of othering in their everyday interactions with peers, children and their families. Incorporating a reflexive approach in one's personal and professional lives is not just a matter of being aware of one's prejudice and standpoint, but also 'recognising that through language, discourse and texts, worlds are created and recreated in ways of which we are rarely aware' (Usher and Edwards 1994: 16).

Deconstruction

As discussed previously in this chapter, within a feminist poststructuralist perspective, language is a critical site of the construction of the subject. Consequently, deconstructing the language that we use every day is an important step in understanding how power relations are constructed and operate in our daily lives. It is an important process in doing social justice education from a feminist poststructuralist perspective. Deconstruction, stemming from the works of the French poststructuralist, Jacques Derrida, is a critical pedagogical tool that is utilized to expose the multiplicity of possible meanings, contradictions and assumptions that are perpetuated through texts (Davies 1993; Alloway 1995; MacNaughton 2009). Deconstruction involves identifying the various discourses that are operating through texts (for example, stories, movies, television, images, advertisements, newspapers); acknowledging the various subject positions that these discourses make available to the reader; and analysing the power relations that underpin the knowledge they are constructing. Davies (1993: 8) points out that 'Deconstruction, or putting a concept under erasure, is a political act. It reveals the generally invisible but repressive politics of any particular form of representation.'

The process of deconstruction seeks primarily to identify the normalizing discourses that constitute common-sense understandings that define, restrict and regulate representations of subjectivities and identities, limiting the subject positions perceived possible to individual subjects. For example, many of the popular texts read by children tend to restrict their gendered subject positions to traditional narrow understandings of what it means to be a boy or a girl. Consequently, deconstruction is primarily about disrupting and destabilizing the cultural binaries that underpin much of the common-sense knowledge that we take up as 'truths' or 'reality'. Cultural binaries such as male/female, adult/child, heterosexual/homosexual and white/black are explicit or implicit in the normalizing discourses that operate in texts; they operate to constitute and perpetuate artificial hierarchical relations of power between the paired concepts, which are perceived as polarized opposites. For example, deconstructing the gender binary male/female would involve exploring the power relations that are inherent within polarized knowledge about boys and girls: boys are tough, loud and physically active, while girls are quiet, softly spoken, and prefer to sit, read or talk with friends.

Thus, the process of deconstruction involves critically unpacking the normalizing discourses that construct knowledge of identities, including those operating in our everyday lives (see MacNaughton 2009). The following steps are involved in this process:

- detecting the cultural binaries underpinning the knowledge operating in the text;
- identifying the discourses perpetuated through the stories or images;

- examining the values and assumptions constituted within these discourses;
- acknowledging the purpose of the discourses;
- exploring how particular subjects are positioned within these discourses – that is, exploring what cultural scripts are implicit and explicit in the texts, and how they work to position the reader;
- identifying who benefits from these discourses and who does not;
- examining how these discourses contribute to the policies and practices of broader social, economic and political structures; and
- acknowledging different possible readings of the text, asking different questions that highlight and challenge how particular ways of doing identity are normalized to the point that they become unquestionable.

The process of deconstruction is not just valuable for building children's critical thinking and opening up different possibilities for doing their identities, it is also a useful tool to deconstruct the different knowledge that operates in the daily lives of all of us.

Implications for policy and practice

The theoretical framework outlined above has significant implications for the way that educators and community-based professionals work with staff, children and their families, particularly in the context of doing social justice education. It is also invaluable in terms of demonstrating the importance of educators being aware of their own locations within discourses, which will impact, consciously and unconsciously, on their practices and daily interactions with others.

It is important that educational settings and community-based services reflexively review their policies around diversity and difference to ascertain if they are inadvertently perpetuating normalizing discourses that continue to other those who are perceived as different. Policies as texts can be deconstructed and reconstructed in order to identify the cultural binaries and the discourses that are operating within them that exclude difference, and maintain and perpetuate hierarchical relations of power – for example, the naming of particular groups in policies and excluding others; or assuming and privileging a particular family type. Hence, policies need to be regularly evaluated and critiqued in relation to who is represented and who is left out. As pointed out in Chapter 1, early education and community-based services are microcosms of the broader society and will thus reflect the normalizing discourses that prevail to sustain the status quo.

Being reflexively aware of how one perceives difference is import-ant to how one communicates and negotiates with families from a range of diverse socio-cultural backgrounds. The location of individual subjects in discourses of diversity and difference will impact on the relations of power that operate around these relationships. Educators and community-based professionals may, through their everyday practices, be othering families, children and staff who are different. For example, educators and community-based professionals who are positioned in the discourse that perceives gay and lesbian families as abnormal and immoral may operate, consciously and unconsciously, to exclude and marginalize these families.

The construction of subjectivity has important implications for pedagogy and the curriculum. Children's subjectivity and identities are constituted in discourses and they, too, are capable of taking up subject positions in different discourses, depending on their desire and understanding of power relations. Childhood educators and community-based professionals need to observe children's positioning in discourse in their setting, and to link their interpretations of these observations to programming and planning – for example, bilingual children's rejection of their home language, or the young boy who bullies other children as a performance of his masculinity. Being aware of how families, educators and other staff are positioned in discourses is also crucial; for example, parents from religious backgrounds may express homophobia as a result of their location in that religion. It is important that observations of children's location in discourse are followed up in a range of different programming and pedagogical strategies; for example, discussions, experiences, the use of resources, and integration across a range of curriculum areas are crucial.

The subjective positioning of childhood educators, community-based professionals and families in discourses around issues of diversity and difference will be crucial in constructing children's knowledge in this area and influencing their subjective position in discourse. Understanding the construction of one's subjectivity, through the process of subjectification, is crucial to educators in order to see its effects on us and on the learning environments we collaboratively produce (Davies 1994).

Children, like adults, are constantly negotiating power relations with one another and with adults. It is important to observe and identify on a daily basis the dominant and alternative discourses available to children operating in early childhood settings, which are either limiting or extending their knowledge of the world, or limiting the subject positions they have available to them; for example, the discourses perpetuated through educators' responses to the young boy who likes to dress up in women's clothing.

As knowledge is socially constructed in discourse, it can be deconstructed and reconstructed. Individual subjects are not fixed but are changing beings. Engaging children in critical thinking and reflection on the normalizing discourses that operate in terms of identities, difference, power relations and inequality can enable racist, sexist, homophobic and classist discourses, among others, to be disrupted and challenged, opening up new and more equitable ways of looking at the world. As pointed out in this chapter, language is the place where identities are constituted, maintained and challenged, so it is an important site of subjective change. Deconstruction of the discourses in which people are positioned to identify the power relations operating is a critical tool for developing critical thinking.

Conclusion

This chapter has provided an overview of the theoretical frameworks that we have utilized in our research and teaching over the past ten years, with a particular focus on feminist poststructuralist perspectives. Our readings of these perspectives have also been significantly influenced by the works of Foucault, especially those around discourse, power and subjectivity. We feel that the process of subjectification is critical to doing social justice work with both adults and children. It provides an invaluable theoretical framework in which to understand how individual subjects become who they are, and how they actively participate in the construction of their own subjectivities and regulate those of others. Feminist poststructural perspectives also remind us that we are flexible, complex and contradictory shifting subjects with multiple identities. This is critical to an understanding of power, identity and social inequality.

Recommended reading

Ball, S.J. (2012) *Foucault, Power and Education*. London: Routledge.

Foucault, M. (1974) *The Archaeology of Knowledge*. London: Tavistock.

Foucault, M. (1978) *The History of Sexuality, Volume 1: An Introduction*, trans. R. Hurley. New York: Vintage Books.

Foucault, M. (1980) *Power/Knowledge*, trans. C. Gordon. New York: Pantheon Books.

Mills, S. (2004) *Discourse*. London: Routledge.

Weedon, C. (1997) *Feminist Practice and Poststructuralist Theory*, 2nd edn. Oxford: Blackwell.

3
Constructions of childhood and the changing worlds of children

Introduction

As briefly pointed out in Chapter 1, postmodernist and feminist poststructural perspectives have challenged fixed and universal understandings of childhood inherent in modernist humanist thinking, and have offered different ways of looking at childhood and children's learning (for example, see Davies 1989, 1993; James and Prout 1990; Walkerdine 1990; Cannella 1997; MacNaughton 2000; Grieshaber 2001; Robinson 2002, 2005b; Cannella and Diaz Soto 2010). Postmodernist and feminist poststructuralist perspectives have highlighted the social construction of childhood – a social process in which understandings of what it means to be a child are constituted within historical, cultural and political discourses. The social construction of childhood focuses on the multiple ways in which childhood is viewed and experienced within and across different cultures, geographical locations (e.g. urban and rural), and historical timeframes. Childhood experiences are also significantly influenced by other factors such as children's gender, social class, ethnicity, sexuality, abilities and family values, including those based on religious, faith or agnostic principles. A focus on the social construction of childhood has meant that many of the perceived 'universal truths' assumed about the child and childhood have been challenged and disrupted. The social construction of childhood provides a critical counter-narrative to the biological determinist views that fix what it means to be a child in human biology, and constitutes childhood in a binary oppositional relationship with adults – that is, what it means to be a child is defined in opposition to what it means to be an adult. In this critical counter-narrative, developmental theories of childhood framed within modernist humanist perspectives of the universal child and Western binary logic have been critiqued and decentred. New discourses about childhood have emerged that view children as social, political and agentic actors in the construction of their own subjectivities and of the worlds in which they live.

This chapter explores the social construction of childhood, and the multiple ways in which childhood is viewed and experienced globally. Childhood is a fluid and heterogeneous period of life that is all too often ideally represented through middle-class, white and Western images. This discussion examines the ways in which the child has been constituted and regulated through socio-cultural, political, educational and economic discourses that are foundational to adult–child binary thinking. Several main areas are addressed in this chapter. First, a brief overview of the postmodern and feminist poststructural critique of the hegemony of modernist humanist theories of child development, such as those of Piaget, in understandings of and approaches to the child and childhood is provided. However, in contrast, some child developmentalist perspectives have considered the role of the social as being central in children's development. Second, this chapter explores the discourse of childhood innocence and its centrality to the regulatory practices surrounding childhood (and adulthood and adult citizenship), and its perpetuation of the adult–child binary. Generally viewed as being biologically inherent in the child by parents/ guardians, educators and other adults, this chapter argues that childhood innocence is a socially constructed concept that is utilized as a technology of power. When childhood innocence is transgressed by educators, parents or even by children, moral panic often results, operating as a powerful social control. Third, a brief overview is given of the ways in which the notion of childhood innocence is utilized to regulate children's lives, especially in terms of their access to knowledge, and the implications this has for children's health and well-being. In addition, we look at the notion of 'difficult knowledge', and how this influences the ways in which educators and parents and guardians work with children (Robinson 2013). Fourth, children's relationship to citizenship is addressed in this chapter. Acknowledging children as agentic subjects contributing to the world we live in is key to children being considered citizens in their own right, rather than in the process of 'becoming' citizens in adulthood. Finally, this chapter explores the changing lives of children in the twenty-first century, and what being a child means in a world that is rapidly changing through global and mobile technologies. It also examines the ways in which children in Western developed countries have become central to advertising in both the consumption and selling of products for large corporate profits, while many children from developing countries are steeped in poverty. Childhood is ever changing and, for many, is a vastly different childhood from that experienced by their parents or guardians. It is critical that children are provided with the skills needed to successfully navigate these new and changing landscapes in order to become competent, resilient and ethical subjects.

Challenges to mainstream child development theory

Postmodern and feminist poststructural perspectives disrupt and challenge the hegemony of modernist humanist perspectives of the universal
child. The child is born into society as an embodied being who grows and
physically matures over time, but postmodern and feminist poststructural theorists dispute the notion of a universally shared experience of
childhood inherent in human biology, arguing that children experience,
negotiate and contribute in their daily lives in the early years in multiple
and different ways (James and Prout 1990; Gittins 1998; James, Jenks and
Prout 1998; Jenkins 1998). Piagetian theory of child development, which
continues to dominate understandings of childhood and children's learning, is an example of a hegemonic modernist humanist perspective of
childhood. This theory is based on the perspective that children from birth
proceed to develop along a biologically predetermined, clearly articulated
linear process towards becoming adults. In this view it is held that all children proceed through this process, reaching certain emotional, physical
and cognitive development stages that correlate with particular chronological ages. In this perceived linear process of development, adulthood
is marked by the ability to engage in abstract and hypothetical thinking.

Modernist humanist perspectives are imbued with binary logical
thinking and, in Piagetian understandings of child development, children
are viewed oppositionally to adults. That is, childhood is defined in opposition to what it means to be an adult; in which case children are viewed
as not being able to cognitively and emotionally engage in the world as
adults do. Consequently, children are viewed as being inherently different
from adults and in a process of 'becoming' adult rather than in a state
of 'being', where they are social actors in their own right, with agency
contributing to the construction of their own childhood.

This process creates the 'world of the child' and 'world of the adult'
binary – separate, distinct and often mutually exclusive spaces in which
differential relations of power are reinforced and maintained between
adults and children. Childhood has also been romanticized by adults, and
'childhood innocence' has been critical in justifying the way that adults
have kept children separate, especially from the public domains of active
citizenry. Gittins (1998: 111) points out that 'Images of children are invari-
ably constructed *by adults* to convey messages and meanings *to adults*.'
This separation of children and adults, perpetuated within this binary logic,
underpins current taken-for-granted or common-sense understandings of
childhood and children, which continue to dominate and influence how
educators, community-based professionals and others work with children
in their early years and beyond. It also underpins many parents/guardians'
interactions with their children. This binary logic has largely determined

what knowledge is accessible to children, and the expectations of what children are capable of achieving and comprehending. This latter point has some serious consequences for children's health and well-being (Robinson 2013), a point that is discussed further in this chapter.

Feminist poststructuralists view childhood as discursively and materially constituted. Within this perspective it is acknowledged that childhood is not fixed in biology but is experienced in multiple ways, influenced by the socio-cultural values, historical periods of time, geographical locations and political contexts in which children grow up. There are multiple and competing discourses of childhood globally that define what it means to be a child and work to regulate socio-cultural practices around children. The discourses of childhood that prevail locally and nationally in different cultures shape perceptions about when childhood 'begins' and 'ends', and how children are treated and included in the everyday politics of daily life, both inside and outside of the family. Experiences of childhood are also inflected by various aspects of one's subjectivity such as gender, socio-economic status or social class, ethnicity, age, body abilities, family structures, and so on. Despite the diversity in experiences of childhood, the dominant discourse that is perpetuated through Western media, popular culture and children's literature tends to be Eurocentric, white and middle class, romanticizing an image of the 'innocent child'.

Political ideologies and socio-cultural inequalities, such as poverty, continue to impact meanings of childhood and children's experiences in their early lives, particularly in terms of work and schooling. Colonization that has prevailed in many countries has had a profound impact on how childhood is perceived and experienced, especially in terms of work and schooling (Cannella and Viruru 2004; Katz 2004; O'Donnell 2015; Wells 2015). For example, colonization and the inherent racist discourses that operate within this process have significantly impacted the early educational experiences of many Aboriginal and Torres Strait Islander children in Australia since white settlement (see Chapter 5).

Feminist poststructuralists critique mainstream theories of child development, like that of Piaget, primarily for: the assumed biologically determined universalism; the generalizations from small groups to *all* children; the perceived linearity of development; the failure to recognize the importance of individual subjectivity, socio-cultural, historical, economic and political factors that abound in these theories (James and Prout 1990; Gittins 1998; James, Jenks and Prout 1998; Wulf 2002; Kontopodis, Wulf and Fichtner 2011). The universalizing categorization of children's behaviours within chronological 'ages' and 'stages' reinforces normative understandings about children's developmental pathways, especially if viewed from middle-class, Eurocentric perspectives. Mainstream universal theories of child development reinforce dominant power relations and define otherness. As Lubeck (1998: 301) points out, the 'idea of stages does not orient us to think in any but normative terms about children whose developmental trajectory might differ'.

In terms of constructions of childhood more broadly, feminist poststructuralists and postmodernists are concerned with several main issues: challenging the hegemony of scientific 'truths' that underpin **authoritative knowledge** and concretize definitions of childhood; the way that the dominant discourse of childhood is founded within the cultural oppositional binary adult/child that perpetuates hierarchical power relationships between adults and children; how the dominant discourse of childhood has perpetuated white, Western and middle-class values that have historically been linked to strong religious and moral discourses; how such modernist humanist perspectives have tended to silence children's voices and compromise their positions in society as citizens; and the impact that such discourses of childhood have had on understandings of children's learning and their access to knowledge.

Such critiques have increased awareness of the need to view child development and children's learning within different social, cultural, political and economic contexts of childhood. Some cultural-historical psychologists, often influenced by the works of Vygotsky (1978), and historical anthropologists, also critical of mainstream Western developmental theories and educational practices, are exploring and conceptualizing child development and children's learning in the contexts of culture and history (Wulf 2011; Kontopodis, Wulf and Fichtner 2011; Moro 2011). Within these perspectives emphasis is placed on the diversity of human life, communication, semiotic processes, the use of artefacts, pictures, technologies, performativity, everyday actions, schools, family and community practices to explore child development. For example, Moro's research with pre-verbal infants points out that:

> During pre-verbal development, the mind is specifically mediated by material culture through artefacts and non-verbal signs other people use to transmit the use of the object in triadic interaction, allowing the construction of new inferences about the material world by the child . . . The material object is the source of cognitive development through signs and public meaning shapes the mind in the very early developing mind. (2011: 69)

Wulf (2011) argues that children experience the world through the process of mimesis. Mimetic processes are the means through which children relate to others in their lives and in doing so take part in cultural processes. Children participate in the performances (rituals) and skills of their social group, adopting its cultural knowledge. Wulf points out that children have a mimetic desire to copy those around them – adults, older siblings and peers – in order to become like them. Robinson and Davies (2015) point out that children are eager to engage in cultural rituals, such as having a boyfriend or girlfriend and marriage, which children generally view as rites of passage into adulthood. Children rehearse these cultural rituals, where mock weddings, 'special' relationships and emulating family relationships are often central to their play. However, mimetic engagement in rituals does not mean that the ritual is always enacted in the exact same manner. Kontopodis, Wulf and Fichtner (2011: 8) point out 'rituals do not only guard societal and cultural continuity, they also cause change'. As a result of the regularity and repetition of performative mimetic rituals, children both confirm and modify practices, relationships and relations of power (Butler 1997).

According to Wulf (2011), it is through mimetic processes that young people learn the values, attitudes and norms embedded in cultural institutions (e.g. family, school, workplace). In the process of learning, children's knowledge, experiences and understandings of their environments increase, enabling them to encounter a broader range of discourses constituting the world in which they live. Largely through their encounters with conflicts and crises, children learn to become more reflexive and aware of power relations and the consequences of transgressing cultural norms. Through the process of reflexive learning there is the potential to change one's location in socio-cultural discourses. Kontopodis, Wulf and Fichtner (2011: 5) point out, 'Being in the world is transforming the world, not adapting to it . . . Human development is the process of the purposeful transformation of the world, a process which is collaborative.'

In humanist modernist discourse, children tend to be viewed as in a process of 'becoming' an adult rather than in a state of 'being' social agentic subjects. Emphasis and importance are placed on what the child will be rather than what the child is (Uprichard 2008). This perspective reinforces the binary notion of the child as being dependent and incompetent, while the adult is considered to be the independent and competent subject. There is a suggestion that only adults can be competent beings and not children. This is, however, demonstrably untrue: one only has to watch young children navigating computer and mobile technologies while some adults watch on in bewilderment at the children's competencies and their own limitations. Competency and dependency are socially and relationally contextual (Uprichard 2008). Viewing the child as either in a state of 'becoming' or of 'being' is problematic, Emma Uprichard (2008: 303) argues, pointing out that seeing the child as 'being and becoming' increases the agency children have in the world. Uprichard (2008: 311) states: 'The "being and becoming" discourse extends the notion of agency offered by the "being" discourse to consider the child as a social actor constructing his or her everyday life *and* the world around them, both in the present and the future.' The process of ageing throughout life is not just an embodied experience for both children and adults, but is simultaneously a social and relational experience. Children's anticipation of adulthood contributes to the ways that they experience their childhood (Qvortrup 2004: 269). This latter point is reinforced in Robinson and Davies's (2015) research, in which children considered 'becoming' adult as a rite of passage many were anxious to achieve. Children often rehearsed how they perceived their adult lives to be in their everyday play, mimicking adult behaviours and engaging in social relations of power. The process of 'becoming' is always relational, performative and ever changing as individuals encounter, negotiate and impact everyday experiences, places, spaces, objects and other bodies (Katz 2004).

Childhood and 'difficult knowledge'

As pointed out previously in this chapter, the modernist humanist binary logic that underpins dominant current perspectives of Western childhood has artificially constructed and maintained the separate spheres of the 'world of the child' and the 'world of the adult'. One significant consequence of this process has been the categorization of certain knowledge as being suitable for adults only and inappropriate for children (Robinson 2013). As Michel Foucault (1980) argues, knowledge is framed within struggles for power that are exercised through competing discourses. In this 'power/knowledge nexus', whose knowledge dominates as the 'truth' and who can access knowledge is largely about power relations.

'Difficult knowledge' is a term that stems from the work of Deborah Britzman (1998), the Canadian educational philosopher. Britzman uses difficult knowledge within her explanation of affective pedagogy. Using a psychoanalytic lens, Britzman (1998: 118) argues that to learn there needs to be a point of resistance on the part of the learner. Difficult knowledge challenges one's subjectivity, resulting in a point of crisis in the self and a critique of, or interference with, the ways in which one looks at the world. Robinson (2013: 23) extends this understanding of difficult knowledge within a Foucauldian framework to include the tensions that exist around relations of power inherent in knowledge.

Children's knowledge and their access to knowledge are bound up in such relations of power. The knowledge that is considered inappropriate for children tends to be that which is often associated with highly emotive, challenging and difficult topic areas for many adults to address – for example, death, sickness, war, divorce, poverty, violence and sexuality (Silin 1995). Some adults view these broader socio-cultural, political and economic issues as developmentally inappropriate topics to address with children, based on the perspective that children are 'too young', will not understand and that the information will compromise their childhood innocence. These topics have become part of what is generally considered by some adults as 'adults' knowledge'. Sexuality, for example, is a particularly difficult topic for many adults to discuss with children and young people. This is largely due to the socio-cultural taboos that exist around sexuality, the discomfort and embarrassment that may be experienced by individuals as a result of the effects of these taboos, and the regulatory impact of hegemonic discourses of childhood and sexuality that constitute this information as developmentally inappropriate for children (Silin 1995; Robinson 2013; Bhana 2016). Robinson (2013) and others (Kontopodis, Wulf and Fichtner 2011; Wulf 2011) argue that the discourse of childhood innocence operates as a powerful regulator around children's access to knowledge and perpetuates the belief that children need to be 'protected' from 'difficult knowledge' in order to maintain their innocence for as long as possible. Robinson (2013) points out that this perspective can have a serious impact on children's health and well-being, raising the question, who benefits most from the discourse of childhood innocence, children or some adults?

Many of the educators, parents and community-based professionals in the various research projects foundational to this book presumed that children were 'too young' and 'too innocent' to comprehend or think critically about what they considered to be 'adult issues' – for example, difference, power, 'race', sexuality, domestic violence, gender inequality. As pointed out in Chapter 1, there is a hierarchy of differences or of rights that exist among educators, community-based professionals working with children and among parents/guardians. This hierarchy reflects the degree of comfort and commitment that individuals have to addressing various equity and social justice issues with children and their families. Those issues that are the most controversial tend to pose the most personal discomfort and are often connected to areas associated with difficult knowledge. Sexuality – especially same-sex families and lesbian and gay equity issues – is generally located at the bottom of the hierarchy and considered an issue less relevant and less appropriate to address with children. Despite the increased awareness of same-sex relationships and families, and of the considerable legal gains they have received in recent years across many Western developed countries, including equal marriage rights, this area of equity and social justice continues to be seen as less relevant to children, and remains a controversial and difficult topic.

Many issues that are relevant to children's everyday lives, perceived to be adults' knowledge, are excluded in children's early education in the name of protecting their 'childhood innocence', backed up by arguments that it is developmentally inappropriate. However, there were some educators, parents and community-based professionals who believed that it was important to address these issues with children, and argued that it can be done, and is being done, in a manner suitable for children. Addressing these issues with children is important for beginning the process of building an awareness of equity, social justice and ethical relationships early in life – a process that is continuously built upon over children's schooling. Children are engaging in building their own knowledge around these issues from the bits of information they receive from parents/guardians, siblings, peers, media, schooling and other significant adults in their lives. However, much of this information is based on stereotypes and misinformation.

The social construction of young children's identities within the social categories of 'race', class, ethnicity, gender, sexuality, language, and so on, tends to be under-theorized by educators and community-based professionals working with children (Robinson and Jones Díaz 1999; Davies and Robinson 2012). There is limited recognition by educators of the broader sociological frameworks, which position children's learning and development within the socio-cultural, historical, political and historical contexts in which they live.

Childhood, regulation and vulnerability: the impact of moral panic

It has been argued that the greatest change in childhood has been the historical shift from viewing and valuing children as economic resources contributing to the family income to viewing and valuing children as emotional investments (Cunningham 1995). This shift was largely the result of changing social, political and economic circumstances arising from the Industrial Revolution in the eighteenth and nineteenth centuries, resulting in the rise of capitalism and middle-class ideologies, and the emergence of the modern nuclear family. Children, especially those from the middle classes became increasingly restricted to the confines and privacy of the family home, under the care, surveillance and protection of parents and other family members (Holland 2006). The introduction of compulsory public schooling in many Western countries was a means through which to fulfil the need for a more literate workforce, to exert greater control over the development of children's moral and Christian values, and was an extension of the process of separating children from adults. The emotional capital invested in childhood, infused with sentimentality, romanticism, nostalgia and innocence, became increasingly reflected through the hegemony of the nuclear family, and the primacy of social, political and economic investments in children's care, welfare and protection more broadly in society.

Children's perceived dependence on adults is a central aspect of the modernist humanist hegemonic discourse of childhood in many Western cultures. How children's dependency has been defined and experienced is variable across history, age, gender, ethnicity, social class, ability and other aspects of subjectivity. Children and young people, to varying degrees, are materially dependent on adults for a period of time, socially and economically. Children are also generally vulnerable to a range of abuses and exploitations from adults and older children as a result of their age, size, gender and the limited power they are able to mobilize in some contexts. The perceived material vulnerability of children is intensified through the discursive constitution of children as vulnerable and dependent subjects. The discourses of childhood, childhood innocence and mainstream child development theory contribute significantly to the construction of children as dependent, incompetent and vulnerable (Robinson 2013). These discourses perpetuate certain beliefs and practices around childhood that reinforce children's dependencies on adults, and undermine the development of children's agency, resilience and competencies. How societies view children, the role children are considered to play in communities, how perceived vulnerabilities are managed, and how power inequalities between adults and children are addressed, is crucial to children's everyday lives.

In Western countries, childhood has become the most regulated period across the human life span (Rose 1999). The regulation of childhood has been especially strict in the context of sexuality and children's access to knowledge in this area (Robinson 2103). Chapter 10 of this book provides an in-depth discussion of these issues, but it is important to acknowledge sexuality in this context as an area in which the regulation of childhood (and adulthood) has been extreme. Parents'/guardians' and community fears and anxieties have escalated in recent times in regards to children's perceived vulnerabilities to harm, especially physical and sexual abuse and exploitation associated with 'stranger danger'. These concerns have resulted in a myriad of social and legal policies and practices that do not just regulate children's behaviours but also those of adults, institutions, business practices and those of communities more broadly. This regulation can be seen in the censorship and rating of films and television programmes, the internet, the music industry and advertising. A highly successful industry has emerged in developing devices and software (e.g. Net Nanny) aimed at preventing and/or managing children's access to certain information in the home and at school – information deemed inappropriate and dangerous to children and young people. Schooling curricula are regulated according to what information is considered developmentally appropriate at certain ages, and discussions of significant socio-political issues – for example, marriage equality for same-sex couples – are censored. This latter example is typified in the recent censorship of the airing of the film *Gayby Baby* (2015) in secondary schools in the state of New South Wales (NSW), Australia. This documentary, directed by Maya Newell, follows the lives of four children who are living in same-sex families. Newell, who grew up with lesbian parents, made the film to counteract the lack of children's voices in the marriage equality debate in Australia. Children's lives have become increasingly and strictly monitored in and outside the home in terms of where they can go and with whom, what they can see, what information they are given, and with whom and what they can play.

When the social regulations around childhood are transgressed, or perceived to be, it can result in moral panic among some members of society. The censorship around the showing of the film of *Gayby Baby* due to public concern is an example of moral panic; or perhaps, more realistically, an intervention by the conservative NSW state premier to avoid moral panic on his watch. The fear of being caught in a moral panic is often enough to lead to censorship, greater regulations and the shutting down of public conversations on the issues. This fear can also lead to self-censorship – that is, individuals choosing to exclude discussions of issues considered controversial, or choosing not to challenge the inequities often associated with such issues. Individuals risk becoming the personal and professional target of media and public scrutiny if they have included the discussion or challenged the inequities, potentially losing their job. In the example of *Gayby Baby*, it was not the schools censoring the film on same-sex families and creating a moral panic, indeed there was support from schools to air the film, but rather it was a conservative Australian newspaper that reported parental concerns about the film being shown to young people in schools. In moral panics, it can take one person to express concerns to the media, who then play a major role in tapping in to the fears and anxieties of conservative members of the public in order to put pressure on those who have the power to reinstate the status quo – generally a reinstatement of conservative values. As this example shows, moral panic is an effective political tool – or technology of power, to use a Foucauldian term – for maintaining the status quo; that is, reinforcing the hegemony of dominant discourses and maintaining current power relations (McRobbie and Thornton 1995; Hier 2003; Ben-Yahuda 2009). Robinson (2013) points out that, in more recent years, a moral panic has arisen around children's and young people's access to knowledge about same-sex relationships and families whenever the marriage equality debate in Australia seems to be favouring the legalization of same-sex marriage. Due to the emotional capital invested in children, they are a fruitful foundation in which to manifest social anxiety and moral panic, often for political gain (Irvine 2006).

Despite the regulations being perceived to be 'in the best interest' of children and for their protection, many of these regulatory practices, especially regarding access to vital knowledge, can have major negative consequences for many children. Gittins (1998: 107) points out: 'Children, generally well looked after and protected, are none the less extremely vulnerable as a result of their own dependencies, isolation, silencing and disenfranchisement.' Robinson (2013) and others (e.g. Kitzinger 1990) have argued that the regulation of children's access to sexuality education, often *in the name of protection* and *in the best interests* of the child, can ironically contribute to making children more 'vulnerable'. That is, children need access to such knowledge, which can be built on over the schooling years in order to foster awareness, critical thinking, resilience, well-being and ethical practices in the early years (Robinson 2013). Resilience, well-being and ethical practice are considered here within multiple interactive relationships, involving individuals, communities, organizations, social structures and systems, rather than within discourses of individual pathologies (Ecclestone and Lewis 2014).

The changing nature of childhoods: technology, social media, popular culture and the child consumer

There has been growing public concern and anxiety over the past three decades or more about the perceived loss of childhood or disappearance of childhood in contemporary Western societies (Postman 1982; Palmer 2006). Mary Jane Kehily (2010: 16) points out that 'media commentary and public discourse on childhood commonly invoke a notion of "crisis"', or moral panic. This concern, more generally expressed through adults' nostalgic longing for a romantic ideal of childhood, is based on the notion that childhood is in crisis and is not what it once was – carefree, adventurous, playful and innocent; children were perceived to be part of a private world separated from the everyday hardships and concerns of adults. This alleged crisis in childhood is viewed to be the consequence of major social changes including, but not limited to, the impact of technology, social media, consumerism, popular culture and fears around children's safety, especially from 'stranger danger'. Despite the evidence to the contrary, children's safety is generally perceived to be at greater risk today than in previous generations (Levine 2002). Many adults lament that children can no longer play outdoors without adult supervision as they could in their own childhood due to the potential risks of abuse, abduction or even childhood accidents. One of the consequences of living in a risk-averse society is that children are subject to greater regulation and surveillance. Children are spending far more time indoors under the protection and close watchful eye of parents or another adult than in any previous generation.

The world and individual lives, including those of children, have changed in many ways through the impact of information and communications technology (ICT), especially mobile technology devices and social media. Access to vast amounts of information 24 hours a day, seven days a week; instant communications with friends, family and work colleagues living virtually any where in the world; online shopping; and the constitution of identities and the documentation of lives through social media sites such as Facebook and Instagram are everyday realities for many adults and children (Buckingham 2013). Many children have developed a sophisticated knowledge of technology usage that often surpasses that of their parents, and they enjoy a sense of power from this expertise (Kincheloe 2002; Zevenbergen 2007). However, David Buckingham (2013: 11) questions the discourse of a 'digital generation' as a characterization of children today, pointing out that technological change affects us all, including adults. Buckingham views the term more as a representation of marketing rhetoric – a set of imperatives about what children and young people should be or need to be, rather than what they are. Buckingham (2013: 11) maintains that very few children and young people 'are interested in technology in its own right, and most are simply concerned about what they can use it for'. Broad systematic differences may exist between adults and children on what they do with technology, Buckingham argues, but any essentialist assumptions about the differences between children and adults need to be challenged.

Children and young people in Western countries do spend more time engaging with technology and computers than the average parent. In European Union (EU) countries, children 0–8 years old are increasingly spending time online (Holloway, Green and Livingstone 2013). In the UK, approximately 33 per cent of 3 and 4 year olds access the internet using computers, 6 per cent via tablets and 3 per cent via mobile phones. Eighty-seven per cent of 5 to 7 year olds use the internet, which has risen from 68 per cent in 2007 (Ofcom 2012: 5). In the Netherlands, 78 per cent of toddlers and preschoolers are online and 5 per cent of babies under 1 are going online (Holloway, Green and Livingstone 2013: 8). In Australian research with 604 children aged 8 to 11, 95 per cent had accessed the internet over the four weeks prior to the start of the research (Australian Communications and Media Authority 2012: 6). Research in the USA, conducted with 1051 children 0 to 6 years old, shows that 75 per cent of participants watched television and 32 per cent watched videos/DVDs for 80 minutes on average on a typical day, while 27 per cent of 5–6 year olds used a computer on average for 50 minutes a day (Vandewater *et al.* 2007). Although television is arguably still the most popular activity for children, the platform on which it is being watched is changing, with tablets and smartphones the most commonly used devices. Interestingly, mobile devices such as tablets and smartphones have become the new pseudo-childminders for some parents, keeping children occupied, entertained and quiet. It is not uncommon to see children totally preoccupied with these devices while their parents do their business or engage in uninterrupted conversation with other adults. Mobile technologies and the internet are entrenched in everyday life, structuring daily activities, educating, building skills, entertaining and managing children, developing new languages, and contributing to the constitution of children and young people's identities.

Children's relationship to computers, social media and the internet has raised a number of important questions for parents, educators, community-based professionals and researchers, as follows.

- *What are the access and equity issues associated with children's access to computers and the internet* (Zevenbergen 2007; Buckingham 2013)*?* Not all children live in digitally wealthy home environments and the 'digital divide' has important implications for children's early learning opportunities. Robyn Zevenbergen (2007) points out that children come to early childhood settings and schooling with a digital habitus that varies across experiences of technology access and usage in the home environment. Zevenbergen (2007) argues that children's formal early education has the potential to address the gap between those who come to preschool with a wealth of experience with technology, or digital capital, and those who come from technology-poor family households.

- *What are the implications of this relationship for children's social and educational development?* Computers and the internet provide considerable educational opportunities for young children, especially in terms of access to information and the possibility of building online communities with other children. Research conducted by Marilyn Fleer (2011) examining children's practices of using technology in the home, either as utility (e.g. the everyday usage of technology to run a household) or through play, highlights the need to consider the technological construction of childhood in the development of the early childhood education and primary school curriculum. However, children's lives have become much more sedentary as a result of the time spent on computers and the internet. This could also be attributed to children's greater confinement to the indoors and the home, as discussed previously.

- *What is the balance between online opportunities and risks for children and their families, and how is this achieved?* The opportunities available to children through their engagement with computers, the internet and social media are significant in terms of education, skill development, access to information, communication with friends and family, and entertainment. It is also important to acknowledge that children and young people get a great deal of enjoyment and pleasure from this relationship with technology, and it is central to the formation of identity, relationships and friendship communities for many (Davies and Robinson 2013; Livingstone and Bober 2013). However, children's perceived vulnerabilities to paedophiles, cyber-bullying or accessing information that is considered inappropriate for children are fears that parents are confronting. These fears often result in stricter regulation of children and young people's (online) lives, which can increase conflict between children and their parents. Robinson (2013) argues that increasing children's critical thinking skills, providing them with more knowledge and opening up channels of communication between children and their families are critical in finding this balance between opportunity and risk.

Popular culture and consumerism have also been viewed as changing the nature of childhood and negatively impacting children's lives. The consuming child, or the desiring child, has been viewed by some to be representative of a 'childhood in crisis' due to modern social changes – the shallow, greedy and self-centred child who wants, buys, gets and finds happiness in material goods (Palmer 2006). Children in Western developed countries have increasingly become the targets of corporate advertising, the production of material goods and company profits; in most cases children are also used to sell these products. This has become known as the 'corporatization of childhood'. Consequently tensions arise around the agentic child, who undermines the possibilities held on to by some of 'preserving' the discourse of romantic idealized childhood (Cunningham 1995).

Children's relationship to popular culture and consumerism is complex. It is important to acknowledge the role that popular culture and consumerism play in the 'everydayness, spatialities, material cultures, bodily practices and affectivity of children and young people's social and cultural lives' (Horton 2012: 5). Children's relationships with a range of cultural phenomena, such as pop groups, toys, films, celebrities, television programmes, fashion, books and collectables, as John Horton (2012: 5) points out, have 'remarkable ubiquity, currency, urgency and vitality' in their lives. Material goods are integral to children's social interactions and participation in the world (Cook 2013). Cook (2013: 425) argues that through the consumption of and interaction with popular culture, children experience 'a sense of belonging and exclusion, difference and sameness . . . Goods and material things enable and activate the creation of culture and social relationships.' Thorne (2005) states that material things are used to 'mark and negotiate difference'. The equity issues associated with children's access to popular culture and material goods are central social justice concerns in children's education and to the development of their friendship groups.

Childhood has changed and it is different in many ways from the lives of the parents and grandparents of children today. Childhood is always changing across historical points of time, with children adapting to new social developments perhaps more easily than their parents or grandparents. The dominant discourse of childhood that constitutes children's lives as adventurous, carefree, innocent and untouched by the everyday social, political and economic circumstances of their families, or by broader social issues and upheavals, is fantastical. Children are not immune to what is going on around them, and they are actively involved and central to the socio-cultural practices of the worlds they live in. Children are forever piecing together information they receive from multiple sources to build on their knowledge and versions of the world (Davies and Robinson 2010; Robinson 2013). In this process they are not just adapting to the world, they are contributing to transforming it (Wulf 2011).

Children and citizenship

The discourses of childhood that prevail in families and in broader communities are foundational to the ways in which, and to what degree, children are encouraged and supported to participate in the everyday social, political and economic practices of these sites. Children's agency arises out of social and cultural contexts. As discussed above, children and young people are social actors who are making contributions to transforming the worlds in which they live every day. However, in many contexts, children's agency is always compromised by the fact that the discourse of vulnerability intersects with the discourse of children's rights to be active, agentic participants in the world (Mitchell 2010; Robinson 2013).

The notion of children or young people's citizenship does not fit easily within hegemonic discourses of citizenship (McCleod 2012; Robinson 2012, 2013). This is largely due to children being viewed as citizens *in potentia*, or in the process of becoming citizens when they become adults, rather than being viewed as citizens in their own right (Mayo 2006). Adult governance of the child, including decision making, has been generally viewed as a key role of parents and the state in Western society. Cossman (2007: 2) argues that all subjects are in a process of *becoming* citizens, not just children. The process of *becoming* citizen highlights the regulatory aspect of hegemonic citizenship involving the production of a particular normative subject. Cath Larkins (2014) points out that dominant contractual and universal definitions of citizenship exclude children from the status of citizenship as they are perceived to lack competencies associated with citizenship such as rationality and independence, perceived as adult characteristics. She advocates for a difference-centred relational understanding of children's agency in citizenship, indicating that adults and children live in relationships of social interdependence and, at various points, both children and adults will each experience dependence on the other.

Although citizenship is a highly contested concept across disciplines, key concepts, such as membership, belonging, inclusion, participation and representation in a national culture tend to be central aspects of defining citizenship (Cossman 2007). These concepts, encompassing social and political agency, are as central to children's lives as they are to those of adults. Based on research in the UK and France with 5–13 year olds living in areas experiencing significant levels of poverty, Larkins (2014: 18) promotes an understanding of children's citizenship as 'Acts of citizenship'. Her research demonstrates that children do 'Acts of citizenship' such as: negotiating rules and creating selves; contributing to social good; contributing to the achievement of individuals' rights; and 'transgressing existing boundaries of citizenship to dispute balances of rights, responsibilities and status, enacting activist citizens answerable to justice'. Larkins comments:

> Citizenship is not only practised by those children who engage in formal participatory processes negotiating rules of social coexistence, such as through councils, committees, forums and decision-making processes. Children also enact themselves as citizens through practices at least as diverse as negotiating rules of social coexistence (wherever this may be), contributing to socially agreed good and fulfilling their own individual rights. (2014: 18)

It is critical to acknowledge and value how children 'enact citizenship of a different kind' in understandings of citizenship more generally (Larkins 2014: 19).

In varying ways, and to varying degrees, both adults and children exercise responsibilities and participate in social life in public and private spaces, such as in homes, schools, businesses, organizations and communities (Qvortrup 2008; Alderson 2010). Children's parliaments (e.g. in the UK, Scotland, India and Pakistan) have been established in which children work at the grass-roots level to enact change in their communities and beyond (Robinson 2013). Cindi Katz's (2004) research in Sudan highlights that children play a central role in the daily activities of the village in which they live. Children's involvement in these activities is crucial to the socio-cultural, political and economic success of the village. In order to prepare children to be active members or citizens in their villages, teaching and learning starts in early childhood.

Implications for policy and practice

It is important to be aware of the ways in which educational settings and other organizations working with children perpetuate certain discourses of childhood, and how this might impact on the children and families with whom they work. The Early Years Learning Framework for Australia (EYLFA) highlights that children are actively constructing their own understandings and contribute to others' learning. The framework also states that children are agentic subjects who have the right to participate in decisions that affect them, including their learning (DEEWR 2009: 9). As pointed out in this chapter, mainstream developmentalist perspectives of childhood tend to be foundational to practices and policies associated with children's learning, what is considered 'normal' and what children are perceived to be capable of understanding and achieving at certain ages. The EYLFA points out that drawing on a range of theories about childhood to inform pedagogical approaches to children's learning and development can challenge traditional ways of seeing children and teaching learning. Actively engaging in theoretical discussions can lead to an understanding about childhood and pedagogy that recognizes the potential limitations of certain theories, and the liberatory potential of others that can lead to working fairly and justly with children and families (DEEWR 2009: 11). It is important to include alternative ways of looking at children's development and learning that incorporate awareness of children's subjectivity and of the broader socio-cultural and historical factors that influence children's lives.

Examining individual values, and workplace policies and practices around children's access to knowledge, is also important for understanding how certain discourses underpin approaches to children's learning that, despite being viewed to be 'in the best interest of the child', can actually increase children's vulnerabilities. Children's access to knowledge is critical for building their resilience and well-being. Having a reflexive approach to practice encourages awareness of how daily interactions with children can and do reinforce binary understandings of adults and children. Reinforcing this binary thinking can undermine attempts to foster children's abilities to be agentic, responsible, resilient and ethical subjects. Workplace, family and community education on the constructions of childhood is important in order to work collaboratively around these issues.

It is essential that the diversity and complexities of children's contemporary lives are reflected in policies, practices, pedagogies and schooling curricula. Popular culture, social media and technology play central roles in many children's daily lives, structuring relationships and friendship groups, constituting identities, building skills and contributing to their education. Despite these areas being a great source of pleasure for children, they are often the basis of anxiety for many adults. Workplace, family and community education on these issues is important. Working collaboratively with families to build children's critical thinking skills and understandings of equity, social justice and ethical practices can support children's safe and successful navigation of these areas of their lives.

Children make significant contributions to families and communities as young citizen subjects. It is important to acknowledge the work children do and the potential they have for being actively involved in families and communities. Encouraging children to be agentic subjects and providing opportunities for them to contribute to daily activities builds a sense of community in children's lives.

Conclusion

This chapter has provided an overview of the social construction of childhood and the changing nature of children's lives in contemporary society. It has been argued that the dominant discourse of childhood innocence, reinforced by mainstream developmentalism, contributes to the construction of children as vulnerable subjects. The changing nature of children's lives is at odds with these discourses. In order to foster children's health and well-being, agency and resilience, there is a need to reconsider the influence these discourses have on perceptions and understanding of contemporary childhood.

Recommended reading

Alderson, P. (2010) Young children's individual participation in matters that affect them, in N. Thomas, and B. Perey-Smith (eds) *A Handbook of Children and Young People's Participation: Perspectives from Theory and Practice*. London: Routledge.

Buckingham, D. and Willett, R. (eds) (2013) *Digital Generations: Children, Young People and Media*. London: Routledge.

Kontopodis, M., Wulf, C. and Fichtner, B. (eds) (2011) *Children, Development and Education: Cultural, Historical, Anthropological Perspectives*. Dordrecht: Springer.

Robinson, K.H. (2013) *Innocence, Knowledge and the Construction of Childhood: The Contradictory Nature of Sexuality and Censorship in Children's Contemporary Lives*. London: Routledge.

4

The changing nature of families in the twenty-first century

Introduction

'Family' is a powerful and pervasive word in our culture and represents a highly unstable and contradictory space, in which an individual's sense of belonging and identity can be affirmed on the one hand, or dismissed and denied on the other. Thus, 'family' is a contentious space, which encompasses a variety of social, cultural, economic and symbolic meanings that shift across socio-economic class, ethnicity, gender, 'race', age and sexuality. How we 'do' family, define families, live in families, and who we live in them with, are all highly contested issues. Despite the diversity in how we 'do' family, normalizing discourses of the traditional nuclear family (that is, heterosexual, married, monogamous, mother and father with children) continue to underpin dominant representations of appropriate and successful family life. This discourse of the nuclear family, which tends to encompass Western, white, middle-class, Christian values and morals, impacts on the way that non-nuclear or Other families are often perceived and judged. Rather than embracing the diversity of family that exists, different families, particularly same-sex families and single parents, are frequently viewed as social problems, destabilizing the foundations of strong and moral family life and social values (Carrington 2002). There is widespread agreement that society is undergoing a process of rapid and radical economic, political, legal and social change, but the political rhetoric of the times, influenced by neoconservative values, upholds that the family should remain unchanged (Silva and Smart 1999). Thus, the traditional nuclear family is often mythically linked to a false expectation that it is the 'natural' foundation of a stable, safe and economically vibrant society, and has shifted 'from being a particular family shape to becoming a prescriptive recipe for living' (Carrington 2002: 8).

The field of education perpetuates the dominant discursive values and practices that operate in the broader society. Despite recognition of the need to encompass family diversity, based primarily on the philosophical position that family is critical to children's positive and successful educational experiences, practices in education still largely represent and perpetuate normal family relations within the discourse of the white, monolingual, middle-class, heterosexual nuclear family. Consequently, the values and perspectives of different families tend to be othered, marginalized and silenced, rarely receiving the official institutional validation given to the nuclear family.

In this chapter it is argued that, in order to acknowledge both the rapidly changing nature of family life and the diversity that exists, it is critical that understandings and representations of family shift away from universalized prescribed structures that normalize the nuclear family and exclude others. The nuclear family, although it may be the most prevalent in Western societies, is but one of many different types of family living practices that occur in society. Therefore, incorporating a feminist poststructuralist framework, we argue that it is more useful and inclusive to begin to reconceptualize families as multiple discursive performative social spaces that are fluid and changing across and within different cultural contexts over time. Further, recognizing different family relations in terms of 'localized networks of choice' (Carrington 2002: 140) acknowledges the agency that individual subjects have in making family networks, rather than being perceived to just passively inherit them.

This chapter on family examines a number of critical issues that pose significant challenges for the ways in which educators and other professionals working with families and children understand, represent, embrace and include family diversity in their policies, programming and practices. It explores whether traditional gendered roles in families have changed over the past decade and examines issues that include: perceptions of family; the need to reconceptualize family in order to be more inclusive of diversity and difference; current social, political and economic impacts on doing family; prominent social theoretical understandings of the role of family in society; social constructions of motherhood and fatherhood; sexual, domestic and family violence and power relations in families; families with disabilities; families of choice; the impact of globalization and **neoliberalism** on family relations; and the social construction of childhood and the position of children in families. The chapter concludes by highlighting the implications that these issues have for childhood education and community services.

What is a family?

What seems to be on the surface a rather simple question, 'What is a family?', is far more complex than perhaps many of us would first imagine. However, this is a highly political and controversial question, where opinions are diverse and contradictory, based on vastly different personal experiences of being in families, or indeed not being in families. Official and social definitions of family can vary greatly according to legal, cultural and religious influences, and often exclude many people's 'realities' of family life. This exclusion and lack of recognition can have significant social and economic implications for those individuals living in families that do not 'fit' the discourses of family that are socially sanctioned. For example, the discourse of the single-parent family is primarily one of deficit and dysfunction, in which children's experiences are often viewed as lacking as a result of the absence of the influence of either a mother or father. Consequently, any 'problems' experienced with children from single-parent families are often attributed in the first instance to their perceived dysfunctional family life. Similar views are held about same-sex families.

Generally, the family is perceived to be fixed in that it is constructed as a 'natural' expression of human biological relationships. This perception is encompassed within the dominant discourse of family in Western society, represented in the narrative of the nuclear family. Through this discourse, the nuclear family is privileged and normalized through the official stamp of support that it receives from other social institutions such as the church, the law, government and education. It is represented as the social norm, and as the only natural, normal and successful family relationship. This normalizing discourse of the nuclear family permeates all aspects of everyday life through individual interactions and institutional practices. Western cultural celebrations around 'Mother's Day' and 'Father's Day' continue to reinforce the importance of nuclear family relations, despite the complexities around such relationships in many children's lives due to family breakdowns and new family reconfigurations.

In 2012–13 in Australia, 84 per cent of all family types were opposite-sex nuclear families. One-parent families with dependent children accounted for 14 per cent of all families and the remaining 2 per cent were categorized as 'other'. Same-sex couple households accounted for 0.7 per cent of all families in 2011 in Australia, with 12 per cent living with children (Australian Bureau of Statistics 2015a). In the USA in 2010, 1 per cent of family types were estimated to be same-sex families, with 19 per cent having children (Lofquist 2011). In the UK in 2015, of the 18.7 million families approximately 13,000 were same-sex married families, with 3000 of these families having children, and 90,000 were same-sex cohabiting couple families, with 3000 living with children (Office of National Statistics 2015). Interestingly, the Australian Bureau of Statistics (ABS) does not collect data on **transgender** families or on children raised by transgendered parents, and it is difficult to consider the prevalence of extended family relationships in reported statistical data on families. Consequently, official numerical representations of family do not necessarily provide an accurate or 'real' picture of the way family is practised or experienced. However, what these figures do demonstrate is that a significant and growing number of families do not fit in to the normalizing discourse of the nuclear family. In fact, the number of single-parent families is increasing significantly, primarily as a result of marriage breakdowns in Western societies. There may be greater tolerance for single-parent families on one level in society today, but there is still a sense of silence that operates around their 'private' circumstances, which works to exclude them on another level. The discourse that constitutes these families as somehow deficient and dysfunctional continues to marginalize them in society. It is important to point out that many single women in Australia, both heterosexual and same-sex attracted, are redefining family through choosing to have and bring up children alone, with many of these women accessing in vitro fertilization (IVF) and other assisted reproductive technologies (Smock and Greenland 2010; Graham 2012). IVF is a process by which the egg is fertilized outside the body.

In answering the question what is a family, it is critical to highlight that there is no one universal way of doing family, despite the prevalence of the normalizing discourse of the nuclear family. How individuals define family and do family is a very subjective process. Personal experiences of growing up in families, what Bourdieu (1990, 1993) calls family habitus, have a fundamental impact on how individuals view family, what they think families should be, and how they do family relations in their own lives. Ultimately, individual subjects' perceptions and practices of family are constituted within the discourses of family that are culturally available to them. The increasing diversity of how individuals choose to do family life today is undeniable.

Reconceptualizing family as performative social spaces in the twenty-first century: a feminist poststructuralist perspective

Feminist poststructuralism, which informs our discussion in this chapter, highlights a very different way of looking at family and is critical of the fixed and rigid structures that operate to normalize the nuclear family. In this perspective families are viewed as discursively constituted social sites in which multiple ways of doing family are possible and real. Consequently, family is not fixed within rigid and static structures, but rather constitutes dynamic and unstable sites that are influenced by individual and social change. When we say that families are discursively constructed, this means that the perceptions or meanings that make up understandings of family come from the different discourses of family that are culturally available. The nuclear family is the dominant or normalizing discourse of family that operates in Western societies. However, there are other competing discourses of family that allow for different meanings and possibilities of doing family life, but these discourses are not given the same official sanction in society, so are less powerful and less supported by individual subjects. The discourse of the nuclear family, which constitutes this way of doing family as the only normal, stable, successful and Christian way possible, in Foucault's terms, operates as a regime of truth in society, through the ways in which it is supported and normalized by other social institutions and through the practices of individual subjects. It is also normalized within Western modernist dualistic thinking depicted in the cultural binary nuclear family/ alternative family. While the nuclear family signifies the normal, alternative families are defined in opposition to this and signified as abnormal, unsuccessful, unstable, dysfunctional and often unchristian. Location in discourses can be influenced by a range of issues, including one's gender, ethnicity, sexuality, religious faith, personal experiences, cultural and language practices, and so on.

Continuing to define 'the family' within homogeneous, rigid and universalized prescribed structures denies the diversity of family life that exists; it also perpetuates the social, legal and economic inequities experienced by alternative families. Consequently, it is critical to begin to reconceptualize family in a more inclusive framework. Feminist poststructuralist perspectives of family provide a useful framework in which to begin to view family as socially constituted within discourse, and as dynamic and shifting. Butler's (1990) concept of performativity (see Chapter 9 for an in-depth discussion) is valuable in extending these understandings, highlighting how meanings of family are normalized through the everyday repetitive discursive performances of family life embodied by individual subjects. In terms of Butler's theory of performativity, it is the repetitiveness of the performance that both constitutes the realness of doing family (in that it conforms to regulatory norms), as well as providing a means through which different meanings of family are made possible (Butler 1990, 1993). The taking up of the nuclear family discourse is critical to the performance of heterosexual gendered identities, especially for getting these performances correct in the eyes of others. However, the repetitions of family performances are not stable and within 'different contexts and times a repetition can take on a different meaning, undermining and subverting the dominant norms' (Alsop, Fitzsimons and Lennon 2002: 103). For example, challenges to rigid family binaries constituted within heteronormative relationships, through gay and lesbian families, have provided a context in which different performances of family are made possible. Thus, family can be viewed as performative social spaces in which individual subjects take up specific and different performances of family life.

Families also need to be depicted as strategic local and globalized networks of choice rather than founded on biological connections or cultural/racial profiles (Carrington 2002). This perspective not only disrupts the normalizing discourse of the nuclear family, but also the homogenizing and essentializing stereotyped understandings of family, such as the notion that there is a single 'Greek family' or a 'Lebanese family' or a 'Vietnamese family' or even a 'gay and lesbian family' profile. A focus on families as performative social spaces in which similar and different performances of family life are embodied, provides not only an understanding of these social relationships as being fluid, contradictory and contextualized, but also a framework in which individual subjects have agency about how they do family. That is, it shifts understandings away from the perspective of individual subjects passively residing within pregiven structures, to a reading of individual subjects actively in the process of creating and recreating their family life performances. Viewing families not as signifiers for exclusion but as more flexible and fluid allows for the inclusion of other non-nuclear characteristics and processes in understandings of family life.

Social theories of 'the family'

Historically, the family was neglected as an area of study primarily because it was generally perceived to be a private issue, in which the state was considered to have no role. The family was also regarded as having little importance in relation to the broader social structure of society. However, this perspective has changed dramatically; the family is now seen as playing a crucial role in perpetuating dominant social discourses, in the construction of children's subjectivities and in perpetuating dominant power relationships that exist in society. Thus, families as performative social spaces are agents of self-reflexivity, actively interacting with the broader society. Families are no longer viewed merely as passive foundations for other social structures, but as sites in which individual subjects are redefining the multiple possibilities of intimate relationships (Graham 2012; Claster and Blair 2013; Davies and Robinson 2013). Although we have utilized a feminist poststructuralist framework throughout this discussion, the following sub-sections provide a brief overview of other social theories that have influenced understandings of family relations and the role of family as a social institution. Some of these theories still have considerable influence on perspectives of family and the role that they play in society.

Structural functionalist theory and the naturalization of the nuclear family

Structural functionalism, a grand narrative view of family, considers the family as an adaptive unit that mediates between the individual and society, with its main role considered to be that of meeting the needs of individuals for personal growth, and for physical and emotional integrity. Apart from this central purpose, the family is considered to have a larger role in relation to meeting the sexual, reproductive, economic and educational (socialization of the young) needs of the society at large. These basic functions are perceived to be the prerequisites for the survival of the society. However, the family is seen as being largely separate from the political processes operating in society, which are perceived to be played out through other public institutions such as the government, law, education, and so on. Thus, the family in this perspective is theoretically depoliticized, and considered not to have an active role in the public arena of politics and economics. Structural functionalists view the patriarchal nuclear family as the natural primary unit of a stable, harmonious and healthy society. It is a neutral safety zone, a retreat and safe haven for individuals to escape and recuperate from the rigours and demands of their public working lives. Within this perspective, the smooth functioning of society is dependent on members of the society adhering to 'agreed' core values in a society. Individuals and families who do not share these values are considered deviant and dysfunctional, and problematic to society. Their lack of conformity is seen as a result of poor socialization as children, which can lead to social and systemic dysfunction.

There have been major criticisms of structural functionalism, based primarily on the way this perspective depoliticizes and mythologizes the nuclear family; how it is based on misconceptions of society as harmonious and founded on identifiable core values that everybody agrees upon (the prevalence of domestic violence is difficult to explain away in this perspective); how the system is exempted from contributing to the existence of social problems and difference is generally perceived as individual deviance; and how inequities are legitimized as natural through perceived biological differences. Power differences and inequalities are viewed as a reflection of the natural order of things. For example, differences in children's perceived intelligence are considered the natural result of children's genetic make-up, with high intelligence naturally occurring in white, middle- and upper-class professional families.

Although structural functionalism as a social theory was particularly influential during the 1950s and 1960s, the perspectives and values inherent in this approach can be heard in the rhetoric of neoconservatism that has emerged as a political force throughout the world today.

The neoconservative call for a return to the 'traditional nuclear family' of the 1950s, and to the mythical core set of social and moral values that it was perceived to be founded upon, is reflective of structural functionalist principles. The dismissal of difference as being problematic and deviant is certainly a central argument that has been utilized against alternative families, who continue to lobby for social and official recognition.

Marxist theories, the family and social reproduction

Marxist perspectives, originating primarily from the works of Karl Marx (1818–83) have been influential in highlighting the role that the nuclear family plays in the **social reproduction** of power relations in society. Like structural functionalism, it provides a grand narrative view of family in society. These various perspectives stress that the family is an 'ideological state apparatus' through which ideologies upheld by the state are reproduced and perpetuated through family members, generation after generation. In contrast to structural functionalism, Marxist perspectives provide a political view of the family, concerned with identifying and exploring the process of ideological domination in shaping and creating the individual subject. The bourgeois patriarchal nuclear family is seen as the primary site of social and class socialization and reproduction.

Marxist theorists are particularly concerned with how the structure of domestic labour is integral to the system of capitalism. Neo-Marxists, such as those critical theorists who were part of the Frankfurt School in Germany (1923–50), were interested in the relationship between the nuclear bourgeois family and authority, especially in terms of how dominant patterns of subordination and domination in the family reflected those operating in broader social structures. This resulted in an increased awareness of how gender role differentiation in the family was linked to the needs of the capitalist economy. For example, the role of women in the household was to provide a caring and nurturing environment for men, who were considered the major economic providers of the family as well as the major source of workers for the capitalist system. Contented and loved workers at home were considered to be healthy and productive workers in the capitalist system. Thus, women were seen to play a critical role in the emotional stability of workers, ultimately contributing to the stability and productivity of the workforce. The patriarchal nuclear family, based on strict gender-differentiated roles, was viewed to be critical to the continued success of the capitalist system.

Family social relationships were viewed to operate around a public/private split, in which family, marriage and domestic life became strongly linked to core values of privacy and intimacy, while economics, work and politics were considered public matters. Different gender roles in society were analysed in terms of how they conformed to the public/private split – that is, women and their influence were aligned with the private world of the family, while men dominated public matters. The nuclear family under capitalism was considered to be critical in providing an environment in which individuals could be emotionally supported through the deprivations and alienations they experienced in an advanced capitalist society. Thus, as a result of this process, as Morgan (1996: 7) points out, by default 'the public worlds of business and politics could continue unchallenged'.

Feminist theories and the family

Feminists have been the most influential social theorists in recent times to extend understandings of the role of family in society. However, there are many variations of feminism (for example, liberal feminism, radical feminism, socialist feminism, psychoanalytic feminism, feminist poststructuralism) providing different perspectives on family relations and how they operate to perpetuate gender inequalities. Feminism operates largely as a grand narrative, but feminist poststructuralism, as pointed out previously, has emerged as a different approach that does not take on the perspectives that are inherent in universalizing grand narrative social theories. As feminist poststructuralism has been outlined in depth previously in this chapter, brief overviews of other feminist perspectives are given here. Feminists from various perspectives have been primarily responsible for critiquing the normalization and maintenance of the public/private split in gendered social relationships in society. They have also highlighted the family as a major political institution in which individual subjectivities are constituted and inequalities of power that operate broadly in society, especially those between men and women, adults and children, are maintained.

Marxist feminists uphold that women's oppression is tied largely to the operations of the capitalist system. Incorporating the principles of Marxist theory into their social critique, they view the family as central in reproducing gendered and class relations in society and in bolstering capitalism through its role in reproducing labour power – that is, reproducing and socializing children to be future workers in the capitalist system. This perspective upholds that women's oppression and inequality in society are linked primarily to their economic dependence on men as a result of their unpaid role in the home, as well as their lack of access to well-paid, full-time employment in the workforce. Thus, the family is generally viewed as an oppressive institution for women. Equality for women, according to Marxist feminists, will be achieved only through the elimination of capitalism.

Socialist feminism arose largely as a result of some Marxist feminists' dissatisfaction with Marxist theory and its failure to deal adequately with gender issues. Marxists tended to view workers' oppression as being more critical than women's oppression. Socialist feminists argue that the lives of women in non-capitalist systems are not substantially different or transformed from those under capitalism – that is, they are still oppressed by patriarchy. Thus, socialist feminists uphold that women's liberation must not be analysed solely in terms of capitalism, but must include an analysis of patriarchy (a system of male dominance and power) and how both systems simultaneously oppress women. The patriarchal nuclear family is considered central to the perpetuation of gender and class inequalities.

Radical feminists linked the nuclear family to women's oppression, but unlike Marxist or socialist feminists, they fundamentally view women's oppression as a result of patriarchy and men's control over women's bodies. The nuclear family is considered to be a primary source of the perpetuation of patriarchal power relations among men and women, with women being largely oppressed and victimized in their homes as well as in public arenas. The patriarchal nuclear family, its intimate links with marriage and strict gender differentiated roles (for example, child care), operate to subordinate and oppress women in society. Radical feminists have been instrumental in highlighting the 'reality' of family life, focusing on the extensiveness of domestic violence, rape in marriage and child sexual abuse occurring in the home.

Psychoanalytic feminists view the family as the primary site of the construction of the gendered subject. Incorporating Freudian psychoanalysis, this perspective focuses on the ways in which our subjectivities and cultures are constructed from our earliest unconscious embodied experiences as children. The 'passionate emotional entanglements' that arise from these experiences in families impact on the way we perceive ourselves and how we interact with others in the world (Alsop *et al.* 2002: 40). These experiences are perceived to be critical in shaping individuals' desires and in constructing the social world. Deleuze and Guattari (1987) utilize psychoanalysis and view the nuclear family as being complicit in the repression and moulding of individual desires. Carrington (2002), incorporating the perspectives of Deleuze and Guattari, and Bourdieu's concept of habitus formation, argues that the desires of individual subjects are shaped primarily through the family in the way they take up, purchase and consume this highly particular architectural form.

Changing practices in a changing world: current challenges to families

Families are highly responsive to individual and social changes. Births, divorce, death, migration, wars, political upheavals, geographic mobility, economic shifts, partnering and remarriage, among other factors, can impact significantly on family structures and practices, resulting in different and new ways of doing family life that significantly challenge traditional perspectives of the family. New and different family formations and performances are reflective of increasingly complex, contradictory and shifting individual subject positions. The following phenomena are examples of major social, economic and political challenges impacting on the normative nuclear discourses of family life.

- *Increased Westernization.* Western influences perpetuated through processes of globalization, technological change, media representations and migration to the West continue to challenge non-Western families and traditional cultural practices. Migration to other countries can result in generational changes in cultural value and linguistic practices as well as family practices and structures.

- *Women's liberation movement.* Feminism has significantly challenged traditional patriarchal discourses of family life, including strict gender role differentiation. Demands for more equitable partnerships in family relationships and in care for children have in some families resulted in changes in family practices performed by men and women – for example, some men choosing to stay at home with children while women work.

- *Individuals marrying later, divorcing earlier and remarrying.* Romantic discourses of love and marriage often leave individuals (particularly women) frustrated and dissatisfied when the realities of marriage and family life do not match their preconceived expectations. Almost one-third of families end in divorce for various reasons, including domestic violence. Thus, perceptions of marriage are changing, especially for women, who are less likely to remarry as quickly as men.

- *Cohabitation and children born outside marriage.* Changing perceptions of marriage have increased the number of couples who choose to live together and have children outside marriage.

- *Planned pregnancies, and fewer births at later ages.* Contraception has provided many women with the option to plan families around careers, or to choose not to have children at all. Legalized abortion has also been an option for some women. Generally women are having fewer children and are having them later in their lives. Overall, couples are becoming parents at later ages and families are smaller.

- *Drop in fertility rates.* The fertility rate in Western countries has dropped in past decades and is equated with, among other factors, access to contraception, women choosing to have children later in life, or women choosing not to have children at all.

- *Generational changes.* Family practices are changing across generations. This is particularly so in immigrant families, where children take up the dominant cultural practices of their new homeland, often rejecting those that belong to their previous homeland or to the parents' birthplace, resulting in family conflicts.

- *Unemployment.* High levels of unemployment are impacting on families from all ethnic groups and social classes. Poverty and welfare dependency impact on the well-being of family members, their access to resources and their life choices. The decline of manufacturing in industrialized countries has resulted in the loss of many jobs, particularly those that have traditionally been filled by men. Consequently, many families who have relied heavily on male breadwinners have experienced challenges to traditional gender role differentiation in family practices.

- *Financial commitments.* Large financial commitments, associated with the cost of living and the desire for commodities, have meant that both parents often have to work to meet the family's obligations. Consequently, there has been an increased reliance on women's paid work. Family financial commitments can place great pressure on family members, particularly at times of economic and employment instability. In recent years, there has also been an increase in the role of grandparents in caring for children while both parents work.

- *Children's rights.* In the past decade there has been a greater focus on the rights of children, which are impacting on parental practices in some instances – for example, disciplining children. An increased awareness of the prevalence of child abuse has resulted in greater surveillance of families and of adult–child relationships more generally, and has increased legislation to protect children. This has been accompanied by an increased understanding of children's agency and of their citizenship rights to be consulted and to participate in decision-making processes that affect their lives.

- *Gay, lesbian and transgender rights movements.* These movements challenge the social, political and economic inequities that face same-sex attracted, gender diverse and transgender people. A major focus of the gay and lesbian movement has been the legal recognition of same-sex marriages and families and their equal access to resources and rights similar to those experienced by heterosexual parents and families. These movements are challenging dominant discourses of marriage and the nuclear family.

- *Reproductive technology and self-insemination.* Reproductive technologies have increased the opportunities for some heterosexual couples to overcome fertility and conception problems in order to have children; they have also given single women and lesbians the option of having children without male partners. Self-insemination is also an option that has been utilized by single women and lesbians.

- *Ageing population.* With an increase in life expectancy in developed and industrialized countries, and a decrease in fertility, these countries are experiencing an ageing of their populations. Consequently, governments are being forced to consider the health and well-being, including housing and care, of increasing numbers of elderly people. In many instances, the care of the elderly is seen by governments as the primary responsibility of their immediate families, reducing the extent of welfare provision offered by governments.

- *Single mothers.* Within recent years the number of families headed by single mothers has been on the increase. As discussed in Chapter 8, in Australia, single mothers comprise the majority of lone parents, with 33 per cent of single-parent families living below the poverty line (ACOSS 2014: 8). In the United States, in 2010, 32.7 per cent of white single mothers with children under the age of 18 years were living in poverty, compared to 47.1 per cent of black single mothers and 50.3 per cent of Latina single mothers (US Census Bureau 2011, cited in Broussard, Joseph and Thompson (2012: 190). In both countries poverty and disadvantage for women are on the increase where the material and discursive forms of inequality place women in female-headed households at a major disadvantage.

Habitus, cultural capital, symbolic violence and family

Bourdieu's concepts of habitus, capital and symbolic violence are useful in helping to understand how the family impacts on individual subjects and on the shaping of the social world. According to Bourdieu, social reality is a construction that is reproduced through the existing power relations operating in society that serve to foster and maintain the position and status of particular groups over others. The family is a critical site of social reproduction. The narrative of the nuclear family is a construction that serves particular ideological visions and political agendas, and is normalized through other social institutions, such as education. For example, it reproduces neoconservative values and morals that maintain heterosexual privilege, such as the greater access of heterosexuals to socially and legally sanctioned marriage. Thus, nuclear families have more cultural capital in society than alternative families.

Bourdieu's concept of symbolic violence is exercised upon individuals that involve complicity (Bourdieu 1990; Bourdieu and Wacquant 1992). This involvement is neither a passive acceptance nor free adherence to conformity; it provides an explanation of how social inequalities can continue largely unabated. Within this perspective, individual subjects are subjected to various forms of violence, such as being treated unfairly or denied resources, or are limited in their social mobility and aspirations, but they do not tend to see it that way; rather it is misrecognized by individual subjects as the natural order of things. Gender domination in the patriarchal family is an example of symbolic violence in operation. Through habitus formation in this context, women are often confined emotionally, socially, economically and physically, and the perception that women were inferior to men in the home and more generally in society is perpetuated. Women's misrecognition of this violence as 'natural' and 'normal' gendered relations in the world provides a habitus of thinking, perceiving and operating through complicit forms of domination constructed in hegemonic masculinity and femininity.

The social construction of motherhood and fatherhood

Just as the normalizing discourse of the nuclear family operates to maintain a particular social order, so do the normalizing discourses of motherhood and fatherhood. Motherhood is often perceived to be the essence of what it means to be a woman, which is perpetuated through the belief that motherhood is a 'natural' and instinctual process in women's lives, due to their biological make-up and reproductive capabilities. However, both motherhood and fatherhood are discursively constructed social practices that are actively negotiated, taken up and recreated by individuals rather than instinctively linked to and fixed in biology; that is, cultural understandings of meanings of motherhood and fatherhood are constituted within the various discourses socially available to individual subjects at particular points in time. Motherhood and fatherhood, as socially constructed practices, are integral to the performance of hegemonic gendered identities (Gregory and Milner 2011). The link that has been socially fostered between motherhood and women's biology has primarily been utilized to maintain a social system of gender inequality based on the 'natural' delegation of women as the sole carers of children and as homemakers. In this respect, motherhood can be seen to be another example of Bourdieu's symbolic violence; that is, the inequities that operate in women's lives associated with being socially delegated the prime and often sole responsibility of mothering and caring for children and other family members, and as homemakers, are often misrecognized as the natural order of things. There is no reason, apart from the way it has been discouraged within dominant socially constructed meanings of masculinity, why men cannot mother.

The dominant discourse of motherhood idealizes, glorifies and romanticizes this role and often demands women to be altruistic; that is, their actions are primarily for the benefit of others, even at the expense of their own needs and wishes (Goodwin and Huppatz 2010). In Australia in recent years, this discourse has emerged in political rhetoric around discussions focusing on the country's critical negative population growth. However, the status of motherhood tends to be diminished quickly within the limited social, political and economic supports provided to mothers once they have children. The 'good mother', as constituted in the dominant discourse of motherhood, is highly attentive and sensitive to the needs of her children, puts her children's needs first, is always there when needed, and provides a stimulating learning environment for her children from the time they are born. Interestingly, the 'good mother' is still often perceived to be one who stays home and cares for her children in their early years; ironically, this is a perspective that is strongly supported by many of the pre-service early childhood educators we have worked with.

The 'good mother' is also perceived to be able to successfully juggle her time and other roles as wife, homemaker and, increasingly, paid worker (full-time or part-time). This discourse is responsible for constructing successful 'good' mothers as being 'superwomen' who can efficiently fulfil all these demanding roles simultaneously. There are some mothers who continue to successfully fulfil the superwoman discourse, but for most the 'good' mother benchmark is unattainable, not through any fault of their own, but as a result of the often unrealistic goals that this discourse places on women. Consequently, mothers' behaviours and practices become the focus of public scrutiny; they are continually judged (often judging themselves more harshly than others) as 'good' or 'bad' mothers, depending on how successfully they perform and cope with these multiple roles. For many, it is often an impossible task posing critical implications for their health and well-being. In educational contexts, including early childhood education, judgements are often made about 'good' or 'bad' mothers based on the various criteria raised above; these criteria are based largely on white, Western, middle-class values associated with the nuclear family lifestyle.

'Good fathers', on the other hand, have traditionally been viewed in terms of their abilities to provide for their families economically and as effective disciplinarians. This primary defining role of fatherhood has meant that many men have played a secondary role in the everyday raising of children, becoming more actively involved in family and homemaking activities on a weekend or holiday basis. Motherhood and fatherhood

have primarily been constituted within the gendered cultural binary male/
female, in which meanings of motherhood have been defined in opposition to meanings of fatherhood, based on gender role differentiation. The
dominant discourses of fatherhood and motherhood operate to reinscribe
the perceived 'naturalness' of the patriarchal heterosexual nuclear family.
Good mothers and good fathers are married and heterosexual, reinforcing
the perceived deviance and unnaturalness of non-heterosexual relationships and families. However, in recent times more men are taking up different performances of masculinity and extending their roles in families to
include caring for children on either a shared or full-time basis. Still, they
can often become the targets of harassment from other men (and some
women) for taking up 'women's roles' and stepping outside the boundaries
of hegemonic masculinity. Interestingly, fathers do not tend to experience
the same public scrutiny that is directed at mothers in relation to raising
children; this is most likely associated with their primary responsibilities
being viewed as being located largely in the public sphere of work, which
limits their time with family.

Families with a disability

Families with a disability face many challenges that impact on family
life. Discourses of disability permeate at all levels of these challenges,
including discrimination, and the application of normative and deficit
assumptions that construct disability in the cultural binaries of normal
vs abnormal. However, poverty and hardship, particularly for single
mothers with disabilities, presents with multilayered challenges where
these women face severe disadvantage associated with poverty, unemployment and gender inequality, racism and parenthood (Parish, Magaña
and Cassiman 2008). Parish and colleagues also argue that gendered policy and practice impact on the lives of single mothers with disabilities
at re-occurring intersections of disability, poverty and motherhood that
impact on successfully parenting their children.

Families of 'choice': doing family differently

The destabilization of the normative myths around family that we have
identified so far in this chapter is opening up spaces and opportunities
for individuals to choose different performances of family. The normalizing discourse of the nuclear family is also being disrupted through different performances of gender – for example, as indicated in the previous
section, where some men are taking on more responsibilities for caring
and nurturing children, either on a full-time or shared basis. As discussed
earlier in this chapter, it is important that we begin to reconceptualize

THE CHANGING NATURE OF FAMILIES IN THE TWENTY-FIRST CENTURY

families as globalized and localized strategic networks of choice. The following families are examples of how individual subjects are doing family differently through choice.

Gay and lesbian families

Lewin (1998: 25) points out that 'same sex commitments are nothing new; only the demand for equity and recognition has changed the landscape'. In many contexts, same-sex families still have to battle for social recognition and acceptance, despite gaining legal equality in many Western developed countries for same-sex relationships and same-sex marriage. In Australia, same-sex couples have gained considerable legal recognition for their relationships, comparable to heterosexual couples, but they do not have access to marriage equality. The global marriage equality movement has resulted in the legal recognition of same-sex marriages in a number of countries in Europe, Scandinavia, South America and North America (e.g. UK, Ireland, USA, Canada, New Zealand, Norway, Sweden, Brazil, Argentina, France and Spain). Neoconservative religious discourses associated with relationships, marriage, family values and childrearing, as well as homophobia, undermine the legal recognition of same-sex marriage and relationships in other countries.

Research points out that gay, lesbian and transgender families are still marginalized in the field of education (Robinson 2002; Surtees and Gunn 2010; Avertt and Hedge 2012; Cloughessy and Waniganayake 2014). This is largely a result of the pervasiveness of homophobia, transphobia and heteronormativity in education, especially in the schooling years (DePalma and Jennett 2010; Wright 2011; Robinson et al. 2014). This research also highlights the importance of including these families within children's broad education of family diversity. This is largely in order to acknowledge the experiences of many young children who come from gay or lesbian families, and to counteract the myths and stereotypes associated with gays and lesbians that children encounter daily. Robinson (2002, 2013) points out that gay and lesbian families, or gay and lesbian equity issues more generally, continue to be largely excluded from early childhood and primary school curricula and social justice agendas for several reasons, which include: the prevalence of homophobia and heterosexism operating in many early childhood settings; the taboos that exist around children and sexuality; fears around dealing with sexuality due to its controversial status, especially parental concerns; the perception that these families and equity issues are irrelevant to most children's lives; the assumed absence of significant gay or lesbian adults in children's lives; the pervasiveness of the discourse of compulsory heterosexuality; and the assumed absence of gay and lesbian families in early childhood settings (see also Chapter 10).

There are many concerns that face gay and lesbian families in relation to their children's education. Many gay and lesbian parents are wary about 'coming out' but do so in some circumstances; they fear 'coming out' may result in their children experiencing discrimination from educators and other staff. Many are also concerned that their children will experience discrimination from other children and parents if their children talk openly about their family experiences in schools (Lee 2010).

How educational settings and community-based services approach family diversity can affect how open gay and lesbian parents are with their children's educators. If settings include gay and lesbian families in their social justice agendas, curriculum on family diversity, and organizational policies and practices, it sends a strong message not just to gay and lesbian parents, but to all parents, educators, community-based professionals and children, that family diversity is recognized and respected.

Interethnic and interracial families

Interethnicity and interraciality are markers of family shifts throughout the Western world, primarily as a result of the impact of globalization, migration, increasingly sophisticated technology and communications, as well as increasingly mobile populations. This has resulted in an increase in ethnically and racially mixed marriages and families. For example, in the United States, the US Census Bureau reported that, in 2010, numbers of interracial and interethnic marriages had grown by 28 per cent since 2000, with a 7 per cent increase from 2000 to 10 per cent in 2010 (US Census Bureau 2010). Family hybridity is the bringing together of two different racial and/or ethnic cultures from which new and different family practices emerge. Intermarriage refers to unions that intersect with class, language, sexuality, caste, nationality, ethnicity, racial and religious difference, and is an important site in which shifting social values emerge, such as those around childrearing and gendered expectations. Within these family contexts, tensions in cultural negotiations can arise around family practices, such as childrearing, which can stem from different cultural constructions of childhood. In addition, these families can experience racial discrimination in everyday experiences where racialized norms, assumptions and inequalities are played out (Harman 2010).

Interracial children's recognition of their racialized identities is contingent upon meanings of racism, which construct understandings of themselves in discourses of whiteness, racism and monolingualism (Ali 2003; Jones Díaz 2015). For bilingual children from interracial and interethnic families, hybridized identities are often mediated across cultural, linguistic and racial lines, as evidenced in the following quote from a father in Jones Díaz's (2016): 'paracido ellos saben que hay una cultura en el medio de mama y papa' [It appears that they know that there is a culture in between the mother and father]. Moreover, as argued by Jones Díaz (2015: 119), the various forms of cultural, linguistic and racial hybridity are evident in the ways in which children negotiate the 'third space' positioning them in 'multiple, hybridized and transformative and often competing discourses of identity' (see Chapters 1, 6 and 7).

Families from culturally and linguistically diverse backgrounds

Many of the issues faced by children and their families from culturally and linguistically diverse (CALD) backgrounds are addressed in Chapters 6 and 7, but it is important to briefly highlight here some of the main concerns facing families. People from CALD backgrounds come from a diverse range of ethnic, racial and cultural backgrounds, and cannot be viewed as a homogeneous group. This diversity is shaped by differences across ethnicity, culture, religion, age, gender, sexuality, languages, occupation, social class, and length of residence in their current country. CALD families face a number of barriers to equal access and use of services, including but not limited to: a lack of knowledge about or access to existing services and resources; the inability of services, including childhood education and community-based services, to meet the specific needs of these families in culturally and linguistically appropriate ways; reduced employment opportunities due to levels of English language proficiency; lack of recognition in many instances of overseas qualifications; employment experiences often associated with low-paid service industries; unemployment; and the challenges that face families that have recently arrived in their new countries of residence, including social dislocation, isolation and racism (Cass 1995; Sawrikar and Katz 2008).

Domestic, family and sexual violence in Australia

Within recent years, domestic, family and sexual violence has re-emerged as a mainstream criminal justice issue in Australia. The murder of Rosie Batty's 11-year-old son, Luke, by his father in 2014 and Gerard Baden-Clay's murder of his wife, Alison, in 2010 have attracted media attention and put domestic violence back in the spotlight (Goldsworthy and Raj 2014). Domestic violence definitions broadly refer to violence that covers a wide range of behaviours committed in the context of intimate relationships involving family members, children, partners, ex-partners and caregivers. It includes physical violence, sexual assault, verbal, emotional, social and spiritual abuse, psychological and economic harm, and is found in all cultural and socio-economic groups (Mitchel 2011; ABS 2012d; Goldsworthy and Raj 2014; Phillips and Vandenbroek 2014).

The majority of violent behaviours occur in the privacy of people's homes and are committed by men against women (ABS 2012a). In 2012, an estimated 17 per cent of all women aged 18 years and over, and 5.3 per cent of all men aged 18 years and over, had experienced violence by a partner since the age of 15. Similarly, in 2012 an estimated 25 per cent of all women aged 18 years and over and 14 per cent of all men aged 18 years and over had experienced emotional abuse by a partner since the age of 15 (ABS 2012a). Women are more likely than men to have experienced emotional abuse by a partner since the age of 15 (ABS 2012a). The Australian National Research Organisation for Women's Safety (ANROWS) reported that, within a two-year period (2008–10), 89 women were killed by their current or former partner (ANROWS 2014). Furthermore, a recent ABC media report noted that, by April 2015, there had been 31 women killed. That represents two Australian women per week being murdered as a result of domestic violence (Bowden 2015).

From a feminist perspective, the issues associated with sexual, domestic and family violence are located in gender power relationships that exist in the broader community, which in turn are played out within the private confines of the family home and family relationships. Rather than it being understood as a women's issue, many campaigners against domestic violence have asserted that it is a men's issue since the majority of the perpetrators are men.

Yet despite more than 40 years of work, principally by feminists, to challenge and educate the public, including politicians, about the complexity and pervasiveness of sexual, domestic and family violence, myths and misconceptions continue to circulate unabated in our society. Such myths include, but are not limited to: 'women ask for it', 'provoke it' or 'perpetrators can not control their anger'; 'it occurs only in poor, dysfunctional families and undereducated communities'; 'victims often falsely report sexual violence', and so on.

Furthermore, Bumiller (2008) argues that, in the context of neoliberalism, the state has little to offer due to its decreased responsibility for welfare, including the protection of women and children whose experiences of violence have rendered them homeless, traumatized and disrupted. She argues that a large professional apparatus has now misappropriated programmes supporting women and children experiencing sexual and family violence. This system has created a professional language to account for, intervene and prevent it through the rationalization that it is a chronic yet treatable problem.

In Australia, it is clear that the state has failed in its response to the increasing and disturbing incidences of sexual, domestic and family violence. For example, in NSW the domestic assault rate has increased

1.5 per cent over the last five years, and Victoria recorded a 72.8 per cent increase between 2004–05 and 2011–12 (Goldsworthy and Raj 2014). Therefore, for educators and community service professionals, it is likely that many of the children and families with whom they work experience sexual, domestic and family violence. While child protection regulations require mandatory reporting of child abuse, incidences of violence experienced by mothers remain hidden and under the radar.

Since the early 1990s research has been documenting the prevalence of child abuse (sexual, physical, emotional) within families and in the home (Breckenridge and Carmody 1992; Easteal 1994). Much has been written on children's physical, sexual and emotional abuse and neglect in the home. In the context of this book and its limitations on space, we can only acknowledge this critical issue as a major concern in any discussion of violence in the home. What needs to be reiterated here in relation to this critical social problem is that child abuse and neglect is a direct result of the power differentials between adults and children, between older children and younger children, and males and females. In more recent years, there has been a growing awareness of the various forms of abuse (physical, sexual, emotional) that are perpetrated against younger children by older children with more power. There is also growing concern about abuse perpetrated against parents from adult children.

In order to significantly counteract the vast abuse that occurs, particularly in the home, it is critical to deconstruct the cultural binaries adult/child and male/female that constitute the power relations that exist between adults and children and in gendered relationships. In terms of child abuse, it is critical not only to look at these relations of power, but also to address the impact that the discourse of childhood innocence has on children's vulnerability to abuse. Robinson (2013) argues, in the efforts to protect childhood 'innocence', which is ultimately a cultural construct, children have simultaneously been made more vulnerable (see also Chapter 3).

The impact of globalization on doing family

As discussed in Chapter 8, globalization has penetrated many aspects of our lives, including social relationships and family structures. It has been a critical driving force that is restructuring the social order around the world and families are at the centre of this change (Trask 2010). Globalization has opened up opportunities for different and new family practices that significantly challenge traditional notions of the family and normalizing discourses of motherhood and fatherhood.

Transnational families

Globalization has impacted significantly on families in relation to issues associated with mobility within countries and across national borders. In Australia, due to globalization, changes in immigration policies, increased flows of labour, 'doing family' across national and state borders have become a significant reality. These families live their lives across geographical distance, yet retain a sense of collectivity and kinship in the context of 'doing family' with the assistance of social media, email and telephone (Baldassar and Merla 2014).

In transnational families the main financial provider (most often the father/male in these instances) is located in a different geographical location from the family, returning for short visits or on special holidays with the family. This is primarily a result of the need to follow employment opportunities, or employers' expectations that their employees will be mobile and willing to travel to various work locations. Technology, communications and air travel make these demands possible. In some cases, families may move constantly with the parent to different employment locations, which can alter child care and education arrangements.

However, the global movement of women from Latin America, the Philippines and India to provide child care for middle-class and wealthy families in the United States, Europe and Saudi Arabia, means that their children are often left in the care of substitute mothers, their fathers or extended family members (Trask 2010). In this context Baldassar and Merla (2014) argue that family members are simultaneously caregivers and care receivers where 'circuits of care' that involve close family members and broader family networks operate. Normative Western discourses of 'good mothering' and 'bad mothering' that mandate physical closeness and direct involvement are challenged by transnational mothering, and in this process new versions of mothering that may be different to normative white middle-class discourses of mothering are constructed (Trask 2010; Baldassar and Merla 2014). Baldassar and Merla challenge the ideal of proximity, which assumes that distance between family members automatically prohibits the exchange of caring. They argue that such ideals lead to stigmatization of transnational mothers as deficit, 'at risk' and 'bad mothers'. Fog Olwig (2014) adds that the physical proximity of mothers and their children is not universally viewed as necessary for the successful upbringing of children. Rather, she argues that, in transnational families, extended family networks become activated in transnational childrearing.

People are increasingly shifting across multiple locations for varying lengths of time, moving in and out of numerous communities, while at the same time maintaining satisfactory social and familial relations across all these sites. Moving populations are not just migrants or guest workers moving from one part of the globe to another, either voluntarily or involuntarily, but rather, people generally are on the move globally and nationally, challenging traditional framings of static and homogeneous families and communities.

Refugee and asylum-seeker families

As a result of continuing social and political unrest throughout the world there has been an increase in the number of individuals and families seeking asylum in other countries that are seen as more politically stable and economically prosperous. For many refugee families it is about fleeing actual or potential human rights abuses in their home countries. Consequently, refugee families may be experiencing severe personal traumas when they arrive in other countries to resettle; this can especially be the case for young children. This trauma can also be associated with the loss of close relatives and friends. Refugee families often arrive in countries with few resources. As evidenced in Chapter 6, young people and children comprise a significant proportion of Australia's refugee intake. The Forgotten Children Inquiry (Australian Human Rights Commission 2014: 54) reported that, in March 2014, there were 56 unaccompanied children in detention centres in Australia. On the mainland, there were 17, 39 on Christmas Island and a further 27 unaccompanied children were detained in Nauru. The majority of these children are from Iran, Afghanistan, Myanmar and Somalia, and they are all teenagers between 15 and 17 years old.

The various policies on refugees in each country will impact on their refugee status and how successfully they are resettled, if at all, into a new country. As discussed in Chapter 6, in recent times there has been an increase in the rejection of refugees, especially those who seek asylum as 'boat people' and attempt to land 'illegally' on foreign shores. This has been the case in Australia in recent years, resulting in the refusal to take these refugees or recognize their international refugee status. Further, refugees, including children, who do arrive 'illegally' in Australia, can experience long periods of mandatory detention while waiting on the investigations of governments to determine their refugee status. The Forgotten Children Inquiry (Australian Human Rights Commission 2014) noted that, under Australian law, there is no prescribed time limit for which a child can be detained, and asylum seekers have no information as to when their refugee status will be assessed or about the duration of their detention. Furthermore, the inquiry reported that 41 per cent of the children detained gave 'fear of life or safety' as the main reason for coming to Australia; the second most common reason was 'escaping persecution by government' (2014: 52). Consequently, and ironically, the personal traumas experienced

by refugees in their home countries can be prolonged by government policies in the various countries in which they seek asylum.

The experiences raised above can pose significant issues for educators and community professionals working with refugee children and
their families once they settle in to their new communities. Children's
experiences of trauma can significantly affect their health and well-being,
their sense of confidence and security, as well as their learning. Different
traumatic experiences associated with war, dictatorial regimes, terrorism,
torture, famine, poverty and living in extreme fear can have serious short-
and long-term effects on developing trusting relationships with individuals, particularly those in institutional locations.

It can often take a lot of time and effort on the part of educators to
build trusting relationships with children to the point that they begin to feel
secure in their new environments. There are also issues for refugee children and families associated with settling in to new environments away
from the familiarity of their home countries, and away from the family
and friendship groups they have left behind. Finding appropriate, secure
and affordable housing, building new networks of support and friendship,
language issues, challenging cultural differences, financial and employment concerns, and accessing available government and non-government
support services are a few of the concerns that face these families daily.
Negotiating language differences will be a particular issue in terms of
meeting children's educational needs. Furthermore, refugee children and
their families may experience discrimination in their new communities,
which can exacerbate many of the fears and insecurities they may already
be dealing with.

Implications for practice in education and community services

As the world becomes increasingly interconnected and diverse, it is crucial that educators and community service professionals understand the
dynamic nature of globalization and its relevance to families. This chapter
has raised many important issues associated with family diversity, and
the following implications offer suggestions that promote family diversity
in policy, direction and implementation, communicating with families, and
working with staff, families and children.

It is important that early childhood educational settings review their
organizational practices, policies and philosophies in terms of how realistically they reflect family diversity. It is critical that the inclusion of family
diversity is achieved through a whole-setting approach, and is monitored
and reviewed at regular intervals. In practice, for example, this would
involve reviewing written materials, such as policies and forms, to check
that they use language that is inclusive of single-parent, gay and lesbian,

and other non-nuclear families; and using more inclusive terms such as 'parent/guardian' rather than mother/father. It is also important to include diversity issues even if there is the perception that they are somehow irrelevant to the current children and families utilizing the setting. For example, policies and practices need to include equity issues associated with gay and lesbian families, even if they are perceived to be absent in the setting. These equity issues are relevant to all children and families, as homophobia and heterosexism are primarily practised by heterosexual children, staff and families, whether there are gay or lesbian families present or not.

Educators and community service professionals are faced with the challenge of how to support and include the many different families that are part of children's lives. It is important that strategies are developed to include those families that tend to remain on the margins of settings' activities. For example, non-normative families, such as CALD families, refugee and asylum seeker families, interethnic and interracial families, gay and lesbian families, single-parent families, families with a disability and transnational families, need to be supported and encouraged to participate in setting organizational, social and educational activities. Achieving this may require the development of employment strategies that target staff who represent the communities to which these families belong. Reaching out to different families through newsletters and special educational and social events is also a useful strategy. Additionally, it is important not to assume that gay and lesbian families are not using the setting; many choose not to be openly 'out', fearing discrimination. Therefore, by establishing supportive communication with families that is inclusive of and responsive towards diversity, secure, respectful and reciprocal relationships are established, which in turn facilitate effective partnerships with families (ELYF 2009).

Settings need to review their available resources to see if they provide educators and children with a range of different family representations. Resources that reinforce normalizing discourses of family can be deconstructed with children to provide different discourses of family, identify power relations inherent within the narratives, e.g. gender power relations, and recreate new and different storylines that represent multiple performances of family and of gender. The processes of deconstruction and reconstruction are useful pedagogical tools for developing children's critical thinking around normalizing discourses and social inequities, providing children with new and different options in the world.

Taking a reflexive approach to pedagogy and practice is important in order to examine how the perceptions and everyday interactions of staff, children and families either perpetuate or disrupt normalizing discourses associated with the 'legitimation' of family and gendered relations. It is a process that requires time, commitment and long-term planning; it cannot happen overnight, and its focus on personal and professional change makes it potentially 'risky' for some, so this must be respected. Community courage, where individuals share the personal and professional risks in incorporating, upholding and defending policies, philosophies and practices that reflect family differences, is critical for its success. This involves developing networks of personal and professional support within and across various organizations to advocate for the representation of family difference in early childhood education.

Conclusion

This chapter has provided a critical overview of the changing perspectives of family, including the current social, political and economic challenges facing families today. It has argued strongly that, in order to be more inclusive of the diversity that exists in families, it is imperative that we begin to shift away from normalizing discourses of the nuclear family that perpetuate fixed structural definitions of family based on biological connections. This discourse primarily operates to dismiss family diversity as problematic, reinforcing social inequities in the process. Viewing families as performative social spaces in which similar and different performances of family are possible, as well as being localized and globalized networks of choice, is an important step in the process of acknowledging how families are constantly negotiated and recreated by the individual subjects living within them. Educators and community service professionals have a critical advocacy role to play in challenging narrow normalizing discourses of family that undermine the vast diversity of family experiences of the children and families with whom they work.

Recommended reading

Claster, P.N. and Blair, S.L. (eds) (2013) *Visions of the 21st Century Family: Transforming Structures and Identities*. Bingley, UK: Emerald Group Publishing Ltd.

Cutas, D. and Chan, S. (eds) (2012) *Families: Beyond the Nuclear Ideal*. London: Bloomsbury.

Trask, B.H. (2010) *Globalization and Families: Accelerated Systemic Social Change*. New York: Springer.

White Ribbon Australia (n.d.) Fact Sheet 10: Ten common myths and misconceptions. Available at: www.whiteribbon.org.au/uploads/media/updated_factsheets_Nov_13/Factsheet_10_Ten_Common_Myths_and_Misconceptions.pdf.

5

Indigeneity

Introduction

This chapter critically examines the historical and social constructions of Indigeneity, with a critical focus on racialization processes for Indigenous children, families and communities. It provides a historical overview of the colonization, dispossession and construction of whiteness, 'race' and racism in Australia. Within this discussion a focus on forms of racism is described, with particular examples provided. Discourses of deficit applied to Indigenous Australians are examined with reference to the impact this has on Indigenous identity and disadvantage. Critical 'race' theory and postcolonial studies are presented as frameworks within which critical understandings of the construction of 'race' and racism are central to working with Indigenous children, families and communities. This chapter also highlights the significance of Indigenous languages, identities and cultural practices in postcolonial nation states such as Australia. Issues of language revival and extinction are addressed along with health and education issues for Aboriginal children and their families in education and community services. By drawing on multiple sets of data from research conducted by Jones Díaz, Chodkiewicz and Morgan (2016, in review) and Robinson and Jones Díaz (2000), issues pertaining to assumed absences, identity and engaging Indigenous families and children in literacy are investigated. Implications for educators and community service staff working with Indigenous children, families and communities are discussed, and links to the EYLFA (DEEWR 2009) are provided.

Prior to British colonization, it is estimated that the Indigenous population was between 700,000 and 800,000, and their presence as the first Australians can be dated back to between 60,000 to 100,000 years (Hollinsworth 2010). In 2011, they represented 3 per cent of the overall Australian population (ABS 2014). It is widely accepted that Indigenous Australians are regarded as having the oldest living cultures in the world, made up of communities with diverse cultural and social practices, religious beliefs, lifestyles and languages (Hollinsworth 2010). Prior to British colonization, there were up to 700 languages and dialects spoken

(SNAICC 2008). Accompanying the colonization and dispossession of fertile Aboriginal lands, the destruction of many of these languages, the introduction of European diseases such as smallpox, the raping of Aboriginal women and the sporadic massacres of Aboriginal people, continued well into the nineteenth century (Hollinsworth 2010).

Australia's colonial history, embedded in Eurocentric constructions of white supremacy, racism, genocide, linguicide and cultural assimilation, has produced social, economic and linguistic oppression and marginalization for Indigenous communities that continues today. Inscribed and rooted in the hegemonic power relations between the colonizers and the colonized, the enforced marginalization institutionalized in social policy has left legacies of dispossession, forced removal of children, economic and educational disadvantage, language death, high mortality rates and poor health outcomes (Jones Díaz 2014a). For example, for more than a century, the colonial narrative of 'terra nullius' (land with no legal ownership) was entrenched in constitutional and property law, resulting in the systematic dispossession, marginalization and genocide of successive generations of European migration to Australia (Tuffin 2008).

The social construction of 'race'

The term 'race' is a social construction and has no biological reality. Rather, it is a historical and social invention, and a politicized justification of real and imagined differences (Hollinsworth 2006; Elam and Elam 2010). As Elam and Elam eloquently note, '"race" as we know is it both a lie and a truth' (2010: 3). This invention, informed by social Darwinism and Eurocentric constructions of 'race', predominantly prevailing in European scientific discourse of the late nineteenth century, was particularly directed at Indigenous Australians. Categories of 'race' were used to assert Eurocentric assumptions of what is meant to be 'civilized': in this instance, Christian, 'white' and European (Moreton-Robinson 2004; Hollinsworth 2006).

The European obsession with categorizing and classifying people into racial typologies effectively asserted white supremacy based on Eurocentric assumptions that being civilized was Christian, white and European. Further, the eugenics movement that followed (which is based on the perceived inferiority of the 'unfit', poor and Irish), from the 1840s onwards, set about constructing a theory of 'race' aimed at enforcing and policing the differences between Europeans and non-Europeans. Hollinsworth argues that scientific racism 'was applied to African races to justify slavery and in Australia to excuse massacres and explain the abandonment of efforts to protect Indigenous people or improve their lot' (2010: Section, 2, para. 3). Furthermore, scientific racism and social Darwinism was used by colonizing British and European interests as a convenient and suitable justification for the dispossession of land, slavery, rape, disease, and the erosion of languages and cultures, which engendered a theory and practice of human inequality towards Indigenous people colonized by Europeans (Young 1995; Hollinsworth 2006, 2010).

Forms of racism: institutional, individual and discursive

Racism operates on three levels: institutional, individual and discursive. Individual forms of racism are expressed through attitudes, values and beliefs held by individuals based on ethnic, cultural or 'racial' grounds (Hollinsworth 2006). Institutional forms of racism operate at the material and institutional level. It is explicit and highly organized into systemic operations within social institutions to discriminate, oppress, misrepresent and control minority groups. Discursive forms of racism are evident in institutions, individuals and groups, informed by racialized discourse, narratives and ideologies.

Notable examples of institutional racism in Australia include legislation that discriminated against Indigenous Australians up until the 1970s (Hollinsworth 2006). On an international level, this included legalized slavery in the Americas up until the late 1880s and apartheid in South Africa up until the 1990s. In Australia, it was not until 1967 that Indigenous Australians were counted in the national census by a referendum. While this invoked social recognition of Indigenous people as citizens, Moreton-Robinson (2011) argues that it was not a formal recognition of citizenship rights as it has often been wrongly upheld. Rather, some of these rights associated with citizenship were already granted to Indigenous people prior to the 1967 referendum. However, Hollinsworth (2010) notes that this legislation symbolized the gradual rolling back of discriminatory legislation, and paved the way for equal pay and the Racial Discrimination Act.

Other examples of institutional racism in Australia include the forced removal of children from their families (the 'Stolen Generations') and the more recent interventionist policies of the Northern Territory (NT) introduced by the Howard government in the 1970s (Hollinsworth 2010). The 1975 Racial Discrimination Act was suspended to enable the NT Intervention to proceed. This was because, under this act, it was racially discriminatory. The Intervention was responsible for the enforced quarantining of social security payments to families whose children do not attend school, and the banning of alcohol and drugs (Moreton-Robinson 2011). Furthermore, troops were sent to 'restore order', Indigenous townships, land and services were taken over by five-year leases and managers sent into these communities by the Australian government

(Hollinsworth 2010: Section 8, para. 1). Such racialized policy was not directed at any other group in Australia, and therefore is by definition a form of institutional racism.

Institutional racism is legitimized and sanctioned, and often explicit. However, Hollinsworth (2006) argues that it is also implicit, official and unnoticed, implemented through institutional practices, policies and procedures at federal, state and local levels through service provision, education and pedagogical practice. It can also operate discursively on individual levels within institutions that involve prejudice, stereotypes, bias, ethnocentrism and xenophobia. For example, in education, these forms of racism can be expressed through having low expectations of Indigenous children and their families, based on assumptions that the children lack motivation and their families are uninterested in their children's education.

In Chapter 1, we discussed the concept of discourse as a meaning system expressed through language, text, representation, images and statements. Discourses are also belief systems that embody social relationships, power and subjectivity. As our sense of self and the ways in which we relate to the world are informed by discourses, we locate ourselves within these discourses. Individuals or groups who take up positions in racialized discourses of ethnocentrism, xenophobia, racialized stereotypes, prejudice and bias will be positioned by these discourses and as a consequence have available to them a range of taken-for-granted assumptions, narratives and ways of speaking about cultural groups and practices other than their own. While discourses are not necessarily a determinant of belief systems, Moore (2012) notes that the social frameworks of the social world play their part in limiting an individual's capacity to go beyond their influences. In discourses of ethnocentrism, individuals or groups uphold the belief that one's culture and cultural practices are superior to those of other cultures. Moore notes that those positioned in this discourse and who subscribe to its belief systems are informed by limited social references and worldviews.

Xenophobia is having a fear of foreigners, with recent examples of **Islamophobia** currently circulating at both global and national levels. Morgan and Poynting (2012) argue that the globalization of contemporary Islamophobia constitutes elements of demonization of Muslims as terrorists where their communities are suspected of harbouring terrorists. Within this ideology, Morgan and Poynting argue that Muslims are represented as 'enemies of the nation' (2012: 2), a corrosive influence, who refuse to integrate into mainstream society while undermining national values. While Islamophobia is an offshoot of xenophobia, stereotypes found in media representations of cultural groups, in particular Indigenous Australians and non-'white' immigrants, effectively construct racialized stereotypes.

These stereotypes include: 'Aboriginals are lazy', 'Aboriginals get special treatment and receive additional welfare payments', and 'Aboriginals are primitive and nomadic'.

More recent stereotypes that have emerged in the Australian media portray Indigenous men as sexual predators, and Indigenous women and children as helpless, passive, vulnerable and in need of protection by white mainstream Australian society. These same stereotypes construct Indigenous communities as dysfunctional and violent. Indeed it was these stereotypes that prompted the Howard government to legislate the Northern Territory Intervention policy that forced Indigenous people into reciprocal arrangements with the government in return for basic services that the government has the responsibility to provide for all Australians (Due 2008).

Regardless of our understanding of how racism operates at institutional, individual and discursive levels, for Indigenous Australians the end result is poor health and educational outcomes, lower life expectancy rates, higher incarceration rates compared to non-Indigenous communities, and an Indigenous unemployment rate that is four times higher than the national figure (Hollinsworth 2010: Section 1, para. 2). Of note is an emerging field of research investigating the links between personal experiences of racism and poor health that indicate consistent findings associating racism with mental health conditions and psychological distress (Paradies 2006; Paradies, Harris and Anderson 2008). Therefore, the impact of racism, inequality and marginalization on Indigenous communities in Australia is of major concern for all Australians. Hollinsworth rightly argues that without a genuine acknowledgement of the extent and impact of racism towards Indigenous Australians, there will be little change or improvement to the stark disadvantage and marginalization they experience.

Discourses of deficit and the impact on Indigenous communities

Fforde *et al.* (2013) argue that discourses of deficit are embedded in representations of Aboriginality that have constructed Aboriginal identity since colonization. They use the term deficit discourse to describe 'a mode of thinking, identifiable in language use, that frames Aboriginal identity in a narrative of negativity, deficiency and disempowerment' (2013: 162). They argue that, rooted in the history of cultural relations in Australia, assumptions of Indigenous deficiency are key components of racism through which the dominance of Eurocentric representations about Aboriginal and Torres Strait Islanders have been the singular reference points and understanding for non-Indigenous Australians.

While Fforde *et al.* (2013) argue that discourses of deficit have been historically constructed, they point to more recent representations in policies of the Intervention, Closing the Gap and other educational English literacy campaigns. Here, underlying assumptions of deficit remain unchallenged, thus potentially reinforcing Indigenous disadvantage.[1] For example, they cite the work of Bamblett (2013), who reported that the Wiradjuri community had disengaged from mainstream schools as a result of continual reference to cultural and social deficit.

Whiteness and nation building

In Australia, it was not until Federation in 1901 that whiteness became the official defining racial marker of the Australian nation, racially defined by the 'White Australia' policy as evidenced in exclusionary policies of all non-whites (Hollinsworth 2006; Moreton-Robinson 2009). However, this is not to suggest that Australia was devoid of racism and racializing practices prior to Federation. On the contrary, Australia's colonial past is rooted in Eurocentric constructions of white supremacy and authorized racism.

The Immigration Restriction Act of 1901 (more commonly known as the 'White Australia' policy) aimed to restrict non-European immigration to Australia and deported immigrants already residing in Australia. For example, many Pacific Islanders, Chinese, Indians and 'Afghans'[2] were denied citizenship and voting rights, and experienced employment restrictions. Pacific Islanders were deported back to their countries of origin despite having spent many years in Australia working as labourers in the sugar cane, gold mining, rail and other industries (Hollinsworth 2006). Apart from the fact that this act banned all 'coloured' immigration to Australia, it also excluded Indigenous Australians from citizenship (NSW Government, Education and Communities 2013). In this context, racism and nationalism were almost synonymous (Hollinsworth 2006), and constituted as such in the 'White Australia' policy. Anglocentric whiteness became the 'definitive marker of citizenship' (Moreton-Robinson and Nicoll 2006: 70) in which the Australian state was a racial state; Indigenous Australians were categorized as 'different' from other Australians and, as a result, not destined to contribute to the emerging nation (Hollinsworth 2010).

Institutional racism directed at Indigenous Australians took many forms, including but not limited to: the establishment of missions and reserves; the denial of civic rights and forced removal of children; the control of property; illicit sexual relations; exclusion from schools, swimming pools and community services; poor provision of health care, nutrition, housing and education; and the exploitation of their labour

(Hollinsworth 2006, 2010). Embedded in this history, Australian national identity and constructions of 'race' have aimed at enforcing and policing the marginalization of Indigenous Australians since colonization.

Interestingly, these racialized constructions are barely acknowledged in discourses of multicultural pluralism, which have been with us since the mid-1970s. Shiells (2010) notes that it has been only in the last 20 years that academics in Australia have started to name and study whiteness in a similar way to other 'racial' categories. As a result, there has been a very recent yet fundamental recognition that notions of 'race' (including whiteness) are constituted in a dynamic set of social relations contingent upon and informed by historical, social, cultural, political, institutional and discursive practices and values (Apple 1999; Guess 2006). Such practices are implicit in the relations between Indigenous and non-Indigenous people, which effectively serve to normalize and sustain the existing inequitable relations of power constructed through 'discursive reproduction of social, cultural and historical processes' (Moore 2012: 3).

In multicultural discourses there are tensions and silences in national ideals of cultural diversity in terms of how Indigeneity is addressed. Curthoys (1999: 286) argues that multicultural pluralism subsumes issues of Indigeneity, which has brought about an uneasy tension and silence as Indigenous Australians have 'protested against being incorporated within the "multicultural" and seen as just one ethnicity among many'. As Curthoys reminds us, Indigenous people have stressed that their situation is different from that of immigrant Australians (including Anglo-Australians). Their Indigeneity to the Australian landscape has meant a special and unique relationship to the land. Patrick (2012) observes that Indigenous people around the world are survivors of colonialism and resource exploitation of their land. Indigenous Australians are no different in that they, too, rightfully demand recognition of their unique status as the first Australians, original inhabitants and owners of the land.

Indeed this recognition is only now just beginning to be evident in upcoming changes to the Australian constitution to recognize Indigenous Australians as the first Australians. The dispossession of land and institutionalized racism inflicted upon them have meant that the social, cultural and political histories of Indigenous Australians are central to the construction of Indigenous identities in their everyday realities of racism and racializing practices in Australia.

Within this tension between pluralist multiculturalism and Indigeneity, there are unanswered questions about the relationship between whiteness and Indigeneity. As May (1999) points out, this tendency to ignore Indigenous voices and concerns is evident in the debates on multiculturalism in Canadian, North American, Australian and New Zealand literature. To this end, it is imperative that critical examinations of whiteness in multicultural societies acknowledge the complexities of the historically and politically situated specificity of racism as experienced differently by Indigenous peoples from those of immigrant backgrounds.

Postcolonial studies and critical 'race' theory

Australia is a postcolonial state. As Ashcroft *et al.* (2013) remind us, all postcolonial societies still continue to be influenced in various ways through overt and subtle forms of neocolonial domination. A significant impact of this domination is evident in the power relations between Indigenous and non-Indigenous people that operate at both discursive and material levels in Australian society. Postcolonial studies and critical 'race' theory critique and challenge these unequal power relations constituted in the social, historical and cultural constructions of 'race' as a result of colonialism and subsequent immigration policies. In particular, postcolonial studies are 'based on the historical fact of European colonization, and the diverse material effects to which this phenomenon gave rise' (Ashcroft, Griffiths and Tiffin 2006: 2). Consequently, the implications of colonization are embedded in social, political, economic, historical and linguistic domination derived from slavery, migration and oppression of Indigenous communities (Ferfolja, Jones Díaz and Ullman 2015).

The discussion that follows begins with an overview of postcolonial studies. It focuses on key concepts such as hybridity, the 'third space' and essentialism, to highlight their relevance for educators and community service professionals working with *both* Indigenous and non-Indigenous children, families and communities in contemporary postcolonial multicultural Australia. The discussion then introduces critical 'race' theory and two of its practical applications: as a useful tool in critically understanding how de-constructions of 'race' and racism can effectively destabilize homogenous ideals of unified identity; and to make visible embedded racial assumptions produced in pedagogical relationships and educational discourse.

Furthermore, Ashcroft *et al.* (2013) argue that postcolonial analysis of colonial power is even more relevant in today's globalized neoliberal world. They note that issues of global warming, environmentalism, ecofeminism, speciesism and ecological imperialism are beginning to take prominence in postcolonial critiques as the connections between colonist treatment of Indigenous flora and fauna and colonized people are highlighted. Therefore, frameworks of postcolonialism continue to provide useful and critical tools in understanding contemporary social, cultural, linguistic, political, economic and environmental complexities that face societies at global and local levels.

Hybridity and the third space

As a key postcolonial theorist, Hommi Bhabha (1994, 1998) has critiqued colonialism and Western superiority from various viewpoints. His work has been pivotal in applying postcolonial thinking to issues of inequality, racism, marginalization, essentialism and hybridity. Bhabha's idea of hybridity focuses on the creation of new cultural forms and practices mainly derived from multiculturalism or the mixing of cultural groups, which are characteristic of postcolonial societies. Building on notions of transformation from the old to the new, he introduced the concept of the 'third space' (1998) to describe how minorities and marginalized people construct historical narratives from fragmented archives, and their subjectivities are often located or dislocated through exclusionary practices.

In this sense the 'third space' is a renegotiated space and hybridity is the strategy that enables for minorities the deployment of 'the partial culture from which they emerge to construct visions of community, and versions of historic memory, that give narrative form to the minority positions they occupy: the outside of the inside: the part in the whole' (Bhabha 1998: 34). In recent times postcolonial theory has made use of these terms to challenge fixed notions of 'race' and ethnicity informed by biological determinist theories of racial science. By examining hybridity and the 'third space' through a postcolonial lens, identities constructed through difference transcend beyond 'race', ethnicity, linguistic and gendered categories.

Central to Bhabha's (1994) thinking is the concept of essentialism. As discussed in Chapter 2, essentialism is when characteristics about a group become naturalized and normalized representations in which they become defined by a singular aspect of their identity. Essentialism constructs identities as fixed, based on forms of biological and cultural uniqueness. In educational and community services, essentialist views of Indigenous children and their families often prevail (Kaomea 2000; Davis 2007; MacNaughton and Davis 2009). Davis (2007) argues that this provides the justification for continued oppression and discriminatory colonial practices, as Indigenous people are routinely positioned as primitive, exotic and uncivilized.

There is a tendency in education and community services to essentialize Indigenous cultures and their communities, despite their good intentions. This is apparent where Aboriginal culture becomes exoticized and reified, celebrated as fixed within essentialist traditions in which cultural artefacts such as boomerangs and dot paintings become exemplars of Indigenous cultures. As a result, the racism, marginalization and disadvantage experienced by Aboriginal families and children on a daily basis are largely dismissed. In highlighting issues of representation of cultural minority groups, Andreotti (2011) draws on Bhabha's questioning of 'authentic representation' and asserts that no representation exists outside of cultural or ideological categories. As a result, systems of representation are layered and interwoven in other systems of representation, suggesting that the idea of authenticity is difficult to justify.

Still, in education and community services, the representation of Indigenous cultures as fixed and stable is highly problematic as it ignores the very existence of hybridity, difference and diversity in the construction of representation. Bhabha's concept of hybridity and third space highlights the fluidity of culture and identity, which effectively resists essentializing discourses that position Indigenous children and their families at the margins. Bhabha writes:

> This third space displaces the histories that constitute it, and sets up new structures of authority, new political initiatives, which are inadequately understood through received wisdom . . . The process of cultural hybridity gives rise to something different, something new and unrecognizable, a new area of negotiation of meaning and representation. (Cited in Kameniar, Imtoual and Bradley 2010: 13)

Critical 'race' theory and whiteness studies

Drawing from critical 'race' theory (CRT hereafter) to examine whiteness is one way of conceptualizing the political and historical specificity of Indigenous Australians. As discussed in Chapter 5, whiteness studies draws attention to its invisibility and unnamed identity within a 'racial' category. Whiteness studies examines the social construction of whiteness and white privilege that operates within normalizing discourses to produce taken-for-granted positions of advantage that are legitimized in everyday social practices, discursive power relations and educational pedagogies (see Chapter 5). Taylor (2009) argues that whiteness is a legal and political framework grounded in ideologies of Western supremacy and colonialism. As previously discussed, this is evident in Australia's colonial history and treatment of Indigenous Australians, in which constructions of Aboriginality were rooted in the legal and political structures of the 'White Australia' policy, the 'Stolen Generations' and assimilationist policies (Hollinsworth 2006).

CRT as a framework, then, offers an unravelling of how the supremacy of whiteness has continued to subordinate people of colour to reify racial inequality (Frankenberg 1993; Villenas and Deyhle 1999; Gillborn and Ladson-Phillips 2010; Zeus 2015). CRT and whiteness studies draw on the lens of cultural studies and postcolonial theory to critically locate the positions of dominant white identity and privilege. However, central to the scholarship of whiteness is not an attack on 'white' people; rather it critically challenges the socially constructed and reinforced power of 'white' identifications and interests (Gillborn 2007).

Since the category of 'white' is an unnamed identity, its constant evasion of scrutiny and interrogation reinforces its social privilege. As Ashcroft *et al.* (2013) argue, it has a special force of normativity, while other racist discursive terms, such as 'black', 'brown', 'yellow' and 'red', continue to be named as 'racial' groupings. Therefore, it is precisely this invisibility of whiteness as a 'racial' signifier that results in the structural and subjective constructions of normative whiteness. Whiteness, like other identities, is historically, socially and culturally constructed, and it too is subject to and mediated by contemporary global changes resulting from economic and political instability.

Indigenous languages, identities and cultural practices

As discussed in Chapter 10, of the 700 languages and dialects spoken prior to British colonization, 120 of these languages are spoken today, with as few as 13 of these languages considered strong (SNAICC 2008; Marmion, Obata and Troy 2014). In recent years, there have been some efforts to increase the availability of Indigenous languages offered in primary schools, particularly in NSW (NSW, December 2011). Purdie (2009: 2–3) notes that, nationally, there are more than 80 Indigenous languages taught in schools. Yet most of these languages are not spoken by students at home. Only 28 per cent of the programmes are first language programmes, including bilingual programmes offered to students in the early years of school. Approximately 12 per cent of programmes are second language learning programmes, and the remaining 60 per cent are language revival programme or language awareness programmes. As noted by Loakes *et al.* (2013), today Indigenous Australians are far less likely to speak their traditional languages in preference for speaking Aboriginal English.

Indigenous communities place high value on bilingual education, and some of the most multilingual communities are remote Indigenous communities. Despite this, however, bilingual education for Indigenous children has remained controversial. This is most evident in the Northern Territory. In 2008 bilingual education was dismantled in remote Indigenous schools, determining that the language of instruction must be in English (Simpson, Caffery and McConvell 2009). In spite of the Declaration of the Rights of Indigenous Peoples (United Nations 2007) signed by Australia in 2009, and the extensive body of evidence substantiating the intellectual, linguistic and cultural benefits of bilingual education for Indigenous and immigrant background children (see Chapter 10), Australia lags behind other countries in providing opportunities for

Indigenous children to retain and strengthen their Indigenous languages and learn English as an additional language and dialect (EALD). As Hobson notes, Australia remains 'the world's worst steward of Indigenous cultural heritage' (cited in Maslen 2011: 37).

Therefore, in postcolonial nation states such as Australia, Aotearoa New Zealand and countries within Latin America with an Indigenous presence, and in African nation states, issues of language revival, retention and access to quality language education programmes are of major concern to Indigenous communities, families and educators. Education and community contexts can powerfully inhibit or prohibit opportunities of bi/multilingual Indigenous children to attain maximum linguistic, cultural and social potential. Invisibilizing Aboriginality, deficit thinking by educators and community professionals towards Indigenous children and their families, racism, whiteness and lack of representation of Aboriginal and Torres Strait Islander perspectives do little to challenge the racialized inequality that Indigenous Australians continue to experience today. Crucial to addressing these issues is the understanding that pedagogical practices, staff attitudes and curriculum in mainstream and Indigenous-specific settings can make a difference in challenging such inequalities.

Research investigating pedagogical practices, engagement with Indigenous families, and practitioner attitudes towards Aboriginal and Torres Strait Islander issues

In the discussion that follows, the data presented draw together two studies by Robinson and Jones Díaz (2000) and Jones Díaz et al. (2016, in review), to highlight how pedagogical practices can be sites of positive engagement for Indigenous families, or conversely places where Indigenous people's lived realities of racism and inequality are dismissed and perceived by educators as irrelevant to children's lives.

The two studies reported here investigate the role of safe spaces for Indigenous women and their children attending an informal playgroup setting (Pennycook et al. 2010–2011; Jones Díaz et al. 2016, in review), and the views and perspectives of early childhood staff on matters relating to Indigenous issues as they impact on children and families (Robinson and Jones Díaz 2000). These studies were conducted in separate community-based settings in NSW over different periods of time, and used qualitative methods incorporating ethnography and participant observation in the form of informal conversations with the women and staff, as well as observational and field notes (as in the case of the Pennycook et al.'s 2010–2011 study), and questionnaire and informal interviews with early childhood practitioners (as in the case of the Robinson and Jones Díaz's 2000 study).

Safe spaces that privilege Indigenous knowledges, texts and cultural/linguistic practices

Engaging Australian Indigenous children and their families in education and community settings requires responsive pedagogical approaches that draw on the cultural and linguistic strengths inherent in Indigenous knowledges, texts and cultural practices. Selected data from a larger study investigating early literacy practices in informal playgroup settings (Pennycook *et al.* 2010–2011) focused on a case study site that was a safe Aboriginal supported playgroup in Greater Western Sydney (GWS).

The mothers attending the playgroup identified strongly as Aboriginal women and valued the opportunity to attend an Aboriginal service led by an Aboriginal family support professional. Moreover there were a number of support services available to the families attending the playgroup. Hence there are two key findings evident in this case study: the significance of safe space for Indigenous families and their children; and the engagement of the children and their mothers through the privileging of Indigenous knowledge, texts and cultural/linguistic practices.

The significance of safe space

In this study, it was apparent that there was a safe Indigenous space for the women and children to come together. For example, the children had opportunities for a variety of learning experiences, while their mothers were able to socialize, make connections with one another, and receive advice and support from the different community-based based professionals. Below, Roslyn,[3] a senior Aboriginal local Darag woman, who was one of the researchers acting as a participant observer with the playgroup participants, reflects on the atmosphere of the playgroup:

> The whole playgroup – mums and children – is very, very relaxed; very easygoing. The mums and the children are quite comfortable there, with each other, with the workers. Everything just seems to flow. There's no pressure on anybody. The mums I think feel safe there. It doesn't matter what they're doing, how they're dressed, what they're saying – they're accepted for who they are without anyone even considering where you come from because a lot of the girls have experienced similar things; they've had some amazing traumas in their lives – domestic violence, illness, drugs . . .

As the year progressed, it was observed that the mothers became more involved with their children's play and learning experiences, as evidenced by Roslyn's observations in the extract below.

Yes – and if there's counting, or colours, or clapping, or any sort of actions, the mums will become involved, with the children. What I've found also is – moving from that social support and the mums spending most of their time chatting to each other while the children played independently – the mums are becoming more involved with the children.

In educational research, Bhabha's notion of 'third space' has been applied to notions of safe space (Conteh, Martin and Robertson 2007). Conteh and Brock (2010) describe the ways in which diverse communities create for themselves opportunities for meaning making through co-constructed meaningful relationships between educators and learners. For example, the mothers' increased interests in their children's learning and engagement in literacy activities at the playgroup was increased through a strategy of integrating literacy activities at morning tea time. At this playgroup, the mothers would sit with their children and read stories to them, as well as chat with the other mothers and children. Thus the mothers gained a sense of ownership and belonging as they gradually became more engaged with their children's literacy learning.

As a result of having a safe space, opportunities for meaning making and learning were facilitated through a sense of belonging and trust. Inherent in this process is the recognition that educational settings are sites where culture is co-constructed, mediated and sometimes contested, where families and their children are at the centre, and there is a recognition that learning is influenced by complex social, political, ideological, historical, cultural and linguistic factors (Conteh and Brock 2010). In this case study site, a crucial element to setting up an Indigenous 'safe space' was the employment of Indigenous staff in which the representation of Indigeneity and connection to local community were high priorities. The playgroup was known to the wider local community as 'safe Aboriginal women's space', in a disadvantaged and under-resourced area, which provided various culturally appropriate services specifically for families and children (Morgan, Chodkiewicz and Pennycook 2015).

Privileging of Indigenous knowledge, texts and cultural/linguistic practices

At the playgroup setting, connections to country, language and culture were acknowledged. Also the incorporation of cultural representations and connections to the children's cultural, linguistic and social realities facilitated the children's engagement with literacy learning, which in turn provided opportunities for the mothers to be involved in their learning (Jones Díaz *et al.* 2016, in review). For example, throughout the year there were diverse learning experiences programmed for the families, which included Aboriginal cultural and literacy events, excursions, and the incorporation of Aboriginal children's books that featured Dreamtime stories, Aboriginal English, Aboriginal languages and cultural practices. Many of these books were written by Indigenous Australian writers and included Aboriginal drawings. Some examples included *The Rainbow Serpent*, *Honey Ant*, *Bush Bash*, *My Place*, *Nan, You and Me* and *Two Mates*.

Given that there were difficulties in accessing age-appropriate urban Aboriginal stories with Aboriginal languages featured, one of the researchers (Jones Díaz) sourced and presented to the children a book written in Dungutti (an Aboriginal language from the mid-north coast of NSW). The book, entitled *We All Clap Hands Together! Sorry Day 2011*, was developed by a primary teacher based in a Sydney school where 'National Sorry Day' is an annual event.[4] The book was based on the nursery rhyme 'Heads, shoulders, knees and toes', and included photos of Aboriginal children pointing to the body parts labelled in Dungutti standing in front of an Aboriginal flag.

The observation from Roslyn below illustrates the children's engagement and interest in learning the Dungutti words.

> Criss sat with children on mat to sing 'Heads, shoulders, knees and toes' . . . as she went through the words, when the song came to knees [Bugga Bugga in Dungutti] Ben said, 'two'. Brock, Haiden and Isaiah were singing along and doing actions and using words learned with Criss.

While the children in this playgroup were unfamiliar with Dungutti language,[5] their connection to the images and new words introduced was apparent. Ben's ability to connect the Dungutti word 'Bugga Bugga' [two knees] to the number 'two', was facilitated through the image of an Aboriginal girl crouched with her two hands on both knees. Brock, Haiden and Isaiah's involvement in singing the song, and pointing to the various body parts while learning the Dungutti words, demonstrates the benefits of incorporating texts, Aboriginal images and words through a familiar nursery rhyme. In this case, such strategies enabled the children to make successful cultural and linguistic connections to the book, which in turn enhanced their literacy learning.

Practitioners' perceptions of Aboriginal and Torres Strait Islander issues with children, staff and families in early childhood education and community-based settings

In the Robinson and Jones Díaz (2000) research, while many participants expressed positive views about the importance of raising Indigenous issues with children, just under half acknowledged that Indigenous people experience stereotyping and racism. Only a few respondents recognized the possibility that children from Indigenous backgrounds had experienced discrimination from children, staff and families at their setting.

Assumed absences and invisible identities

Assumptions about children's daily interactions and direct experiences with Indigeneity were confined to the adults' knowledge of children at the setting rather than their knowledge of children's experiences outside the setting, in their community or home contexts. Many of the respondents' comments were drawn from their observations of children at the setting, based on an assumed absence of Indigenous families and children attending the setting. The comments below illustrate how, for many of the participants in this study, Indigenous issues were relevant only when there were Indigenous children attending the setting.

> If the children [were] in my group, I would actively incorporate this area into planning and programming but because they aren't [in my group], I only sometimes cover this.
>
> . . . there are no Aboriginal families in our setting but if there were, then that would be important.
>
> This is not the majority background at our centre, so it is not incorporated actively.
>
> Again, considering all the other 'issues' that we would be incorporating into our daily practice . . . , [it is] not possible to do it [Aboriginal perspectives] all the time.

This assumed absence, that there are no Indigenous families and children attending the setting, is problematic particularly since some Aboriginal people do not appear to have the 'Indigenous look'. Due to this, their lived realities and experiences of Aboriginality and racism are constantly denied and therefore perceived as not relevant. It appears that Indigenous issues were seen as relevant only when children and families from 'visible' Indigenous backgrounds were attending the setting. This denial of Aboriginality based on physical appearance is a form of essentialism in which skin colour is synonymous with Aboriginality through which universalized, naturalized and normalized singular representations of Indigenous identity is constructed.

Implications for educators and community service staff

This chapter has raised pertinent issues relevant to educators and community services staff working with Indigenous children, families and communities. The discussion that follows offers suggestions that effectively incorporate Indigenous perspectives in daily pedagogical practices in mainstream services that are informed by the following principles: knowledge of historical, cultural and social constructions of 'race' and racism in Australia; a critical reflexive approach to how these issues impact on children, families and communities; policy that embeds Indigenous perspectives, knowledge and voices; authentic representations of Indigenous culture that are incorporated throughout the curriculum; providing safe spaces and active recognition; and harnessing of Indigenous languages, literacies and cultural practices on a daily basis. Across these areas, it is crucial that local Aboriginal and Torres Strait Islander communities are consulted and the inclusion of Indigenous voices, expert knowledge of elders and ways of relating, being and belonging are shared throughout these processes. Furthermore, it is important that a whole-setting approach is underpinned by collaboration that also recognizes the role of ongoing professional development for all staff as the starting point for ongoing critical conversations that inform pedagogical practice.

Knowledge of the historical, social and cultural constructions of 'race' and racism in Australia

It is essential that staff are knowledgeable about historical and social constructions of Indigeneity, whiteness, 'race' and racism in Australia, in view of how these constructions were the end result of colonization, dispossession and marginalization for Indigenous Australians. Unfortunately, Eurocentric constructions of white supremacy still play out today in the minds of parents and communities who are poorly informed by racialized media reports, stereotypes and racism. There is a need for critical understandings of how historical policies such as the 'White Australia' policy and contemporary social policies including multiculturalism and Intervention policies have shaped Indigenous disadvantage in contemporary Australia. When staff are informed about how local and national histories, policies of dispossession, assimilation and language loss continue to impact on children, families and communities, pedagogical practices are enhanced.

This relates directly to the principle of 'ongoing learning and reflective practice' identified in the EYLFA (DEEWR 2009: 10). Specifically, the framework invites us to question how philosophies, understandings and knowledge can assist in better understandings of what may be observed or experienced in view of how they may or may not inform practice.

A critical and reflexive approach

Being a critical reflexive educator or community worker relies on dispositions that are informed by contemporary theoretical frameworks. By drawing on CRT and postcolonial studies, educators and community-based professionals are able to draw critical connections between theory and practice by understanding how local and national issues impact on Indigenous Australians. This will inform their work, enabling them to respond in ways that are equitable, just and responsive to the issues that face Indigenous Australians. CRT and postcolonial studies equip staff with tools to critique the various deficit assumptions often applied to Aboriginal and Torres Strait Islander people. They also assist in understanding how forms of racism that operate at institutional, individual and discursive levels uphold and reproduce discourses of deficit disadvantage and inequality. Through the lens of such theories, a greater appreciation for Indigenous identity, languages and cultural practice is afforded.

A critical, reflexive practitioner is mindful of the links to the principles of ongoing learning and reflective practice identified in the EYLFA (DEEWR 2009), which encourages a move beyond normative ways of knowing and belonging (Sumsion and Wong 2011). Indeed the focus for reflection incorporates a questioning disposition informed by theory to help better understand the complexities and challenges in working with Indigenous children, families and communities.

Policy that embeds Indigenous perspectives, knowledge and voices

Regardless of whether there are Indigenous children and families attending the setting, Indigenous perspectives, knowledge and voices need to be incorporated into the policy and philosophy of the setting. This will enable pedagogical practices and procedures that authentically represent and incorporate both traditional and contemporary social and cultural practices, Indigenous languages including Aboriginal English, and employ Indigenous staff wherever possible. An example of this includes the Acknowledgement of Country, which is a statement of respect for and acknowledgement of Indigenous Australians' custodianship of the land performed at the commencement of gatherings. Acknowledgement of Country pays respect to the local Indigenous languages and groups of the area in which the gathering is taking place. Other examples include statements about what Indigenous languages and cultural practices are represented in the programme and how this representation will occur.

As with all policy development and implementation, collaborating with families, children and communities is essential if their voices are to be heard. Through consultation with local Aboriginal organizations, land councils and elders, collaborative partnerships and trusting relationships can be formed where Indigenous knowledge underpins policy content and procedures. Policy that incorporates Indigenous perspectives also acknowledges the importance for staff to engage in professional development opportunities where knowledge and critical insights are gained and brought back to the setting to share with staff. As in the case of all policy development, such policy is open to evaluation and change. Therefore, through policy, educators are able to acknowledge 'Indigenous people's worldviews, social structures and pedagogy as a legitimate foundation upon which to construct new meanings or knowledge alongside Western traditions and ways of knowing' (Bouvier and Karlenzig 2006: 17).

Representation and incorporation of Indigenous perspectives in the curriculum

As previously discussed, essentialism constructs identities as fixed, homogeneous and singularly defined by cultural stereotypes. Authentic representations of Indigenous cultural and linguistic practices go beyond the exoticization and celebration of cultural practice as something fixed in the past. As discussed in Chapter 5, approaches that are confined to celebratory and superficial representations of cultural practice reinforce ideas to children and families that identity is fixed and singular, rather than fluid, multiple and transformative. For educators and community service professionals, then, it is important to critically reflect on the appropriate use of Indigenous resources to ensure that such issues of representation are addressed accordingly. For example, using simplistic and stereotypical representations of boomerangs and dot painting merely teach cultural stereotypes to children. It is essential that educators and community service professionals challenge essentialism by representing everyday social, cultural and linguistic practices evident in Indigenous communities, including the negotiation of political struggle against racism, whiteness and inequality evident in Aboriginal and Torres Strait Islander communities.

Providing safe spaces

As discussed in the findings reported in this chapter, providing 'safe spaces' for Indigenous children and their families in childhood and community-based settings fosters engagement, a sense of belonging and trust. In both mainstream and Indigenous-focused settings, it is important that pedagogies allow space for Aboriginal ways of knowing, and being able to recognize and respond to local cultural knowledges and practices. Such pedagogies embrace practices that are 'locally defined, culturally appropriate and relevant to the values of the local community' (Guilfoyle *et al.* 2010: 68). Crucial in this process is the employment of Indigenous staff members who represent the communities to which the children belong.

A safe space draws on understandings that, for Indigenous people, family includes both immediate family members but also extended family members such as aunties, uncles and cousins, grandparents and kinship connections, and community members with whom the child is connected (Warrki Jarrinkaku ACRS Project Team 2002, cited in Guilfoyle *et al.* 2010). Therefore it is crucial that significant family, community and social networks are included in programmes where Indigenous children are present as this provides families with access to informal support networks where information and advice are available. This also involves Indigenous community-based professionals being readily available on site or within the local community.

Three key principles of the EYLFA (DEEWR 2009), which focus on 'secure, respectful and reciprocal relationships' (p. 10), are relevant in fostering safe spaces for Indigenous children and families. This is dependent upon establishing a welcoming environment where there is a two-way flow of information (Beecher and Jones Díaz 2014) and relationship building (Board of Studies 2008) that fosters collaboration and trust between educators, community-based professionals and families.

It is important to recognize that there are complexities and contradictions in communication practices. The ability to recognize and negotiate communication protocols requires forms of cultural literacy. This involves having knowledge of diverse meaning systems, but also the ability to negotiate and read different ways of communicating in different social and cultural contexts (Reid, Jones Díaz and Alsairari forthcoming). Acknowledging and observing Indigenous protocols in communicating is especially important in establishing trusting and respectful relationships. Local Aboriginal communities can provide assistance in finding out about specific protocols that need to be considered (NSW Board of Studies 2008). This in turn establishes ongoing and collaborative partnerships with families, where parents and families feel safe in exchanging information about cultural, linguistic and social practices that can effectively inform pedagogy, curriculum and policy.

Active recognition and harnessing of Indigenous languages, literacies and cultural practices on a daily basis

As previously discussed, Australia has a long way to go in catching up with other countries in providing children with opportunities to learn Indigenous languages and dialects. Critical to challenging these issues is the legitimization of Indigenous languages and dialects in educational and community settings. As a starting point, setting up the visual environment through consultations with elders, grandparents, family members and local Indigenous community groups so that it represents Indigenous languages, literacy and cultural practices will enable culturally relevant representations of stories, songs, symbols and images. This process develops connections to traditional local language and cultural practices as well as those contemporary practices, both of which are vital. Finding out about local Indigenous languages, either spoken in the past or spoken today, through making contact with the Aboriginal community, education, health and legal consultative groups will ensure a more informed and sensitive approach.

Still, it is important to acknowledge that, while Aboriginal and Torres Strait Islander people may identify strongly with their Indigenous identity, they may not speak their languages and may have little contact with speakers of their languages. However, they may have multiple connections with more than one Aboriginal community. By representing the languages that are spoken in the region, these connections can be strengthened.

Furthermore, most Aboriginal people today speak varieties of Aboriginal English and their first language (Eades 1995). Aboriginal English is a variation of English that uses certain words, phrases, expressions and grammatical features as a way of maintaining group membership (Harrison 2011). It is important that educators and community-based professional recognize this as a legitimate and valid dialect, and incorporate its use throughout the daily programme providing enriched language-based experiences where both Australian Standard English and Aboriginal English are promoted and supported.

Integrating Indigenous literacy and language practices throughout the curriculum through Aboriginal and Torres Strait Islander dance, movement, mime, drama, music, poetry, rap, storytelling, books and multimedia will facilitate learning outcomes identified in the EYLFA (DEEWR 2009: 10), where Indigenous children have a strong sense of identity and well-being, are connected to their world, are effective communicators, and confident and involved learners.

Conclusion

This chapter has critically examined the historical, social and racialized constructions of Indigeneity that have shaped processes of inequality and marginalization for Aboriginal and Torres Strait Islander people throughout Australia's history. It has discussed ways in which policies of colonization, dispossession and nation building have produced forms of racism that construct deficit discourses of Aboriginality embedded in Australian society. By drawing on CRT and postcolonial studies, educators and community service professionals are able to develop critical understandings of how racialized constructions of deficit pervade educational policy, curriculum and pedagogy. This chapter has also highlighted the significance of Indigenous languages, identities and cultural practices, including an examination of issues relating to language extinction and revival, health and educational disadvantage. By drawing on two studies, the findings highlight how the educational setting can be both a site of positive engagement of Indigenous families or, conversely, a negative site of dismissal, embedded in staff attitudes towards Indigeneity. Finally, implications for educators and community service professionals were offered and links to the EYLFA (DEEWR 2009) were considered that are relevant for both Indigenous focused and mainstream settings in the incorporation of Indigenous perspectives into pedagogical practice.

Within recent years, the Apology and policies of Closing the Gap have in some ways addressed the issues of disadvantage and marginalization of Indigenous Australians. However, Australia still has a long way to go to fully challenge the institutional, individual and discursive forms of racism that continue to exist there. In 2016, the proposed Referendum to ask the Australian people about the inclusion of Indigenous Australians in the Constitution as the first Australians will be a further testing ground for laying out a foundation for change.

Notes

1. Closing the Gap is a national strategy that aims to reduce Indigenous disadvantage in education, health, life expectancy, early childhood education and employment outcomes, endorsed by Australian government in March 2008.
2. The 'Afghans' were imported mainly from Afghanistan, Pakistan, but some arrived from Turkey, Iran and Egypt as camel handlers. As they were considered a homogenous cultural group, they were categorized together as 'Afghans'.
3. In order to protect the identity of the participants in this study, the names used in this chapter are pseudonyms.
4. National Sorry Day is an annual cultural Australia-wide observance held on 26 May every year. It acknowledges Australia's 'Stolen Generations', who were Indigenous Australians forcibly removed from their families and communities. Many schools and community organizations take part in this event to demonstrate commitment towards national reconciliation.
5. Dungutti language is an Aboriginal language spoken from the mid-north coast to the northern tablelands in the west of NSW.

Recommended reading

Maslen, G. (2011) Lost for words, *About the House Magazine*, December: 37–39.
New South Wales Board of Studies (2008) *Working with Aboriginal Communities*, rev. edn. A guide to community consultation and protocols. Sydney: Board of Studies. Available at: www.boardofstudies.nsw.edu.au (accessed 14 October 2014).
Sarra, C. (2011) *Strong and Smart – Towards a pedagogy for emancipation: Education for first peoples.* Oxfordshire: Routledge.
Secretariat of National Aboriginal and Islander Child Care (SNAICC) (2008) *Foster their Culture: Caring for Aboriginal and Torres Strait Islander Children.* North Fitzroy, Vic.: SNAICC.

6

Critical multiculturalism: policy and practice

Introduction

This chapter examines multiculturalism in terms of how it has informed and shaped childhood education and community service delivery. It begins with an overview of how multiculturalism has influenced Australian society for more than 40 years, and provides a critique of its limitations in challenging legitimized and institutionalized social inequalities. Australian multicultural policy is examined within contemporary contexts of post-multiculturalism in which a critical overview of the global and local responses to refugees and asylum seekers is provided. Within this discussion there is a focus on how refugees and asylum seekers are constructed in political agendas and media debates within the broader contexts of current moral panic and Islamophobia. The chapter then examines the limitations of plural multiculturalism in current practices with regard to their limitations in providing equitable and innovative pedagogies that are responsive to the impact of globalization, **superdiversity**, intensified global immigration and racialization. By drawing on frameworks of cultural studies it also aims to examine 'whiteness' as a social construct that operates in many of the dominant cultural practices embedded in childhood education and community services. Educators' perceptions of children's understandings of 'race', ethnicity and power are examined and new insights from recent research that highlights children's negotiations in challenging whiteness, racism and marginalization are offered. The chapter concludes with a range of implications and strategies that can assist practitioners in implementing contemporary pedagogies that embrace critical approaches to multiculturalism in a globalized world.

Australia as a post-multicultural superdiverse nation state

Australia, like many countries today, is a superdiverse post-multicultural nation state, which has within the past 20 years received a steady flow of immigrants from almost every part of the world. For example, the Australian Bureau of Statistics (ABS) (2015b) reports that 28 per cent of the population was born overseas. ABS (2011) reports that 43.1 per cent of people have at least one parent born overseas. However, in Greater Capital Cities such as Melbourne and Sydney, this increases from 21 per cent to 30.7 per cent. The term superdiversity encapsulates the intersections of ethnicity with other powerful variables such as immigration rights and restrictions, globally transient labour markets, influenced by gender, sexual diversity, religious traditions, changing family structures and diversity of social values, and practices evident in post-multicultural societies (Vertovec 2007; Vertovec 2010; Jones Díaz 2016). Discourses of superdiversity is an emerging perspective on change and unpredictability in social and cultural contexts (Arnaut 2012), which are influenced by intensified and integrated global labour markets, economies often with free market trade agreements, technological advancement, free flow of labour movements across borders, international political instability and conflict.

Multiculturalism as policy and practice

In Australia, since the 1970s, an important social policy shift was legislated by the Whitlam Labor government that changed many aspects of Australian life. As a result, assimilationist thinking, informed by the Immigration Restriction Act (see Chapter 5), which expected all cultural and racial minority groups to take up dominant Anglo-Australian mainstream social practices and identities, shifted to more liberal discourses of pluralism, where cultural, social, language and religious differences could coexist. Within this discourse, there is tolerance and acceptance of religious, ethnic and social differences among and between groups. Therefore, in Australia, since the mid-1970s, successive governments have endorsed multiculturalism, but with increased emphasis on social cohesion. Even though multiculturalism is still somewhat controversial, it is accepted as integral to Australian national and cultural identity. Along with Canada, Australia has enjoyed the reputation of a 'model country' in terms of successfully crafting its immigration policies (Walsh 2008). Hence, most Australians consider themselves to live in a pluralist society where cultural and social diversity are accepted and even appreciated, despite localized grievances experienced by cultural minority groups, which have prompted debate about Australian national identity, nationalism and racism (Castles, Vasta and Ozkul 2014).

However, since the events of 9/11 in the United States, there has been a widespread backlash against multiculturalism (Castles *et al.* 2014) where concerns for security and social cohesion have dominated political and media narratives. Indeed, as Papastergiadis remarks, since 2001 multiculturalism has 'slid into the twilight zone of a zombie concept' (2013: 1), with recent declarations from German Chancellor Merkel, the French President Sarkozy and British Prime Minister Cameron declaring that it has failed. Meanwhile, in Australia, recent immigration policy has shifted its focus away from family reunion policies to skilled migration. Within the past five years Australia has seen a significant increase mainly driven by net overseas migration including international students and temporary skilled migrants (Phillips and Klapdor 2010).

Australia, like many other Western immigrant-receiving nation states, is indeed in a post-multicultural era. Post-multiculturalism, described by Vertovec (2010), is where changing conditions and contexts of diversity due to the intensification of migration have led towards conditions of superdiversity, diasporic identities and transnational immigration, anti-multicultural public debate and policy discourses. Still, given these changes, multiculturalism in Australia remains as official social policy. The updated 2011 policy maintains a focus on themes relating to preserving cultural identity, social equality and maintaining social cohesion. However, there is a more concentrated focus on social cohesion, community harmony and the maintenance of democratic values. In addition, there is attention to the valuing of economic, trade and investment benefits that have resulted in Australian multiculturalism, and greater commitment to addressing intolerance, discrimination and racism. A further addition to the policy is greater emphasis on shared rights and responsibilities, highlighting the responsibilities of citizenship in its relationship to loyalty, adherence to Australian law, and respect for rights and liberties. This is couched in the context of entitlement to cultural heritage, cultural practice and language within the boundaries of the law free from discrimination. The policy is explicit in drawing attention to the broader aims of national unity, community harmony and maintenance of democratic values (DSS 2011). Consequently, these new additions reflect a response to increased global population movements and cultural diversity in nation states (Chiro 2014), and recent global political tensions.

Despite these recently updated themes, Australian multiculturalism continues to embrace both structural and cultural pluralism (Hollinsworth 2006). Cultural pluralism pertains to the social, linguistic and cultural practices that express cultural identity. Hollinsworth (2006) argues that cultural pluralism is overwhelmingly private in as much as language, religious, cultural and culinary practices are largely confined to the private space of the home or within local ethnic communities. Structural pluralism, on the other hand, refers to the public domains of the legal, educational, health, welfare and other key state institutions. Hollinsworth (2006) argues that in the public arena monoculturalism remains unchallenged, often viewing the presence of linguistic and cultural difference as a problem rather than an asset.

Despite the emphasis on access and equity in Australian multicultural policy, the interrogation of access and equity remains confined to institutional barriers of participation rather than discursive social practices that render cultural minorities as marginal and excluded. For example, the limited participation of cultural minority groups in the Australian media, and the misrepresentations of diverse social, cultural and language practices are largely confined to cultural stereotypes. Since 9/11, the media has played its part in the demonization of Muslims as terrorists or fundamentalists, or Muslim women as oppressed, submissive and passive victims of Islamic fundamentalism through the wearing of the hijab/burqa (Hebbani and Wills 2012).

Limits to multicultural pluralism

While multicultural pluralism is fundamental to the importance of cultural identity, the attainment of social equality and the maintenance of social cohesion, much of the criticism of Australian multiculturalism has centred around its inability to challenge the social, legitimized and institutional inequalities that exist based on 'difference' and the ways in which individuals can become marginalized as a result. As Daniel (2008) suggests, pluralist approaches to multiculturalism are limited in their ability to critically examine the structural causes of racism, patriarchy and economic disadvantage. Yet, as Kincheloe and Steinberg (1997: 15) argue, pluralism has become the mainstream articulation of multiculturalism, which 'typically links "race", gender, language, culture, disability and to a lesser degree sexual preference in the larger effort to celebrate human diversity and equal opportunity'.

Much of the criticism around pluralist multiculturalism highlights the fact that, while cultural differences can be appreciated and tolerated, the structural inequalities that marginalize cultural and racial minority groups from institutional and social power are reproduced. As hooks (1997: 166) reminds us, 'evocations of pluralism and diversity act to obscure differences arbitrarily imposed and maintained by white racist domination'. While cultural pluralism embodies recognition of cultural difference, it has limited commitment to equality of opportunities; the frameworks for challenging the social, legitimized and institutional inequalities based on 'difference' are also limited (Kincheloe and Steinberg 1997). For example, in Australia, white, middle-class, heterosexual, monolingual and Christian values, voices and narratives dominate in social, linguistic, political, economic, educational and cultural terrains. In relation to the arts and literature Cahill (2014) argues that migrant narratives are domesticated and reductively positioned as stereotypes of survival and confrontation, where literature has become an economic commodity co-opted to tokenize and curate difference.

Furthermore, in discourses of pluralist multiculturalism, identity is conceived as fixed or unchangeable, predetermined and unified. Categories of ethnicity are constructed as homogenized entities, in which social and cultural histories are silenced. Within this silence there is a conflation of culture and identity, and both are conceptualized as fixed and static, marked by the foreclosure of values and beliefs, languages, lifestyle choices and religion, rather than shifting and unstable due to hybrid cultural practices and diasporic experiences. This results in presumptions that within cultural groups there are points of solidarity, cohesion and homogeneity, where essentialist notions of ethnicity construct a singular category of one's identity void of other identities including sexuality, gender, class, (dis)ability, age and religion (Ang 2014; Watkins 2015; Jones Díaz and Walker 2017: forthcoming).

In discourses of Australian multiculturalism, these assumptions are applied to many cultural minority groups living in Australia, in which the impact of migration, neocolonialism, superdiversity, globalization and neoliberalism has silenced significant cultural histories and biographies of individuals. For example, the Latin American and Caribbean community in Australia is often constructed as a homogenized community, ignoring the impact of postcolonialism in terms of the relationship between Europe and its former colonies (Langer 1998), and the national, political, regional, racial, language and cultural differences between Central, Caribbean and South America.

Whiteness and multiculturalism

Since the late 1980s and 1990s, critical work on white identity has emerged, originating from the USA and Europe. In the USA white hegemony has been seriously challenged primarily due to the unequal racialized positioning of African, Asian and Latino/Americans (Larbalestier 1999), but particularly of African Americans, in spite of their inclusion as citizens and despite discourses of liberal pluralism, which continue to discriminate against African Americans (Stratton and Ang 1998). In Australia, as discussed in Chapter 5, Indigenous and non-Indigenous scholars informed by critical 'race' theory (CRT) have deconstructed white identity, exposing its agenda of invisibility and privilege to reveal the relationship between whiteness, power and social policy (see, for example, Moreton-Robinson 2004; Martin-McDonald and McCarthy 2008; Moore 2012).

Sociologists, as well as cultural, critical and feminist theorists, examine whiteness as a social construction, its place in the making of subjectivity and its relationship to structural institutions (see, for example, Frankenberg 1997; Gillborn and Ladson-Billings 2010; Leonardo 2010). The central aim of such work is to examine how 'white dominance is rationalized, legitimized, and made ostensibly normal and natural' (Frankenberg 1997: 3). This means that questions are raised as to how whiteness is normative and authorized in institutional policies, procedures and everyday social practice.

As discussed in Chapter 5, the need for critical understandings of the impact policies have on normalizing whiteness, is crucial. Therefore through the lens of 'critical multiculturalism' possibilities for interrogating the structural and subjective workings of normative whiteness as universal and homogenized are possible. Critical multiculturalists are concerned with white positionality and its relationship with 'race', class and gender inequality (Kincheloe and Steinberg 1998). Whiteness, like other racial categories and social identities, is a socio-historical construction and, in this way, whiteness is subject not only to political, social, economic and cultural histories but also to contemporary shifts and changes in a globalized world. Consequently, it is not a fixed, stable or biological entity, but rather, as Kincheloe and Steinberg (1998) point out, it can be invented, lived, modified and discarded.

As an unmarked identity, whiteness constantly evades scrutiny while maintaining social privilege. It is a refusal to acknowledge white power, and those who are white are often unknowingly implicated in social relations of privilege, domination and subordination (McLaren 1998). Frankenberg (1997: 6) argues that there is fundamentally a co-constitution of whiteness and racial domination, and it 'makes itself invisible precisely by asserting its normalcy, its transparency, in contrast with the marking of others on which its transparency depends'. McLaren (1998) adds that whiteness functions through normative social practices of **assimilation** and cultural homogenization.

However, in Australia, the taken-for-granted assumption about what it means to be white is evident in the media – for example, normative and singular representations of families as white, nuclear, middle class, heterosexual and monolingual. These images imply that whiteness is normative and homogeneous. In contrast, whenever any 'other' families, or non-traditional gendered practices, are represented in the media, they are usually stereotypes – for example, the 'happy' Italian family eating pasta, or the 'incompetent' husband attempting to change a baby's nappy. The Australian media are still yet to represent same-sex families in everyday practices of family life. Such racialized and gendered cultural stereotypes and heteronormative silences are constructed in discourses of normative whiteness, where relations of social inequality remain unchallenged and stabilized.

Yet there are many ways to be white, and the intersections between whiteness and other social identities such as class, gender, sexuality and age bring about different subjective locations and 'lived experiences'.

According to Frankenberg (1993: 233), 'whiteness, masculinity, and femininity are co-producers of one another, in ways that are, in their turn, crosscut by class and by the histories of racism and colonialism'. Examples of how whiteness intersects with other social identities are apparent in limited research that documents white women's experiences in interracial couples where class, gender, sexuality and 'race' foreground everyday social relations and practices (see, for example, Frankenberg 1993; Luke 1994; Reddy 1994; Harman 2010). While there is research documenting the experiences of racism in interracial families, the primary focus is directed at the child, with relative silence around the experiences of white mothers of interracial children (Harman 2010). Luke (1994) argues that white women in interracial families negotiate gender and sexuality, marked with 'race' in their unique experiences of racism by association with persons of colour.

Clearly, for white women whose identities are intimately shaped by 'race' and racism, there is both significant conscious and unconscious awareness of racial inequality experienced through shifting histories of racism and varying material relations constructed by 'race' (Frankenberg 1993). However, for white women, while their whiteness renders them as invisible and unmarked, in reality, through their association with their children and/or partners of colour, issues of 'race' foreground their daily social practices and relationships, power relations and material well-being.

As a white woman living in an interracial family, I (Jones Díaz) share experiences of whiteness and racializing practices similar to those described by Luke (1994) and Frankenberg (1993), and the women in their studies. When my brown-skinned children were growing up I observed numerous occasions of racialization, including overt scrutinization by shopkeepers and teachers, racialized slurring at school by peers, tokenism and ridicule. For example, at my oldest son Dominic's Year 12 graduation, his ultimate schooling experience was met with humiliation through racialized ridicule of a 'mock award' given to him as a joke for 'not being black enough'. This award was in response to Dominic's continual defence of his mixed 'race' identity, as an Afro-Dominican Australian, often met with racialized retorts and jokes from his peers. Moreover, to this day, my Afro-Dominican-born partner has experienced countless instances of police surveillance while driving in Sydney, Australia. During the normal course of daily events, he has been stopped and asked to show personal identification for no apparent reason.

Collins (1990) suggests that white women often become the 'front runners', and cultural and racial brokers, as 'their identities change from being insiders within their own dominant culture to becoming an "outsider within"' (quoted in Luke 1994: 59). Consequently, my 'in between' status positions me as the 'front runner' and 'cultural broker' of the family.

Bank tellers, government officials, school personnel, doctors, work colleagues, and so on, look directly at me and occasionally glance uncom-
fortably at my partner to merely acknowledge his existence. Some have
even refused to include my partner in negotiations or transactions. Hence,
my negotiation of the insider/outsider nexus is evident in the ways in
which my partner and I tenuously deal with these daily encounters. The
disapproving looks, glances and ambiguous body language are all just
part of the everyday politics and tensions of racializing practices that we
experience. These strenuous relationships are more often than not constructed within and contextualized against markers of 'race', language
and gendered power relations within normalizing discourses of whiteness.

Global and local responses to refugees and asylum seekers

In a post-9/11 world, global responses to multiculturalism, immigration,
refugees and asylum seekers have hardened as a global resurgence of
social and political conservative critiques of liberalism and multiculturalism is on the rise. Critical multiculturalists in Australia called for multiculturalism to address issues of racism, whiteness and the recognition of
gender, sexuality, language and class in shaping multiple identities and
negotiating power relations; however, on global levels and particularly in
Europe, the backlash to multiculturalism had already begun. Paradoxi-
cally, Papastergiadis (2013) argues that this conservative hostility towards
multiculturalism had begun with John Howard in the 1990s. He argues that
Howard's conservative discourse rebuked the excesses of political cor-
rectness and multiculturalism was accused of exaggerated racial injustices, which unfairly rewarded minorities to distract attention away from
the achievements of the Australian settlement. Meanwhile, within recent
years, the continual increase of forcibly displaced people has propelled
a global and local response with 60 million forcibly displaced people in
the world today (UNAA 2015a) representing the worst humanitarian crisis
since the Second World War.

The UNHCR (2014) claims that, by the end of 2014, 59.5 million
individuals were forcibly displaced worldwide, which is an increase of
8.3 million people on previous years and the highest annual increase on
record. The current conflict in Syria has lead to more than 4 million fleeing that country and left 7.6 million internally displaced (UNHCR 2014).
In 2015 alone, there were more than 2800 deaths incurred on the dangerous journey to Europe.

Recent discussions at the European Commission failed to reach an
agreement on a collective response to binding quotas across the conti-
nent (UNAA 2015a). The commission reports that, despite Germany's ini-
tial welcoming response to the refugee crisis, it has recently announced

the reintroduction of border controls. These initiatives were met with approval by countries such as Hungary as the fence along its border with Serbia was completed. Legislation in Hungary was passed to allow authorities to imprison illegal immigrants for up to three years. Other countries, such as the Czech Republic, have responded with increased border controls. Meanwhile, in the United Kingdom, 20,000 refuges will be resettled (UNAA 2015a). While other refugee emergency hotspots continue to emerge across the world, and political instability persists, the UN has urged the EU to work towards 'cooperation, compromise and solidarity' in establishing a more internationally cohesive approach (2015a: 4).

Historical and contemporary responses to refugees and asylum seekers in Australia

Despite Australia's controversial immigration history, it has always been an immigrant-receiving nation state, beginning with colonization in which Indigenous Australians were dispossessed by immigrants from British, colonist and convict backgrounds (Castles *et al.* 2014). Prior to the commencement of Australia's official immigration programme of 1945, according to the Refugee Council of Australia (RCA 2015), the first identifiable group of refugees were the Lutherans who settled in South Australia more than 170 years ago. They were followed by other refugees escaping religious, political and racial persecution from Hungarian, Italian, Polish, Russian, Greek, Bulgarian, Armenian, Assyrian and Jewish backgrounds, who were permitted to settle provided that they met restrictions imposed by the Immigration Restriction Act (the White Australia Policy hereafter).

In 1945 Australia reached its peak, with the arrival of seven million immigrants (DIC 2010). Since Federation, Australia has provided protection for an estimated 800,000 refugee and humanitarian entrants (RCA 2015). However, it was not until 1975, due to the arrival of Indochinese 'boat people', that the government developed a specific refugee policy (Phillips and Klapdor 2010).

However, within the last 20 years, policies of immigration and asylum have remained controversial. Castles *et al.* (2014) argue that, even though Australia has a significant immigration heritage, the tensions and controversies evidenced in the 2001 and 2010 federal elections are representative of politicians and the public's failure to come to terms with changing drivers and characteristics of migration to Australia. This was apparent in the 2001 federal election, dubbed 'the Tampa election' (Martin 2015), in which the then Howard government refused to allow the Norwegian freighter MV *Tampa* to enter Australian waters because it was carrying 438 rescued asylum seekers, mainly Hazaras from Afghanistan (ABC News 2001). This crisis was a catalyst for a new border protection regime leading to the Pacific Solution. While there was international criticism, including a diplomatic dispute between Australia and Norway, there was widespread approval within Australia.

The Pacific Solution commenced in 2001 and comprised a series of policies, which excised small islands around Australia from the official migration zone. This enabled the Australian government to turn back the boats to Indonesia and process asylum seekers in offshore detention centres on Manus Island, a province of Papua New Guinea (PNG) and Nauru (Jabour 2013). While the Pacific Solution officially ceased in 2007, it unofficially continued under the Gillard/Rudd Labor governments' Regional Resettlement Arrangement (RRA) through the provision of naval resources in the interception of boats and the continued processing of offshore detention in PNG (RAC 2015).

According to the Asylum Seeker Resource Centre (2015), as at 31 October 2015, there were 1949 people detained in onshore detention facilities, 112 of whom were children; 621 people in Nauru offshore detention centre, of whom 95 were children; and 929 people in Manus Island detention centre. There are currently 632 people detained in the community, of whom 354 are children. This represents a total of 4131 people in some form of detention facility. Meanwhile, the Children out of Detention website reports that 4013 children are living in the community on Bridging Visas where their parents have no employment rights and limited access to government support (Children out of Detention n.d.).

According to *Forgotten Children: National Inquiry into Children in Immigration Detention (2014)* (Australian Human Rights Commission 2014), the average period of time people are held in detention facilities was more than 413 days. This period of time steadily increased from 75 days in 2013 to 459 in January 2015, with a slight decrease in August 2015 (DIBP 2015).

Recently, Australia's response to the current Syrian refugee crisis indicated a softening of its hard-line approach to immigration policy in which a one-off intake of 12,000 Syrian refugees has been accepted, with AU$44 million in funding to support housing, processing and integration (UNAA 2015b). While this not only represents a highly contradictory stance to recent offshore regional processing policy, it is a drop in the ocean in terms of the estimated 4 million refugees waiting in countries bordering Syria, Turkey, Lebanon and Jordan, in addition to an estimated 7.6 million who are internally displaced within Syria (UNHCR 2015b).

However, as Australia increases its humanitarian response to the Syrian crisis, it continues with its morphed policies of the Pacific Solution to the current 'offshoring' of refugees and asylum seekers to poorer countries who are often non-signatories of human rights agreements. This has left hundreds of people in limbo, living in ambiguous and temporal situations with limited information about their status, in unsafe and vio-lent conditions[1] where human rights abuses transpire (Mountz 2011). Such policies, informed and shaped by xenophobic political narratives, poli-ticians, media personalities and community attitudes, have effectively undermined a successful settlement history of refugee and humanitarian entrants (RCA 2015).

Within the current global political climate, where border protection dominates, anxieties around border control and real or imagined threats from illegal immigrants often constructed as terrorists and security threats are reminiscent of the White Australia policy where non-white foreigners were feared and mistrusted (Tazreiter 2010). Indeed, as Tazreiter (2010) asserts, it is often in periods of crisis that politicians resort to past narratives from collective national memory of Australia's early days of white settlement in which themes of protection from exter-nal threats hold currency and potency in Australian mythology.

Still, what remains in Australia is a raft of issues for Australian policy and its people to contend with as a result of its response to detention and asylum. Issues such as forced detention, offshore processing, strong possibilities of forced return, unsafe and substandard detention facilities, limited access to family reunion opportunities, negative public and political debate, and a continual state of ambiguity and temporality (Mountz 2011; RCA 2015) have adversely affected refugees and asylum seekers.

Moral panic and Islamophobia

Cohen (2011) argues that sites of moral panic are connected with border control, refugees, asylum seekers, immigration and multicultural absorp-tion. However, moral panic over non-white immigrants and xenophobia are not new to Australia, and indeed are rooted in the White Australia pol-icy evident in the fears and anxieties about Australia's national identity (Martin 2015). Historically, waves of panic have circulated in political and media debate. For example, fear of Chinese immigrants in the nineteenth and twentieth centuries and then, later, the fear of an 'Asian Invasion' spurred on by Pauline Hanson[2] represent a continuity between racism, the White Australia policy and Australia's response to asylum seekers arriving by boat (Mares 2011).

More recent and perhaps disturbing examples of localized moral panic fuelled by racializing discourses of Muslims did not necessarily begin with 9/11, but they did gain traction due to media reports, and xenopho-bic media and public debate. The demonization of all Muslims as terrorists and 'anti-Australian' spurred on variations of anti-multiculturalism, 'race' debates and anti-immigration discourses that were marked by the Cronulla 'race' riots in 2005. Racial conflict in the southern beachside suburb of Sydney resulted in mass 'race' riots and violence fuelled by text messages and media sensationalism inciting mob violence against those of 'Middle-Eastern appearance'. This was in retaliation for an alleged attack on two Cronulla Beach lifesavers by ethnic Lebanese youths the previous week.

The riots were also incited by commercial media, which published headlines such as 'Not on our beach: Cronulla police vow to defend Australian way' (Gee and McIlveen 2005) and commercial talkback radio stations encouraging callers to assert racist opinions against Lebanese and 'Middle-Eastern' men. Furthermore, text messages exhorting 'Aussies' to attack 'Lebs' and 'Wogs' at the beach, and T-shirts with slogans such as 'We grew here, you flew here', were just part of the many racializing slurs directed at Lebanese and Middle-Eastern Australians. Despite this, Prime Minister John Howard firmly denied that the riots were linked to racism in the community and that Australia was inherently a non-racist society.

The Cronulla 'race' riots were an undermining of Australian multiculturalism. Discussion and debate on commercial media polarized issues and dichotomies of 'us' and 'them', shifting much of the blame on to the ethnicity of youth gangs that refuse to adopt 'Australian ways', rather than focusing on the reactions of insular, xenophobic and racialized views constructed in discourses of monoculturalism and whiteness (Jones Díaz 2007).

Ten years to the day on which these riots took place, the newly formed far right-wing Party for Freedom called for a rally to mark the decade since the Cronulla riots. Both the NSW Supreme Court and the Federal Court ruled against the proposed rally, declaring that if it went ahead it would be unlawful. Hundreds of Cronulla residents posted Facebook messages to support the courts' ruling and condemning the party's leader Nicholas Folkes (Dale 2015). While the ban prevented the memorial from going ahead, the ruling did not determine that it was unlawful for any other individual or group to gather. Meanwhile a Facebook campaign, 'Cronulla Riot Never Again – Anti Racist Convergence', was launched on 12 December 2015, calling for a rally against the party and racist violence.

Contemporary forms of permanent moral panic and xenophobia

Morgan (2014) argues that Australia is in the midst of intense moral panic about Islam, not helped by emotive media narrative and hyperbolic public debate, which construct Sydney suburbs like Lakemba as 'hotbeds of Jihadism' (2014: 1). Indeed, as argued by Martin (2015), moral panic over asylum seekers has become a normalized and permanent state of alarm, equating refugees and asylum seekers with Muslim terrorists, in what has now become global moral panic over fundamentalist Islam, essentially demonizing all people of Middle-Eastern origin and/or appearance.

Distinctions between refugees, asylum seekers and migrants have been obscured by political and media debates (Mares 2011). The recent Gillard Labor government's campaign to deter asylum seekers arriving by boat depicts images of navy personnel with a voiceover from the then Prime Minister expressing Australia's commitment to 'stronger borders' and 'cracking down on people smugglers'. This resulted in widespread confusion regarding the impact of asylum seekers on Australia's population. For example, Mares (2011) reports an opinion poll conducted in 2010, which found that a quarter of the respondents thought that illegal boat arrivals accounted for approximately 25 per cent of Australia's total annual immigration intake.

Other forms of widespread confusion in Australia are the abundance of myths that have circulated about asylum seekers and refugees, some of which include: they are 'cashed up' because they can afford to pay people smugglers; they are queue jumpers; they are not genuine refugees; they take the place of genuine refugees in overseas camps; they do not contribute to Australia in any meaningful way; and they pose a security risk to Australia (RCA 2014). In reality, it is British nationals who pose the single biggest 'risk' to Australian borders since they are more likely than any other foreign citizen to overstay their visas in Australia (Martin 2015).

In post-9/11 politics, Morgan and Poynting (2012) argue that the West has made use of collective insecurity, which taps in to popularized xenophobia and constitutes certain elements of immigrant cultures such as Muslim minorities as 'an inscrutable and inherently volatile presence, as a subversive influence, immune to the interpellations of citizenship' (2012: 8). They point to examples of Western global cities where there have been Islamophobic campaigns calling to disallow the building of mosques, the banning and/or over-scrutinizing of Muslim schools and prayer rooms, the banning of the jibab or burqa in schools and rights to free expression of 'demonized minorities' such as Muslims.

Of most concern are the horrific Islamophobic comments recently expressed by Donald Trump, Republican candidate for the 2016 US presidential elections, who denounced all Muslims as being a terrorist threat to the security of the United States. In a dangerous and divisive rant on ABC's *Good Morning America*, he called for 'a shutdown of Muslims entering the United States . . . until our country figures out what is going on' (BBC News 2015).

Clearly, global and local responses to intensified immigration, and the ongoing refugee and asylum crisis are of major concern for educators and community service professionals as they address issues of xenophobia, racism, cultural difference and marginalization given the ongoing global instability, and changes in both global and local cultural, social, economic and political circumstances. The discussion below locates current practices and pedagogies informed by multiculturalism, and offers a critique of current approaches to cultural, racial and social difference adopted in Australian education and community services over the past 40 years.

Multiculturalism in education and community services

In childhood education and community-based settings, approaches to cultural, racial and social difference have been informed by broader social policy of multiculturalism based on normative understandings of socio-cultural difference. In Australia, multicultural pluralism influenced many pedagogical approaches to difference and diversity during the 1970s and 1980s. Multicultural education centred on teaching children about other cultures. Specifically, this involved children learning about particular cultures and cultural difference, with intent to dispel ignorance and combat racial prejudice. However, this approach most often translated into a tokenistic, celebratory and superficial respect for cultural differences where cultural and linguistic differences were highly trivialized and manifested into what Castles *et al.* (1988) termed 'spaghetti and polka' understandings about cultural difference, more commonly known to early childhood educators as the 'tourist approach' (Derman-Sparks and the ABC Task Force 1989).

Both celebratory and anti-bias approaches to multicultural education aimed to develop children's positive attitudes towards diversity through the reflection and acknowledgement of socio-cultural difference, and therefore explanations about difference were often couched in terms of 'celebration' and 'tolerance', harmony and pluralism. Moreover, anti-bias approaches were also seen to provide effective ways of including all types of differences, whether they be racialized, gendered or classed. However, in its attempts to incorporate the complexity of diversity that is presented in early childhood settings, it has relied upon 'add on' conceptual approaches to addressing diversity, which package difference and diversity into fixed social boundaries where notions of double or triple oppressions apply.

Consequently, superficial, celebratory and 'add on' approaches to multiculturalism and diversity fail to fully acknowledge the interrelationships between social categories and difference in relation to how children are actively involved in the construction of their own identities and subjectivities. In this context there is limited understanding of the historical, embodied, social and cultural construction of subjectivity, and how subjectivity is constituted in how children experience their identity. As a result, tolerance and acceptance of difference are emphasized at the expense of critiquing the relationships between difference, power and inequity; our capacity to work towards a pedagogical agenda that critically addresses the various social inequities based on 'difference' is limited. Moreover, social, cultural, political and economic inequities based on difference rarely become focal points when working with children and families in educational and community-based settings, as explanations of and conversations about social inequalities are constrained. Children's and adult's experiences with difference and inequality do not go beyond descriptions of particular circumstances and are often confined to staff understandings of children's developmental stages of growth and development. As one respondent in our research commented, 'If issues are dealt with positively and appropriately to children's development, they will understand some issues and have a positive basis for the future' (Robinson and Jones Díaz 2000: 114).

Liberal pluralism in childhood education and community services

In recent years, in education and community services, 'diversity' has tended to replace 'multiculturalism' as a popular term for the coexistence of social, cultural and class differences that exist in society. Paralleling the broader social contexts of liberal pluralism, diversity in these contexts has largely emphasized tolerance and acceptance of difference, despite pedagogy that has been inherently embedded in monocultural and monolingual Anglo-Australian cultural practices, which until recently have remained unchallenged. From this perspective, the term 'diversity' used alone is insufficient in analysing issues related to inequality.

Furthermore, simplistic pluralistic notions about diversity do not give educators and community service professionals the necessary conceptual tools for analysing and understanding how inequalities are constructed and perpetuated by individuals, social groups and social structures. This is particularly significant to the field of early childhood education since the relationships between people, the learning experiences of children and the management practices that operate within it are crucially linked to broader societal processes, policies and practices. Apple (2012) argues that schools (including early childhood and community services) are not separate from the political and moral realities of broader society, but are indeed embedded in them. He also points out that any separation between the politics of education and the politics of society is artificial since education is a crucial part of the larger society. He emphasizes that education is precisely the social field where possibilities of critique and interrogation of social inequality are more likely to be explored.

This tendency to separate education from broader societal realities was evident in our research. In our study, there was less attention to and concern for the impact of discrimination, racism and inequality operating in society and in children's and families' lives. Hence, ways in which individuals are marginalized as a result of inequality seemed poorly understood. For example, few respondents acknowledged adult's and children's experiences with racial inequality. While a little more than half of the respondents did agree that cultural diversity, difference and power were worth critically raising with children, few connections were made between structural inequalities, discrimination and critical thinking.

Moreover, this contradiction in respondents' views was also evident in issues associated with children's experiences of racial discrimination and inequality. Respondents ranked children's experiences with discrimination at the lower ends of the scale, perhaps indicating that practitioners' awareness of children's experiences with inequality and discrimination is limited. It follows, then, that in this study educators were largely unaware of the broader socio-political inequities that are prevalent in our society, particularly with regard to how discrimination and racism implicitly and discursively impact on children in their daily lives.

Whiteness and mainstream early childhood curricula

In education and community settings working closely with young children and their families, the predominance of child development theories informed by developmental psychology has had a powerful and significant influence on policy, pedagogy and practice. This is despite research that challenges the universalizing and hegemonic positions of developmental theory (Robinson 2013) and in Australia the national adoption of the EYLFA (DEEWR 2009), which aims to broaden educators' pedagogical practices beyond developmentalism to incorporate a range of theoretical perspectives including critical and poststructural theories.

Developmental theory is largely informed through middle-class Eurocentric and colonist perspectives that promote a singular and linear view of childhood, based on **biological determinism**, with limited regard for the broader socio-cultural contexts that influence learning (Alloway 1997; Cannella 1997; Cannella and Diaz Soto 2010; Pacini-Ketchabow and Taylor 2015). In this sense, developmental psychology colludes with discourses of whiteness through its preoccupation with objective Western science, emphasizing rationality, reason and objectivity. As a result, whiteness is shaped by its association with science and the disciplines of psychology and educational psychology (Kincheloe and Steinberg 1997).

Developmental psychology emerged from the Enlightenment and post-Enlightenment/modernist eras of rational and scientific thought, which viewed human beings as rational, objective and universal. To this end, whiteness is constituted through Eurocentric discourses in which developmental psychology plays a key role. Through the aggressive expansion of masculinized European colonization, objectivity and masculinity represented the highest expression of white achievement and white privilege, which today continues to inform everyday social relations, service delivery and pedagogical practices in childhood education and community services (Kincheloe and Steinberg 1998; Saraceno 2012).

Whiteness in the construction of deficit identities, othering and marginalization

Normative understandings of identity as hierarchical, linear, chronological, universal and fixed are informed by developmental psychology. These understandings are also aligned with Western science, which privileges Eurocentric discourses of whiteness in its preoccupation with reason and rationality. When these understandings are applied to children from diverse social and cultural communities, there is a denial of the multiplicity and contradictory realities of social, cultural and linguistic practices from which children's identities are mediated, transformed and negotiated.

Bhabha (1994, 1998) and Spivak (1999), drawing on the work of Hall (1992, 1996) in relation to identity negotiation, point out that identity is not a fixed end product but rather fluid and transformative, which is always subject to the 'play of difference' (Hall 1996). This 'play of difference' is socially constructed through the social contexts in which people are situated, which in turn influence and shape their identity. Identity is constructed through lived experience, which is constantly undergoing change and transformation (Hall 1996). It is through daily lived experience and relationships with others that children, like adults, experience their identity in multiple and often contradictory ways. As a consequence of marginalization, racialized minorities are in constant processes of adaption and transformation due to hegemonic whiteness.

Researching educators' responses to children's understandings of 'race', ethnicity and cultural difference

In our research it was clear that while many educators held positive views and attitudes towards the importance of multicultural and anti-racist education, their perceptions of children's experiences of and understandings about 'race', ethnicity and cultural difference appeared to be underacknowledged. For example, as discussed in Chapter 5, a little more than half of the respondents claimed that children do not understand Indigenous issues, exemplified by statements such as 'I think that children in the nursery room are too young to be aware.' There appeared to be more emphasis placed on children developing healthy self-esteem and cultural identity than on their understanding of Indigenous issues, racism and power. Yet, children's capacity to locate themselves in racializing

discursive practices ultimately affects their own thinking about themselves. Rizvi (1993) reminds us that children's constructions of 'race' are
inherently connected to the broader discursive practices and social relations in which racism is produced in Australian society.

Furthermore, many educators commented that children's ability to
understand issues of 'race', ethnicity and cultural difference is largely
based on difference in physical, language and cultural practice, as highlighted in the following comment, also discussed in Chapter 5: 'Children
realize that children look different but do not fully understand the issues
of race and cultural identities as this is an "internal" aspect of multiculturalism.' This assumption that children's understandings are limited to
the physical and obvious aspects of racial and ethnic difference denies
children's lived experiences of living in families and communities that are
affected by normative discourses of whiteness and racializing practices.

Children's experiences of whiteness, racism and marginalization

The discussion that follows draws on extracts from my study (Jones Díaz
2007) to highlight how non-white bi/multilingual children's experiences
of negotiating whiteness and meanings of 'race' in their daily lives have
implications for their subjectivities through which they experience their
identity. The data reports on Martín, Julia and Emilia's experiences of
their daily negotiation of 'race', difference and language. These experiences provided them with various meanings about themselves and those
around them that are shaped through their difference.

Rubie and Martín

At the time of this study, Martín was 9 years old; he is my son. He is from
an interracial family and his father is Afro-Caribbean from the Domini-
can Republic. He attended a primary school situated in the inner-west of
Sydney. More than half of the school's population consisted of children
from non-white backgrounds and many spoke at least one language other
than English at home. From my observations, the families of the children
ranged from disadvantaged working-class families to upwardly mobile
double-income middle-class professional families. The diversity of class,
cultural, racial and linguistic representations at this school is characteristic of many inner-west schools in multicultural Sydney.

Martín had taken a liking to an Anglo-Australian girl in his class.
He regularly told me about his plans to 'get Rubie to talk to me', 'to get
Rubie to sit next to me' and, more importantly, 'to get Rubie to play with
me'. However, Martín's progress with Rubie (pseudonym) had not gone
according to plan. One afternoon Martín arrived home from school,

entered the room in which I was working and slung himself down on the chair sighing:

Martín: Mummy, I don't want to be brown any more.

Criss: Uhh, why not?

Martín: I'm sick of being brown, it's not working. I can't attract Rubie's attention, and anyway she likes Joseph more than me.

Criss: Joseph? But isn't that because they are friends outside of school?

Martín: Yeah, but he's white and Rubie's white and she talks to him a lot.

Criss: [a long pause of silence and hesitation] But, but . . . oh maybe, you know that, you know that, you have beautiful brown skin and oh, Martín, when you say that you don't want to be brown any more, that really upsets me. I get really sad.

Martín: But it's true.

Criss: Yeah but there are lots of black and brown kids in your class and you are not the only one.

Martín: Yeah but Joseph isn't black and Rubie is starting to like him more than me.

As a white mother of Afro-Dominican Australian bilingual boys, issues of language and 'race' emerge on a daily basis. They form part of the ambience of everyday lived experience in our family. There are always ambiguities and uncertainties around such issues in which racialized and heteronormative discursive practices arise. However, my subjective realities of being white and living in a black family bring into question my own shifting and transformative location in 'whiteness'. For my family, 'whiteness' is always interrogated and visible, yet its shifting, contradictory and transparent character in regards to the interplay of day-to-day social and power relations and experiences is highly ambiguous and often difficult to locate. Because of this, my response to Martín's outburst was one of hesitance and struggle. My reply, 'but there are lots of black and brown kids in your class and you are not the only one', was an attempt to defuse his concern. Perhaps this comment also reflected the limitation of my own ability to deal with the power of normative whiteness and racializing discourses in Martín's life. Yet, for Martín, the issue was not related to how many other children in his class were black or brown.

Later, I asked Martín:

Criss:	Martín, can I ask you a question about the Joseph thing and sitting next to Rubie?
Martín:	What?
Criss:	If Joseph were black or brown, would it still worry you that he gets to sit next to Rubie?
Martín:	No.

Martín's response to my question was firm. He perceived Joseph (pseud-onym) to have a structural, spatial and temporal advantage in sitting next to Rubie. From Martín's perspective, his ability to access Rubie was limited as he perceived that Joseph's cultural capital accumulated in his whiteness would ultimately prevail. This was aggravated by the spatial and temporal set up of the seating arrangements in this classroom.[3] While Joseph was in the right place at the right time, his whiteness gave him additional symbolic advantage, despite being among a racially diverse group of children, where he was potentially in the minority: 'Yeah but Joseph isn't black and Rubie is starting to like him more than me' (Martín).

You racist bastards!

Martín's attempts to challenge racism at La Escuelita[4] are apparent in the extract below when he observed two girls making faces at the video camera that Martín was controlling. It was break time at La Escuelita and most of the children were outside playing except Martín, Barbi and Marianna, who remained in the classroom. Martín had borrowed my video camera and placed it on the floor of the classroom. Two girls, Barbi (8 years old) and Marianna (5 years old), bent their heads down to the level of the camera. A Spanish book was on a table nearby, the girls pretend to read it in Chinese:

Barbi:	King Kong Ching Cha.
Mariana:	[imitates Barbi]
Barbi:	King Kong Ching Cha. [bends down to the camera and squints her eyes]
Martín:	I can see your eyes.
Martín:	Look how racist you are. You are racist. You are so racist.

A few seconds later, Marianna and Barbi went outside. Martín bent down to the camera and made dinosaur faces, noises and hand movements.

Barbi returned to the camera and continued to squint her eyes into the camera. Martín addressed her, 'Hello bloody racist guy.'

Martín's attempt to capture the girls' racializing play script on camera, 'I can see your eyes . . .', shifts to an attempt to disrupt their play: 'Look how racist you are. You are racist. You are so racist'. However, this intervention appeared to be ignored by the girls as they left the room. Martín persisted in drawing attention to the racism by swearing at Barbi upon her return, 'Hello bloody racist guy.'

Julia and Emilia: speaking back in Cantonese

Emilia (9 years old) and her sister Julia (11 years old) speak Cantonese at home. At the time this study was conducted they had recently arrived in Australia after living most of their lives in Venezuela where they learned Spanish at school and spoke Cantonese at home. Here Julia talks about their experiences of being teased in Venezuela for speaking Cantonese at school:

> No one ever would ever believe us . . . you know in Venezuela [at] school there [were] a lot of kids [that would] tease us 'Chinese girl, Chinese girl' and we would always say back in Cantonese 'shut up, shut up' and I said 'Can't you ever be quiet' in Cantonese . . . you know in Cantonese shut up means Saosang . . .

Julia's account of the racialized teasing that they endured from other children in Venezuela is an illustration of children whose linguistic and physical 'difference' requires daily negotiation in their dealings with racism. For Julia and Emilia the harassment and racialization from other girls was ongoing, which they found difficult to challenge: 'No one ever would ever believe us.' However, despite their ostensibly powerless position with the other girls, they adeptly turned the teasing back on the perpetrators, to reposition them through the use of their Cantonese: 'we would always say back in Cantonese "shut up, shut up" . . . "Can't you ever be quiet".' In this instance, speaking back in Cantonese, 'Saosang' [shut up], was effective in dealing with the other children's racist comments. In this instance the girls' agented use of Cantonese served to gain social control in a classroom context where girls make use of their superdiverse linguistic and cultural capabilities to challenge racism (Jones Díaz 2016).

Towards critical multiculturalism in childhood education and community services: implications for practice

The extracts above raise issues for educators in their work with young children particularly from interracial families, Indigenous and cultural minority backgrounds, but also generally for all children who grapple with conflicting and fluid experiences of identity construction. Critical multiculturalism offers educators a lens through which to interrogate normative practices constituted in discourses of whiteness from a critical standpoint. A recognition of and willingness to interrogate how culture is connected to the discursive frameworks of power and inequality (Giroux 1997) are an effective starting point for educators. This requires educators to recognize that 'pedagogical and institutional practices produce, codify and rewrite disciplinary practices, values and social identities in relation to, rather than outside of, the discourse of history, power and privilege' (Giroux 1992: 9). In this sense, educators and community service professionals need to acknowledge that their contribution to reproducing educational practices in their setting is directly connected to broader social, political, historical, cultural and global influences that impact on their work with children, families and communities with whom they work.

It is crucial that educators gain contemporary insights into the various ways in which children negotiate racialized identities within a context of whiteness that operates discursively in education and community services. Approaches that address issues of diversity and difference need to incorporate the voices and experiences of children as they mediate their emerging identities across the various social fields of their daily life, including home and community contexts. This is of particular importance regarding interracial children and children from racial minority groups, given that much of their unique experiences of negotiating visible whiteness and meanings of 'race' in their daily lives is unknown to educators (and to some of their families).

Going beyond culture as 'celebration' and the fetishization of cultural practice

Childhood educators and community service professionals are in a position to critically recognize the limitations of multicultural pluralism, which is confined to celebratory, superficial and cultural tokenism that fetishizes cultural practice and identity as categorically fixed in tradition. Cultural identities are not fixed in tradition, but are fluid and multiple, constantly being rearticulated through contemporary global expressions, and hybrid and diasporic experiences derived from living in superdiverse multicultural societies. Educators and community service professionals need to go beyond simplistic understandings of diversity as 'tolerance' and culture as 'celebration', and recognize that cultural differences and ethnicities are situated within a particular place in time that involves cultural experiences that are not necessarily fixed and contained by that experience (Hall 1992).

In practice, acknowledging diversity, cultural difference and the fluidity of identity means that educators find ways of representing children's cultural practices that are contextual and reflective of their everyday lived experiences. This may include employing staff of the same cultural and language backgrounds as the children, and engaging in ongoing conversations with families and children about important events, activities and relationships. In so doing, everyday narratives and practices are represented throughout the curriculum in routines, learning experiences and the environment. To this end, children will have a strong sense of identity and well-being, be connected with their world and be confident learners (DEEWR 2009).

Moreover it is crucial that educators acknowledge the 'multiple, contradictory, and complex subject positions people occupy within different social, cultural, and economic locations' (Giroux 1992: 21). Rather than constructing children, whose identities are intersected by issues of 'race', class, gender or sexuality, as victims of double or triple oppression, it is more useful to understand how their subjectivities and identities are shaped and mediated against a backdrop of intersecting, often conflicting and multiple discursive identities constructed through discourses of femininity, masculinity, monolingualism, heterosexuality, (dis)ability, whiteness and class.

Therefore, the challenges that critical multiculturalism presents to childhood educators and community service professionals call for new ideas and pedagogical strategies that are capable of constructing pedagogies that are relevant, respectful and responsive to children's and families' everyday lived experiences that may also include negotiating racializing practices and normative whiteness. Pedagogy informed by frameworks from postcolonial theory, cultural studies, critical theory and feminist poststructural theory will effectively disclose the workings of inequality, marginalization and racism derived from normative whiteness, which ultimately serves to marginalize children and families from cultural and racial minorities. As discussed in previous chapters, pedagogies and practices that draw on a range of contemporary theories and perspectives (DEEWR 2009) that challenge normative views of childhood and identity, and promote diversity and difference, will result in high levels of engagement with children, their families and local community.

In this context, educators recognize the significance of providing opportunities for children to engage in critical thinking or argument in the context of difference, inequalities and power relationships. To do this effectively, educators need to observe children taking up subject positions in discourses of whiteness and racism, in order to fully appreciate the complexities and contradictory positions through which many children are positioned.

Adopting a reflexive stance towards cultural and racial differences

Central to the process of adopting a reflexive and critical stance when working with children, their families and local communities, there is a willingness to engage in a process of deconstructing whiteness and decentring normalizing practices that privilege white dominance as normal and natural. This involves a preparedness to reflect on preconceived and unexamined discourses of whiteness that operate in institutional policies, procedures and everyday social practices authorized in childhood and in community settings. For example, in early childhood education, educators have many opportunities to reflect on how the routines undertaken in daily practice are directly informed by dominant white Anglo-Australian cultural practices, such as sleeping, eating, feeding, toileting, reading and communicating.

In adopting reflexive and critical approaches, educators and community service professionals need to decentre their location in discourses that pathologize difference as abnormal or deficit, as well as acknowledge and incorporate differences in childrearing, family and language practices that are represented by the families and children attending the setting. This involves actively deconstructing myths and stereotypes that circulate in the community and in the media regarding refugees and asylum seekers. This also requires the implementation of pedagogies and practices that create safe spaces for refugee children and their families through the validation and use of their languages and representation of their cultural practices (Harvey and Myint 2014). Moreover, the need to challenge pedagogies that have low expectations for children from culturally and linguistically diverse backgrounds is crucial as is the recognition that children progress well when there are high expectations for their learning (DEEWR 2009).

Spivak (1990, quoted in hooks 1997: 178) points out that 'the holders of hegemonic discourses should de-hegemonize their position and themselves learn how to occupy the subject position of the other'. Learning to occupy the subject position of the Other requires educators and community services professionals to locate their own subjectivity and examine how 'the knowledge or "truths" one holds about the world and the . . . power one experiences . . . in different contexts, are all constituted in discourse' (Robinson and Jones Díaz 1999: 35). This requires white educators to locate their own 'whiteness' as an unmarked identity of invisibility and transparency, particularly with regard to how they are located in discourses of whiteness, which have inscribed much of the collective memories, histories, use of language and cultural practices of Indigenous communities and non-white Australians.

Conclusion

This chapter has provided a critical overview of Australian multicultural-ism and its limitations in addressing issues of equity and social justice in an era of post-multiculturalism characterized by superdiversity, globaliza-tion and intensified global migration, and asylum. It has critically exam-ined pedagogies informed by pluralist multiculturalism and constructions of whiteness to highlight their limitations in challenging racialized and unequal power relations that exist in multicultural superdiverse societies. Dominant curriculum and pedagogical approaches informed by develop-mental psychology have also been examined to illustrate the relationship between developmental psychology and discourses of whiteness in early childhood education. The chapter has also discussed early childhood edu-cators' perceptions of how children understand and experience 'race', ethnicity and power relations. By drawing on recent research into young children's experiences of whiteness, racism and marginalization, the argu-ments raised highlight the need for further work in this area. The chapter concluded with a range of implications that can assist educators and com-munity service professionals to adopt critical and reflexive dispositions in their work with children, families and communities that afford equity and social justice for all.

Notes

1. The recent rape of a 23-year-old woman Iranian asylum seeker, 'Nazanin', who was raped while on 'day release' from detention in Nauruis, is one such example (Stein 2015).
2. Pauline Hanson is an Australian politician and leader of the far-right political party One Nation. She is well known for her conservative and anti-immigration stance on multiculturalism.
3. In Australia, primary schools with composite classes will often combine children from two year levels. In Martín's class, there were Year 2 and Year 3 children, and the seating arrangements were devised by the teacher. According to Martín, when the children were working at their tables they were assigned to particu-lar areas of the room in which Year 2 and Year 3 children did not sit together. Consequently, part of Martín's frustration is related to the teacher's seating arrangement and hence his inability to sit closer to Rubie.
4. La Escuelita is a pseudonym that refers to the case study site, which was a com-munity language Spanish school that the participants in this study attended.

Recommended reading

Jones Díaz, C. (2016) Growing up bilingual and negotiating identity in globalised and multicultural Australia: exploring transformations and contestations of identity and bilingualism in contexts of hybridity and diaspora, in D. Cole and C. Woodrow (eds) *Superdimensions in Globalisation and Education*. Singapore: Springer.

Watkins, M. (2015) Culture, hybridity and globalization: rethinking multicultural education in schools, in T. Ferfolja, C. Jones Díaz and J. Ullman (eds) *Understanding Sociological Theory and Pedagogical Practices*. Cambridge: Cambridge University Press.

Harvey, N. and Myint, H. H. (2014) Our language is like food: can children feed on home languages to thrive, belong and achieve in early childhood education and care? *Australasian Journal of Early Childhood*, 39(2): 42–50.

See also the relevant pages at the New South Wales Department of Education and Communities website for a range of resources and policies pertaining to anti-racism, refugees and multicultural education: www.schools.nsw.edu.au/learning/yrk12focusareas/antiracism/index.php.

7
Languages, identities and bi/multilingualism in childhood

Introduction

The majority of the world's population is bi/multilingual (Romaine 2013), and it appears that this is a normal everyday expression of cultural, linguistic and social practice. Australia is one of many multicultural/multilingual nation states in the world, with 19 per cent of the population of five years of age and above speaking a language other than English at home (ABS 2012b). The 2011 census reports that there are more than 300 languages, including Indigenous languages, spoken in Australian households (ABS 2012c) and, in the community, almost 400 languages are spoken (ABS 2010). In 2011, Australians identified with more than 300 ancestries, observing diverse cultural and religious traditions (ABS 2012b). Consequently, many children grow up in bi/multilingual families and communities, located in urban, rural and isolated regions across Australia. However, for children growing up with two or more languages and dialects, who attend 'English only' education and community-based settings, the use of their home language/s or dialect/s can be severely restricted, particularly when there is limited institutional and educational support for their use.

This chapter examines the socio-political forces involved in the retention and learning of home languages and dialects in childhood. It begins with a critical discussion of the significance of the cultural, social and political processes that affect languages retention and languages learning in contexts of globalization. A conceptual reframing of bi/multilingualism, language/s retention and identity in young children is offered, and data from Jones Díaz's (2007) research highlighting practitioner perceptions towards home language retention and additional language learning are examined to demonstrate how broader socio-political forces and power relationships operate and position young bi/multilingual children, families and educators into marginalized situations in everyday relations and social practices.

Global languages, community languages and Indigenous languages

The six official languages of the United Nations, considered to be global languages, are Arabic, Mandarin, English, French, Russian and Spanish (Crystal 2010; Fung 2010). These languages not only have many speakers, but enjoy greater legitimacy over minority languages due to their adoption as official languages both at the United Nations and in their respective countries. As a result, they are more powerful and prestigious than other languages. Crystal argues that, while world languages facilitate international communications, they need to be viewed as part of global multilingualism, in which minority languages also contribute to the flow of ideas, cultural resources, processes and products.

There are important ideological and political distinctions between global languages, community or immigrant languages, and Indigenous languages. From a socio-critical perspective, these differences are understood as being directly linked to ideological and political issues that underlie the politics of language, which together shape the retention, use and learning of these languages in educational and social contexts. Drawing on Bourdieu's concept of legitimate language, Heller argues that 'certain language practices and language forms are considered legitimate in educational settings, while others are not' (1996: 141). Hence there are structural and discursive power relations between global languages and other languages that are at the top of the hierarchy.

Minority languages: Indigenous and community languages

Language ideologies that reify monolingualism serve to reinforce the power relations through entrenched homogeneity and colonialism (Gogolin 2011; May 2012; Cooke and Simpson 2012; Macedo and Bartolomé 2014). Such ideologies have limited regard for multilingualism as a communicative and social practice evident in our contemporary global world. In the case of Australia, monolingual approaches that constituted social policy have seen the death and destruction of many Indigenous languages. Of the 700 languages and dialects spoken by Aboriginal and Torres Strait Islander people, prior to British colonization, today there are approximately 120 languages spoken (SNAICC 2008). Of these, as few as 13 can be considered strong. There appear to now be around 100 languages that are described as severely or critically endangered (Marmonion, Obata and Troy 2014).

In Australia, community languages are commonly known as immigrant languages that have been brought to Australia as a result of social policies including colonization, assimilation and multiculturalism.

The top ten community languages are Mandarin, Italian, Arabic, Cantonese, Greek, Vietnamese, Filipino/Tagalog, Spanish, Hindi and German (ABS 2012d). Interestingly, three of these languages, in addition to English, enjoy official status in the United Nations.

While the extent of linguistic diversity is clearly apparent in Australia, Scarino (2014) argues that this is set against a multicultural agenda that has become more politicized than ever before. This is in a context where national goals of education present highly abstract expressions of goodwill towards linguistic and cultural diversity, yet fail to recognize the significance of languages and cultural practices in learning. Moreover, she notes that the fragility and ambivalence in the learning and teaching of languages in schools is evident in the absence of coherent national and state languages policy. While these concerns primarily directed at primary and secondary levels of languages education are of significance, what remains highly troubling is the total lack of policy at national and state levels for the provision of home language for children from birth to 5 years of age (Jones Díaz 2014b). The absence of coherent languages policy from birth to Year 12 has resulted in Australia lagging in the teaching of languages. As few as 12 per cent of high-school students study a second language in their final year of school, compared to 50 per cent in the USA and UK (Cruickshank 2012).

English as a global language

Power relations that exist between nation states in our society are directly linked to modes of production, trade, commerce and media that operate at global levels. Within these modes of production, communication technologies are paramount, many of which are transmitted in English. Hence, English is currently considered a globalized and international language, which has gained much prominence and power over other languages (Crystal 2010; Jenkins 2013).

While the majority of the world's population does not speak English as their home language or dialect, there are more speakers of English as an additional language than there are 'native speakers' (Crystal 2010; Romaine 2013). The dominance of English is not based on inherent linguistic or grammatical features, or the numbers of people who speak it, but rather on the political, economic, religious and military might of the nation states that adopt it as their official language (Crystal 2010). Because it is a powerful language, everyone in the world wants to speak it. Jenkins (2013) notes that English has penetrated societies and individuals to an extent that has no parallel in human history, across fields of education, trade, media, diplomacy, politics, digital technologies, tourism, finance, trade, culture, fashion, politics and war.

As a consequence of globalizing English, 'English only' policies and politics in the United States, Britain and Australia have emerged (Crystal 2010; García 2011). For example, in education, 'English only' policies in the United States and Australia have seen the dismantling of bilingual programmes in preference for 'English only' programmes (see, for example, Simpson, Caffery and McConvell 2009; Gandara and Hopkins 2010). On the other hand, in Asia and Europe, it is common for bilingual schools to teach English at early childhood levels. Gogolin (2011) notes that many immigrant minority languages in Europe are afforded few privileges, and very few speakers have access to education and literacy in these languages.

While globalization and the dominance of English are on the rise, language remains a significant marker of identity, inextricably linked to the ways in which we understand others and ourselves. Despite the desire to pass on to children the language through which local identities are expressed, families are under considerable pressure to abandon their home language or dialect in favour of English. Parents see the benefits in their children speaking English, but this is often at the expense of the home language or dialect. Nevertheless, the disappearance of languages remains a serious threat to global linguistic diversity, knowledge systems, and varied cultural and social practices. Linguists predict that, of the 7000 languages spoken in the world, half will be extinct by the next century due to death, which is currently occurring at a rate of one language every 14 days (Nettle and Romaine 2000; Russ 2014).

Learning English at the expense of the home language

More than 50 years of research have consistently pointed to the social, cultural, intellectual, linguistic, familial and economic benefits associated with bi/multilingualism, and bi/multilingual education (Pearl and Lambert 1962; Reyes and Azaura 2008; Bhatia and Ritchie 2013; Bialystok 2013; Bialystok and Calvo 2013). Despite this, the dissemination of these findings, and their potential to inform educators and families alike, has remained relatively scant in terms of there being accessible and reliable information sources that parents, educators and caregivers can utilize. For young bilingual children, the retention of the home language or dialect will most likely be inhibited when they are exposed to dominant English-speaking environments such as day care and school, without sufficient support for the home language or dialect.

There is consistent support in research findings indicating that language shift takes place rapidly in minority communities, and that strong institutional support for the home language or dialect is essential in order to slow down this process (Jeon 2008; Jones Díaz 2014b). Given the lack of research into early childhood language shift in Australia, where the impact of monolingual or dominant English-speaking environments has been relatively under-studied, one can only assume that in bilingual communities the processes of language shift may parallel the processes of linguistic and cultural assimilation. Consequently, the relationship between language shift and cultural shift is of great significance to early childhood educators working closely with children and families, in terms of understanding young bilingual children's construction of bi/multilingual/ bi/multiliterate identities in diverse socio-cultural communities.

Therefore, there appears to be limited regard for the lack of representation of languages other than English in mainstream education as the unequal distribution of linguistic resources renders other languages marginal (Priven 2008). Furthermore, there is limited recognition of the intersections between language retention and identity construction in the early years of children's lives, where the formation of identity is constantly negotiated, transformed and changed amid a background of hegemonic English-speaking social fields such as preschool, school and community contexts (Jones Díaz and Harvey 2007). For example, within the social fields of childhood, the use of language is central to the construction of social relationships, which are often constituted in power relations, discourses and identities.

However, studies informed by socio-critical, poststructural and cultural theory frameworks focus on childhood bi/multilingualism and languages learning to examine the relationship between power, equity, discourse and identity, particularly in relation to how bi/multilingual children and their families negotiate issues of language and identity in educational and community settings (see, for example, Bourne 2010; Jones Díaz 2011, 2015; Gardner and Martin-Jones 2012; Heller 2012). These scholars argue that it is essential to examine discursive practices and discourses evident in the daily life of educational institutions. They point out that the language practices in multilingual settings are constituted in the legitimization of power relations among cultural groups. These language practices are embedded in the pedagogical discourses informed through such processes of legitimization most often found in childhood education and community-based settings.

More recent work on bi/multilingualism in children and languages education adopts a multilingual focus, emphasizing the essential role in **'translanguaging'** hybrid language practices (García and Sylvan 2011). This work highlights the plurality and heteroglossic contexts in which languages operate (Creese and Blackledge 2010), and goes beyond conceptualizing language as more than an autonomous skill to an understanding that multiple linguistic repertoires are used in purposeful ways for meaning making that most often parallel the translanguaging practices of the community. In education and community-based settings the focus, then, is on the plurality of languages building on all language practices, rather than promoting a specific language or languages (García and Sylvan 2011). In this way, minority languages, including Indigenous languages, are also privileged alongside global languages.

Yet despite research that points to the impact of broader societal and global processes of children's linguistic repertoires and the negotiation of their home languages, in early childhood education the preoccupation with Piagetian and developmental frameworks remain. These frameworks underpin and legitimize narrow monolingual pedagogical approaches to language learning, resulting in the unintentional exclusion of information and disregard for children's use of and learning in their home language/s or dialect/s. This is apparent in the singular use of 'language' rather than reference to the child's languages in observation and assessment procedures in preschool settings where children's developmental profiles draw on observations and interpretations of children's language development. In such exclusions, 'English' becomes synonymous with 'language' as educators draw on normative monolingual developmental pathways with little regard for the complexities in learning and negotiating two or more linguistic codes in the early years of life. This often results in early childhood educators adopting deficit and dismissive approaches towards bi/multilingual children's cognitive and linguistic capabilities, positioning these children as less capable than English-speaking children. The discussion that follows is an attempt to reframe educators' and community-based professionals' understandings of the broader sociological factors that impinge on children's negotiation of identity construction in using/ learning languages.

Critical understandings of equity in language retention and language learning

Critical frameworks for understanding bilingualism, identity and language learning are essential, particularly in relation to how schooling and early childhood education reproduce inequality and power relations between various cultural and language groups with differing cultural and **linguistic capital**. Bourdieu's (1993: 78) analogy of the **linguistic market** provides a useful framework from which we can understand the production of linguistic inequality in the early childhood field. His model of **linguistic habitus** + linguistic market = linguistic expression can be effectively applied to 'English only' early childhood settings, where the sole use of English throughout the day is normalized social practice. Linguistic habitus is the product of social conditions, which produce utterances and linguistic behaviours adapted to the requirements of a given social situation, which Bourdieu refers to as social fields or markets.

For Bourdieu (1993: 79), the linguistic market exists when 'someone produces an utterance for receivers capable of assessing it, evaluating it and setting a price on it'. This price is the value of the linguistic performance, which depends on the laws that are determined by the market operating in various social fields.

Bourdieu's notion of linguistic capital is the power to control the mechanisms operating within the linguistic price formation to one's advantage and social power. In this way, Bourdieu emphasizes that every linguistic interaction is determined by micro-markets, which are ultimately dominated by broader structures. Therefore, in 'English only' early childhood settings, the micro-market operating is regulated through the broader legitimization of English overriding other languages spoken by children and staff, rendering them with little social power while privileging English. The power relations evident in these settings mean that children and adults are subject to a 'unified price formation', which is embedded in dominant 'English only' environments and social interactions. Bourdieu (1993), then, asserts that the linguistic market is the place where forms of linguistic domination are secured.

In understanding how linguistic markets secure their domination, the notion of 'habitus' provides a significant contribution to the analysis of social and cultural practices in both educational and non-educational settings. Habitus is the 'system of schemes for generating and perceiving practices' (Bourdieu 1993: 87), which involves the durable incorporation of dispositions, practices and perceptions realized both spontaneously and generatively at the moment of social practice within a social field (Bourdieu 1990). 'The habitus is an unpredictable yet often systemic representation of the social condition in which it is produced . . . , a transforming machine that leads us to "reproduce" the social conditions of our own production, but in a relatively unpredictable way' (Bourdieu 1993: 87).

More specifically, then, in relation to the use of languages and dialects, the linguistic habitus involves the production of utterances, speech and communication adapted to a particular social field or market. The forces within the linguistic market of daily interactions that allocate social power will regulate this production of meaning through language in a given situation, and the dispositions and tendencies to speak in certain ways become congruent with discourses and 'rules' operating within the linguistic market (Bourdieu and Wacquant 1992). Hence, for bi/multilingual children and adults, the linguistic habitus generated in speaking English and home language/s or dialect/s will undergo various adaptations and transformations within the various social fields they encounter, which can either prohibit or promote the use and learning of their home language/s or dialect/s. As Bourdieu (1993: 87) writes, 'the situation is, in a sense, the permissive condition of the fulfilment of the habitus'. This means, then, that unless the home languages and dialects of children are authorized and legitimated in early childhood, primary and community-based settings, the linguistic habitus generated in speaking home language/s and dialect/s will be replaced by English, and the habitus of speaking English may override children's interest and proficiency in using their home language/s or dialect/s with their family and community.

Bourdieu's theory of social practice offers a comprehensive framework for understanding the production of educational and linguistic inequality. In particular, his emphasis on cultural capital as cultural currency or social power assists our understanding of the impact of hegemonic monolingual pedagogies on bi/multilingual children's capacity to exchange social and cultural power. For Bourdieu, human activity is conceptualized as 'exchanges' that occur within an 'economy of practices', which can yield or not yield material and symbolic 'profits' (Olneck 2000). These 'profits' constitute three different forms: embodied cultural capital, objectified cultural capital and institutional cultural capital (Bourdieu 1986). Embodied cultural capital includes modes of interaction and expression, cultural preferences and affinities, and ways of knowing and reasoning (Olneck 2000). For bi/multilingual children, the languages, knowledges and communicative practices in which they are represented become 'embodied' (Jones Díaz 2011). Objectified capital includes representational cultural texts transformed by and institutionalized through the media, art, music, popular culture, literature, digital technologies, the internet, education and globalization (Jones Díaz 2011; Moustakim 2015). Finally, institutionalized cultural capital includes titles, qualifications and certificates authorized by institutions, which are legitimized by federal, state, corporate, professional and community-based institutions (including educational settings).

Consequently, for young children, having proficiency in home language/s and dialect/s will generate differentiated forms of cultural capital depending on how the linguistic market accommodates and validates the required linguistic habitus. However, as children enter 'English only' childhood education and community-based settings, their potential for accumulating embodied cultural capital constituted in learning their home language/s and dialect/s will be constrained as their learning of English may transform their linguistic habitus accumulated through the objectified cultural capital represented through curriculum, pedagogy and policy. Conversely, bi/multilingual children can have opportunities to exchange and accumulate embodied and objectified forms of cultural capital transmitted in both English and the home language or dialect. This can occur through their family, cultural and community networks, or within childhood education and community-based settings that promote and extend children's home languages and dialects.

Researching bilingualism and multilingualism in childhood settings

Two important studies investigating adults' and children's practices and perceptions of bilingualism, language retention and language learning reveal significant findings relating to questions of identity, bi/multilingualism and languages learning (Robinson and Jones Díaz 2000; Jones Díaz 2007). The first is the research that we (Robinson and Jones Díaz 2000) conducted with early childhood educators, which investigated perceptions, practices and policies in long day care and pre-school settings within the inner-west and south-west areas of Sydney, Australia. Of the five different areas relating to diversity and difference under investigation in this study, questions relating to bilingualism and biculturalism were examined. The second study, conducted by Jones Díaz (2007), investigated educators' work with bi/multilingual children in general, and with Latino/a children in particular. The data drawn from 34 teacher/caregiver questionnaires raised issues about bi/multilingual identity and how teacher/caregiver attitudes shape children's identity construction. It also highlighted the voices and views of some of the children who participated in the broader study, which investigated families and children's different and similar perspectives on growing up and living with two or more languages and dialects. This included how families negotiated and reconstructed identity, while simultaneously facilitating their children's languages retention and learning in everyday social practices of childhood.

The hegemony of English: structural and institutional constraints in the provision of home languages/dialects support

Gramsci's concept of hegemony refers to ways in which power operates between dominant and minority groups occurring both at local and global levels, due to political and economic domination through various ideologies and discursive strategies of consent and coercion. For Gramsci, hegemony operated through 'moments of consent' via cultural leadership rather than top-down mechanisms of force, constraint, legislation, police intervention or military might (Fontana 2008: 86). In the case of English and its dominance in the world today, Gramsci's description of hegemony has much to offer in understanding the consensual processes of language shift to English (Ives 2013), whereby language minority groups willingly abandon their languages for the lure and promise of English. Through this interplay of consensus, coercion and persuasion, hegemony operates through 'a dialectical relationship enabling those in power to maintain power, while apparently giving the people exactly what they want' (Davis 2004: 7). We can apply this term to ideological power relations that exist between languages, speakers of different languages and the resources available in society that support multilingual diversity. Priven (2008) argues that, in order for minority languages to survive, there must be acknowledgement of the hegemonic structures of power evident in the unequal distribution of resources between monolingual and bilingual education.

Therefore, the power relations between languages and speakers of languages are constituted in hegemonic relations that subordinate minority languages and speakers of those languages to the dominant language and culture within society. In Australia, while there is a vast array of community languages spoken and 'tolerated', there appears to be unequal distribution of linguistic resources in educational, political and social fields within the community. Community and Indigenous languages are considered minority languages, and hence often afforded a lower status and rendered invisible (Liddicoat and Jowan Curnow 2014). In many Australian schools, the provision of community languages (CL) is limited, with the much of the responsibility for languages education being relegated to 'ethnic' communities through state subsidies (Jones Díaz 2014b).

In Jones Díaz's study (2007), the power relations between languages were apparent and there appeared to be a relationship between the lack of institutional and structural support for community languages and children's interest in using their home language or dialect at the educational setting. The data below illustrate practitioners' awareness of children's understanding of the minority status of their home languages:

I believe that children are aware that their home language may be a minority language and to some extent feel threatened by that.

Children often display embarrassment about using their native tongue in the classroom. It clearly makes them feel exposed to teasing or ridicule.

The marginal status of home languages was also highlighted in the participants' expressions of perceived limitations and frustrations in their work, particularly as CL teachers. These teachers work in CL programmes,[1] offered after school by various ethnic communities. These programmes often receive limited support from local, state and federal levels of government. Hence, the day-to-day management and administration operates through the voluntary sponsorship of different ethnic communities. In order for them to provide a teacher to teach the language, they rely on parent fees and volunteer management committees to sustain their viability in running the programme (Jones Díaz 2014a). Further, due to the diversity of language proficiency and retention rates in many bi/multilingual communities, these CL classrooms will often have a diverse range of language levels, across kindergarten–Year 6 age ranges. Hence, teachers in these classrooms encounter many difficulties and limitations in providing quality language pedagogy (Jones Díaz 2014a). The following comments highlight some of the participants' frustrations.

Teaching the language after school, children are too tired [and] [h]aving mixed ages (6–12).

Tú sabes lo que paga el, el government en grants por las escuelas, muy poco. ¿No es cierto? A pesar de todo esto también está un poco un asunto de, política porque así el, el government se desentiende. (CL teacher, La Escuelita)	You know that the government pays very little in grants to the schools. True? In spite of this, this is also a political matter because the government doesn't want to know about it. (CL teacher, La Escuelita)

Either-or-dichotomies; monolingualism vs bi/multilingualism

Bourdieu's (1993) concept of the linguistic market demonstrates how linguistic inequality is produced in social fields (including childhood education and community-based settings) in which English is used throughout the day as normalized social practice. In Australia, these settings produce linguistic markets regulated through curriculum, policy and practice, which is promoted and normalized, effectively securing the domination of English at the expense of other languages. For bi/multilingual children entering English-only or English-dominated settings, in order to survive, make friends, and get the teacher's attention, the learning of English is perceived as imperative. In Jones Díaz's (2007) study, discourses of monolingualism reinforced for children either-or-dichotomies of monolingualism vs bi/multilingualism, resulting in children's desire to learn English at the expense of the home language.

Learning English at the expense of the home language/s

The data below represent practitioners' beliefs and observations of the bilingual children with whom they work, as to whether they were in the process of losing proficiency in their home language. Some responses included:

Some children are beginning to reply to parents in English even though they are spoken to in home language.

> Many kids understand but only speak when necessary or encouraged. Children understand their home language but rarely use it to communicate.

> Children that arrived with little or no English now speak English at school and at home. We no longer hear them speak their home language.

> To be able to communicate successfully at school children often drop their home language.

> At the beginning of the year they would talk a lot more in Spanish/ Vietnamese/Cantonese and now they express themselves in English, they avoid their home language. (Teacher, prior-to-school setting)

Furthermore, parental anxieties about their children's English language development were apparent in some of the educators' comments relating to working with parents to encourage bilingual children to speak their home language. Some examples were:

> Parents wanting their children to learn English as quick as possible.

> Parents (some) believe their children are attending the setting to learn English customs rather than it being a reciprocal learning experience.

> Parents want their children to speak English to 'fit in' and 'get on'.

> Parents want their children to be like us because they live in Australia.

> Staff difficulties using the home language. Parents want children to only use English to prepare for school.

Constructions of the 'deficit' bi/multilingual child

In Australia throughout the 1950s and 1960s, the theory of cultural deprivation, or 'deficit theory', was directed at working-class, immigrant and Aboriginal communities. Genetic deficiency became a popular explanation for the educational failure of many working-class, immigrant and Aboriginal children (Germov 2004). In Australia, these deficit theories were also driven by assimilationist social policies of monoculturalism in which cultural difference was equated with cultural deficit. Children from linguistic, cultural and racial minorities were constructed as underachievers and deficient learners. In educational contexts, such pervading assumptions suggested that there was something wrong with the child, the family and the whole community to which the child belonged. The child's cultural and language background was viewed as a deficit and the only way to help this child was to teach him/her English so the handicap would be overcome.

While Fforde and colleagues (2013) argue that deficit discourses continue to construct dominant narratives and representational formations of Aboriginality in Australia, the issues they raise are also of important relevance to how recent social policy informing the delivery of children's services have shaped early intervention and prevention strategies within recent years. Constructions of 'at risk', 'vulnerable and needy' and 'hard to reach families' are buzz words commonly used in the field. These strategies have unwittingly reinvented and renewed deficit discourses applied to Indigenous communities, but have also been extended to immigrant and bi/multilingual communities, economically disadvantaged individuals and families, and children with disabilities.

Consequently, discourses of deficit very often permeate many educators' and community-based professionals' expectations of bi/multilingual children and low expectations of their potential are often held. This was apparent in Robinson and Jones Díaz's (2000) research, as the majority of the participants tended to construct bilingual children's lack of English as a deficit and locate children in discourses of 'need'. Acceptance of other children and integration into the dominant English-speaking setting was of considerable concern, as the data below illustrate. Some comments were:

> Children from NESB [non-English-speaking backgrounds] have specific needs that affect development based on their previous experiences.

> Any children who are bi [bilingual] will have some additional areas of need in their life compared to children with monolingual/monocultural backgrounds.

Further, in discourses of monolingualism, children's ability to mix effectively with other children (in being able to accumulate social capital in an English-speaking dominant environment) is measured against the ability to speak English. Hence, what counts as cultural capital for these children is the ability to 'fit' in to the monolingual 'English only' setting, rather than an appreciation of and willingness to draw on the cultural, linguistic, social, economic and familial strengths in being bi/multilingual.

In our earlier research (Robinson and Jones Díaz 2000), the practitioners' preoccupation with 'fitting in' is synonymous with 'survival' in 'English only' settings or environments where languages other than English have little currency and legitimization. This further reinforces the dichotomy of monolingualism vs bi/multilingualism, constructing a 'natural' authority embedded in the linguistic market of 'English only' based on language norms informed by monolingual English-speaking practices. Defaulting to monolingualism masks the reality that it is precisely the linguistic market of 'English only' within which the 'needs' are constructed, rather than questioning how the monolingual 'English only' environment works to impede children's capacity to accumulate social and cultural capital in their home language/s or dialect/s. Bourdieu reminds us that education is one of the most significant social fields in which the linguistic market determines social and cultural power. Hence, linguistic markets operating in education and community-based settings need to go beyond the cultural binary of monolingualism vs bi/multilingualism to legitimize bi/multilingualism in accordance with global linguistic markets whereby multilingualism and diverse forms of practices are normalized, rather than marginalized as deviant or illegitimate. In building on Scarino's (2014) call for an 'unlearning of monolingualism', what is required in education and community-based settings are policies, curriculum and pedagogies that promote opportunities for children's bi/multilingualism as essential communicative practice for all children in the twenty-first century.

Educators' perceptions towards home language/s retention and additional language learning

Rhetoric but not reality

Within these two studies significant issues emerge relating to language retention and the impact on the home language or dialect. In both studies, there is a clear demonstration of goodwill and awareness of the importance of bi/multilingualism, but the rhetoric and strong support for the retention of children's home languages and dialects does not match the reality. For example, in our research (Robinson and Jones Díaz 2000: 76), disparities between what educators believe to be important and what they actually claim to implement in terms of programming and planning for home language retention were evident. Similarly, in the second study (Jones Díaz 2007), the incongruence between ideology and practice is also evident. For example, while the majority of the participants were bilingual, less than half reported using their language with children, and only about a quarter of the 34 participants reported using the home language 'all the time' with children to promote the children's cultural and linguistic identity. In other situations, the use of the home language to assist children in the learning of new concepts, and promoting family involvement, received lower scores.

Further, in the second study, of the 59 languages listed by participants as spoken by the children in various settings, only seven are identified as part of the settings' community language or home language support programme. These languages included Spanish, Vietnamese, Arabic, Assyrian, Chinese, Thai and Italian. Furthermore, of the 19 participants who worked in preschool settings, the majority indicated that their setting did not offer any form of bilingual support to children. This contrasted with the reality that in preschool settings there was a greater proportion of bilingual educators employed than in primary school settings. Yet more than half of the participants across both preschool and primary settings indicated that their setting did not specifically employ bilingual educators for their language skills.

The depoliticization of linguistic inequality

All the participants across both studies strongly supported bi/multilingualism, with most respondents demonstrating adequate insights into the socio-cultural, linguistic and cognitive benefits of bi/multilingualism. However, it was evident that participants' frame of reference was principally informed by developmentalism. Concern for broader sociological issues relating to language rights, access to the home language and linguistic inequality were not apparent. The majority of participants rated 'self-esteem' as the principle reason for promoting bilingualism with children, rather than other reasons relating to cultural identity, family cohesion, and overseas links with family and community.

This preoccupation with self-esteem is an indication of how developmental psychology predominates in education and community-based settings, which tend to depoliticize or downplay the equity issues in not having access to the home language or dialect, hence masking linguistic inequality. Given that socio-cultural and socio-political assumptions are at the centre of teaching and learning (Nieto 2013), it is important to acknowledge the interplay of cultural, linguistic, social, economic and political realities that impact on children's access to educational equity. In both studies, concerns for children's individual 'self-esteem' were of higher priority than concerns for children's lack of opportunities to use their home language/s at the setting with other children in social interactions to extend their learning. It is important that bi/multilingual children have access to their home language/s in education and community-based settings. To this end, also important is the recognition that languages learning is a social experience and linguistic markets reflect the diversity of languages spoken by all children at the setting, including the kinds of codes of interactions and communication styles used.

Critical approaches to linguistic diversity and difference

In both studies, the vast majority of participants considered that children did indeed have understandings of language and cultural differences. Participants identified many reasons for this relating to children's exposure to 'difference' through living in diverse communities, the setting's approach to diversity, and children's experiences with diversity in friendships and their subsequent awareness of different cultural practices. Comments from the second study include the following.

> Our school is approximately 95 per cent NESB. They see constant examples of cultural and linguistic diversity through multicultural events, items and very vibrant LOTE [language other than English] and community language programme which operates within the school.

> English-speaking children label the non-English-speaking children 'naughty' as they use actions to get what they want, not language.

> Children are very smart to notice language and cultural differences. They can distinguish colour, different clothing worn by cultural groups that are different from their families. They also have the ability to discover whose children speak the same language as them during playtime.

There was clear acknowledgement in both studies that children were not only aware of language, cultural and racial differences, but also capable of constructing negative attitudes based on these differences, as the comments below indicate.

> They mention that they can't understand what a child is saying and will avoid playing with them sometimes.

> Children often laugh and repeat and/or ask what is being said.

> Especially older children [who ask questions such as] 'Why do they talk funny?'

> Children are aware of when adults/children are not using English. [They comment] 'What are they saying?' or 'They don't speak properly.'

> Yeah, I was born in Australia, but my mummy was born in Peru . . . So I speak Australian and Spanish. (Barbi, 5 years)

> Si, ella por supuesto se considera Australiana pero se considera Peruana. Se identifica con el país, con las costumbres, con la música . . . [Of course she considers herself Australian but she [also] considers herself Peruvian. She identifies with the country, with the customs, with the music . . .] (Carol, mother of Barbi)

> . . . y pienso que ella es Australiana, su idioma es inglés pero ella también entiende que sus raíces son de Latinoamérica. Somos de sur América de habla espanõl también. [. . . and I think that she is Australian, her language is English, but she also understands that her roots are from Latin America. We are from South America and we speak Spanish.] (Miryam, mother of 12-year-old Alison)

Parents' awareness of their children's negotiation of two cultural worlds in which identity is mediated across cultural, linguistic and racial lines was skilfully expressed by one parent (Raul) of two boys from an interracial and interethnic family:

> Parecido ellos saben que hay una cultura en el medio de mama y papa. [It appears that they know that there is a culture in between the mother and father.]

Lola, who is 11 years old, lives with her mother, grandmother and older sisters. Her father lives in Panama and is of Greek background. In the conversation below, I (Jones Díaz) ask Lola what it means to speak Spanish and have a Latin American background.

Criss:	Do you know what your culture is?
Lola:	Maybe, I don't know. My mum's Uruguayan.
Criss:	So what does that make you?
Lola:	Spanish.
Criss:	Spanish?

Lola identifies herself as Spanish and conflates her mother's cultural background with the Spanish language. She positions her own identity in relation to this homogenized category, 'Spanish', which is often applied to all Latin Americans and Spaniards. However, this is a problematic generalization because it works on two distinct levels. First, it implies that the Spanish language is unique to Spain and that Latin American cultures are duplicates of Spanish culture. Second, 'Spanish' refers to the generic language group, spoken by both Spaniards and Spanish-speaking Latin Americans. However, Lola's identification as 'Spanish' reifies and homogenizes both Iberian and Latin American languages and cultures as one unified homogeneous category.

In this second study, it was evident that there were significant intersections between language and identity, and while there were differing points of identity positions between the children and their parents, for the most part the parents' perceptions of their children's identity claims included a strong allegiance to their Latin American cultural heritage. Similarly, the educators and caregivers who participated in this study also had perceptions of how children negotiate and identify with their cultural background. Many of the practitioners reported that the Latin American children with whom they work do indeed identify with their cultural heritage:

> [They are] very much part of the family culture and family experiences such as visiting relatives.

> To varying degrees [they identify with their heritage] . . . Some are very vocal and full of information. Some sit back, like all children.

> I perceive that many can relate to their Latin American culture and community as many of them discuss things they have done on the weekend. Such as going to Latin parties, Mexican festivals and some children do Colombian and Flamenco dancing.

However, not all participants agreed with the sentiment raised above:

> They usually consider themselves Australian even when they are coming from [a] Spanish-speaking country.

Feelings of shame and reluctance to use the home language

In the second study, participants highlighted a number of difficulties encountered when trying to encourage children to speak their home language. Many of the teachers and caregivers reported that the bilingual children with whom they worked felt ashamed and embarrassed to speak their home language. Some comments were:

> I believe that children are aware that their home language may be a minority language and to some extent feel threatened by that.

> They are not fully fluent in their home language. They are embarrassed. It's not cool!

> Children often display embarrassment about using their native tongue in the classroom. It clearly makes them feel exposed to teasing or ridicule.

> Many children feel shy and embarrassed about speaking in their home language. It's about having confidence, being able to speak in your home language very well.

> Children [are] not confident to speak at all (even preschoolers) to teachers.

Poststructural, critical and cultural perspectives highlight agency and subjectivity as critical components in the social construction of the 'self'. The 'self' is considered as an active and conscious thinking subject whose understandings, interpretations and meanings about the world, and the social relations between people, institutions and social practices influence daily life. Children, like adults, are capable of shifting and changing their thinking and behaviours according to the social context in which they are involved (see Chapters 1 and 2). For bi/multilingual children, choices in language use are contingent upon the social context and their subjectivity. Clearly, from the participants' comments above, children's reluctance and shame in speaking their home language is an illustration of children's capacity to locate themselves in normalizing discourses of monolingualism.

Implications for policy and practice

As childhood educators and community-based professionals working with children and families in changing times characterized by globalization of English and its technologies, as well as increased cultural, social and linguistic diversity, our negotiation of difference in personal and professional lives in our local communities calls for greater reflection, knowledge and understandings about children's experiences of growing up bi/multilingual. The following discussion centres around key areas of practice that can assist childhood educators and community-based professionals working with bi/multilingual children, families and communities.

Reframing understandings of bi/multilingualism and languages learning

Moving beyond Piagetian developmental frameworks will enable pedagogies to be more inclusive and recognizant of ways in which bi/multilingualism is shaped and mediated by broader societal processes. By understanding that 'English only' educational and community settings produce monolingual and normative approaches to the use of languages and languages learning, educators and community-based professionals acknowledge how this can limit bi/multilingual children's potential in negotiating cultural and linguistic capital at the setting.

Through the recognition that there are diverse ways in which children experience languages learning and languages, normative monolingual discourses can be challenged. By drawing on the principals, practices and learning outcomes of the EYLFA (DEEWR 2009), inclusion of home languages and dialects in assessment and programme planning will accommodate and validate children's bi/multilingual identities rather than ignore or dismiss them as unimportant and irrelevant to children's lives. For example, the principals of ongoing learning and reflective practice, high expectations of equity and a respect for diversity (2009: 10) acknowledge the importance of learning about and incorporating critical and cultural theories informed by Bourdieu (1990, 1991a), Foucault (1980) and Hall (1996). This enables us to challenge assumptions embedded in normative monolingual approaches embedded in curriculum. From these principals, responding to and assessing children's bi/multilingual repertoires through intentional teaching of children's home languages wherever possible will enable learning outcomes that strengthen children's multiple identities and build on children's dispositions as engaged, confident bi/multilingual communicators.

Disrupting the power relations between languages: critical thinking with children and adults

Understanding the discursive and political use of language brings awareness of the power relations and equity issues that exist between languages in our dominant English-speaking societies. Therefore, when educators and community-based professionals are mindful of their location in monolingual and normalizing language practices, particularly when interacting with speakers of languages 'othered' through English, they effectively draw on the principals of 'secure, respectful and reciprocal relationships' and partnerships with families that involve practices of 'cultural competence' (DEEWR 2009: 10). In communicating with bi/multilingual families and staff, educators and professionals take time to draw on their experiences with children's home languages or dialects to find ways to represent these experiences in the daily programme.

Further, as children are capable of producing discriminatory practices when adults are not around, the need to understand how children take up multiple yet contradictory subject positions in discourse is crucial. Hence, going beyond feel-good and fuzzy statements such as 'It is not nice to make fun of the way Raul talks' does little to help children acknowledge that there exist power relations between adults and children, adults and adults, and children and children, particularly in the context of cultural, racial, linguistic and social differences.

Therefore, it is essential that educators and other professionals have an understanding of the broader contradictory and complex mechanisms operating in children's lives – for example, the acknowledgement that issues of **linguicism** and racism are 'collective' experiences of inequality, and worthy of discussion and critique with children, will lead towards pedagogical practices that go beyond superficial and tokenistic approaches towards linguistic and cultural differences.

Representations and explanations of linguistic difference need to go beyond oversimplified and individualistic representations – for example, the emphasis on a child's home language or dialect as 'his/her language', 'that's Raul's language', individualizes the child's linguistic difference. Rather, a more appropriate representation of a child's home language or dialect is discussion about the language as a community or Indigenous language that is spoken in our society by various communities. Here the emphasis is on the diversity of languages spoken in our society rather than confining it to the realm of the child's individual ways of speaking. By focusing on the collective use of language, this locates the language in its broader societal context, enabling children to better understand its dynamic and communicative function within the community.

Reframing understandings of identity construction in the lives of bi/multilingual children

For many bi/multilingual children and their families, 'experiences of identity and the use of the home language are mediated and negotiated against a backdrop of dominant English-speaking contexts' (Jones Díaz 2003: 331). This brings about constant negotiation and transformation of identity, which is intersected across social fields in which the hegemony of English as a dominant and global language affords it greater cultural, linguistic and social capital. Hence, a move away from understandings about identity as fixed and stable will enable us to understand how bilingual children experience their identity as multiple and transformative. For example, meanings about themselves are often shaped by their experiences of growing up with two or more languages or dialects, which may have less cultural, linguistic and social capital in our society.

Consequently, educators and community-based professionals need to take the time to find out about family language and cultural practices that are significant to children outside the setting. In this way, learning experiences for children are more meaningful and connected to their everyday lives. It is crucial to understand that the relationships between culture and language are not stable, and that therefore cultural practice is fluid and dynamic. The practice of cultural competence (DEEWR 2009: 10) involves moving beyond the fixation of culture as celebration and towards an appreciation of cultural practice as part of everyday life. This will enable educators to implement experiences that enhance and acknowledge diversity across families, cultural groups and communities, enabling the outcome of a strong sense of identity (DEEWR 2009: 10).

Creating a linguistic marketplace that legitimizes languages other than English

Settings can promote and extend children's home languages and dialects by making available opportunities for their use with other bi/multilingual children and educators. This will contribute towards children identifying positively with their language. Hence, their interest and willingness to continue to speak their language or dialect may follow. This means that all languages spoken by the families of the children attain forms of institutionalized cultural capital (at the setting) in which the policies, pedagogies and curriculum approaches provide enabling linguistic markets through the provision of opportunities for the use of languages spoken by children, families and educators. The following suggestions can assist educators and community-based professionals in implementing experiences that go towards creating a linguistic marketplace that legitimizes the use of languages and dialects spoken by children and families at the setting.

Policy direction and implementation

In order to effectively address the socio-cultural and language learning issues affecting bilingual children, early childhood settings (including schools and community services) need to implement language and literacy policies that reflect contemporary theoretical and pedagogical approaches. Such policies may include home language support, full bilingual programmes and learning English as an additional language. These policies should be updated regularly and re-evaluated in consultation with staff, families and children at the setting. Further, policies that enable educators to access professional development, in the form of in-service, conferences and resource development, are crucial.

Working with bi/multilingual staff and families

Bi/multilingual educators and community-based professionals that represent the languages and cultures of the children at the setting should be employed to support children's home languages or dialects. Bi/multilingual educators who use their language/s with children from the same language/s background can effectively 'nourish trusting relationships, restore safe spaces and affirm bilingual identities for teachers and children from refugee [and CALD][2] backgrounds' (Harvey and Myint 2014: 43). They also play a crucial role in observing, planning and implementing experiences collaboratively with other staff members in which their language expertise is valued and integrated across curriculum areas.

It is crucial that families receive encouragement to continue speaking their home language or dialect to their children. This is especially important because, as children's proficiency in English increases, their preference to use English at home with parents and siblings will also become apparent. This can also result in English unknowingly 'taking over' family interactions, and the work involved in sustaining conversation in the home language or dialect becoming arduous. Therefore, early childhood educators can offer support and encouragement by being sensitive to families' concerns regarding their children's bi/multilingualism.

Furthermore, families (including grandparents and older siblings) are encouraged to contribute their language and cultural expertise through storytelling, conversations, routines, and so on, so that bilingual children hear their language spoken by adults and children at the setting, and other children, who don't speak that language, are exposed to the use of languages other than English, as well as their home language or dialect.

Communication practices and interactional strategies

In order for children to maximize opportunities in language learning, quality communication and interactions strategies are crucial. Educators and community-based professionals need to ensure that they provide dynamic, fluid and sustained interactions and conversations across a variety of functional and communicative contexts throughout the day in both English and children's home languages and dialects. Bi/multilingual staff are encouraged to use their language/s, particularly with children who speak them and, by doing so, develop close relationships with children. However, it is important that educators and community-based professionals understand the complexities in raising children bi/multilingually, especially in interracial or interethnic families where more than one language or dialect can be used. Staff need to offer ongoing support to families through the provision of up-to-date information about bi/multilingualism and ways to support the home language or dialect in the setting of the home. For example, pamphlets, websites, bi/multilingual retail outlets and newsletters should be available in a range of languages at the setting. These resources can be accessed from local libraries, the internet and educational resource settings.

It is also vital that bi/multilingual staff read books in their languages and dialects in small groups, making sure that there are more children in the group who speak the language or dialect than do not. This strategy encourages those children who do not speak the language to pay close attention to gestures and visual cues that can aid comprehension. For the bi/multilingual children who do speak the language, their engagement with the text will not only model listening skills but also valorize the linguistic capital in that language. Bi/multilingual staff should not rely on translation methods when reading bilingual books – for example, reading one page in the home language and translating the same page into English. This only encourages the children to focus their attention solely on English, distracting them away from attempting to pick up cues and listen to the story in the home language or dialect.

It is also important that bi/multilingual staff are not used solely for the purpose of translating and communicating between parents and other staff members. Their language and cultural knowledge should be seen as a resource for the children's learning, and it is likely that they are not trained as professional translators.

Programming and planning

With thoughtful programming and planning, educators and community-based professionals can provide relevant experiences to children that will enhance their language learning. For example, practices of 'assessment for learning' (DEEWR 2009) include observations and assessment procedures that are informed by information about children's use of their home languages and dialects outside the setting, as well as at the setting. By gathering information from families about the different social and cultural practices within which home languages and dialects are used, practitioners can gain a better appreciation of children's experiences with their home languages and dialects. The information collected about children's use of language is then integrated across different curriculum areas and implemented in daily experiences where 'intentional teaching' leads to outcomes that demonstrate children as effective communicators, and confident and involved learning (DEEWR 2009: 10).

For example, grouping children in language groups based on age and interest can also provide opportunities for both bilingual staff and children to use their home languages and dialects. This not only supports the development of relationships between bi/multilingual educators and children, but also enables bi/multilingual children to extend and develop their linguistic repertoires. It also provides opportunities for children who speak minority languages in the setting to access social and cultural capital in that language.

It is important that realistic linguistic, cultural and social practices of the children, their families and communities are represented in the setting. This can be done through the use of posters, books, CDs, images, songs and other resources. Furthermore, stereotypic images need to be avoided, and a thoughtful balance of resources that represent both traditional and contemporary images of cultural and language practices provided. Texts in children's languages, including books, newspapers, games, electronic media, popular culture texts, and so on, are used throughout the day across different curriculum areas and not confined to book corner or language sessions.

Conclusion

In globalized English-speaking nation states, there are cultural, social and political processes that significantly impact on children's and families' experiences of bi/multilingualism, languages learning and identity construction. Bi/multilingual children, families and educators are often positioned as marginalized subjects, particularly in 'English only' settings in which the broader socio-political forces and power relations have a marked impact on negotiating cultural difference, identity and cultural capital. Also, their capacity to use their home languages and dialects in functional and communicative contexts can be minimized through discursive pedagogical practices of monolingualism, which can counteract the intellectual, social and cultural gains in being bilingual. Therefore, it is crucial that educators develop critical and contemporary understandings of the relationship between identity negotiation and languages learning and usage in bi/multilingual children, in order for them to provide quality-based and equitable pedagogies representative of all children in childhood and community-based settings.

Note

1. In Australia, CL schools and programmes provide languages education including Indigenous languages for primary- and secondary-aged students. These programmes aim to support the retention of the home language, and cultural and linguistic practices of the children attending these schools. In the UK, these settings are known as 'complementary programmes', in Canada and the USA they are referred to as 'heritage language' programmes, and in Europe they are called 'mother tongue maintenance' programmes.
2. In Australia and Aotearoa, New Zealand, the acronym CALD is used to denote people who are culturally and linguistically diverse.

Recommended reading

D'Warte, J. (2015) Reflections on language and literacy: recognizing what young people know and can do, in T. Ferfolja, C. Jones Díaz and J. Ullman (eds) *Understanding Sociological Theory and Pedagogical Practices*. Cambridge: Cambridge University Press.

Jones Díaz, C. (2015) Silences in growing up bilingual in multicultural globalized societies: negotiating languages, identity and difference in childhood, in T. Ferfolja, C. Jones Díaz and J. Ullman (eds) *Understanding Sociological Theory for Educational Practices*. Melbourne, Vic.: Cambridge University Press.

Podmore, V., Hedges, H., Keegan, P. and Harvey, N. (eds.) (2016) *Teachers voyaging in plurilingual seas: Young children learning through more than one language*. Wellington, NZ: New Zealand Council for Educational Research.

8
Social class and inequalities: deconstructions of poverty and disadvantage

Introduction

Within the last 30 years major political, economic, social and cultural changes have occurred on a global scale that have influenced everyday lived experience. In the words of Blommaert, '[t]he world has not become a village, but rather a tremendously complex web of villages, towns, neighbourhoods, settlements connected by material and symbolic ties in often unpredictable ways' (2010: 1). Our everyday lives are continuously marked by the impact of increased **globalization**, communication technologies, free markets, and increased flows of human and non-human resources and capital. At the centre of these changes, the impact on and intersections of social identities – such as class, 'race', ethnicity, language, gender, sexuality, religion, (dis)ability and social relations – are significant. Due to increased widening of global markets facilitated by rapid advancements in media and communication technologies in which trade, commerce and the flows of human and non-human capital are readily apparent, social identities, cultural practices and power relations take on new forms of negotiation in which meanings about class and inequality are reframed.

Educators and community service professionals working with young children and their families witness every day the impact of globalization in terms of how children's life chances are affected by the declining provision of health care, welfare services and education. In terms of childhood education, children's access to affordable, high-quality programmes that address issues of equity and social justice is crucial in maximizing children's learning opportunities. On one level, the impact of globalization is relatively straightforward as its effects can be seen everywhere in almost every aspect of our lives. However, on another level, the cultural, social, political and economic implications of globalization are relatively unknown to educators and community service professionals.

Hence, this chapter offers a starting point from which issues of class, globalization and neoliberalism can be understood. It begins with an overview of globalization, and argues that the economic, political, cultural and social impact of globalization on our lives is powerful. The relationship between neoliberalism and globalization is examined and there is also focus on the impact of neoliberalism on the role of the state in the provision of the 'public good' and the construction of neoconservatism. Further, this chapter highlights the need to reframe traditional theoretical frameworks of class. It argues that contemporary understandings of class are needed in order to understand that, within a globalized world, disadvantage and poverty remain closely tied to increased inequalities at local and global levels. This chapter also examines the complexities facing children and families in negotiating discourses associated with neoliberalism, consumerism and corporate constructions of childhood.

Therefore, as educators and community service professionals working with young children, critical understandings of globalization are crucial if we are going to make a difference to children's lives. This chapter therefore discusses the phenomena of globalization, neoliberalism, poverty, disadvantage and consumerism issues in relation to how they impact on young children and their families.

What is globalization?

Globalization is the construction of world systems that merge finance, trade, labour, modes of production, consumption, services, media and communication technologies. It also involves the interconnections of linguistic, cultural and social ideologies across multiple sites of economic, cultural, social and political fields, which are characterized by rapid change, free markets and capitalism at global levels (Marginson 1999; Baylis, Smith and Owens 2014). Thus, globalization is a part of our social reality that impacts on every aspect of our daily lives. However, apart from the effect that globalization has on our lives, there are the economic imperatives that shape and constitute political, social and cultural spheres of society.

While globalization is often equated with Americanization and cultural **imperialism**, Tierney (2004) argues that it is more complex than a basic imposition of a homogeneous culture on other cultures. This means that it is evident not only at the surface level of homogenizing cultural and social practices, but also in how societies define and construct political, economic, social and cultural structures and practices that take place at a much more complex level. From a cultural studies perspective, globalization does not necessarily directly imply Western homogenization of cultural discourse and social practices. Rather, as Nederveen Pieterse (2015) argues, the multidimensional characteristics of globalization operate simultaneously across hybrid yet specific economic, cultural, social, legal, political and institutional landscapes. Nederveen Pieterse (2015) describes how globalization involves processes of cultural hybridization that give rise to a global mélange. Take for example the hybrid influences in much of contemporary world music genres, which have reinvented and popularized music from Africa, Latin America, Asia, India and the Middle East.

There are a number of themes inherent in definitions of globalization, which include transnationalism, consumerism, global inequality and the role of the state in providing for 'public good'. First, globalization takes on a transnational impetus in the articulation and mediation of technology, free markets, migration, labour markets, free trade deals, profits and consumerism across the globe. Transnationalism can be defined as global interconnections, exchanges and practices that operate across nation states on social, cultural and economic levels (Mau 2010). Where transnationalism operates at economic levels, corporations commonly known as multinational or transnational corporations function across geographical borders with for-profit capitalist agendas. On social and cultural levels, this involves social interactions, relationships, mobility, affiliations and networks (Mau 2010). For example, email, Facebook, Twitter, Instagram, and so on, provide platforms for the establishment of social networks and relationships on personal and professional levels.

Second, much of the success of globalization is in its reliance on consumption, where consumers are transformed through commodity flows produced in global advertising (Appadurai 2015). Tierney (2004) suggests that globalization produces forms of cultural logic, which maintain that happiness and meaning are to be found in goods and services, based on assumptions that consumerism is necessary for the world and individuals to function. Sklair (2015) adds that without consumerism global capitalism does not have a reason to exist and is ultimately constrained. Sklair argues that global capitalism produces ideologies of consumerism that can be observed globally, not only confined to the 'first world', but in shopping malls around the world where large numbers of workers and their families flock to consume using credit cards.

Advocates of globalization argue that the world has become a global community, and wealth is more abundantly shared across nation states. They cite the growth of capitalism as a major cause of integrating large numbers of people into the global economy (Hamelink 2015). However, sceptics assert the contrary: the global economy is an economy made up of just a few rich countries that belong to the Organization of Economic Cooperation and Development (OECD) (Hamelink 2015).

Third, globalization has produced and maintained forms of global inequality despite some debatable assertions such as those above that economic globalization alleviates poverty and lessens the gap between the wealthy and the poor. For example, in Australia and most OECD countries, Fletcher and Guttmann (2013) report that while labour income inequality has declined, overall income inequality has increased since the mid-1990s, with the very highest income earners showing strong increases to their share of national income. Moreover, Milanovic (2015) argues that, as the world becomes more globally integrated, dimensions of global inequality are likely to become increasingly relevant. He argues that as a result of global flows of information, ideas, labour and connectivity, communities and individuals become more aware of how others in other parts of the world live and how much money they make. As a result, they are able to make direct comparisons of global income distribution. While inequality between nation states has declined slightly in recent years, Milanovic (2015) warns against rushing to conclusions that this represents an irreversible decline in global inequality. Adding to this cautionary approach, Hung and Kucinskas (2011) argue that unless the economic growth of China and India spreads to other developing countries, global inequality will rise within the next 25 years.

However, the reality is that there are many countries in Africa, Central Asia and Latin American that are the poorest in the world. Collier (2015) argues that, despite economic globalization, many of these countries remain in poverty traps caused by civil war, high dependency on natural resources, being landlocked (in the case of Bolivia, Rwanda and Kyrgyzstan), resource scarcity, poor governance and malfunctioning economic policies. Stiglitz (2015) notes that in Latin America, despite the short burst of growth in the early 1990s, recession has set in. Gilbert (2014) adds to this, reporting that, in the same region, the number of people living in poverty has increased. Hence, globalization is yet to alleviate such tensions in these countries.

Finally, the role of the state in providing for 'public good' is questionable. According to Tierney (2004), the role of the state is increasingly seen as not having much to do with equity in a globalized world. He suggests that transnational corporate economies are the engines that drive action; the focus is not on public goods aimed at social justice, such as public schooling, health and welfare. Rather, the state's goals and purpose become focused on ensuring that corporations are competitive. Thus, the principles of the corporate economy take precedence over ensuring appropriate provision and delivery of public services, which include schools, community services and early childhood settings. Subsequently, the profitability and competitiveness of businesses, rather than the creation of jobs, educational opportunities and welfare for its citizens, are the goal of the state. The emphasis is increasingly on profit at the expense of the 'public good', as social and communal goals are given less prominence and competition, and 'for-profit' agendas become the priority. Consequently, expectations of the state shrink or evaporate, leaving individuals to sink or swim in a borderless economy (Tierney 2004).

Thus, in today's fast-paced capitalist and globalized world, for educators and community service professionals working closely with families raising young children an appreciation of the economic dimension of globalization is fundamental. The likelihood that early childhood settings, community services and schools comprise both wealthy and poor families calls for the need to be sensitive to ways in which increased consumerism, the widening gaps between the wealthy and the poor, and the demise of the provision of public services will ultimately impact on working poor and disadvantaged families. Since economic resources for many families are constrained by the increasing costs of raising children, educators and community service professionals need to be cognizant of how their programme may or may not exacerbate discursive inequality and power relations between children, families and staff mediated by financial constraints, material possession and choice.

Neoliberalism

Almost every aspect of our daily lives is influenced by neoliberal policies and practices, most evident in the regulation of social life through market imperatives that result in the increased commodification and finance of food production, leisure time, care, work and childhood (Langley 2008). Neoliberalism involves the transformation of social relations into exchanges through modes of political and economic rationality that are characterized by **individualism**, privatization, deregulation and withdrawal of the state from the common good (Lingard 2009; Gill and Scharff 2011). It involves political economic practices which propose that well-being can be advanced within instructional frameworks to promote entrepreneurial freedoms and skills characterized by free markets, free trade and private property rights (Harvey 2005, cited in Gill and Scharff 2011).

Neoliberalism is also a substantial global capitalist enterprise (Walkerdine and Bansel 2010) and worldwide phenomenon. It can be defined as a political, economic and cultural strategy through which policies are designed to devolve the state's responsibility for welfare, education and health services to the community, the family, the individual and private enterprise. Walkerdine and Bansel (2010) argue that the state is no longer responsible for social security, health, education (including early childhood education and community services) and welfare, where organizations and individuals take on the responsibility for their own well-being. They assert that the 'self' is fashioned 'simultaneously as consumer and commodity; as buyer of goods and services and as a seller of oneself in the market' (2010: 5), which is constructed through a discourse of entrepreneurship.

Davies and Petersen (2005, 2010) argue that discourses of neoliberalism constitute self-enterprising mechanisms and hyper-individualism, which combine with management techniques to produce increased competition and vulnerability. This manifests into individual strategies of 'survival of the fittest' with little emphasis on well-being. They argue that institutions shape workers as individualized, vulnerable, competitive and useful subjects, where compliance becomes a normalized everyday work practice. Hence, within this discourse, the emphasis on 'performance' renders our subjectivity as dispensable while simultaneously producing dispositions of competitiveness and acquiescence, which ultimately constructs normalized and naturalized unequal work practices and relations.

Within a neoliberal discourse there is also an assumption that all social groups will ultimately benefit from the effects of corporate profit, regardless of the fact that it increases the wealth of the already wealthy. Yet, in reality, neoliberal agendas aim to reduce labour costs, decrease public expenditures and make work more flexible (Bourdieu 1998). This decreased public expenditure and the commitment from governments to take less responsibility for social welfare, education, housing and health operate alongside attempts to weaken trades unions and other employee representative bodies. For poor families and the working poor, this means that they are more likely to be exploited, as their incomes remain low and their ability to access services is increasingly compromised.

In the end, neoliberalism has implications for the working poor, children and disadvantaged groups in our society, because they are the ones most likely to be affected by government policies on health, welfare, housing and education. Once these services become 'enterprising' concerns from which 'for profit' desires operate, economically disadvantaged groups and minorities are positioned at the mercy of market-driven agendas from which they are least likely to benefit. Moreover, the increasing gap between children from middle- to upper-class families and children from working poor families means that single-parent families, low-income families and families dependent on welfare are especially vulnerable to cuts in social, welfare and education services. Therefore, macro-economic policies driven by globalization and neoliberal agendas impact on the most disadvantaged and marginalized children in both developing and developed nation states.

Neoliberalism, the state and neoconservatism

Apple (1999) argues that in neoliberal discourses the idea of the consumer is fundamental, and the world is a massive supermarket where 'consumer choice' is an imagined guarantor of the democratic rights of its citizens.

Apple (2013) asserts that, under the conditions of neoliberalism, education becomes a marketable commodity, like cars, television or food, in a for-profit market in which metaphors of business dominate. Subsequently, at the very core of globalization, neoliberal discourses position the state in a subordinate relationship to global corporations as 'the principles of the corporate economy take precedence' (Tierney 2004: 11). Hall (2011: 706) argues that the neoliberal model is grounded in the idea of the 'free, possessive individual', and that it views the state as oppressive and tyrannical. The state must not intervene in the 'natural' mechanism of the free market, or interfere with the right to make profits and accumulate personal wealth. Couldry (2010) adds that markets function as a reference point for organizing how governments must operate, and overrides other political principles of social welfare and the provision of goods and services. Hence, private enterprise is considered to be the answer in the delivery of essential services such as education, health and welfare. For example, early childhood programmes in the United States, Australia, Aotearoa New Zealand, Canada and the United Kingdom have not escaped the neoliberal agenda that privileges private enterprise at the expense of state-funded and state-regulated services. As a result, state intervention is viewed as not necessary, except on behalf of targeted minorities and the very poor.

Apple's (1999, 2001, 2013) notion of neoconservative restoration is a clear example of the connections between neoliberalism and globalization, which Apple (2013) notes has been increasingly powerful in Australia, Aotearoa New Zealand, the United States, Canada, England and Wales. Neoconservatism is reflected in ideologies that have gained a strong grounding in the broader society, including early childhood education and community services. The emergence of neoconservative thinking is the result of a successful struggle by the right to form a broad-based alliance between neoliberals, who are guided by visions of the weak state, and strong individualized and private enterprising technologies. In education, this results in the over-regulation of content and pedagogy through national curriculums, 'high standards', discipline and national testing regimes (Apple 2013). He argues that, as a result, schools (including early childhood education) become more similar and more committed to traditional, monocultural and standardized pedagogies. Together, the forces of neoliberalism and neoconservativism combine with authoritarian popularism in which dominant and normative discourses of masculinity, femininity, heterosexuality, heteronormativity, monolingualism, whiteness and the nuclear family become even more entrenched in the narratives of educational reform and media debates on falling educational standards.

Education, globalization and neoliberalism

Apple (1999, 2001, 2013) argues that neoliberalism is a powerful element in the current conservative movement in education. Neoliberal agendas view schools, universities, early childhood education and community services as 'black holes' into which money is poured without results. Economic rationalism underpins almost every aspect of this discourse in which there are misguided assumptions that there exist fairness and justice in 'for profit' markets (Apple 1999). Public funding is measured against economic rationalist criteria limited by 'for profit' outcomes, rather than by outcomes that indicate quality and equity, which are at odds with economic rationality.

Traditionally, education has been seen as for everyone, not just a privileged few, and **affirmative action** policies, such as those associated with access and equity for minority groups, would be addressed through education. In this sense, education for social justice is not new; rather it forms the fundamental basis from which we build democracy (Saltman 2009). However, as argued by Saltman (2009), the world of 'high stakes accountability' has positioned educators concerned with social justice at the crossroads where making conscious and proactive decisions for public education is challenged by increasing threats of privatized education, essentially serving to maintain the status quo.

Despite these recent challenges to social justice and public education, there have been considerable reforms in addressing issues of inequality in education. These reforms are, informed by critical, cultural and feminist poststructural theorists, such as Bourdieu (1990, 1991a, 1991b, 1998), Foucault (1974), Apple (1999, 2001, 2013) and Davies (1994, 2008). Such theoretical frameworks have addressed ways in which education operates to reproduce power relations of dominant and privileged groups within society. For example, Apple (1999, 2001, 2013) has argued that what is taught in the curriculum and regarded as 'official knowledge' is bound up with the struggles and history of class, 'race', ethnicity, gender, sexuality and religious relations. Academics and teachers with a critical social justice agenda, who have been informed by theorists such as Bourdieu, Foucault and Freire, take a critical approach towards pedagogy and curriculum. They question what constitutes 'official knowledge' within the mainstream curriculum in order to reshape and contest the power of dominant groups. Issues of representation of minority groups, such as people of colour, those from minority language backgrounds, women, gays and lesbians, and people with disabilities, who traditionally have been excluded from the mainstream curriculum, have been highlighted to reduce inequality in education.

However, Tierney (2004: 15) argues that despite these recent gains in educational reform that incorporate a social justice agenda, in the United States in particular, within a globalized market economy, 'the state no longer has a role as a cultural arbiter and shaper of the public good, so education has lost its purpose as well'. According to Tierney (2004), knowledge and the purpose of education are being reshaped. 'Competence' has become the purpose of education, which is evaluated through the process of 'testing'. This reflects the concerns of Cannella and Viruru (2004), who point out that the new colonialism in early childhood is perpetuated through the process of standardized testing of children from very early ages, particularly in the United States; but this process is also operating in other countries such as Australia and the United Kingdom. What is considered 'official knowledge' is replaced with an emphasis on 'skills' and 'competence', which is being redefined by neoliberal economic agendas as 'cultural codes are equated with the competence one displays on standardized tests' (Tierney 2004: 16).

In recent years, standardized testing regimes have been readily applied to position minority groups as subordinate to dominant groups. In Australia, the United Kingdom and the United States, neoliberal discourses have engineered a renewed emphasis on standardized testing (Lingard 2010; Giroux 2011; Apple 2013). Constituted in competitive neoliberal discourses in education, children who succeed are constructed as competent and capable, while those children who fall below standardized average score counts are constructed as deficit. Furthermore, as Reay (2010) argues, when the focus remains on testing, tracking and streaming, social class inequalities are reinforced rather than alleviated. Hence, 'globalization's purpose for education reinscribes a theoretical justification for the dominant to be dominant' (Tierney 2004: 16).

Thus, for families with young children, there is increased anxiety around competence and academic success at school. Parents are increasingly under pressure to ensure that their children succeed and survive the education system. In Australia, the private 'coaching colleges' offering tuition in maths and English are experiencing increased levels of participation from students whose parents are anxious about children's academic success. Further, explicit in the pedagogies of such 'coaching colleges', exam techniques are taught, equipping children with the necessary skills and techniques enabling them to compete for competitive places in various selective schools administered by the state education departments. Since public education is woefully underfunded, and private schools in Australia are well beyond the financial capacity of many working- and middle-class families, the competition is fierce. Good-quality education becomes a hot commodity despite the public rhetoric of quality public education.

In the preschool years, neoliberal parenting subjectivities emerge as a result of the anxiety parents have for their children's academic success. A growing number of middle- to upper-class families have their preschoolers enrolled in ballet, music, gymnastics, drama and 'pre-reading' tuition. Parenting magazines and newspapers have abundant advertisements from private ballet, music, coaching schools and colleges, proposing the benefits of such extracurricular activities for intellectual, social and creative development towards a 'good start' to academic success at school. The fees of these private institutions are well beyond the means of many low-income and working families.

These anxieties become even more entrenched, particularly for marginalized families, and families from cultural and linguistic minorities, where all children entering primary school in Australia participate in an 'on entry' assessment programme, which requires children to respond to a variety of tasks that measure their knowledge of English literacy and numeracy. For bi/multilingual parents, the prospect that their children are likely to 'fail' their very first 'test' in English serves to reinforce the pressure for families to abandon their home language/dialect in favour of English (see Chapter 7).

Hence, in neoliberal discourses operating in education, time is considered a critical commodity and it is perceived that the investment in our children's education needs to begin in the early years. Starting the process in the early years is perceived necessary in order to procure the skills required to enable children to succeed in education and to develop a competitive disposition to participate in globalized markets. Tierney (2004) suggests that, as the emphasis changes from public to private education, so too does inequality; within this process there is an amplification of social differences but fewer public dollars going towards public education. This calls in to question the role of teachers in these changing times.

Discourses of managerialism pervade the education system, in which teachers become managers who provide students with the techniques to pass a test. Models of accountability clench pedagogy where students are educated to acquire market-oriented skills in order to compete in the global economy. Schools pressure teachers to teach to a test and, if students do not pass, teachers are held accountable (Giroux 2011). This move away from teachers as 'transformative intellectuals' (Giroux 1988, 1997), informed by principles of social justice and equity, is lost in a neoliberal, globalized world. Moreover, Giroux (2011: 9) argues that today new forms of 'neoliberal pedagogy' have emerged and dominate education at all levels, stifling critical thought for a pedagogy that promotes 'rote learning, memorization and high-stakes testing', while simultaneously producing student passivity and teacher routinization (Nussbaum 2010, quoted in Giroux 2011: 9). Consequently, the potential for equity, social justice and critical pedagogy in education is displaced by a training agent role, as in business, industry and competitive modes of production, which are the fundamentals of neoliberalism and globalization.

Corporatization of childhood

As a consequence of globalization, traditional Western views of childhood as a time of innocence are slowly being disrupted. Steinberg and Kincheloe (1997) point out that, due to rapid social, economic and technological changes, childhood is increasingly shaped by media, popular culture, globalization, technology and capitalism, and as a result 'notions of childhood and youth are more complex, more pathologized, and more alien to adults who educate and parent' (Steinberg 2011: 2). Therefore, they argue that we can no longer make use of traditional assumptions about childhood as a time of innocence and naïvety. Rather, the postmodern globalized childhood encompasses meanings about children as consumers, who are informed by a variety of sources, such as television, movies, video games, books, toys, friends, social media, the internet, digital media and popular culture. Through these various sources, they also have access to adult information and 'adults' worlds'. Thus, children are knowing and not necessarily innocent; the binary of 'adults' worlds'/'children's worlds' is being disrupted. Yet, traditional views of childhood are constantly upheld in contrast to the reality that many children have in-depth knowledge about what are generally perceived to be issues relevant to 'adult worlds'.

As children gain greater access to 'adult worlds', it seems that corporate constructions of childhood also position children at the centre of consumerism. The historian Paula Fass (2003: 975) makes the pertinent point that 'it is foolhardy to discuss globalization, the cultural politics of globalization, and the social consequences of globalization without firmly situating children in that discussion'. She argues that children will become greater consumers of play goods as the process of globalization and deregulated market economies increase children's access to these goods. For example, with the increased access to technology, children in the West are exposed to sophisticated digital, electronic and mechanical gadgets in toys, such as computer games, video games and electronic media texts.

The computer and electronic gaming industry is a multimillion-dollar project that has in recent years outgrown other industries. For example, global video market games revenue and software expenditure combined is currently valued at 152.75 billion US dollars (Statistica 2016). Consequently, global corporations that produce entertainment, food, clothing and toys increasingly target children; books and so on have become a significantly important consumer group for multibillion-dollar corporations. Therefore, there is no doubt that children and youth have become an increasingly significant consumer group (Mayo and Nairn 2009), and the children's and family entertainment industry is big business. For example, Nudelman (2015, citing Disney Yahoo Finance) reported that the Disney Corporation generated 48,813 billion US dollars' worth of revenue in 2014 stacking up as the third most successful media network in the world. Its global success is attributed to its cross-marketing of films, animation, theme parks, interactive online games, media networks such as Disney channels and other cable networks whose icons appear on children's clothing, breakfast cereals, school bags, toiletries, frozen food, and so on, influencing childhood and children's consumption of entertainment and toys. It is no wonder that childhood is viewed as an enterprising and profitable industry. Children and childhood are being bought and sold in new ways, coercing children into avid and fervent consumerism.

Furthermore, Giroux and Pollock (2011) observe that youth now inhabit a cultural landscape where they recognize themselves in terms preferred by the market. They note that multibillion-dollar media corporations have a commanding role over commodity markets and this plus support from governments has emerged as the primary educational and cultural force in shaping how youth (and children, including very young children) define their interests, values and relationships to others.

Kasturi (2002: 51) states that, within corporate constructions of childhood, metanarratives generated by these corporations engender in children the 'need' to buy certain products, and coerce parents into thinking that the 'ideal' or 'natural' childhood involves the 'continuous consumption of these corporate promoted products and services'. For children, then, the social and cultural capital accumulated through the consumption of these products and services becomes a driving force in the continual acquisition of such products and services. For example, children's group memberships and social relations with one another are often constituted in their interests around popular culture, as they engage in complex talk about the narratives, moves and characteristics applicable to the various types of popular culture in which they are interested (Jones Díaz, Beecher and Arthur 2002).

Further, corporate consumer constructions of childhood defined by Western perspectives homogenize childhood as white, Western, urban, monolingual and middle class. The metanarratives of popular culture found in Disney toys, high-tech wearable gadgets, zoetrope toys and 'smart figures' such as Yu-Gi-Oh!, Barbie, Bratz, Playmation, Disneyvision, and so on, present normative discourses of femininity, masculinity, heterosexuality; whiteness and the nuclear family (to name just a few). In many of the narratives associated with these items, children and adults from diverse socio-cultural groups, such as people of colour, people from Indigenous cultures, gays and lesbians, and people with disabilities, are underrepresented. These discourses and narratives effectively position and silence minority groups as 'problems' or 'bad guys', while simultaneously privileging and normalizing the perspectives and voices of dominant cultural groups.

Apart from the homogenizing and commercializing effects of globalization on children, the corporatization of childhood is also reflected in the way that early childhood education in Australia has become a 'hot' commodity on the Australian stock market in recent years. As with other stock market companies, the quality of service can be compromised, as shareholder profits become the focus of company philosophies and strategies. How this stock-marketization of early childhood education impacts on the field more broadly remains to be seen, but it has the potential to influence curricula, pedagogies, professional standards and service costs to families, as decisions are influenced by economic rationalism and shareholders, who may not necessarily be those utilizing early childhood services or those with an understanding of children's early educational needs. Poor families may find it increasingly difficult to meet the financial costs of their children's early education. What is particularly alarming is the potential for increased class distinctions across the different types of early childhood services that families can afford to utilize.

The discussion below examines disadvantage in view of children's and families' experiences of poverty, not confined to within families but externally due to lack of health, education and welfare service, poor infrastructure and isolation. It begins by deconstructing poverty and disadvantage to broaden understandings of poverty in childhood. It examines macro and economic policies that impact on children and childhood, and also critiques contemporary deficit views of marginalized and working-class families that exist in education and community services.

Class relations in a globalized world

Traditional understandings about social class are principally based on the work of Marx (1967) and Engels (1974), in which social inequality was related to material wealth and the ownership of labour. Marxism, a structuralist and modernist theoretical framework, posits class inequality within binary distinctions between the ruling class or bourgeoisie, who owned the factories, business and land, and the working class or proletariat, who worked for the ruling class (see Chapter 1 for an overview of Marxism). Marxism claimed that the only means to attaining equality was through a proletariat class struggle in which workers could use their labour as the bargaining chip to improve working conditions and workers' rights, and ultimately redress inequalities between the ruling class and the working class to bring about the collective ownership of the means of production. Karl Marx's work was a response to the massive changes triggered by the Industrial Revolution, which saw the growth of secular and democratic institutions, such as the political parties advocating for 'the working man' and the union movement, and increased emphasis on technologies and the mass production of goods and services (Kell 2004).

While Marxism was applicable in understanding the relationship between the Industrial Revolution and capitalism in society, Kell (2004) argues that, as postindustrial societies globalize due to technology, communication, trade and commerce, Marxist theory has become inadequate in explaining the complexities and contradictions emerging in these societies, particularly when exploring uncertainty and ambiguity. As film, literature, music, the arts and architecture become increasingly important sites of cultural analysis and representation, different ways of knowing and meaning-making provide a platform from which diverse cultural knowledges can provide tools for analysing society (Kell 2004). Further, with increasing mobility of the population across the world, diversity rather than homogeneity is apparent, and social identities, such as class, gender, 'race', ethnicity, sexuality and (dis)ability, are constructed and understood in relational terms to one another, rather than in isolation.

In postmodern thinking, the overlaps and intersections between identities across different cultural meaning systems are emphasized. For example, a growing number of studies examining parent–teacher partnerships reveal that for parents the work involved in negotiating and advocating for their children's academic success is mainly gender related (Reay 1998, 2010; Lareau and McNamara-Horvat 1999; Lareau and Weininger 2008; Vincent 2010; Taylor 2011; Huppatz 2015). Childrearing, homework, school liaison, parent involvement and children's organized leisure are mostly assigned to mothers. These studies also reveal that much of this gendered work operates in the deployment of and access to social, cultural, economic resources in which class is a major factor. Further, Taylor (2011) examines the cultural contradictions among mothers by 'race' and class, arguing that white women in the United States experience class privilege by being able to employ marginalized women to provide services such as child care.

Consequently, in this new postmodern period characterized by capitalism and globalization, meanings about class relations and class identity take on new hybrid forms. Hall (1997: 2) points out that, by deconstructing traditional assumptions about class relations as a dichotomous struggle between the 'workers' and 'owners', 'we can hope to understand the socially constructed and historically contingent ways in which economic interests are articulated and pursued in the everyday capitalist world'. These economic interests cut across relations of class, 'race', ethnicity, gender, sexuality and (dis)ability. However, dismantling the binary relations between 'workers' and 'owners' does not imply that class is no longer significant. Indeed, there is a negative impact of globalization on the working-class urban poor in terms of job security, the casualization of the labour force and the volatility of competitive market-driven economies. Globalization does not lack a socio-economic dimension; rather, it sharpens material inequalities and economic marginalization based on class, gender and ethnicity (Heron 2008; Carpentier and Unterhater 2011).

Questions about equity in a globalized world become even more pertinent as new modes of work practices determine economic security or insecurity, particularly for those minority groups, such as the working poor, marked by gender, ethnicity, 'race', sexuality and (dis)ability. For example, in Australia, the most disadvantaged groups are single parents (mainly women), Indigenous Australians, people with a disability, the unemployed, immigrants from non-English-speaking backgrounds, private renters, single parents (mainly from female-headed households) and carers (Saunders 2011; ACOSS 2014).

Poverty and disadvantage: global comparisons

On a global scale, children living in poverty are more likely to die before the age of 5 or fall ill from a communicable or environmental disease (Tierney 2015). Due to the numbers of large countries that have moved from being low-income countries to middle-income countries, in 2007–08 three-quarters of the world's population, or 1.38 billion people, live in middle-income countries (Sumner 2010: 10). Sumner notes that, according to these trends, poverty is turning from an international to a national problem where the distribution of the global poor has shifted. Still, while China decreased its share of global poverty, poverty in India (despite its entry into global markets) and sub-Saharan Africa is on the increase (Sumner 2010). However, in the United States alone, there are at least 16 million children in poverty (DeNavas-Walt and Smith 2013, cited in Tierney 2015). Tierney (2015) adds that, in 2012, the Census Bureau recorded the greatest number of Americans living below the poverty line since records were first documented in 1959. Inequality in the United States has risen to levels beyond those seen since the 1920s (Tierney 2015).

In Australia, despite 20 years of economic growth, the Australian Council of Social Services' *Poverty Report* (ACOSS 2014: 8) revealed that poverty is growing, with an estimated 2.5 million people, or just under 13 per cent of all people, living below the internationally accepted poverty line (measured by 50 per cent of median income). Further, 603,000 children (17.7 per cent of all children under the age of 15 years) were living below the poverty line. These figures represent one in seven adults and one in six children. Key findings of the report also revealed that women, children, older people, immigrants from non-English-speaking countries, Indigenous Australians, people with disabilities and single-parent households face higher risks of poverty (ACOSS 2014: 10). Specifically, 30 per cent of single parents lived in poverty and, as a consequence, 36.8 per cent of all children living in poverty were in single-parent households (2014: 10).

Deconstructions of poverty and disadvantage

In the education and social science research literature about poverty and disadvantage, Zeus (2015) identifies three different perspectives. The first is the materialist view of material deprivation, which is essentially informed by Marxist theory. In this view, poverty is created as a by-product of capitalism in which its evolution has caused education to devolve from a place of learning to a site of social control. Indeed many scholars argue that, while education has been seen as the way out of poverty, it has also been seen as the site where inequality and disadvantage is reproduced (Bourdieu 1986; Reay 2010; Tierney 2015).

The second view of poverty that Zeus (2015) outlines is that the material conditions of poverty produce cultural practices and dispositions that come with a set of repertoires produced through the architecture of poverty that is created from disadvantage. Early research informed by this perspective was highly problematic in its tendency to take on deficit assumptions and pathological assumptions blaming culture and individuals rather than systemic causes of disadvantage and poverty. However, the limitation of this perspective in its pathological view of culture underestimates the ability of people to thrive in conditions that most would find abhorrent (Zeus 2015). In response to these limitations, this perspective has been reconceptualized within the last 40 years, principally informed by Marxism, poststructuralism, cultural theory and critical theory, where working-class culture from different racial and cultural perspectives is considered to transform education. Moreover, within these reconsiderations, there is the recognition that cultural practice can maintain relative autonomy from economic deprivation, a way to go beyond it rather than escaping it (Zeus 2015).

Finally, the third perspective of poverty is ideological and draws on critiques of whiteness to illuminate its role in transforming human bodies into racialized ones (Zeus 2015; see also Chapters 5 and 6). The inability of educational settings and community services to address poverty is masked by ideologies of whiteness that inform discourses of deficit applied to children from racial and cultural minorities. Zeus argues that when educators (including professionals working with children and families) make sense of poverty there is a risk of reifying racism and class systems that construct their subjectivities.

For educators and community service professionals working with disadvantaged communities, acknowledging that there are different perspectives of poverty and disadvantage is crucial. However, a useful approach to addressing childhood poverty and disadvantage is to understand that they operate on a multidimensional level that not only involves material deprivation, but issues of exclusion and inclusion at discursive and institutional levels, which are equally as important. Moreover, understanding of the role of agency in children's lives is fundamental, too. As discussed in Chapter 2, the poststructural and cultural studies view of agency adopted in this book draws on the notion that individuals construct their identities and are capable of critical reflection to enact change and exercise choice.

In terms of how agency operates in the lives of children living in poverty and dealing with institutional and discursive forms of inequality, Redmond (2009) draws on the work of Giddens (1984), who proposes that agency involves reflexive thinking or monitoring, and exercising choice to act in certain ways to deal with various situations. Giddens (1984) links agency to structure and the recognition here is that the two do not exist in isolation from each other or that the latter does not exist without the former (cited in Redmond 2009). While agency is constrained by structure, Finch (1989, cited in Redmond 2009) argues that it is at the same time a resource upon which people draw in their interactions with others. Therefore, as Redmond (2009) concludes, 'children's agency needs to be understood in the context of economic constraint but also in the context of dependence on, and submission to, the authority of adults' (2009: 544). Within this relationship, he claims that poverty both constrains and facilitates children's agency, and economic constraints compel children to make decisions that they would not normally have to make.

A recent Australian study that has drawn on this perspective (Skattebol *et al.* 2012) explored the perceptions of children and young people who experience economic adversity. This study revealed insights into their daily experiences of negotiating disadvantage within their social and familial networks. The authors of the study (Skattebol *et al.* 2012) acknowledge that economic adversity does not exist in singular but multiple forms through which the participants in the study negotiate not only economic disadvantage but also 'complex domestic lives, caring and other responsibilities, unsafe neighbourhood, sub-standard schooling, and few options for out-of-school activities' (2012: 1). The study's aim was to understand children's relationship to economic disadvantage, and explore their use of agency in protecting themselves and their families from the effects of poverty and disadvantage. The findings revealed that the children in this study were not passive but active agents in their negotiations of poverty and disadvantage. The findings challenge conventional approaches to researching children's experiences of poverty, which often position them as passive and vulnerable. While not ignoring the systemic causes of economic and educational disadvantage, lack of access to services and unaffordable transport facing the participants, this study highlighted the significance of agency in the lives of children and their voice in understanding the impact that poverty and disadvantage have in the lives of children and their families.

Deconstructing deficit discourses: 'at risk', 'vulnerable', and 'hard to reach' in education and community services

As discussed in Chapters 5, 6 and 7, deficit discourses and the pathologi-zation of difference as abnormal have persistently pervaded educational policy, curriculum and pedagogy, particularly in relation to cultural, linguistic and racial minorities and their children. These discourses are also applied to children from economically disadvantaged backgrounds, reflecting deficit views of poverty outlined by Zeus (2015), as discussed above. Gorski (2011) argues that deficit ideologies embedded in beliefs of social inequality assume intellectual, cultural and behavioural deficiencies.

In Australia, within the last 20 years, early childhood policy and pedagogy have seen a resurgence of the perceived deficiencies discussed above, despite critical scholars and educators having challenged such deficit perspectives (see Pacini-Ketchabaw and Schecter 2002; Comber and Kamler 2004; Jones Díaz 2007; Valencia 2010; Gorski 2011; Gowlett 2011; Sleeter 2011). Moreover, as Cheesman (2007) argues, terms used by federal and state governments targeting poor families and children 'at risk', 'vulnerable' and 'disadvantage' frame the child as weak and in need of intervention.

In Australia, Gowlett's (2011) study of teachers' use of deficit labels in an outer-metropolitan high school, recorded that teachers inscribed students into categories of 'underprivileged', 'backward' and possessing 'deficit skills'. In Gowlett's study, the teachers attributed students' misbehaviour to family problems, rather than assigning the problem of disengagement to limitations in curriculum or pedagogical practices that reinforce social inequality at school. The use of language to inscribe children and their families into certain categories as 'at risk', 'vulnerable' and 'hard to reach' is constructed through deficit discourses of disadvan-tage and poverty that ultimately position children as passive and lacking in agency. It also produces low expectations from teachers and profes-sionals of their achievements.

As neoliberal agendas propel ideological shifts away from direct pro-vision of health, education and community services, in Australia a new role for federal and state governments has emerged to principally direct their attention to addressing the 'gaps' and 'targets' in the community, while simultaneously leaving the provision of such services to market forces. In Australia within recent years, much of this new role taken up by governments is apparent in 'early intervention' programmes evident in many early childhood education and children's services. Penn (2009) argues that, while early intervention programmes may provide some respite to children, the systemic conditions that produce poverty will continue, unless other social and economic redistributive actions are undertaken. Early intervention alone cannot address wealth and income inequalities. Furthermore, while many of these programmes may be well intentioned, they are often based on the assumption that adult early intervention is the key to successful development in children. Parents and families tend to be viewed as lacking the willpower, energy or capability to improve their children's circumstances. Such intervention programmes have a limited understanding of the broader political and economic issues that also produce poverty, indebtedness, inequality, mental illness, violence, and so forth. This ultimately leads to institutional constructions of deficit discourses targeted at disadvantaged and minority children, families and communities. Moreover, as argued by Cheesman (2007), early childhood education and educators' expertise is reduced to offering advice on playgroup activities or child development to predetermined programmes. Their role is subordinated, and the complexity and significance of early childhood pedagogy undermined.

Simpson, Lumsden and McDowall Clark's (2015: 101) study of 30 early childhood education and care practitioners found that neoliberal discursive formations of child poverty pathologized disadvantaged parents and constructed child poverty as a by-product of the 'poor and their deficient subjectivities'. Hence, the practitioners in this study attributed child poverty as a problem 'rooted in parents' negative subjectivities, dispositions, behaviours, motivation and/or undesirable values and practices' (2015: 102). One senior practitioner remarked that parents 'are quite happy to sit at home and not necessarily try to find themselves work and better themselves' (2015: 102). Simpson *et al.* (2015) conclude that the practitioners in their study defined poverty as a result of poor parenting, and very few of them understood the systemic operations around poverty.

Hence, as a result of the relentless influence of neoliberal policies and economic agendas on childhood education, and child and family community services, it is crucial that educators and professionals understand poverty and disadvantage as a by-product of the broader systemic processes in society that construct inequality and marginalization rather than attributing poverty to the failure of families and minority communities.

Implications for policy and practice

In working closely with children, families, communities and staff, it is crucial that educators recognize the impact that globalization and neoliberalism have on everyday lived experiences. With increased privatization of preschool settings, and continual downgrading of public education, ways in which teachers ensure that their programmes and pedagogies address issues of equity, affordability, diversity and difference will become pertinent to their work. The following suggestions may assist early childhood educators in addressing issues of neoliberalism and class with families, children and staff members. The discussion that follows offers a range of implications that educators can consider at both personal and professional levels that specifically promote the principal of commitment to equity, and the belief that all children have the capacity to succeed and high expectations are held for their achievement (DEEWR 2009).

Challenging neoliberalism and corporate agendas

It is crucial that educators and community service professionals develop an informed and critical disposition towards globalization and neoliberalism, particularly in relation to the broader social and cultural impact on social identities, such as class, 'race', ethnicity, gender, sexuality and (dis)ability. Central to a critical disposition is the will to challenge inequality and difference with children, staff and families by highlighting the importance of equity in early childhood education. The recognition that, as a result of neoliberalism and globalization, children from middle- to upper-class families and children from working poor families, single-parent families, low-income families and families dependent on welfare are especially vulnerable to cuts in social, welfare and education services is particularly important. Therefore, macro-economic policies driven by globalization and neoliberal agendas impact on the most disadvantaged and marginalized children in both developing and developed nation states.

Educators and other professionals can also develop alliances and collaborations with local and national lobby groups, such as unions, women's groups and local environmental groups through different communication technologies, or participate in interagency or local community events. These alliances or projects can be integrated into daily experiences at the setting in which children and families take a proactive stance towards local issues affected by global processes and neoliberalism, such as promoting environmental sustainability or funding cuts to local services. Through these alliances with both community groups and families, they can help build social capital through collaborating and forging links with local schools and community-based services such as playgroups, family support, community language programmes and other child-based community organizations.

Reframing our understanding of class in a globalized world

Educators need to be sensitive to the increasing costs of education that is becoming privatized. The 'outsourcing' of curriculum in which there is an overdependence on excursions, guest speakers and 'fee paying' activities to 'enhance' the curriculum can often pose additional economic hardship on low-income families. Further, costs associated with purchasing educational resources for children that educators often assume all families can afford need to be carefully considered in terms of the financial burden they place on family incomes, which are already stretched. It is essential that educators understand that while globalization may have some advantages in providing flexible work practices, these work practices may include long hours or shift work, often exclusive to working-class and working poor families. These families often bear the brunt of insecurity in employment through the increased emphasis on competition and productivity.

As education becomes more competitive, educators and community service professionals can develop a critical stance towards the overemphasis on standardized testing, particularly in schools that marginalize children from minority groups and encourage competition between children and parents. Furthermore, childhood educators can engage in conversations to inform parents of alternative ways of engendering 'school readiness' and cultural capital without having to invest in private tuition. In their own practice, they adopt an array of assessment for learning methods that 'capture and validate the different pathways that children take towards achieving outcomes' (DEEWR 2009: 17).

Working with marginalized families and communities

It is crucial that educators and community service professionals are prepared to challenge deficit and normative assumptions about children and families experiencing poverty and disadvantage. In this process, high expectations for learning are applied to all children and the focus is on children's learning in the context of their home and community experiences (DEEWR 2009). Hence, being mindful of how deficit thinking is manifested and sustained through stereotypes and deficit labels such as 'at risk', 'hard to reach' or 'vulnerable', is essential.

In order to work towards adequate representation and participation of minority groups in the decision-making processes of the setting, educators and community service professionals need to critically examine whose voices are heard at the setting. Through this process, they are also able to recognize and respond to the barriers that impact on children's educational success, and are able to 'challenge practices that contribute to inequities' (DEEWR 2009: 13) that may be evident in the setting's policy, pedagogy and practices. For example, it is imperative that minority groups and children's voices are represented on parent and citizen committees, parent management committees and other parent committees. This may mean finding alternative and creative ways of seeking their participation, such as holding meetings at times that are convenient for working families; engaging in ongoing and two-way conversations with parents to gain feedback on policy and programming directions; or sending home brief surveys asking parents for comment.

Working critically with children, families, staff and the community

Educators need to engage in critical discussions and follow-up experiences with children to assist them in developing a critical stance towards consumerism and competition. They can do this by providing experiences that enable children to identify, describe, compare and contrast ways in which popular culture is cross-marketed to children, to encourage them to buy new products. Through these experiences they encourage children (and other staff) to think critically about how normalizing discursive representations of class, gender, 'race', ethnicity, sexuality and (dis)ability are evident in popular culture, computer and video games, children's literature, toys, films, television and advertising that targets children.

Awareness of the digital divide in terms of its impact on children's access to technology in the home is fundamental. Not all children have computers at home, and opportunities to develop competence with technologies associated with computers may be limited. Further, the ever-increasing gap between what children know about information and communication technologies and what their parents and teachers do not know needs to be acknowledged. However, it is also important that educators draw on children's expertise with technology and digital and popular culture by building on the social and cultural capital that children bring to the setting. This can be done through making connections to different curriculum areas such as literacy, numeracy, technology, science and the social sciences.

Conclusion

This chapter has provided for educators and community service professionals a starting point for investigation of the impact of globalization on children's and adults' lives. In capitalist societies, neoliberal discourses underpin economic, political, social and cultural relations at both macro and micro levels. The economic and political agendas of globalization have produced homogenized meanings about childhood as a corporate construction in which children are specifically targeted as powerful consumers. Popular culture and digital technologies play a significant part in this process.

Furthermore, this chapter has offered a reframing of class identity, poverty and disadvantage in a globalized world, in which inequality and the life chances of children are affected by the widening divide between the working poor and the wealthy. While globalization may have some advantages in providing flexible work practices, these advantages are often denied to working-class and working poor families, who bear the brunt of insecurity in employment through the increased emphasis on competition and productivity. Additionally, as governments take less responsibility for the provision of housing, health and welfare services, and quality public education, children and families from disadvantaged backgrounds are most likely to suffer.

Recommended reading

Apple, M.W. (2013) *Knowledge, Power and Education: The Selected Works of Michael W. Apple*. New York: Routledge.

Bourdieu, P. (1998) *The Essence of Neoliberalism*. Available at: https://mondediplo.com/1998/12/08bourdieu (accessed 18 March 2016).

Gorski, P.C. (2011) Unlearning deficit ideology and the scornful gaze: thoughts on authenticating the class discourse in education, *Counterpoints*, 402: 152–173. Available at: www.jstor.org/stable/42981081 (accessed 2 January 2015).

Steinberg, S. (ed.) (2011) *Kinderculture: The Corporate Construction of Child-hood*, 3rd edn. Boulder, CO: Westview Press.

9
Gender in early childhood

Introduction

Over the past three decades, feminist researchers have highlighted the importance of understanding gender, gender identity formation, and how gender differences are constituted and perpetuated in the early years of children's lives (Davies 1989, 1993; Thorne 1993; Greishaber 1998; MacNaughton 2000; Blaise 2005; Renold 2005; Taylor and Richardson 2005; Robinson and Davies 2008, 2015; DePalma 2013; Renold and Mellor 2013; Osgood 2014, 2015; Huuki and Renold 2015; Osgood and Giugni 2015). This body of research demonstrates how children are generally fixed within categories of binary gender – male and female – based on perceptions of biological sex, through discourse and social practices. Young children's perceptions of gender are constituted in the discourses (narratives or cultural stories) encountered in their families, schooling, popular culture and media, about what it means to be a girl or a boy, in that space and time, and how gender is materially played out in their daily experiences. Cultural narratives can provide children with multiple representations of gender, but binary gender is perceived to be the natural expression of gender in the West, with femininity unquestioningly associated with female bodies and masculinity with male bodies. One just has to peruse most toy departments or go to children's birthday parties to see that not much has changed in terms of binary representations of gender. Expectations of girls and boys, from both adults and children, are still gendered in terms of behaviours, practices and future roles in society. This body of research also demonstrates that children have a strong sense of gender by age 3, and are actively constituting themselves as gendered subjects within rigid understandings of binary gender and policing the gender performances of other children according to what they perceive to be 'appropriate' masculine and feminine behaviours. Children who do transgress binary gender norms, especially those who identify as gender diverse or transgender, generally encounter harassment and ostracism from other children and sometimes from adults.

Largely as a result of research and the efforts of feminist scholars and activists, gender and **gender equity** were firmly placed on the educational agenda in primary and secondary schools in many Western countries in the late 1990s and early 2000s. In Australia, gender, gender equity and an acknowledgement of the role that schools play in perpetuating gender differences between boys and girls, were central to national educational policies and equity strategies up until more recent times. However, in what has been termed a 'postfeminist' world, gender and gender equity are frequently perceived to be issues associated with an era that no longer exists. In other words, gender equity has been achieved, women and men have equal opportunities, and the gender glass ceilings of the past have been shattered. Despite the ongoing research evidence that gender issues still matter in education, the workforce, in families and in broader society, there has been a diminished focus on gender in Australian educational policy. Increasing violence against women and girls (e.g. domestic violence, sexual assault and sexual harassment), for example, is a major concern in Australia today. Similarly, the violence and discrimination faced by people who transgress gender norms are also serious issues. These are pertinent issues founded on perceptions of gender and power and diversity and difference that can begin in early childhood. Building respectful and ethical relations around gender in early childhood is a critical component of addressing these issues.

In early childhood education, where children's understandings of binary gender and gender stereotypes begin to consolidate, addressing gender issues with children has tended to be met with varying degrees of commitment. Some educators and families do not see gender as a relevant or significant issue in children's lives, with some indicating that there were more pressing issues requiring their attention (Robinson and Jones Díaz 2000; Davies and Robinson 2012). Unfortunately, the multiple and intersecting inequities that can be experienced by individuals/groups, associated with gender, sexuality, social class, ethnicity, disability, and so on, can be pitted against one another in the jostle for recognition in a time-poor environment with limited resources.

However, there is a 'hierarchy of difference' that exists for educators (and no doubt others), not just in terms of perceived relevance and significance of diversity and difference issues to children, but also in terms of how personally comfortable educators feel about addressing certain issues with children and families. Gender is often located at the lower end of perceived relevance, significance and personal comfort in this hierarchy (sexuality is generally at the bottom). There are some who consider that gender has fallen off the early childhood education agenda entirely for childhood educators and community-based professionals. Despite the gendered lives of children, and the active role they play in the constitution and perpetuation of binary gender, children are often viewed as not being aware of gender and certainly not engaging in gendered power relations.

This chapter explores gender in childhood and includes a focus on: the various dominant theories utilized to understand gender, gender formation and gender differences; Butler's heterosexual matrix, which provides a critical perspective on the relationship between gender, sexed bodies and sexuality; children's active role in the construction of gender in their own lives and in other children; gender diverse and transgender children; educators' perspectives of gender and the role they can play in the perpetuation or disruption of normalizing discourses of gender in children's early education; and implications of the discussions for educators and community-based educators.

Gender regulation: a feminist poststructuralist and queer perspective

Our discussion of the process of gender construction in children's lives is primarily informed by feminist poststructuralist and queer perspectives, which argue that individual subjects identify and make sense of themselves as men and women or boys and girls through the various cultural discourses of gender made available to them. However, children embody particular discourses of gender that they invest in and represent this through their gender expression. In this dynamic cultural process of gender construction, sexed bodies are discursively and materially inscribed with masculine and feminine attributes. Within this perspective, gender is not determined by one's biological sex as perceived in biological determinist explanations, but rather gender becomes an unstable and contested social category whose meanings and representations are susceptible to change across and within different cultures over time and across bodies. For example, what it meant to be a young woman in white, middle-class, Anglo-Celtic Australia or Britain in the 1800s, and the attendant social expectations, are different from those operating today; understandings and representations of what it means to be a boy in Balinese cultures are different from those in Latin American cultures, and can vary within those cultures.

Stryker (2008) points out that transgender and queer identities challenge the dominant relationship of the sexed body and gendered subject, reinforcing the unstable nature of gender and the ways in which it is culturally inscribed on bodies. Transgender identity is when one identifies as, or desires to live and to be accepted as, a member of the sex opposite to that assigned at birth. Robinson's research with gender diverse and transgender young people highlights how many young people today enact their own gender subjectivity, troubling and challenging the sex-gender binary system (male and female). These young people point out that binary gender does not reflect the multiple ways in which they view and express their gender (Robinson *et al.* 2014). Some examples of the ways in which these young people identified with gender are: queer, F2M, M2F, trans*, transman, transwoman, non-binary, queer girl, queer boy and androgynous. Interestingly, Facebook, acknowledging the shift in how many young people perform gender, has more than 50 different gender options to choose from. Butler (1990: 174) argues that 'true gender is a fantasy instituted and inscribed on the surface of bodies'.

There are many different ways of performing masculinities or femininities, which are influenced by other markers of identity such as social class, 'race', ethnicity and sexuality. Halberstam (1998), critiquing the binary gender system, points out that masculinity is also produced and sustained across female bodies. Despite the fact that there are multiple ways of doing masculinities and femininities, within the sex-gender system, some ways of being a boy or a girl are normalized. For example, the belief that boys enjoy being physically active, like climbing trees or play fighting, while girls are more sedate, like sitting and playing with dolls, reading quietly or talking with friends, are discursive and material practices that constitute meanings, representations and expectations of girls and boys. Children learn what society considers the appropriate and correct way of performing their gender and take these discourses up in order to achieve a recognizable identity within the existing social order (Davies 1989).

Feminist poststructuralist perspectives on gender construction have been critical of the way that Western philosophical thought has traditionally divided people into males and females, believing that this is a reflection of the natural order of things. The constitution of the sex-gender binary system was based on the view that males and females were inherently different from one another due to the fact that they were biologically different. Masculinity and femininity have been constituted within a cultural binary – signified as male/female – and primarily represented and defined in opposition to each other (for example, boys are strong and girls are weak). This cultural binary also represents a hierarchical power relationship that is reflective of gendered social relationships operating more broadly in society. De Lauretis (1987: 5) argues that the process of gender 'is always intimately interconnected with political and economic factors in each society . . . [and] systematically linked to the organisation of social inequality . . . assign[ing] meaning (identity, value, prestige, location in kinship, status in the social hierarchy, etc.) to individuals in society'. Within this gender binary, male and female are seen to be complementary yet mutually exclusive. Kimmel (1994: 126), based on his research on constructions of masculinity, points out that 'historically and developmentally, masculinity has been defined as the flight from women, the repudiation of femininity'. Feminist poststructuralists consider that it is critical to disrupt and deconstruct the oppositional thinking constituted in cultural binaries such as the sex-gender system of male/female in order to initiate social change.

These perceived differences between the genders have been highly influential in structuring the pathways open to and chosen by men and women, boys and girls in their lives. The gendered division of labour that operates in the home and in the workplace is reflective of these gendered pathways. Child care, for instance, is a career almost entirely made up of women, while men dominate motor mechanics. Alsop *et al.* (2002: 3) point out that this gendered division of labour 'is dependent upon our cultural understandings of men and women being different and thus more suited to different types of work'. Davies (1989: 12) points out that 'children can take up a range of masculine and feminine positionings if they have access to discourse that renders that non-problematic'. However, normalizing discourses of gender work powerfully on individual subjects, greatly influencing how they perform their gender. Resisting dominant discourses of gender and positioning oneself in different ways of doing gender that are not socially sanctioned generally equate to getting one's gender wrong. The consequences of getting one's gender wrong can be severe and result in social isolation, teasing and bullying, as well as other forms of violence and regulation (Robinson *et al.* 2014).

Sex roles and socialization theory: a critique

Many educators and community-based professionals we have worked with tend to perceive gender as socially constructed, but largely through the process of socialization of young children into particular sex-role behaviours. That is, children are socialized to take up stereotypical behaviours and roles associated with binary gender that form 'feminine characters' and 'masculine characters'. Within the theory of sex-role socialization, the biological basis of gender difference is assumed and naturalized. Children are taught the roles that are related to perceived biological differences considered inherent in male and female bodies and dispositions. Those who transgress specified gender roles and characteristics are generally considered problematic and representative of either failure in the socialization process or individual pathologies (Connell 1987). The family, schooling, popular culture, media and peers are considered to be the main socializing agents in society.

Feminist poststructuralists are critical of this perspective of gender construction, taking issue with the assumed biological basis of socialization theory, a failure to recognize children's agency and resistance in this process of gender formation, and the perpetuation of Western binary thinking. (Davies 1989; Walkerdine 1990; Alsop *et al.* 2002). This perspective does not recognize the active role that children play as agents in the construction of their own identities, nor in the regulation of the identities of others. In general, it does not acknowledge the active and significant part that children play in the organization of the social world (Davies 1989). The process of socialization operates in such a way that children are viewed as 'clean slates' at birth, and become the passive recipients or objects of the social messages that are enforced on them in their early years, largely through their relationships and interactions with adults. In this process, adults become the active agents, not children; and there is perceived to be a straightforward cause-and-effect link that is highly problematic. This process not only relies on and reinforces the traditional Western binary associated with cause-and-effect thinking, but is based on the adult/child binary in which children are perceived to be the dependent and powerless Other to adults. Davies (1989: 6) makes the pertinent point that 'we need to shift the focus away from individual identity to relations of power and to the multiple subjectivities that are available to any one person within discursive practices of our society'. That is, we need to incorporate an understanding in our ways of looking at the world, of the broad social power relations that are operating in society, which work to narrowly and rigidly fix identities within socially sanctioned norms. Sex-role and socialization perspectives obscure the multiple discourses operating around gender, for example, that provide individual subjects with a range of different gendered subject positions to take up as their own.

'Biology is destiny'? The discourse of biological determinism: a critique

As one can tell from the discussions in the previous sections, biological determinist explanations have been influential in understandings of gender, gender formation and gender differences up until more recent times. This view is still influential in education today, especially with the emergence of brain theories that perceive differences between men and women stemming from having variations in brain make-up. Biological determinism refers to the ways in which meanings of woman and man are perceived to be stable and fixed characteristics that stem from one's biological make-up (sexed body, hormones, perceived differences in brains in males and females). Biological characteristics were also perceived to determine and fix other psychological and behavioural dispositions that were associated with maleness and femaleness. Biological explanations emphasized and constituted gender within the sex-gender binary system discussed previously. As scientific discourse was considered to be the 'authoritative' knowledge during the Enlightenment period, research focused on 'discovering' the 'differences' between men and women in their biological make-up. In this process, the essence of femininity and masculinity became located in sex hormones, with testosterone viewed as the driving force behind male domination. Women's bodies in particular were considered to be dominated by the balance or imbalance of hormones, a 'fact' that was used to justify the exclusion of women from important roles in public life (Alsop *et al.* 2002: 19). For example, in Australia, women were excluded from driving trams due to the belief that their hormonal make-up could lead to unpredictable behaviour that could put both driver and passengers at risk. In schooling contexts, biological explanations are often utilized to understand gendered behaviour. The phrase 'boys will be boys' is commonly used to understand the aggressive behaviours, including the sexual harassment of girls engaged in by many boys. These behaviours are often perceived to stem from boys' competitive, natural urges that are often considered uncontrollable, arising from 'healthy' levels of testosterone (Robinson 2012).

Feminist poststructuralists have critiqued essentialist biological explanations of gender, arguing that gender is not fixed in biology, but is dynamic, fluid, and culturally and historically changing as discussed previously (Davies 1989; Grieshaber 1998; MacNaughton 2000). Physical characteristics, such as body hair and voice pitch, are often poor indicators used to differentiate between males and females. Perceived gender differences are often intensified through socio-cultural values and practices. For example, males and females are equally capable of mothering, nurturing and caring, but cultural values can operate to discourage boys and men from displaying these behaviours. Body hair, for example, is actually a characteristic of human bodies performing a specific function, varying across and within males and females. However, some cultures go to great lengths to dehair female bodies (anyone who uses wax strips to dehair their legs knows what is meant by this!) in order to emphasize differences between male and female bodies, reinforcing binary gender differences. Biological explanations of gender universalize and essentialize certain behaviours as characteristic of being male and female; for example, aggressive and competitive behaviours are constituted as male behaviours, while women are constituted as timid and uncompetitive. Males who do not engage in these behaviours can be viewed with suspicion as not being 'real' boys or men in cultures where these types of behaviours in men are valued. Biological explanations of gender do not allow for the vast differences that exist between males – not all men are aggressive or competitive (and not all women are timid and uncompetitive).

New material feminism and posthumanism

New material feminists and posthumanist scholars, taking up the works of Barad (2007), Deleuze and Guattari (1987) Harraway (1991), Braidotti (2006) and others, are influencing understandings of and approaches to gender in childhood (see Huuki and Renold 2015; Osgood 2015). These perspectives seek to rectify an imbalance between the discursive and material ways of knowing and experiencing the world, arguing that discourse alone does not allow for a full understanding of how subjects become who they are and know the world. They point out that discourse has 'real' material impacts and affects. Posthuman perspectives decentre the human subject and highlight the importance of the intra-actions between the human and non-human in the process of knowing. In the context of understanding gender in childhood, these perspectives highlight the importance of exploring how the material (e.g. bodies, buildings, outdoor spaces, sounds, trees, toys and other objects) affects ways of knowing and becoming gendered. Through an analysis of the complexity of the active and constitutive relationships or entanglements that exist between the material, discourse and affect, and how power is mobilized in these spaces that are continually being re-constructed, different experiences of gender can be explored.

The heterosexualization of gender: Butler's performativity and 'heterosexual matrix'

A critical aspect of gender formation that tends to receive limited focus in early childhood education is the way that gender is inextricably constituted within and normalized through the process of 'heterosexualization' (Butler 1990; Blaise 2005, 2009, 2010; Renold 2005; Robinson 2005c; Robinson 2013; Robinson and Davies 2015). As Robinson (2005c, 2013) argues, the construction of children's gendered identities cannot be fully understood without acknowledging how the dominant discourses of femininity and masculinity are heteronormalized in children's everyday lives, including through their educational experiences. What this means is that through the processes of gender formation, children's sexual identities are simultaneously being constructed and normalized as heterosexual (Renold 2005; Robinson and Davies 2008; Blaise 2010; Robinson 2013). The process of heterosexualization that operates in children's lives is rendered largely invisible through heteronormative discourses that normalize and naturalize this process within constructions of gender and as representation of 'normal' child development.

Judith Butler's use of performativity, and her concept of a heterosexual matrix, are particularly helpful in understanding the construction of gender, how it is heteronormalized, and in looking at the ways girls and boys assert their gendered subjectivities. Butler (1994: 33) defines performativity as 'that aspect of discourse that has the capacity to produce what it names . . . this production actually always happens through a certain kind of repetition and recitation'. She further elaborates by pointing out that performativity 'is the vehicle through which ontological effects are established' (Butler 1994: 33) – that is, how and where masculinities and femininities are played out, culturally and historically, is the way in which hegemonic forms of masculinity and femininity get established, instituted, circulated and confirmed (Butler 1994). According to Butler, it is the repetition of the performance of masculinities and femininities that constructs and reconstructs the masculine and feminine subject. Thus, gendered identities are formed from the performances of subjects and the performances of other subjects towards them. Children repetitively perform their femininity and masculinity in order to 'do it right' in front of their peers and others (Butler 1990), and it is through this repetitive process that the feminine and masculine subject becomes defined and constructed. The repetitiveness of the performance makes it seem natural and real. Individual subjects strive to have their gendered performances considered authentic or real through the judgements of others.

As Robinson (2005a) points out, it is important to remember that the concept of gender performance is always one that is enacted within strictly defined cultural boundaries; what counts as a performance of masculinity or femininity is rigidly defined and policed by the socio-cultural context in which one is located over various historical points in time. For young children, getting their gender performance right is critical not only in terms of how they see themselves, but also in the way they are viewed and accepted by others, particularly their peers. If they do not get their gender performance right, and do not conform to what is generally upheld as appropriate boy or girl behaviour, they run the risk of being ostracized or bullied.

Butler's (1990) concept of a 'heterosexual matrix' helps to explain how the 'correct' gender becomes heterosexualized. The heterosexual matrix is 'a grid of cultural intelligibility through which bodies, genders, and desires are naturalized'. Butler (1990: 151) explains this matrix further as a:

> hegemonic discursive/epistemic model of gender intelligibility that assumes that for bodies to cohere and make sense there must be a stable sex expressed through a stable gender (masculine expresses male, feminine expresses female) that is oppositionally and hierarchically defined through the compulsory practice of heterosexuality.

In other words, Butler is arguing that we make sense of gendered bodies and desires through the way that they are discursively unified, naturalized and fixed through compulsory heterosexuality (Rich 1980). The perceived fixed, unified and stable nature of this embodied relationship between gender and sexuality is constituted and perpetuated through the cultural binary male/female, which defines masculinity and femininity as natural opposites.

Alsop *et al.* (2002: 97) argue that in Butler's theory, 'it is the "epistemic regime of presumptive heterosexuality" [Butler 1990: viii] which drives our division into male and female, and which itself structures our understanding of biology'. Thus, in Butler's perspective, it is the presumption of heterosexuality that ascribes bodies as gendered, rather than traditional perspectives, which uphold that the natural distinction of bodies into male and female signifies the normality and naturalness of heterosexuality. Butler argues that it is the way that the construction of gender is assumed to be a natural process given by biology that is critical to these understandings. The effect of the range of gendered performance is to make it appear that there are two distinct natures, male and female. As pointed out by Alsop *et al.* (2002: 99), 'What we take to be "nature" is therefore an effect rather than a cause of our gendered acts.' Thus, the repetition of normalized gender performance polarized within the cultural binary male/female, which is socially constituted, renders this behaviour as being a given from nature, or one's biology.

Butler's works, along with feminist poststructuralist understandings of the formation of gender, provide childhood educators and community-based professionals with a useful theoretical framework to inform their practices and gender programmes with children. Gender formation is a continuous, complex and negotiated process in which children actively construct and reconstruct their performances through the socio-cultural discourses they have available to them. Individual boys and girls will locate themselves within certain discourses of masculinities or femininities, taking up these meanings and social relationships as their own. However, one's subjective positioning is not fixed, but can discursively shift as individuals read their locations within relations of power, claiming or resisting discourses according to what they want to achieve (Hollway 1984). Young boys who engage in bullying behaviour as a performance of their masculinity, which is reinforced through respect from their peers (albeit a respect often based on fear), and societal and media representations of appropriate masculinity associated with aggression (for example, rugby league sporting heroes), will generally not be convinced to change their behaviour based on pleas of not hurting another child's feelings. Getting the performance of this form of masculinity correct, especially in front of peers, is often about public displays of aggression over others.

The 'realness' of doing gender is the ability to compel belief in the performance. For example, for many young boys, the judgement of their male peers is critical to the measurement of how authentic they are at doing their masculinity. Although there is an increasing understanding of how gender construction operates in children's lives, the way in which stable notions of gender, sex and desire are constituted, expressed and normalized through compulsory heterosexuality (that is, how gender is heterosexualized and sexuality is simultaneously normalized as heterosexual) needs greater consideration in childhood education.

Gender diverse and transgender children

Gender diverse and transgender children have recently become the focus of increased public discourse in Western countries such as Australia, the USA and the UK. This is linked to a sharp increase in numbers of children and young people who identify as gender diverse or transgender seeking support and talking more openly about their lives (Hewitt *et al.* 2012). This is despite the fact that **transphobia** is widespread in these societies, and the consequences for children, young people and adults who are open about being gender diverse or transgender can be dire, with harassment and violence a common experience for many (Greytak, Kosciw and Díaz 2009; Robinson *et al.* 2014; Smith *et al.* 2014). Manning, Sansfaçon and Meyer (2014: 5) state that, 'Expressions of gender-nonconformity, whether by a child, teen, or adult . . . challenge a society that is organized largely on the basis of a binary understanding of identity.' Research on gender diverse and transgender children has also increased steadily over the past decade in the social sciences (e.g. education, social welfare), with some of the literature focusing on children in primary schools and early childhood education (Ehrensaft 2014; Meyer and Sansfaçon 2014).

Gender diversity is when gender identity expression is different from societal expectations/stereotypes related to binary gender (male/female). Transgender identity is when one identifies as, or desires to live and to be accepted as, a member of the sex opposite to that assigned at birth. Research points out that feelings of discomfort with one's assigned gender at birth can start as early as age 3, and can persist into adolescence and adulthood (Riley *et al.* 2011; Stark 2014). However, only about 20 per cent of gender diverse young children will persist into puberty, with 99.5 per cent of those persisting at puberty continuing to identify as such into adulthood (Stark 2014). Research highlights that children's awareness and understanding of gender identity starts early in life and, at age 3, they are not only beginning to rigidly regulate their own gender identities according to gender norms, but also those of other children (and adults) (Robinson 2013).

Gender diverse and transgender children experience pressures in all aspects of their lives to conform to normative binary gender behaviours. This pressure can be significant in families and in schools. Transgressions from normalized performances of gender in young children often evoke strong emotive responses from parents (Grossman, D'Augelli and Salter 2006). How parents and siblings react to a child's or young person's gender diversity or transgender identity is critical to that child or young person's sense of self, and their health and well-being more generally. Parents who allow and encourage their children to take up gendered positions that transgress from their assigned sex at birth are often met with criticism and horror from extended family members, friends, educators, other professionals and the broader community. However, there are increasing numbers of parents who openly affirm their gender diverse and transgender children (Manning, Sansfaçon and Meyer 2014).

An increased visibility of gender diverse (and sexuality diverse) young people in schools (Australian Curriculum, Assessment and Reporting Authority 2012) has resulted in greater awareness of their schooling experiences and the urgent need to address the problems they face stemming from heteronormativity, transphobia and homophobia. Research highlights that a pattern of habitual and purposeful homophobic and transphobic abuse is prevalent in schools (Greytak, Kosciw and Díaz 2009; Robinson *et al.* 2014). Children and young people who are gender diverse or transgender encounter transphobia and homophobia from peers and also from teachers; this has a profound impact on their daily lives, and health and well-being. Homophobia tends to accompany transphobia, as it is perceived (or feared) that non-conforming gender behaviours are an indicator of same-sex attraction in children and young people. Transphobia and homophobia in schools can not only result in self-harm, suicide ideation and attempted suicide, but also disengagement with schooling, avoidance of using school toilets, frequently changing schools to avoid harassment, leaving school early with minimal qualifications, and drug and alcohol abuse. Addressing transphobia and homophobia in children's early education and schooling is critical to challenging these attitudes, biases and behaviours that are widespread in society.

A glimpse of educators' perspectives on gender and approaches to gender equity

According to our combined research with early childhood educators, educators' perceptions and understandings of gender and gender formation were largely influenced by discourses that naturalize and normalize gender behaviours in the biological differences between males and females. Most had no formal training in gender theory or gender equity issues;

some had discussed gender in their university training; and only a few acknowledged that they had attended in-service training on gender and gender equity in their places of employment. Consequently, understandings and perceptions of gender were highly influenced by their personal experiences. In research conducted by Davies and Robinson (2012) with early middle childhood educators and community-based professionals in Australia, there were similar findings. In this research, information about gender was primarily gained from personal experience, from newspapers and magazines, and from the internet.

In our combined research (Robinson and Jones Díaz) some educators, who tended to view gender as a social construction in the first instance, resorted to biological explanations in the end when they felt that children seemed to naturally take up traditional ways of being girls and boys, despite the significant efforts they made to provide and encourage alternative gendered ways of being for children. Several educators gave similar examples of this related to the ways in which girls and boys chose to play with traditional gendered toys despite the availability of other non-traditional options. Alsop *et al.* (2002: 35) make the pertinent point that there is a 'naturalizing trick' operating around people's responses to gender – that is, the habitual or 'second nature' of doing gender often leads one to be seduced by the notion that it must be entirely natural and fixed. Most of the educators and pre-service teachers that we have worked with tended to view gender construction in terms of children's socialization into sex roles that assumed a natural biological difference.

Educators generally perceived children to have an understanding of gender stereotypes and of the potential discrimination that can arise from this stereotyping. However, there tended to be less certainty about whether children understood the concept of power and how it operates in gendered relationships. For some educators, children were considered 'too young' to understand power and how it operated, let alone engage in using power in any way, either as boys or girls. This perspective stems from the oppositional thinking that is constituted in the cultural binary adult/child, in which meanings of childhood are defined and constructed in opposition to what it means to be an adult. Within this thinking, power is considered to be a complex adult concept that only they understand or practise; this is based on the view that power is primarily negative and utilized by overbearing and manipulative individuals. Children, on the other hand, are viewed as being naturally unaware of such behaviours, too developmentally immature to understand the concept, as well as being 'too innocent' to engage in such manipulative practices. An early childhood teacher who commented, 'Children aren't aware of these things unless it is pointed out by adults', encapsulated this perspective. Consequently, some educators were concerned that doing gender equity work (or any other social justice work) with children that went beyond increasing children's awareness of the stereotypes perceived to be enforced on them by adults, was entering dangerous territory, in which children's eyes were opened to 'differences' that they would not naturally see.

Some educators were adamant that they treated boys and girls in the same manner, pointing out that they did not have to incorporate a focus on gender equity into their programmes because their everyday philosophy was that 'We are all the same; we are equal.' This philosophical approach to difference often leads to pedagogical practices that deny difference and the politics of power that operate around identities, not just in terms of gender, but around 'race', ethnicity, class, sexuality, and so on. Within this perspective, all difference is overshadowed by the shared element of being 'human', perceived to be the equalizing factor across all cultural differences. This approach appeals to children's perceived innocence, inherent goodness, fairness and thus the ability to look beyond difference. However, the notion of being 'the same' becomes synonymous with characteristics associated with the dominant culture. For example, 'human' designates being 'white', 'Western' and 'male'. The more minoritized cultures take up the practices and perspectives of the dominant culture, the more equal 'they' become. Consequently, this approach to dealing with diversity, including gender, does not adequately allow children to deal critically with their knowledge of difference, different messages received, or the power relations they encounter and participate in every day that are based on difference. Further, it does not provide children with a critical awareness of the broader structural inequalities that exist socially, politically and economically that impact on all children and their families.

Some educators were concerned that some of their colleagues engaged in discriminatory practices with children. This was often linked to the cultural backgrounds of educators and staff, to their age, to their status as casual untrained carers or to a lack of training in gender issues. There was a perception held by some educators that gender issues and gender discrimination were linked primarily to specific cultures that were viewed to be more patriarchal in the way that they treated girls and women. This tended to be associated with educators from non-Western cultures, who were viewed as perpetuating strong messages in their practices that gender differences between boys and girls were natural and 'healthy'. In terms of age, some believed that older members of staff from different generations had traditional stereotyped values and expectations around children's gendered behaviour. From our observations and experiences in dealing with gender equity issues, it is easy to fall into the 'euro/**ethnocentricism**' or 'generation gap' trap that leads one to uncritically equate gender discrimination with the Other, in this case non-Western cultures and older members in society. This perspective is one that tends to operate largely on racialized and aged stereotypes, and the process of essentializing groups – that is, certain characteristics are considered to be natural to all who are part of that group, thus defining and fixing them as such; or the tendency to see one aspect of a subject's identity (often the visible parts) and to make that representative of the whole individual. For example, the stereotype of women from non-Western cultures being oppressed by males is generalized to all and seen as a part of what it means to be a non-Western woman. What the process also does is blind one to the everyday practices of gender discrimination that operate through our own practices and those of the dominant culture, hence depoliticizing the power relations that exist in mainstream society.

As pointed out in the introduction to this chapter, it has been perceived by some childhood educators that gender equity has dropped off the childhood education agenda. However, when gender and gender equity are addressed by educators, this is considered to be an important part of doing social justice and equity work with children, families, teachers and colleagues. Its importance is accredited to the need to counteract the narrow and often stereotypical views that children and some educators, colleagues and families have about what they view to be appropriate behaviour for boys and girls. As one director of an early childhood setting states: 'Children may not verbally express their views about what women and men should do but they certainly make play choices according to gender stereotypes quite often.'

Despite this support for the incorporation of gender equity into programmes, it does not necessarily translate into what individual educators do in practice. In our research, only about half of educators acknowledged that they regularly included a focus on gender issues in their programming and pedagogical practices. In Davies and Robinson's research (2012), the focus on gender and gender equity was minimal and was not an issue that was regularly included in programming or considered in pedagogical practices. In our research, it was not a commitment to an ongoing process of initiating individual or institutional change, but rather it was about addressing problems as they arose or when recognized by educators and other colleagues. For example, as one educator commented: 'We deal with gender discrimination wherever possible; we address issues as they arise.' This was echoed by another educator, who pointed out: 'We ask children about their views and explain things when we hear discrimination between girls and boys.'

Consequently, in many early childhood settings, dealing with gender issues is often unplanned, spontaneous and left to the commitment of individual educators, who have a particular interest in the area – a point reiterated by Davies and Robinson (2012). Most settings have a policy that deals with gender equity, but it is often encompassed within a broader 'umbrella' policy, such as an anti-bias policy, dealing with diversity more generally. Specific social justice or equity issues such as gender can often get lost in broader anti-bias policies if they are not generally considered a problem or a focus of interest for individual settings. They also provide an opportunity not to directly address specific controversial issues that settings choose not to deal with, such as gender and sexuality issues, like same-sex families.

In recent years, critical research has highlighted the need to recognize the relations of power that operate around gender and view children as active agents in the construction of their own gendered identities (Huuki and Renold 2015; Robinson and Davies 2015). Still, many educators in our research rely on gender equity strategies that focus solely on challenging children's stereotypical gendered behaviours, and expanding their views about what roles they can take up as boys and girls. This approach was largely facilitated through supporting children to participate in non-traditional play; encouraging both boys and girls to spend time in various gendered spaces or play centres that are usually dominated by one gender or the other; and through different role modelling displayed in posters and books depicting males and females engaging in non-traditional gendered roles. The following examples given by educators highlight this particular approach.

> Boys and girls are given the same opportunities and are encouraged to participate and be active in all centres, for example, home corner, beauty salons, dress-ups, woodwork.

> Staff challenge children's stereotypes/bias through resources like books and posters showing males and females doing non-traditional activities.

> Challenging children with their beliefs that pink and blue are not for girls and boys respectively and that doctors, nurses, teachers, police can be both male and female.

> We set up activities in a way that both genders play; if boys do not play with home corner we programme blocks in it.

The last comment above highlights a particular strategy often utilized in this approach. When girls or boys do not take up the option of engaging in non-traditional gendered play areas, traditional gendered toys or equipment are used to entice children into these spaces. In the example given, boys are lured into home corner through the use of blocks; in another example, trucks and cars were placed in the shopkeeping area to encourage boys' participation. As pointed out previously, sex-role and socialization theories, which underpin these approaches, do not provide a framework for informing practices that consider children as being active in the process of gender construction and do not allow for an understanding of the way that power works in children's everyday lives. In these approaches, adults are the agents of the resocialization attempts on children's gendered practices, while children are expected to passively take on the new ways of being with minimal resistance. There is also no consideration of how children actively resist taking up different ways of being masculine or feminine subjects if it is not part of how they see the world and how they fit in to this larger picture as gendered, classed, racialized, sexualized beings for instance. Children are constantly negotiating the various gendered discourses that are culturally available to them; either resisting or taking up different meanings of being boys or girls, depending on their perceived investments in taking up particular ways of being over others.

As the comments above indicate, challenging children's stereotyped perceptions of gender and gender roles was the main means through which gender equity practices were instigated. Some educators pointed out that they often invited parents who were involved in non-traditional gender roles and occupations to talk with children and to act as role models. This approach to gender equity highlights the importance of equal access and opportunities not only in the public spheres of work and politics, but also in the private realm of the family and personal relationships. The sharing of roles associated with caring and nurturing of children and home duties, traditionally perceived as 'women's work', is considered crucial to gender equity in both the public and private realms. The gender equity areas believed to be most important to address with children by the majority of the participants reflected this perspective, and related to gender stereotyping, and sharing 'mothering' and household duties.

However, the philosophical and practical approach to gender equity outlined above has been criticized for its lack of recognition of power in gendered relationships, in terms of both the micro everyday interactions and macro structural levels in society. Increasing women's access to non-traditional roles and increasing men's shared involvement in the home through equal opportunity legislation is important but it has not to date changed the overall power imbalances operating between men and women in various contexts. This point is best reflected in the words of a boy aged 5, who commented to one of our early childhood students during her practical experience, 'A lady might be able to be a postman on a bike, but they aren't as good or fast as a man.'

Many early childhood educators encourage boys into the traditionally female-dominated area of 'home corner' or girls into the male-dominated 'block corner', but do not critically challenge children's gendered ways of making meaning in their everyday interactions in or out of these areas. In some instances, as pointed out earlier, if boys do not actively engage in 'home corner' experiences, then blocks are programmed into that area to encourage their participation. Unfortunately, there seems to be limited deconstruction of the gendered power relations operating in such instances, consequently the status quo reigns despite the change of environment and good intentions.

Deconstructing gender and power at all levels of society is crucial to building children's understandings of gender discrimination and inequality. However, among the participants generally in this research, a dominant perspective prevailed that tended to distance children from the broader social inequities that are experienced by individuals, families or minority groups. The links between the discrimination experienced by individuals and broader structural power relations were viewed as less significant and relevant to children's lives. Consequently, children are not challenged, for example, to critically consider the links between stereotyping, gender roles in the home, violence perpetrated against women, children and some men, and the discrimination experienced by women and girls in various contexts, beyond the early childhood setting and the family. Therefore, children do not gain an adequate understanding of the way that gender power relations are intimately inherent in socio-cultural, political and economic structures in society, and how individual practices and interactions on a daily level contribute to these gendered structures, including those in which children are engaged. This practice of distancing children from broader social issues is often founded in dominant social discourses that perpetuate developmentalist understandings of children (see Chapter 3), which view and construct them as being 'too young' to understand or 'too innocent' to be subjected to the burdens of what are perceived to be adults' concerns.

Heterosexualization and heteronormativity in early childhood education

Robinson (2013) argues that heteronormativity in early childhood education is rendered largely invisible through the hegemonic discourses that constitute understandings of childhood and sexuality. The presumption that children are asexual, 'too young' and 'too innocent' to understand sexuality is contradicted by the fact that the construction of heterosexuality and heterosexual desire is an integral part of children's everyday experiences, including their early education; for example, children's literature widely used in early childhood education constantly reinforces a heterosexual narrative (Cahill and Theilheimer 1999; Theilheimer and Cahill 2001). This process of heterosexualization continues largely unnoticed and unchallenged unless it is perceived to be working ineffectively – that is, when the boundaries of compulsory heterosexuality (Rich 1980) seem to be crossed, and when children's heterogendered constructions seem to be unacceptably and inappropriately slipping beyond the norms.

It seems that it is through such transgressions that children learn lessons about what is acceptable and what is intolerable. For example, parents are often concerned about their sons dressing in women's clothes, fearing that this behaviour may lead to homosexuality. It is important to point out that research shows that this is not necessarily the case. According to Lev (2004), children and young people who transgress gender norms are likely to have one of three outcomes: they will mature into heteronormative, gender typical adults; they will grow up to have same-sex attractions; or they will identify as transgender or trans-sexual. Stone Fish and Harvey (2005) point out that heterosexual adults are rarely studied to see whether they report gender atypical behaviours in childhood. Research conducted by Robinson and Davies (2010) investigating adult reflections of gender performances in childhood and sexual orientation in adulthood indicated that some who were gender non-conforming in childhood and adulthood did identify as lesbian. However, there were also some women who were highly invested in femininity in childhood and adulthood who also identified as lesbian. Educators can problematize and discourage young children's desires for same-sex relations if they transgress from what is perceived to be normalized heterosexual gendered behaviour. Wallis and VanEvery (2000) describe an instance of this, where a young boy was actively discouraged by educators from articulating his wish to 'marry' the person he loved best, which was his best male friend.

Play is a critical site of gender construction, but it is equally a significant site in which heteronormative discourses operate. Mock weddings, mothers and fathers, chasing and kissing games, and girlfriends/boyfriends are all examples of young children's narratives of their experiences in early childhood education. Such activities are often viewed as a natural part of children's everyday lives, and are rarely questioned or thought about by educators. Robinson's (2013) research on children's gendered and sexual subjectivities, which involved interviews, focus groups and surveys with parents/guardians and educators, and interviews and focus groups with children aged 3–12 years, highlights this process. Robinson's research highlighted how children engaged in heteronormative gendered children's play, daily conversations and interactions about liking/loving someone, 'special' relationships, kissing, being mothers and fathers, having babies, setting up house, and mock weddings (Robinson and Davies 2015). Alex, a boy aged 9 years old, in a conversation about marriage and relationships, commented that girls and boys in his friendship group sometimes argue about who they are going to marry:

Alex:	We have fights saying who we're going to marry when we're older.
Interviewer:	Really?
Alex:	At school we have like fights. We have fights like the boys say I'm marrying – like the boys say I'm going to marry this girl and then this girl says no I'm marrying this boy and the boy is like no, no I'm marrying this girl.

Ruby, aged 5, talks about being in love and how this is played out in their daily lives at school:

Ruby:	Some of my friends keep falling in love with Tim.
Interviewer:	Who's Tim?
Ruby:	He's like – this guy he's like, he's my friend. I used to fall in love with him.
Facilitator:	Why aren't you in love with him any more?
Ruby:	Then I fell in love with Harry and he's gone now because he's gone to the mountains.
Interviewer:	What does it mean that you've fallen in love with him?
Ruby:	I'm like – on the first day that we both really, really, really happy on that day. Because, guess what? I'm really good at singing the national anthem, but we did get separated because when we were talking when Mr Peters was talking – our teacher said Ruby can you please move away . . . we still make each other happy the whole day, and then we started play- ing at recess and lunchtime. Then on the third day, he says I don't love you any more.
Interviewer:	Oh why did he say that?
Ruby:	I don't know. Because we're not supposed to kiss at school, and we're not supposed to – we're not supposed to like say that.
Interviewer:	That you're in love?
Ruby:	Like we're in love, because like we shouldn't say that because other people will say ah, Ruby was in love with Harry.

Children's play practices are rarely considered part of the normalization of the construction of heterosexual desire and the inscription of heterogendered subjectivities in young children. These heterosexualized activities are not linked to understandings of sexuality, but are seen as 'children being children', a natural part of growing up. Epstein (1995) has argued that the relationship between gender and sexuality is critical to an understanding of sexism and heterosexism in education, pointing out that sexism cannot be understood without an analysis of its relationship with heterosexuality.

The media, popular culture and children's literature play a major role in the perpetuation of heteronormativity in children's everyday lives. Children's literature and films provide numerous examples of the ways in which children's cultures and children's gendered lives are heterosexualized. Giroux (1995: 1) argues that:

> Children's culture is a sphere where entertainment, advocacy, and pleasure meet to construct conceptions of what it means to be a child occupying a combination of gender, racial, and class positions in society through which one defines oneself in relation to a myriad of others.

Robinson (2005c) points out that an examination of children's classic books, such as *Beauty and the Beast* (Disney 1994a), *Anastasia* (Krulik 1997) and *The Little Mermaid* (Disney 1994b), demonstrates the pervasiveness of the fantasized heterosexual happy ending that is about not just constructing gendered identities, but a specific type of gender performance that is heterosexual. Deconstructing children's popular cultural texts provides a critical context in which to disrupt normalizing discourses that perpetuate gender inequalities. The construction of heterosexuality is part of children's everyday lives, including what is learned in their early educational experiences; however, it is rarely ever noticed, and almost never ever thought about (Robinson 2005c). It is important that early childhood educators refocus their critical lens around construction of gender in early childhood in order to understand how gender is heterosexualized through heteronormative daily practices and interactions with peers, family, in schools and other institutions working with children.

Implications for policy and practice

The issues raised throughout this chapter have important implications for the way that gender issues and gender equity are approached in early childhood education. Educators are in a positive position to provide opportunities for children to experiment with different performances of gender through play without feeling like that it is taboo and that they are doing something wrong.

Gender equity policies in childhood education and community services are important documents, which provide direction for dealing with gender in settings and for educating staff, children and families about significant gender issues. It is important to review current policies for sexist language or normalizing discourses that restrict and regulate gendered identities to narrow definitions of what it means to be a girl or boy, woman or man. It is important that settings incorporate a non-sexist language policy that involves staff, children and their families. As with all policies, it is important to include staff, children and their families in developing and revising policies. It is also critical to monitor, evaluate and review policies on a regular basis, and to have a policy on supporting gender diverse and transgender children and their families. This will need to be developed in consultation with families and/or professionals that work with children who are gender diverse or transgender.

A critical understanding of how gender is culturally constructed is vital, particularly when working in diverse communities. Childhood educators and community-based professionals need to be reflexive of their positions, in regards to gender and gender equity, to ensure sensitivity and fairness are considered. It is important that educators encourage family involvement in their gender equity strategies. Many parents are not familiar with how gender is constructed in childhood, and often resort to biological explanations of the gendered differences that they perceive among their children. It is important that gender education programmes are also designed to meet the needs of parents; for example, it is critical to highlight the liberatory potential of children's positioning in non-normative gender discourses, counteracting fears that it impacts future sexualities. Families' awareness of gender issues, including the issues faced by gender diverse and transgender children and their families, can be fostered through community seminars, parent–teacher nights, informal meetings, newsletters, information sheets and organization of different displays (for example, domestic violence issues; International Women's Day information).

Viewing children as active participants in the construction of their own gendered identities and in the regulation of how others do gender is an important theoretical framework from which to begin educating children about gender issues. Current approaches that focus on disrupting stereotypical gender roles do not challenge the power relations that operate around gendered identities. Incorporating a deconstructive approach to children's understandings of gender encourages children's critical thinking around the issues, and focuses on new and different possibilities of doing gender. Working with children to recognize the liberatory potentials in taking up non-normative discourses of gender is important as it increases the options that they feel they have in their lives and disrupts the notion of difference as deviance. Deconstructing children's play themes, popular culture texts, and utilizing texts with different storylines, provide children with new, liberatory and non-traditional gender subject positions to consider. The latter point may mean increasing the resources that educators have access to that provide storylines with non-normative gender subject positions. Feminist post-structuralist perspectives point out that it is important to begin to give alternative discourses of gender status and power, so children will see some personal investments in desiring to take them up.

Addressing diversity and difference, and engaging in equity and social justice education is far more successful if a whole institutional approach is taken to educate management committees, staff, children and families about equity issues. Doing this work is often not easy, especially when individual subjects are located in different discourses of gender. Some of these discourses may not contribute to a different and more equitable understanding of gendered relationships, but rather perpetuate differential treatment for males and females. Different readings of gender may cause some resistance among staff, families and children, but it is important to continue to work through these issues together. Opening up a dialogue that respects different opinions and encourages all to contribute is an important foundation from which to find a point of reconciliation that works in favour of equity and social justice.

Conclusion

Young children learn quickly that if they do not get their gender 'right' and conform to 'appropriate' gender behaviours, they can be ostracized and bullied by their peers, and can be punished in different ways by adults, including their parents. Young boys, for example, who do not like to engage in what are considered typical masculine behaviours, such as aggressive play fighting, or competitive group sports such as rugby, but rather prefer reading, dancing or even playing with girls, can experience a difficult time in their schooling, which can have long-term effects on their emotional and physical well-being. However, children's transgressions from what is generally perceived to be appropriate masculinity and femininity are most likely to be punished in various ways rather than encouraged. Even if any of these young boys do choose to identify as gay in their lives, the consequences of non-conformity are already well understood. The association of violence with performances of hegemonic masculinity has implications not just for those who identify as gay or lesbian, or those perceived to be so by others, but also for women, whose lives are emotionally, physically, socially and economically affected by experiences of sexual violence, sexual harassment or domestic violence. Feminist poststructuralist perspectives remind us that there are multiple ways of doing masculinity, but how these are culturally read and interpreted constitutes the inequalities reflected in broad social relationships in society.

Normalizing discourses of gender diminish the options and choices children have in their lives. Their perceptions of appropriate masculine and feminine behaviours can restrict what they choose to learn, what activities and sports they choose to participate in, how they interact with other children, the feelings that they perceive they can openly display, what they see to be their choices of potential careers, how they envisage their futures, and so on. The construction of gender is about constructing social relationships that impact on us all. Educating children and families around the liberatory potentials of taking up non-normalizing discourses of gender is important for providing children and adults with greater flexibility and options in their lives on many different levels.

Recommended reading

Meyer, E. and Sansfaçon, A.P. (eds) (2014) *Supporting Transgender and Gender Creative Youth: Schools, Families, and Communities in Action*. New York: Peter Lang.

Osgood, J. (2014) Playing with gender: making space for posthuman childhood(s), in J. Moyles, J. Payler and J. Georgeson (eds) *Early Years Foundations: Critical Issues*. Maidenhead: Open University Press.

Robinson, K.H. and Davies, C. (2015) Children's gendered and sexual cultures: desiring and regulating recognition through life markers of marriage, love and relationships, in E. Renold, J. Ringrose and D.R. Egan (eds) *Children, Sexuality & Sexualization*. London: Palgrave: 174–190.

10

Childhood and sexuality

Introduction

Over the past two decades there has been an increased emphasis in research on childhood and sexuality that has highlighted the importance of addressing sexuality issues with young children in their early education (Casper *et al.* 1998; Cahill and Theilheimer 1999; Robinson and Jones Díaz 2000; Kissen 2002; Robinson 2002, 2005c, 2005d, 2013; Renold 2005, 2006; Robinson and Davies 2008; Davies and Robinson 2010; Blaise 2009, 2010, 2013; Surtees and Gunn 2010; DePalma 2013; Gunn 2015; Robinson and Davies 2015). This research has increased awareness of the socio-cultural construction of children's sexual subjectivity; the relevance of addressing sexuality diversity, same-sex families, and lesbian and gay equity issues with children; and the importance of children's access to sexuality education. Robinson (2012, 2013) has argued that these areas are central to children's sexual citizenship. However, despite this research, and the socio-cultural, political and legal gains in recent times associated with same-sex relationships, including the legalization of same-sex marriage in many Western countries, addressing these issues with children continues to be viewed as controversial and problematic. This stems largely from the socio-cultural taboos associated with childhood and sexuality, which have led to strict regulations of children's access to knowledge about sexuality (see also the discussion in Chapter 3).

Consequently, these social advances are not well reflected in policies, practices and curricula in early childhood education or in primary schools, nor in the policies and practices of community services working with children and families (Cloughessy and Waniganayake 2014). There are cases in Australia where parents in same-sex families are still challenging the non-inclusive language used in registration forms in some educational institutions. That is, the names of *mother* and *father*, rather than *parent* or *guardian*, are requested on forms. Fears and anxieties still prevail for many working in early childhood education, community organizations and schools associated with potential parental and community backlash, especially from conservative religious groups, for addressing sexuality and same-sex families in children's early education (DePalma and Atkinson 2009; Flores 2014). Effective social justice pedagogies, policies and practices represent and empower children and families from diverse cultural backgrounds, as well as foster an appreciation of the diversity that exists in society.

Sexuality is not just relevant to early childhood in terms of building children's awareness and respect for cultural and family diversity, but it is also pertinent to an understanding of the construction of children's sexual subjectivities in the early years. Like other aspects of children's identity – for example, gender, ethnicity, 'race' and social class – children's sexual identity is also socially constructed, a point that is discussed in depth in this chapter. Understanding how children's sexual subjectivities intersect with or are influenced by their gender, ethnicity, social class, and so on, is also important. From very early ages children are actively involved in constructing their sexuality, primarily within the context of their heteronormative understandings of gender (Renold 2005, 2006; Surtees 2005, 2006; Robinson and Davies 2008, 2015; Blaise 2010; Surtees and Gunn 2010; Robinson 2013). Access to sexuality education is critical in order for children to have a greater understanding of who they are as sexual and gendered subjects. Children's access to sexuality knowledge can have important implications for children's health and well-being, for developing children's understandings of diversity and difference, and for building ethical and respectful relationships early in life.

This chapter provides an overview of some of the main issues relevant to childhood and sexuality and to children's sexual citizenship (see Robinson 2013). The following areas are addressed: theoretical understandings of sexuality; the relationship between sexuality and gender; dominant discourses around childhood and sexuality; children's sexual citizenship; the regulation of children's access to knowledge of sexuality, and the implication this has for children's health and well-being; the construction of children's sexual subjectivities, and how children are active agents in this process; the role children, parents and educators play in the constitution of children as heteronormative subjects; and homophobia and heterosexism in early childhood education. The chapter concludes with a discussion of the implications that all of these major issues have for policy and practice, pedagogy, working with families, and building respectful and ethical relationships early in children's lives.

Feminist poststructuralism and sexual identities

Feminist poststructuralism is one of the primary theoretical frameworks informing the discussion in this chapter. In this perspective, sexual identity is considered to be a social construction, rather than biologically determined. Sexual identity is viewed as constituted within discourse and as being fluid, flexible and changing. Within the cultural binary heterosexual/homosexual, the normative sexual subject is constituted as heterosexual while non-heterosexual subjects are often constituted as deviant and abnormal (Butler 1990; de Lauretis 1994). Utilizing Foucault's (1977) concept of 'regimes of truth', the normalization of heterosexuality and the social sanction of this view as a 'truth' is discursively constituted through the everyday language, interactions, practices and policies operating in institutions such as the family, schools, the church and government at the macro levels of society. The normalization of heterosexuality is also constituted through the everyday practices of individuals; that is, through the taking up of discourses, which constitute heterosexuality as normal and non-heterosexuality as the abnormal Other. Individual subjects constitute, enact and embody their sexual identities through their location within particular discourses of sexuality that are available to them. As active agents in the construction of their own sexual identities, individual subjects reflexively negotiate the different discourses of sexuality available, taking up those that are perceived to provide more personal investments for them at that point in time. However, heteronormativity operates both consciously and unconsciously as a powerful regime of truth, as indicated previously. Notions of 'choice' become problematic, as can be seen from the consequences of taking up a subject position within a discourse of sexuality that is not socially sanctioned. Foucault's *History of Sexuality Volume 1* (1978) provides a critical investigation of the way in which the sexual identities of individual subjects are constituted within and 'governed' by the discourses operating in society. This includes the discursive construction of the homosexual Other and the consequent policing of *all* sexualities. Foucault argues that powerful techniques of surveillance that are operating in societal institutions, including the government itself, lead to the internalization of self-disciplining techniques by individual subjects. In these ways individuals take up the culturally coded ways of being through their embodiment of the exercise of power at work in and on them through socially sanctioned discourses.

Queer theory and sexual identity

Queer theory has also influenced the approach taken to sexuality in this discussion. This theory stems largely from poststructuralist theoretical perspectives. It reinforces the notion that identities are not fixed or stable, but rather are shifting, contradictory, dynamic and constructed. Queer theory upholds that all identities are performances, and challenges normalizing practices, particularly in terms of sexuality and the heteronormative constructions of gender. It challenges the unquestion-able, natural and normal positioning of heterosexuality as the superior sexuality and the othering of non-heterosexual identities, which is constituted within the cultural binary heterosexual us/homosexual them (see Jagose 1996; Sullivan 2003). The term 'queer' encompasses those who feel 'marginalized by mainstream sexuality' (Morris 2000: 20), including those who see themselves as heterosexual but challenge the conformity constituted and enforced in hegemonic discourses of heterosexuality. Ultimately, queer theory disrupts the notion that one's gender and sex-uality are inherently fixed in one's biological sexed body, upholding the pluralities of sexuality and the multiplicity of gender. Thus, this perspec-tive provides a critical theoretical lens through which one can begin to see the everyday processes of heteronormativity.

Judith Butler's (1990, 1993) work on gender and sexuality has been highly influential for queer theorists. Her concept of performativity (see Chapter 9) advances the argument that gender is articulated through socially endorsed performances constituted in discourses of what it means to be a girl, boy, woman or man. The very fact that these performances are embodied and repeated so frequently results in the appearance that gender is natural and linked to one's biology. The authenticity of how one does one's gender is linked to how others read one's performance. This operates in the same way for sexuality, which is perceived to be socially constructed (Sedgwick 1990; Britzman 1997) rather than linked to biological bodies or fixed gender identities. Performativity opens up the possibility of there being new and different ways of performing gender that operate outside the rigid boundaries of the socially sanctioned cultural binary of masculine/feminine. For queer theorists, it is the visibility of the Other that troubles the normative cultures underpinned by such cultural binaries, allowing a critical space in which individual subjects can take up different ways of being in the world as gendered and sexualized subjects.

Other theoretical perspectives on sexual identity

The following common and competing theories on sexuality have under-pinned many of the social and institutional practices that have managed children's sexuality historically and still do today in some cases. These theories of sexuality have had different impacts on children's lives.

Biological determinism

This perspective views sexuality as originating from one's biological make-up. Some researchers are currently trying to find evidence of a 'gay' gene, and exploring possible brain differences between homosexuals and heterosexuals. However, there is no evidence at this point to support this perspective. Biological determinism is often used to support gay rights in as much as people who identify as gay are perceived to not have a choice in their sexuality. Thus, their rights are viewed within the perspective that 'they can't help the way they are' and therefore need support to live their lives in the most equitable ways possible. Feminist poststructuralists are critical of perspectives that fix sexuality in biology, as they view sexuality as a social construction and as being fluid, flexible and changing.

Social constructionism

Within the perspective of social **constructionism** sexual identity is perceived to be influenced primarily by the values and practices of the cultures and society in which we live. As in the social construction of gender identity, individual subjects are 'socialized' into sexual identities that their culture defines as 'normal' and 'appropriate'. Heterosexuality is generally upheld as the norm, while non-heterosexuality is constructed as 'deviant' and 'abnormal'. Sexuality in this perspective becomes a 'choice' in that one can choose to conform to society's values and practices, or resist and engage in non-heterosexual relationships. However, the idea of 'choice' must be problematized in that there are many different social controls, such as discrimination, threats or actual violence, and potential rejections from families and friends, among others, operating to make individual subjects conform to the normalizing practices of the culture. Although feminist poststructuralists and queer theorists have some similar perspectives on the social construction of sexuality, they challenge the passiveness of socialization theory and sex role theory. That is, feminist poststructuralists view children as active agents in the process of sexuality formation, and emphasize discursive and material power relations in this process.

Freud and psychoanalysis

Freud's theory of sexuality was based on his work, primarily with middle-class women, as a therapist and physician in Vienna in the late 1890s and early 1900s. Freud proposed that infantile sexuality was central in the formation of individual subjects and argued that instinctual drives encountered by the infantile body, essentially from the mother (for example, suckling, kissing, touching), resulted in the child recognizing the origins of and experiencing pleasure and desire, which are then carried unconsciously and consciously by the infant throughout life. Thus, Freud believed that human culture stemmed from our 'convoluted attempts to contain and redirect the energies of sex' (Bhattacharyya 2002: 5). In this process, socialization became focused on redeploying and redirecting our selfish devotion to physical pleasure. Consequently, children's sexuality is interrupted (or becomes latent) and their desires are redirected to more socially accepted practices and objects, learning to achieve satisfaction through other means. However, Freud points out that this disciplining of sexual impulses (or repression) results in multiple and complex neuroses that signify human existence (Bhattacharyya 2002). Freud's theory of sexual identity has been criticized for its heterosexism, through the ways in which he associated neuroses with, among other things, the failure of individuals to conform to the socially sanctioned practices of heterosexuality.

Childhood, innocence and sexuality

The social construction of childhood is discussed in depth in Chapter 3, but there are several points relevant to this discussion of childhood and sexuality that need to be reiterated here. First, feminist poststructuralists and other critical socio-cultural theorists have critiqued fixed humanist biological perspectives of a universal childhood, underpinned by mainstream child developmentalist theory (James and Prout 1990; Kontopodis, Wulf and Fichtner 2011). These scholars stress the importance of understanding how childhood is socially constructed. Second, in humanist discourse, childhood and adulthood are constituted within a binary relationship in which they are defined in opposition to each other. That is, what it means to be a child is perceived to be inherently different from what it means to be an adult (James and Prout 1990; Cannella 1997; Gittins 1998; Dahlberg *et al.* 1999). This oppositional understanding of childhood and adulthood is reinforced by mainstream developmentalist theory, such as that of Piaget, in which the process of children's development and learning is perceived to be fixed according to a linear, predetermined set of biological stages that correlate to chronological age. Third, this rigid binary logic underpins much of the common-sense understandings of childhood, perpetuating the belief that the differences between adults and children are logical, biological and natural, influencing the ways in which children and adults are viewed in the world. This binary thinking artificially creates a 'world of the child' and a 'world of adults', which can generally be perceived as mutually exclusive (Gittins 1998). Finally, childhood innocence (especially sexual innocence) is the ultimate signifier of what it means to be a child. Generally equated with children's age (or in mainstream developmentalist terms – physical, emotional and cognitive immaturity), childhood innocence is constituted as a natural stage of embodied childhood. How childhood innocence has been discursively utilized to: define and sometimes prolong childhood; preserve adult/child binary relationships of power, and regulate children's and adult's behaviours; maintain the hegemony of heteronormative subjects; and to act as a powerful social control, is often overlooked (Taylor 2010; Faulkner 2011; Robinson 2013).

Sexuality, like childhood, has traditionally been viewed as being fixed, biologically determined and linked to developmentalist theory. Physiological sexual maturity in particular is represented as the boundary between adulthood and childhood. In a post-Freudian era, sexuality is largely considered to begin at puberty and mature in adulthood. Children's embodied sexual immaturity is equated with childhood innocence. However, Sigmund Freud's (1976 [1905]) theory of the proto-sexual polymorphous child offers a counter-discourse to the notion that children's sexuality is absent or dormant. Within Freudian theory children have an active sexuality that needs to be expressed, and childhood is viewed as centrally constructed around a flexible sexuality, a polymorphous perversity. Freud argued that, prior to children's understandings of social norms, they found erotic pleasure and sexual gratification in any part of the body. This sexual behaviour was deemed perverse in adults. Once children learned social norms these behaviours were generally suppressed, resulting in the repression of sexual feelings (Robinson and Davies 2015).

Sexuality within poststructuralist and queer theoretical perspectives is considered to be a fluid, non-linear, multifaceted, complex, contradictory and unstable relationship that can vary across cultures and over historical periods of time, according to the discourses available (Foucault 1978; Weeks 1986; Butler 1990; Britzman 1997). Sexuality is imbued with relations of power. As Jeffrey Weeks (1986: 25) points out:

> Sexuality is something which society produces in complex ways. It is a result of diverse social practices that give meaning to human activities, of social definitions and self-definitions, of struggles between those who have power to define and regulate, and those who resist. Sexuality is not a given, it is a product of negotiation, struggle and human agency.

Sexuality is socially and culturally constituted, with desire constructed and policed through powerful societal discourses (for example, particular religious and legal discourses), and social practices that are institutionally and individually supported at both the micro and macro levels in society. However, just as gender is made to appear as being from nature and biology, so is sexuality, with the relationship between the two viewed as symmetrical. Judith Butler (1990) points out that sex/gender/sexuality are socially organized and aligned with biological sex, a process in which sexual desire and gender expression are conflated and heteronormalized. Wilton (1996: 127) states that, 'This profoundly ideological notion of complementary gendered polarity – heteropolarity – has become the mystified and naturalised organising principle which saturates Western culture, structuring thought and social organisation around notions of binarism, complementarity, unidirectionality and polarity.' Through this process of normalization, heterosexuality is upheld as the natural, instinctual, desired, appropriate sexuality, with all other deviations from this behaviour considered unnatural and abnormal. Thus, sexuality, like gender, is perceived as relational, shifting, changing, flexible and fluid; it is produced by society in complex ways, through diverse social practices, and individual and social definitions. As Weeks (1986: 25) comments, 'Sexuality is not a given, it is a product of negotiation, struggle and human agency.'

It is in the context of the social construction of sexuality and childhood that the precarious and volatile relationship between childhood and sexuality emerges. Linked with mainstream developmentalist perspectives of childhood, and reinforced by conservative and religious discourse, children are often viewed as being asexual, 'too young' and 'too innocent' to understand sexuality. Through these relations of power, children's sexual subjectivity is dismissed and sexuality is constituted as an aspect of adult subjectivity. The fact that sexuality is predominantly narrowly viewed and spoken about in terms of the physical act of having sex, rather than an aspect of identity, similar to one's gender, ethnicity or social class, for example, serves to intensify the perception that sexuality is irrelevant or dangerous to children. According to Pepper Schwartz and Dominic Cappello (2001), sexuality is the sum total of our sexual desire, behaviour and self-identity. Deborah Britzman (2000: 37) points out that sexuality is 'a human right of free association' and a *force* that is vital to human passion, interest, explorations and disappointments. Children have a sexual subjectivity and share in their own ways the experience of this *force* in their lives. Sexuality is viewed in this discussion as being experienced and expressed in multiple ways across the life span, which includes the lives of children. Not only has childhood been defined by adults for adults, but so has children's relationship to sexuality (Silin 1995; Gittins 1998; Robinson 2002). Adults have defined what children should or should not be, and should or should not know.

Children's sexual subjectivity

Although the dominant discourse of childhood constitutes sexuality as being irrelevant to and developmentally inappropriate for children, research with children is suggesting something very different (Allen and Ingram 2015; Kromidas 2015; Renold, Ringrose and Egan 2015). In recent years there has been an increased focus on research investigating children's sexual subjectivities, highlighting not only the ways in which children constitute themselves as sexual subjects, but also through the practices of parents and educators (Renold 2005; Blaise 2010; Robinson 2013; Robinson and Davies 2015). What has been commonly found across this research is that children's sexual subjectivities are constituted largely through the social construction of children as gendered subjects in the early years. That is, the construction of gender in children's lives needs be understood in terms of how this process is heteronormalized through children's everyday practices and interactions with others (see the in-depth discussion in regards to gender in Chapter 9). Children's perceptions of sexuality encompass a broad range of behaviours including, but not limited to, having a special person that you love and are 'in love' with, having a boyfriend or girlfriend, marriage, kissing and having children. These life markers are generally viewed through heteronormative discourses of gender in which heterosexuality is assumed and normalized. Mobilizing discourses of boyfriends or girlfriends, children generally play out or rehearse narratives of heteronormative romantic love in everyday interactions with children, especially in play activities such as mock weddings, mothers and fathers, doctors and nurses, and chase and kiss (Renold 2005; Blaise 2010; Bhana 2013; Robinson 2013; Robinson and Davies 2015). In Robinson's research conducted with primary school children, focusing on building ethical relationships early in life through an exploration of the construction of children's gender and sexual subjectivities, young children were asked about relationships. Having a boyfriend or girlfriend was common and such relationships were part of children's everyday activities in the primary school environment (Renold 2005; Blaise 2010). A 6-year-old boy, Ethan, comments:

Researcher:	Do you know anyone that has a boyfriend or a girlfriend at school?
Ethan:	Yes, and I saw them kissing in . . .
Researcher:	Did you?
Ethan:	Yes, down in [the] garden.
Researcher:	So a boy named Bob and a girl named Patty.
Ethan:	There's two Bobs at school and Patty's little sister, she's in, the little sister is in Year [2] and her name is Pip.
Researcher:	So they're boyfriend and girlfriend?
Ethan:	Yes.

Researcher:	Have you ever had a boyfriend or a girlfriend?
Ethan:	Sometimes, but actually before I had a lot, about up to maybe 15.
Researcher:	Really? Wow.
Ethan:	Then it went back down to seven and at the moment it's only one.
Researcher:	So you have them all at the same time?
Ethan:	Yes.
Researcher:	So what does it mean to be someone's boyfriend? What do you think that means?
Ethan:	[You] Like them.
Researcher:	So how do you know that you like them?
Ethan:	Because they're nice, look nice.

What is especially interesting about Ethan's comments is how 'liking' a girl (often more than one at a time!) is linked to girls' appearances, perpetuating the dominant discourse that girls' physical attraction is what counts in their relationships with boys.

Children are developing perceptions of self and about gender, sexuality and relationships through the discourses that they encounter prevailing in their everyday lives. They build knowledge about these aspects of life from the bits and pieces of information they receive from families, schooling, peers, media and popular culture. The concept of marriage is central to the constitution of many children's gendered and sexual subjectivities – that is, children's heteronormative readings of marriage. However, this is not surprising considering how pervasive the discourse of marriage is in children's lives and in broader society. As a parent commented in Robinson's research: 'It's like osmosis!' (Robinson 2013). Heteronormative readings of marriage are legitimized through family photographs, media, popular culture, adult practices and children's early educational experiences (Robinson and Davies 2015). For example, in some Australian early childhood settings, children's mock weddings have been turned into large-scale whole-setting celebrations, with special invitations sent to parents.

The concept of marriage for many children operates as a moral regulatory framework, legitimatizing sexual and romantic expressions of love and having children, intimacy, kissing, gendered and sexual relationships, and constructions of family (Robinson and Davies 2015). Most of the children in Robinson's research viewed marriage as the key signifier of the pathway to intimate relationships, in particular the right to kiss another person. For many children, marriage was the representation of adult maturity and the context in which intimate sexual relations and 'having babies' were enacted and legitimated. When asked about the meaning of weddings, one 6-year-old girl, Ella, commented: 'It means that you're getting married and you're about to have a baby.'

Children are often quick to police other children's transgressive gender behaviours, such as when a boy wishes to marry another boy in mock wedding play. As a result of the hegemony of heteronormative discourses played out in everyday lives, and through the regulatory practices of others, children learn quickly that transgressing heteronormative gender behaviours can have serious consequences. It is in the early years of children's lives that heteronormativity begins to take shape, feeding in to the homophobia and transphobia that are firmly entrenched in the schooling years and beyond. The construction of heterosexual identities and desire in early childhood is a socially sanctioned, integral part of children's everyday educational experiences (Renold 2005; Blaise 2010; Robinson 2013; Robinson and Davies 2015). However, children do have greater access to counter-narratives in more recent times through an increase in public recognition of same-sex relationships and marriage, through media and popular culture, and television series such as *Modern Family*, which features a range of family types, including gay fathers.

Children's sexual citizenship

There are many different forms of sexual citizenship, but 'all citizenship is sexual citizenship, in that the foundational tenets of being a citizen are all inflected by sexualities' (Bell and Binnie 2000: 10). However, sexual citizenship is a useful concept for specifically framing and articulating broad political issues associated with sexual identity, including those of children. As Robinson (2012, 2013) has argued, although children have a difficult relationship with both sexuality and citizenship, in that they are generally perceived to have little bearing on children's lives directly, sexual citizenship does have significant relevance to children. Sexual citizenship addresses a range of issues pertinent to the lives of children and their families. For example, the role love, family and the social play in people's lives (Berlant 1997; Richardson 1998; Weeks 1998), and the sexual citizen as a target of consumerism (Evans 1993), have considerable relevance to children and to childhood. In relation to the latter example, in the process of equating innocence with children's bodies, childhood and children have become fetishized and eroticized, placing children in a precarious position as sexualized subjects, vulnerable to the fetishes of some adults who use their power to abuse and exploit children for their own advantage (Kitzinger 1990; Elliott 1992; Faulkner 2011; Robinson 2013).

Love, family and social relationships are central to children's lives, but are experienced and negotiated by children in different ways. Love, desire and engaging in special relationships are not just the preroga- tive of being an adult, but are part of children's lives and the development of their sexual subjectivities. These relationships may be played out in different ways but the intensity of feelings, emotionally and physically, associated with these interactions can be intense. Learning to negotiate these relationships in ethical ways is a crucial aspect of children's agency, and these early experiences can have important implications for relation- ships throughout life.

Ideal norms of family life, perpetuated through hegemonic discourses of the nuclear family, exclude the experiences of many children who live in different family structures, including same-sex headed families. Broad socio-cultural political debates related to sexual citizenship, such as marriage equality, same-sex headed families and the barriers to equity experienced by those who are LGBTQ are concerns that impact many children directly. These issues impact all children through the strict cultural regulations associated with sexual orientation and gender identity expression regardless of how one identifies in terms of sexuality.

Many children and young people are actively engaged in acts of sexual citizenship demonstrated through their involvement in organizing and participating in schooling or community events that support sexuality and gender diversity. For example, 'Wear it Purple' day, when wearing a piece of purple clothing is a show of support for same-sex attracted and gender diverse young people, and a challenge to homophobic and transphobic harassment and violence. Other similar examples include participating in gay and lesbian events such as Pride Day, the Sydney Gay and Lesbian Mardi Gras or Diversity Day. The organization of Ally programmes in schools, where students of all sexual orientations and gender identities work together to advocate against homophobia and transphobia, is another act of sexual citizenship that many children and young people are engaged in.

Children's sexual citizenship is ultimately about: learning to become ethical gendered and sexual subjects, to respect others in intimate relationships and to understand the implications of consent; building respect for the gender and sexuality diversity that exists in life; having an awareness and understanding of the rights of sexual subjects; being supported in building confidence and resilience in order to become informed sexual subjects; building critical thinking skills and sexuality literacy; and fostering health and well-being. Children's and young people's access to sexuality education is central to sexual citizenship.

Children's access to sexuality education

As pointed out above, children are actively engaged in constituting themselves as sexual subjects. However, dominant discourses around childhood, sexuality and innocence are out of step with the reality of children's everyday lives as sexual and gendered subjects. The discourse of childhood innocence is central to the rigid restrictions placed on children's access to sexuality education. This regulation is generally considered to be in the 'best interests' of the child in order to 'protect' children, primarily to protect 'childhood innocence'. Sexuality education is constituted as being developmentally inappropriate for young children. Critiquing the concept of 'age appropriate' in relation to children's access to sexuality knowledge, Sara McClelland and L.E. Hunter (2013: 61) describe the term as an 'empty signifier' that is 'often beyond the scope of critique'. They point out:

> Deployments of age appropriateness obscure processes of history, politics, social construction, and personal opinion, and insert, instead, a common sense appeal for an agreed upon boundary that is created and maintained, but without structure and often without merit. Appropriateness, as an idea, assumes and pays homage to an omniscient arbiter of right and wrong – an arbiter who is nameless and formless, and as a result, even more powerful in its declarations of appropriate and inappropriate. (2013: 61–62)

The discourses that underpin the regulation of children's access to sexuality education have also significantly influenced what information parents provide children and at what age. Parents often feel that they are under the *gaze* of not just *officials* (e.g. educators, community and welfare professionals), but more importantly of other parents, who can be quick to make judgements about other parents' practices. Parents who provide their young children with sexuality information, generally deemed developmentally inappropriate, often do not talk about it with other parents, and tell their children not to discuss it with other kids or adults (Robinson 2013). This surveillance of behaviours and silencing of open discussions with children emphasizes the taboos around sexuality and reinforces that children cannot talk with adults about these issues. It is the fears around adults' sexual behaviours that are foundational to the panic associated with children's sexuality (Fine and McClelland 2006; McClelland and Hunter 2013).

Comprehensive sexuality education is a broad term that encompasses knowledge of intimacy, relationships, bodies, desire, reproduction, gender and sexual ethics, sexual orientation, social and political issues

226 DIVERSITY AND DIFFERENCE IN CHILDHOOD

about sexual and gender diversity, and sexual health and well-being. These issues are deemed by some adults to be irrelevant or dangerous to children. However, research with children shows that these issues are as integral to children's gender and sexual subjectivities as they are to those of adults (Blaise 2005; Renold 2005; Robinson and Davies 2010; Bhana 2014). The denial of children's access to sexuality education is also linked to some adults' fears that providing children or adolescents with sexual knowledge will directly result in 'causing' youth to have sex prematurely (McClelland and Hunter 2013). However, research refutes this fear, pointing out that access to comprehensive sexuality education actually prolongs the time until young people engage in their first sexual encounter with another person (Levine 2002).

The regulation of children's access to sexuality education is especially strict in terms of information about same-sex relationships and the issues encountered by gays and lesbians. In fact, moral panic often results when children's access to knowledge, or play practices, are perceived to transgress the boundaries of heteronormativity (Taylor 2007; Robinson 2013; Bhana 2014). Children's everyday heteronormative play practices, such as 'chase and kiss' and 'mothers and fathers' are considered a representation of children's 'normal' development (discussed further in the next section on heteronormativity in early childhood education). Moral panic associated with children's access to information about same-sex relationships and families has stemmed from: children's access to resources specifically designed for children that portray same-sex families; schooling curricula that positively represent same-sex relationships (see Section 28 in the UK and Proposition 8 in USA); when children's television programmes are perceived to have gay characters or reflect gay relationships (e.g. Tinky-Winky in *Teletubbies*; and Noddy and Big Ears); and children's access to comprehensive sexuality education. Robinson (2013) has argued that moral panic is used as a political strategy for maintaining the heteronormative nature of the curriculum in schools, the sanctity of heterosexual relationships, and the hegemony of the heteronormative adult citizen and social order more broadly in society. Scholars (Kitzinger 1990; Levine 2002; Robinson 2012, 2013; McClelland and Hunter 2013; Bhana 2014) have argued that the regulation of children's access to sexuality education, often *in the name of protection* and *in the best interests* of the child can, ironically, make them more *vulnerable*.

Heteronormativity in children's early education

Heteronormativity is used to designate how heterosexuality is constituted and represented as the natural and normal sexuality. The normalizing discourse of heterosexuality takes on the privileged and 'unquestionable' position of being the 'true' sexuality, or the representation of the natural order of things, primarily through the way it is linked to the male/female biological binary and to procreation. Heterosexuality is also normalized through the way it is 'encoded in language, in institutional practices and the encounters of everyday life' (Epstein and Johnson 1994: 198). For example, religious discourses and practices significantly contribute to the way heterosexuality is normalized and non-heterosexualities are abnormalized and excluded – for example, in terms of the perceived illegitimacy of same-sex marriages and families. The assumption that is often made on enrolment forms in early childhood settings, that all children come from heterosexual families, is another example of heteronormativity in practice. Thus, the normalization of heterosexuality is a social phenomenon that is actively negotiated, with its dominant discourses and narratives primarily constituted within the socially constructed cultural binary of heterosexual us/homosexual them – a powerful hierarchy in which heterosexuality defines and speaks with perceived authority about the Other. Institutionalized heterosexuality thus becomes the definer of 'legitimate and prescriptive sociosexual arrangements' (Ingraham 1994: 204) and the norm by which all other sexualities are defined as different, illegitimate and abnormal. Within this framework, heterosexuality becomes compulsory (Rich 1980). As Letts (1999: 98) points out, heteronormativity is ultimately about power, a reinforcing of a 'culture of power' associated with heterosexuality. Within this culture of power the normalization of heterosexuality is rendered invisible, and diverts attention and critique away from the macro- and micro-social, economic and political discursive practices, including those that operate in educational institutions that construct and maintain this hierarchy of difference across sexual identities.

There are many contradictions that surround the perception that children are 'too young' to deal with sexuality issues; most are related to the process of heteronormativity. The construction of heterosexuality and heterosexual desire is part of the everyday practices in early childhood settings (Cahill and Theilheimer 1999). The incorporation of mock weddings, the encouragement of various activities in home corner, such as mothers and fathers, and young children's participation in kissing games and girlfriends/boyfriends are common among children. These and many other activities are rarely questioned, but rather are part of the normalization of the construction of heterosexual desire and the inscription of heteronormative gender in young children's lives. For many early childhood educators these activities are considered to be 'children being children', and a natural part of growing up, linked to the process of child development. However, Epstein (1995: 57), based on her work with nursery-age children, reminds us that:

> sexism is, by definition, heterosexist and that sexism cannot, there-fore, be understood in the absence of an analysis of heterosexuality as both political and institutionalized . . . that school is an important locus for the inscription of gender and of heterosexuality and that it is, therefore, also an important locus for challenging dominant discourses of (hetero)sexism.

It seems that, for some, sexuality becomes problematic when it transgresses the boundaries of compulsory heterosexuality, with double standards often disguised and perpetuated through discursive practices that constitute children as being 'too young' to deal with sexual differ-ences and discrimination. This perspective is reflected in the following response from the director of a preschool setting:

> I think children are really too young to deal with sexuality issues. They have no understanding of it; it isn't part of their experiences . . . Like they do get into playing house, mothers and fathers and getting married, that kind of thing, but that's normal everyday play that children like to get into. They see it all the time on television and in their lives. But beyond that, I don't think it's appropriate and it's not part of their experiences.

Homophobia and heterosexism in early childhood settings

Discourses of homophobia and heterosexism that prevail in society define all sexualities other than heterosexuality as abnormal and deviant, thus relegating those who identify as other than heterosexual to the margins, while simultaneously silencing their experiences of discrimination and inequality. In children's early education, addressing same-sex relation-ships and the issues faced by gays and lesbians often encounters resis-tance from some educators, parents and other community members positioned in homophobic and heterosexist discourses. These discourses are strongly linked to conservative, religious, moral and cultural beliefs around same-sex relationships. Many educators allude to their religious values, and those of children's parents, as an important factor in their not dealing with gay and lesbian issues with children. The intersection between religious discourse and sexuality difference is an area that many find difficult to reconcile or negotiate, as demonstrated in the following comments made by early childhood educators:

I don't feel comfortable with these issues at all and wouldn't discuss them with children. It is against my religious and moral values.

We have never had children from a family with two parents of the same sex, probably because of our Christian focus. It is not relevant to our setting.

Children should not have to accept this lifestyle, particularly where it conflicts with the religion taught at home (as in my centre). However, children need to be taught to accept people. Staff and families need to be aware of this.

Educators have a critical role in creating positive learning environments in which all individuals have similar opportunities to reach their potentials, and can feel supported, included and affirmed about who they are. Not only do educators have a 'duty of care' to both children and adults with whom we come into contact, there is also a broader role that involves a communal responsibility for fostering social justice within the communities in which we live and teach. This is reflected in the philosophies of Reggio Emilia, which emphasize the liberatory potential of early childhood institutions as 'civil forums', in which important social issues and events are openly discussed with children, and where social justice perspectives, policies and practices are paramount. Educators who are positioned in discourses that operate to undermine *respect* for the differences that exist in people's lives may have difficulties negotiating and incorporating social justice pedagogies and philosophies into their daily work with children and their families. Negotiating the different discursive locations that exist among educators and families is not easy work, but it is not impossible to find a point of reconciliation across differences that can lead to respect for difference, rather than just 'tolerance'. It is within this context that it becomes possible to begin doing social justice education with a whole-institution approach, but there is no shifting without education, patience, dialogue, or a willingness to take individual and communal risks (Robinson 2005d).

Sexuality is also largely considered to be a matter that should remain within the privacy of the family and is therefore not perceived to be the responsibility of educators. As one child care worker articulated, 'Their private issues are their private issues.' Britzman (1997) argues that this perception that sexual identity is a 'private' affair, which has little to do with public lives, is a powerful myth. It contributes to heteronormativity, and perpetuates the notion that heterosexuality has nothing to do with homosexuality. On the contrary, the cultural binary heterosexual/homosexual operates not just to narrowly and rigidly define the two oppositionally, but what is perceived as possible for those who identify with either of these sexualities. Britzman (1997: 192) points out: 'The fact is that schools mediate the discourses of private and public work to leave intact the view that (homo)sexualities must be hidden.'

Heterosexuality becomes the 'public' voice, definition and representation of 'normal' and 'natural' sexuality. This normalization of heterosexuality is further enforced through powerful gender discourses that operate to constitute socially sanctioned performances of masculinity and femininity as heterosexual, and regulate gender conformity among children and youth. Early childhood education is very much part of this normalization process of the construction of the heterosexual public/ homosexual private binary. This is reinforced in early childhood education through the process in which lesbian and gay identities are legitimized largely and solely within the privatized context of the family. It has been highlighted in our combined research and teaching in this area that the only perceived legitimate and relevant context in which to deal with gay and lesbian issues in early childhood education is within the discourse of family diversity and parenting. As one teacher indicated, 'I think all this comes under family life and shouldn't be separated from that.'

Not surprisingly, then, homophobic harassment and violence experienced by some gay or lesbian early childhood educators in their workplace is an issue that has arisen in our combined research (Robinson and Jones Díaz 2000). This harassment is experienced from other staff and/or from parents of children attending their settings. One teacher pointed out that, 'We have some gay staff and some positive images, but some heterosexual staff still have a problem with it and there is some tension there.' Research in other areas of the workforce, including various educational contexts, highlights that homophobic harassment, discrimination and violence are widespread and have crucial implications for the well-being of individuals who experience these behaviours (Ferfolja and Hopkins 2013; Ferfolja 2014). Such harassment is also in breach of anti-discrimination legislation throughout most Western countries. Homophobia among educators and parents sends strong messages to children about difference.

Heterosexism and homophobic stereotypes and myths can be perpetuated through daily pedagogical practices and everyday interactions between educators and children (Robinson and Jones Díaz 1999). One highly influential homophobic myth that has been prevalent in early childhood educational settings (and within the broader society) is the perception of 'homosexuals' as paedophiles and sexual predators (Silin 1997). This myth has been partially responsible for keeping men in Western nations, regardless of their sexuality, out of the field of early childhood education (King 1997; Wright 2011). Male early childhood educators are located in a range of complex and contradictory discourses. They can be viewed as positive role models for children, through their challenging of hegemonic constructions of masculinity, but, on the other hand, can be viewed suspiciously as potential child abusers. These men are often perceived to be sexually suspicious, as their very employment challenges hegemonic constructions of masculinity and gender roles, which are intimately linked to constructions of heterosexuality. Child care and working with children is considered traditionally to be a 'woman's role', and those men who challenge gender traditions and participate in 'women's work' are often scrutinized by others, particularly other men, who take up hegemonic masculine, heterosexual identities. Not only is their gender questioned but so too is their sexuality, by association.

Dealing with gay and lesbian equity issues with children is also frequently misconstrued as dealing with sex, rather than about the experiences of communities, or about loving or caring relationships. Homophobia operates to define and essentialize non-heterosexuality purely in terms of physical sexual acts. Thus, the focus in non-heterosexual relationships is centralized on the perceived abnormality and deviance of their sexual behaviour. Rendered invisible in this process are the ordinary everyday activities and tasks that are part of the lives of all, regardless of sexual orientation. Consequently, the hypersexualization of gay and lesbian identities results in the perception that doing sexuality work with children is developmentally and morally inappropriate behaviour and perpetuates many of the myths about non-heterosexuals.

Out of sight, out of mind: 'compulsory heterosexuality' and the invisibility of sexual Others

Many early childhood educators do see the importance of addressing gay and lesbian discrimination in children's early education, but some consider the issues not to be relevant to their specific workplaces, so do not include them in workplace policies or practices, or in their pedagogies (Robinson 2002, 2005c, 2013). Whether these issues are considered relevant is based primarily on educators' awareness of working with children with gay or lesbian parents, as indicated in the following comments.

> We haven't dealt with these issues because we haven't had gay and lesbian families in our setting. It isn't really a concern to us.

> At the moment I would only address these issues if I had children from homosexual families, if the children were curious.

> I would consider these issues important when/if gay and lesbian parents use my setting.

The above comments reflect a widely held myth that doing anti-homophobia and anti-heterosexist education is relevant only to those who identify as non-heterosexual and not to those who are heterosexual. However, as pointed out previously, sexuality is a socially constructed social relationship (Weeks 1986; Britzman 1997). The homosexual/heterosexual dualism represents a hierarchical power relationship in which definitions and understandings of homosexuality are defined in opposition to what it means to be heterosexual, and vice versa. Sedgwick (1990) makes the point that gay and lesbian issues are not just relevant to a minority of people who identify as gay or lesbian. Rather the heterosexual/homosexual binary relationship, which largely perpetuates discriminatory thinking towards non-heterosexual identities, is crucial in the way that all people's lives are determined, controlled and regulated across the spectrum of sexualities.

For some, the relevance of dealing with gay and lesbian issues depends on whether the presence of gay and lesbian parents is causing 'problems' for the setting or for the children from these families. Some also perceive it as a potential problem if other children are becoming 'too curious' about other children's same-sex parents. Consequently, it seems that, for many, dealing with gay and lesbian issues is done only as a last resort, and where it is judged that educators could no longer afford to ignore issues or divert children's curiosity. Such perceptions relinquish educators' responsibilities for validating families parented by gays and lesbians, and for providing non-discriminatory educational environments for all children. It also sends a strong message to children that such issues are not to be openly discussed, reinforcing the taboo that already silences discussions in this area.

Childhood educators and community-based professionals often assume that lesbians and gays are not a part of their clientele or community, or members of their own staff. Unlike more visible identity differences, sexuality difference is often not readily recognized, with most people generally assumed to be heterosexual, unless openly stated otherwise. Such assumptions, constituted within the discourse of 'compulsory heterosexuality' (Rich 1980) or 'heterosexual assumption' (Weeks, Heaphy and Donovan 2001), and reinforced through the pervasiveness of heterosexism, are prevalent throughout early childhood education (as elsewhere in society). This results in an assumed absence of gay and lesbian parents or significant adult carers, or even early childhood educators, unless they are publicly 'out' to their children and settings. However, the 'invisibility' and silence of gay and lesbian families are often enforced due to the extent and effectiveness of homophobia and heterosexism within educational settings and in society more broadly. This makes it extremely difficult and potentially risky for gay and lesbian families to 'come out' to their children's educators and/or openly discuss their concerns. Many gay and lesbian families who send their children to daily child care and preschool do not disclose their sexualities and are not out to their children's educators. Some gay and lesbian families actively seek out early childhood settings that demonstrate a commitment, through policies and practices, to diversity and difference (hopefully including sexuality), in order to feel more confident that they will be respected and that their children will not be discriminated against. It is important to point out here that in some cases children from gay and lesbian families attending early childhood settings do on occasion experience discrimination from other children, and from educators and other staff members.

Another assumption often made by childhood educators is that children, regardless of their family structure, do not know or interact with adults who openly identify as gay or lesbian. Many educators, often unfamiliar with children's social lives beyond the setting, generally read children's lives from the context of their own experiences of diversity, which may be limited. In addition, the dominant discourse of childhood, as discussed earlier in this chapter, leads to a misconception that all children are naïve and innocent, and 'suitably sheltered' from what adults' generally consider to be 'inappropriate' issues, such as sexual orientation.

Implications for policy and practice

The issues raised in this chapter have significant implications for practice, policies, pedagogy and the curriculum in children's early education. Addressing sexuality education with children, increasing understandings of children's sexual subjectivities, and building ethical and respectful relationships early in life are important for developing children's sexual citizenship, for developing their resilience, health and well-being, and for fostering greater acceptance of the sexuality and gender diversity that exists in society. Robinson's research with parents/guardians and educators focusing on children's early education around sexuality knowledge highlights a need for a collaborative approach between educators and families in addressing these issues. Working with parents to develop a collaborative approach to children's comprehensive sexuality may require some foundational work in terms of discussing the importance of this teaching and learning in the early years with both families and colleagues.

Diversity and equity policies in educational settings and in community-based services need to name and address the specific needs of same-sex families. They also need to include and address sexuality issues more broadly in the workplace – for example, the needs of educators who identify as lesbian, gay or queer. Addressing homophobia and heterosexism is central to diversity and equity policies. It is important to name and include these areas in policies, even if same-sex families, or lesbian and gay educators and community-based professionals are perceived not to be part of the workplace or family clientele. Broad umbrella policies, such as an anti-bias policy, which are seen to be inclusive of a range of diversity and difference issues, can actually hide, silence and marginalize issues considered more controversial, such as sexuality. Therefore, it is important to review policies in order to ascertain if they inadvertently perpetuate homophobic and heterosexist discourses.

Developing and implementing policies generally involves including staff, children and families in the process. Educating those involved about why it is important to include these perspectives, what the important issues are, and the responsibilities and roles of individuals in the implementation of policies is important to the success of this process. It is also critical that policies are openly displayed in services and are discussed with new families; this is also a crucial part of the education of community members. However, the success of such policies will ultimately be reliant on management supporting educators in actively implementing the policies in daily practice, even if resistance arises. The development of supportive procedures for dealing with resistance from various sources, including parents, managers and other staff members, is important.

It is crucial that educators and community-based professionals do not assume that same-sex families are not utilizing their services. Homophobia and heterosexism make it difficult, and often impossible, for some gay and lesbian parents to come out to educators and community-based professionals. Their silence and invisibility should not be perceived to be an indicator of their absence. Openly including gay and lesbian perspectives in policies will provide a more supportive environment in which to foster trusting relationships between educators and families. Including gay and lesbian parents in the development of programmes that deal with the social, political and economic issues facing their families and communities is also important in developing positive relationships between educators and families. The Early Years Learning Framework Australia (DEEWR 2009) points out that children's and families' lives are diverse and complex, and it is the right of children to see their cultures and identities reflected in the curriculum.

Educators need to encourage children's critical thinking around the normalizing discourses of gender and sexuality that operate in their lives. The process of deconstruction is particularly useful for identifying the discursive location of children in these areas, for acknowledging social power relations, for highlighting stereotypes and myths, and for posing different and new questions that encourage a broader representation of gender and sexuality. Such an educational programme needs to be founded within a theoretical framework which recognizes that children are active participants in the construction of their own identities and those of others. In programmes that are developed around children's interests, sexuality issues can be creatively tapped into through a range of different topic areas that children often raise, especially those that are related to gender identities and families, both of which open up discussion possibilities around sexuality, and gay and lesbian equity issues. Ultimately, encouraging children to take an active interest in current affairs issues and engaging them in critical discussions will provide a plethora of interest-based issues that can include sexuality issues.

Despite the prevalent belief to the contrary, sexuality and gay and lesbian equity issues are relevant to *all* children and their families. Normalizing discourses of gender and sexuality operate to regulate and constrain the behaviours of all individuals, and to perpetuate homophobia and heterosexism. It is important to initiate and maintain an inclusive and continuous dialogue around the issues, concerns and fears of educators and families in order to provide a more supportive environment for the development of effective social justice policies and practices in this area. This needs to be done in conjunction with the development of an ongoing education programme for management, educators, other staff members, and families on the broad socio-political and economic issues facing gay, lesbian, bisexual and queer people. A range of resources is available to address sexuality diversity with children – for example, the *Learn to Include* (Harding 2006) books for children and associated teacher manuals.

Conclusion

This chapter has stressed the importance of dealing with sexuality and sexual orientation issues in early childhood education. It has focused in particular on how the hegemonic discourses of childhood and sexuality that prevail in children's early education (as elsewhere in society) intersect to construct the perception that sexuality and sexual orientation issues are irrelevant to children and their early education. However, it has also been argued that these equity issues are as relevant to children's lives as they are to adults. Further, it has been pointed out that, regardless of whether early childhood settings have known gay or lesbian families utilizing their services, addressing sexuality equity issues need to be a critical component of social justice education for all.

Recommended reading

Blaise, M. (2009) 'What a girl wants, what a girl needs': responding to sex, gender, and sexuality in the early childhood classroom, *Journal of Research in Childhood Education*, 23(4): 450–460.

Cullen, F. and Sandy, L. (2009) Lesbian Cinderella and other stories: telling tales and researching sexualities equalities in primary school, *Sex Education: Sexuality, Society and Learning*, 9(2): 141–154.

DePalma, R. (2014) Gay penguins, sissy ducklings . . . and beyond? Exploring gender and sexuality diversity through children's literature, *Discourse: Studies in the Cultural Politics of Education*, 14 July: 1–18.

Robinson, K.H. (2013) *Innocence, Knowledge and the Construction of Childhood: The Contradictory Nature of Sexuality and Censorship in Children's Contemporary Lives*. London: Routledge.

Robinson, K.H. and Davies, C. (2015) Children's gendered and sexual cultures: desiring and regulating recognition through life markers of marriage, love and relationships, in E. Renold, J. Ringrose and D.R. Egan (eds) *Children, Sexuality & Sexualization*. London: Palgrave: 174–190.

11
Revisiting the challenge of diversity and difference in childhoods

Introduction

Our research and work with childhood educators, community service professionals and pre-service teachers shows that social justice education is generally considered an important aspect of children's early education. However, throughout this book we have highlighted many of the contradictions and complexities facing childhood educators and community-based professionals in doing this with children, families and communities. We have also acknowledged that doing social justice education and building ethical relationships with children in practice can be difficult work, as it frequently involves taking perceived and 'real' personal and professional risks, which can challenge many educators' subjective positions in the world, particularly in relation to their understandings of childhood and in terms of how they view difference (Robinson 2013).

We started this book with a discussion of what we have called a hierarchy of differences. What this means is that some areas of diversity and difference are considered personally and professionally more relevant, worthy of support and consideration, and safer than others. This personal and professional preference for taking up certain areas of difference over others is primarily based on individual (dis)comfort levels around doing work in various areas of diversity. How comfortable one feels addressing specific equity areas will be related to a number of different issues, including level of expertise, and critical understandings across social justice issues and equity, one's subjective location in discourses of diversity and difference, and how supported one feels by colleagues and parents in doing this work. One's location in these discourses will be influenced by personal experiences and cultural and religious beliefs, among other factors. Promoting social justice and equity around sexuality issues, for instance, is an area that many educators and community-based professionals feel uncomfortable addressing. This is primarily due to its controversial status and the perceived risks involved in incorporating these issues into programmes. As some childhood educators have pointed out to us, it is much easier and personally less risky to take up the discourse of the irrelevance of sexuality issues to young children and to pass the responsibility on to secondary educators working with older children. Furthermore, like sexuality issues, other equity issues faced by single parents, or those associated with family poverty, domestic violence, racism and bi/multilingualism can also be marginalized and silenced in the discourse that positions these issues as 'private' family matters. Consequently, many equity issues are placed in the 'too hard' basket and are not included in children's early education, even when children bring the issues up themselves. Children receive strong contradictory messages from individuals, families and institutions such as the media. Where children discursively locate themselves in terms of difference and equity, and how this is played out in their lives, is very much influenced by educators' and professional's discursive and material practices and the contradictory messages they receive.

In many respects, education, government and community-based organizations, as microcosms of the broader society, operate to perpetuate the status quo in society – that is, through everyday practices they maintain the social order or power relations that currently exist in the world. As Kobayashi and Ray (2000) argue, social institutions, such as education, actively participate in defining which social justice issues will be recognized, taken up and challenged, and which social inequalities will continue to be publicly tolerated. Through an awareness of the complexities and contradictions that operate for childhood educators and community-based professionals around diversity and difference, we can collectively begin to deconstruct the barriers that currently exist and prevent the recognition of and engagement with the Other in policy, pedagogy and practice. The representation of day-to-day experiences of minorities, incorporating their interests and perspectives, is central to substantially and appropriately addressing diversity and difference. Individual childhood educators and community-based professionals are a critical component of this democratic project, as their daily work with children and their families is crucial in terms of disrupting the normalizing discourses that perpetuate power inequalities and relationships that are experienced by those who are not part of the dominant culture.

However, it is important that a reflexive approach is incorporated into pedagogy and practice with children and families in order to understand how their subject positions in discourses can perpetuate, consciously or unconsciously, the social inequalities that prevail in society. In other words, as pointed out previously, reflexivity is about developing a critical self-conscious awareness of one's relationship with the Other. As stated by the EYLFA (DEEWR 2009: 13), 'Reflective practice is a form of ongoing learning that involves engaging with questions of philosophy, ethics and practice.' We feel that this is the crucial starting point for anyone who is involved in doing diversity and difference within a social justice education agenda. A reflexive approach to diversity and difference is primarily about deconstructing the discourse of 'tolerance' and 'inclusion' in order to refocus more on the discourse of 'respect' and a deeper critique of what 'inclusive practice' should look like, engaging with minorities on their terms. Many educators and community-based professionals view 'tolerance' as the reflection of the success of their practices. The concepts of 'tolerance' and 'inclusion' are constraining, as they are always about a precarious hierarchical power relationship that has its limits in terms of how long one can 'tolerate' the existence of someone else who is often perceived as an annoyance or irritation. In contrast, respect and building ethical relationships are about accepting people's rights to choose to be who they are in the world that sit equally beside different ways of being, knowing and doing.

In this final chapter, we highlight several critical issues that we feel childhood educators and community-based professionals need to consider when reviewing current approaches to diversity, difference and social justice education with children and their families. They are issues that we have addressed at various points throughout this book and include: promoting theoretical understandings of children, childhood, diversity and difference; enhancing links between theory and practice; acknowledging how diversity and difference are often located in the discourse of deficit; encouraging children's critical thinking and learning; deconstructing the adult/child binary; increasing communications with families and communities; developing policies and procedures that incorporate social justice perspectives; building supportive networks at all levels of childhood education and community-based services; promoting professional development of educators and other staff; and the need for further research into diversity and difference in early childhood education. These implications are reflected in the principles, practices and outcomes of the EYLFA (DEEWR 2009).

Promoting theoretical understandings of childhood, diversity and difference

Feminist poststructural perspectives, as well as the other cultural and critical theories that have largely informed the theoretical frameworks of our various discussions in this book, provide invaluable understandings of the social construction of childhood through different discourses that are historically and culturally available. These frameworks acknowledge the multiple subjectivities of children across different sites of identity, and recognize that children are active participants in the construction of their own identities and in the regulation of the identities of others. For example, through the lens of feminist poststructural perspectives educators can shift their reliance on 'common-sense' oppositional thinking constituted in cultural binaries, such as adult/child, which construct understandings of what it means to be an adult or child. Such knowledge tends to inform many educators' daily practices with children, thus perpetuating the hierarchal relations of power that exist between adults and children.

Incorporating contemporary theoretical and critical perspectives of childhood, diversity and difference into programmes, policies and practices is a critical foundation for effectively doing social justice education with children and their families. Traditional perspectives of childhood and children's learning, based on developmentalism, are still largely viewed by many educators and community-based professionals as the only legitimate and acceptable theoretical tools for understanding children, families and diversity. However, as we have argued throughout this book, modernist perspectives of childhood and children's learning are limited in their potential to inform equitable approaches to diversity, difference and social justice education. Modernist universalized discourses of childhood do not address children's agency or the multiple experiences of what it means to be a child across different socio-cultural contexts, such as gender, sexuality, class, 'race', (dis)ability, ethnicity, religion, and so on. Developmentalism constrains our understandings of children's identity formation, particularly in contexts of diversity in which children's and families' negotiation of their difference is ongoing, complex and often contradictory. Children, like adults, construct multiple identities. Through the entering and re-entering of different discursive fields, children are capable of taking on multiple ways of being, doing, thinking and acting, depending on the power relations operating in a given social field. Children need to be given opportunities to question, analyse, test and critique different versions of 'reality' in ways that are contextually relevant to their daily lives, in order for them to deal with the complexities and contradictions characteristic of a postmodern, globalizing and diverse world.

Educators' and community-service professionals' perspectives of childhood, and of diversity and difference, can impact on the social justice issues considered appropriate to address with children. Children are aware of diversity and difference from very early ages, and this influences their behaviours towards others and their everyday social practices. Like adults, children are acutely aware of the normalizing discourses that operate in society, and actively regulate and police their own behaviours and those of others according to these social norms. However, the discourse of childhood innocence is a powerful influence on how many childhood educators perceive children's experiences and understandings of diversity, difference and social inequalities. Consequently, some aspects of social justice education (for example, poverty, sexuality, death, divorce, domestic violence, racism) are often not raised with children by educators who are located in discourses that construct children as being 'too young' to understand what they (the educators) perceive to be adult concepts.

The hegemonic discourse of childhood and the cultural binary adult/child continue to perpetuate the oppositional thinking that constitutes traditional understandings of what it means to be a child or an adult. These modernist common-sense perspectives are perceived to be representative of the 'natural order of things' and operate to artificially construct different and mutually exclusive polarized worlds for children and adults. Consequently, many childhood educators (like other adults) participate in the construction and maintenance of these separate imagined 'spaces', designated as the 'world of adults' and the 'world of children', through their everyday practices and interactions with children. This polarized constructed relationship between adults and children primarily defines childhood in opposition to what it means to be an adult. In this process certain knowledge, practices and roles become designated as associated with adults and thus are perceived to be irrelevant to children. Broader social, economic and political issues are generally considered to be irrelevant to the 'world of children'; indeed, they become perceived as adult burdens and responsibilities from which children need to be protected for as long as possible. This protection is generally aimed at maintaining their childhood 'innocence'.

The discourse of childhood innocence, in conjunction with perceptions that children are 'too young' to deal with issues perceived solely as associated with adult lives, impacts on the way social justice education is undertaken with children. For example, as pointed out previously, many educators do not see the relevance or significance of relating individual discrimination to broader social, economic and political inequalities when dealing with equity issues with children. It is often felt that children will have no understanding of these broader concerns. This is also reflected in the way sexual equity issues are perceived as irrelevant to children's lives and understandings.

Yet, children are growing up in an increasingly globalized and competitive world, characterized by accelerated and sophisticated media and communications technologies, such as the internet, social media, film, television and computers. As these technologies become more integrated into children's entertainment, popular culture and toys, the perceived dichotomy between children's worlds and adults' worlds is blurred. However, despite the fact that children have greater access to 'adults' worlds' through these technologies, hegemonic discourses of childhood prevail, masking the reality that, today, young children are more knowing and less naïve than earlier generations.

In order to support children in voicing their ideas and concerns about different social issues and current events, and to contribute as active citizens in society in their own right, there needs to be a disruption of and a shift away from the limitations of traditional perspectives of childhood and children's learning. This will enable childhood educators, community-based professionals and children to engage in experiences, projects and programmes that can bring about change.

Positioning children and families within discourses of deficit

Some children and their families who come from minority socio-cultural backgrounds or non-nuclear families are often perceived as being deprived. Children from culturally and linguistically diverse (CALD) backgrounds are often positioned in deficit discourses, and perceived by educators and community service professionals as being unable to integrate effectively and adapt to the setting if they are not speaking English. In terms of bi/multilingualism and language retention, there are greater concerns for children's individual socio-emotional needs and lack of English-language proficiency than with broader sociological issues associated with home language retention and its connections to bi/multilingual identity formation.

Families parented by gays and lesbians are often, consciously and unconsciously, positioned within discourses that construct them as being deficient. As pointed out in Chapter 8, homophobia and heterosexism operate in ways that construct these families primarily as sites of discrimination, which results in children being potentially harassed or teased. Thus, they are rarely constructed in positive discourses that view them as sites of celebration.

It is crucial that childhood educators and community-based professionals build on the cultural, linguistic and social capital of children, families and staff from diverse backgrounds, rather than diminishing and dismissing their 'difference' as deficit. Since childhood educators are at the forefront of young children's educational trajectory, their willingness to challenge normalizing discourses of heterosexuality, heteronormativity, femininity, masculinity, childhood, 'race', monolingualism, motherhood, nuclear family, and so on, can ultimately transform children's early experiences of education from potential failure to guaranteed success. In this way, 'difference' is able to accumulate equality, rather than be the site of marginalization and subordination.

Fostering children's critical thinking around diversity and difference

Developing children's critical thinking around diversity and difference is an important component of doing social justice education with children. Our research indicates that the development of children's critical thinking is not generally given a central focus in the equity work that educators do with young children. Rather, the focus tends to be on identity stereotypes, with limited acknowledgement of how the politics of difference operates in society to perpetuate inequalities.

While our research indicates that the use of resources is seen to be an effective way of introducing diversity and difference, the focus tends to be mainly superficial. There is a heavy reliance on resources as a means of promoting cultural diversity at the expense of fostering children's critical thinking around the issues. Appropriate use of such resources can aid critical thinking, but there is little evidence in our research to indicate that this is a common practice in the field. Consequently, little emphasis tends to be placed on developing and fostering critical thinking in children (and adults) about racism, sexism, homophobia, heteronormativity, racial, cultural and linguistic differences, monolingualism, inequality and power. Moreover there is a tendency to operate in a superficial manner and take celebratory approaches towards diversity in which the provision of resources alone is often considered sufficient enough in reflecting and exploring diversity and difference. Through the 'deliberate, purposeful and thoughtful' practice of 'intentional teaching', as defined by the EYLFA (DEEWR 2009: 15), explicitly making use of strategies 'such as modelling and demonstrating, open-questioning, speculating, explaining, engaging in shared thinking and problem solving to extend children's thinking and learning', will foster critical thinking around pertinent issues of diversity and difference.

The philosophy that 'We are all the same, we are all equal' is commonly articulated among educators. However, this discursive reading of social and cultural equity, where understandings of what it means to be 'the same' are standardized on hegemonic cultural values, dismisses the importance of acknowledging power differences among individuals and across different cultural groups. Consequently, the discrimination and inequalities faced by individuals (educators, community-based professionals, families and children) are not generally linked to broader socio-political and cultural factors. For example, when gay and lesbian issues are dealt with in childhood they are rarely considered within the broader social issues of homophobia or heterosexism. There seems to be a prevalent perspective that dealing with diversity in childhood is not relevant or directly related to broader social issues around discrimination or inequality.

Consequently, for many educators, doing social justice education with children does not currently include analysing how discrimination and inequalities are constituted within broader socio-cultural, political and economic relationships in society in terms of their impact on adults and children in daily life. Inequality and disadvantage are becoming more apparent in recent years due to the impact of globalization and neoliberalism, which brings increased economic hardship to many low-income families, single-parent female-headed families, newly arrived immigrants, refugees and asylum seekers, who are most vulnerable to the decreased levels of commitment from governments in providing equitable and affordable health and welfare services, as well as public education (including early childhood and primary education).

This lack of contextualizing and acknowledging inequalities and discrimination in broader socio-cultural, economic and political discourses is most likely influenced by the prevalence of the discourse of childhood that renders these concerns as irrelevant to children's understandings of the world and to their daily lives. In order for children to understand their own discriminatory practices, it is critical for them to be aware of how power and inequality are constituted within the discourses that are culturally and historically available to them in society. Consequently, it is imperative that social justice education with children is extended to include the development of children's critical thinking about the issues. As pointed out across the chapters in this book, deconstruction is a valuable teaching tool that can be utilized in everyday activities with children to foster their critical thinking.

However, questions for learning and finding out about the world are culturally and socially embedded. In many middle- to upper-class white Anglo-Australian homes, good problem solving encompasses thinking critically and verbalizing ideas accordingly. In other cultures, however, encouraging children to question and verbalize their ideas can be considered offensive and thus culturally inappropriate. Therefore, teaching strategies used to facilitate problem solving and critical thinking may in fact be representative of only one cultural context that is Anglocentric, Western and middle class, with little regard for how children mediate between different cultural, 'raced', classed and gendered expectations and discourses. Getting children to locate how their shifting subjectivities are constituted in discourses is critical if adults are going to be effective in assisting them to deconstruct dominant discourses that produce inequalities. Hence, it is crucial that critical thinking is not used as yet another tool for marginalizing those children who may have less experience of verbalizing, questioning or expressing their opinion.

Unfortunately, there are no 'quick-fix solutions' to dealing with incidences of racism, sexism, homophobia, classism, linguicism, and so on, in or out of childhood and community-based settings or classrooms. What works for one person in one context may not be useful to someone else dealing with a similar or different issue in another context. Critical mediation in these areas of social justice needs to become part of one's daily curriculum and programming, an integral part of how one lives one's life on all levels. In such a context, there is an understanding that disrupting and challenging inequality can be fraught with contradiction and complexity, and is ongoing and never ending. Hence, 'quick-fix solutions' may appeal to many as a way of masking or obscuring difficult issues, but ultimately they will not provide a sufficient means for effectively dealing with issues of diversity and difference.

Out of sight, out of mind

The perceived irrelevance of certain social justice issues to particular childhood and community-based settings is problematic in the field. There is a powerful prevailing discourse which perpetuates the belief that there is no need to address areas of social justice that are not perceived to be part of the communities that individual settings cater for. For example, it is often perceived that it is not important to address racism among a predominantly Anglo-Australian group of children; or that it is irrelevant to deal with homophobia or gay and lesbian issues if there are perceived to be no gay or lesbian families utilizing the service. The relevance of doing social justice education is largely based on the presence of visible and audible differences, such as skin colour, language and cultural practices. Other differences that are not so readily obvious tend to be considered as being absent from settings. Assumed absences can result in perpetuating further invisibility, silencing and marginalization of minority groups. For example, if Aboriginal families with a lighter skin colour, or gay or lesbian parents are not known to educators, they are assumed not to be there. Consequently, in settings where there are many children with obvious physical and language differences, doing social justice education is considered more relevant to these children and their families, than in settings that 'appear' to have more homogeneous clientele groups. Interestingly, the justification for addressing such issues is frequently based on the fear of potential conflicts or on necessity when problems arise. This is particularly so in the case of children who are learning English as an additional language, in which transitional approaches to the home language are utilized to help 'settle the child'. The language is not the focus in this strategy, rather the child's need to integrate into the 'English only' setting is the priority.

There is a need to recognize that all areas of social justice education are relevant to all children and families, regardless of their backgrounds. Indeed, they may be even more relevant in less culturally heterogeneous settings, where dominant cultural values and perspectives prevail and where interactions with minority groups may be more limited. In culturally homogeneous settings, racializing practices or heteronormative assumptions may be more explicit. Furthermore, in homogeneous contexts, where the absence of cultural and social diversity and difference does not always give children opportunities to develop understandings about diversity, negative generalizations and stereotypes can often result. It is equally crucial that the normalizing discourses operating in the lives of children from homogeneous environments are disrupted and challenged, even in the absence of obvious cultural diversity.

It is crucial to understand that difference and its consequences not only are the concern of a minority of people who share such difference, but also have highly significant implications for the way others live their lives, including the 'majority' culture. For example, the heterosexual/homosexual cultural binary that underpins much of the inequalities and common-sense knowledge of sexual differences that prevail in society not only restricts the lives of those who identify as gay or lesbian, but also impacts on others, including heterosexuals. The young boy who wishes to challenge the boundaries of his gender and enjoys dressing up in women's clothing is no doubt familiar with the consequences of not conforming to the rigid and narrow definitions of what is generally considered to be appropriate masculinity, which are highly influenced by such binaries as heterosexual/homosexual.

Developing policies and procedures that critically address diversity and difference

There is a need for childhood education and community-based services to develop policies and practices that reflect a broad range of contemporary diversity issues. These policies are more effective when they are developed in consultation with staff, families, communities and relevant stakeholders so that different perspectives are included. It is important that policies and procedures specifically address the complexity of issues relevant to the communities, children and families using the setting. It is critical that policies and procedures are inclusive of areas often perceived by educators and other staff as 'irrelevant' to their setting or assumed to be absent, as discussed above. The generic 'one size fits all' procedures often indicated in multicultural and anti-bias policies do not allow for diversity of practice and the complexity of issues to be well understood. For example, strategies in providing gender equity in settings that have culturally diverse families require approaches that may differ from those undertaken with middle-class, white professional families.

Communicating with families and communities

Doing social justice work in childhood education and community-based services involves working with families as well as children. The perspectives of families can impact significantly on how diversity and difference are addressed by such settings. We have found that families that are representative of the dominant culture tend to have more power and control over the everyday policies and practice. This is not surprising since they tend to have more cultural and linguistic capital to negotiate formal and informal interactions in educational contexts than families from minority cultures. It is important that all families are encouraged to participate in their children's early education. However, this may mean that educators and community service professionals will have to actively develop a supportive and trusting environment in order for this to happen.

Families can make valuable contributions on many different levels. They can be encouraged to be involved in policy development, decision making and programming. However, it is critical to foster the involvement of those families whose perspectives are rarely acknowledged or are given only tokenistic consideration. Families can be a valuable resource for educators in terms of understanding the children with whom they work. However, we have found in our research that communications with families tend to be limited and often one-way – that is, educators advising families. For example, educators often advise families regarding the importance of home language retention, but few educators are able to report on family perspectives on or concerns about raising their children bi/multilingually. Families are often not encouraged to provide information about their children's experiences at home or in the community, and educators seldom seek out families as a resource for increasing their awareness of diversity issues.

The relationship between families and educators is a complex and often potentially volatile one. It appears that, for many educators and community services professionals, the family should take prime responsibility for particular issues related to children's education around diversity and difference, such as sexuality issues and home language retention. This raises some important points around the perceived responsibilities of educators, community service professionals and parents when it comes to difficult and controversial areas associated with social justice education that are often considered 'private' family matters. However, we feel that working with children and families brings with it a responsibility to foster community and social values that are about upholding human rights across the social justice spectrum. It is our view that there is a more in-depth dialogue between families and childhood educators and community service professionals around controversial social issues, in order to shift these debates to a more productive level, with the aim of reaching a point of reconciliation. Currently, the perceived threat of parental and community resistance is enough to immobilize educators and community services professionals around dealing with more controversial social justice issues, such as gay and lesbian equity concerns. Consequently, these issues continue to be avoided. However, this does little to deal effectively with the inequities and discrimination that surround these areas and serves only to perpetuate the silencing and marginalization of 'minority' groups.

The role of management and leadership

Management bodies, governments and children's services agencies have a critical leadership role to play in supporting educators and community service professionals to develop and implement inclusive social justice policies and programmes. However, we have found that, despite federal and state government policies and programmes relating to access and equity issues, there is often a lack of support or leadership direction provided by management bodies in the areas of social justice education. This further exacerbates the constraints associated with incorporating diversity and equity into programming and teaching practices. Building positive support networks across all levels of childhood education and community services through supportive leadership strategies is crucial to the successful implementation of inclusive social justice education programmes. This becomes especially important when educators and community service professionals need the institutional support in order to tackle more controversial issues. Thus, incorporating a social justice education programme is about fostering a communal courage through collaboration, leadership and shared responsibility by promoting perspectives towards social justice, which involves a whole-setting, institutional and community approach.

The importance of professional development for childhood educators and community service professionals

Pre-service early childhood education courses provided by universities and vocational colleges are in a key position to address contemporary theoretical frameworks and approaches around social justice in childhood. For example, this may include an understanding of how feminist poststructuralism, cultural and critical 'race' studies, critical and postcolonial theory can effectively inform practice. It is essential that in-service and pre-service agencies incorporate professional development programmes that are informed by contemporary theoretical and practical frameworks to effectively address current social issues pertaining but not limited to racism, whiteness, sexuality, globalization, asylum seekers and refugees, neoliberalism, bi/multilingualism, critical multiculturalism and class. In order for pre-service teachers and community-based professionals to fully grasp the complexities associated with diversity, pre-service education courses need to provide subjects that include professional experiences that focus on issues of diversity and difference. These need to go beyond celebratory and superficial multicultural and 'anti-bias' perspectives and the use of stereotypic resources. Pre-service and in-service providers need to critically address and evaluate the manner in which current resources associated with diversity are utilized in settings. It is apparent from our research that resources tend to be utilized on a superficial level. In order to make full use of the variety and quality of resources that are available to childhood settings and community services, critical reflection and evaluation of the use of resources enable educators and children to make realistic connections to children's and families' everyday life situations and practices.

Finally, in facilitating pre-service teacher professionalism, it is important that the pre-service teachers and community-based professionals are equipped with the leadership attributes and critical dispositions necessary for challenging unequal relations of power and privilege that enable them to work equitably with diverse communities, adults and children in a globalized world. To this end, Osgood (2010) suggests that professional confidence for those working with young children involves the engagement in critical reflection on aspects of their work, including understanding the ways in which they are positioned through discourse. Therefore, professional practice is tied closely to the notion of being a critical reflexive practitioner. The preparedness to engage in self-critique and location of their own positions of privilege and power is of paramount importance in their work with children, families, colleagues and communities.

Further research into diversity and difference in early childhood education

Our research is unique in its aim to locate educators' perceptions and practices in contexts of diversity and difference. However, there is a need to juxtapose educators' perspectives with the voices of children, their families and their communities, in order to be cognizant of how current discourses of difference in childhood and community-based settings operate to locate diverse social and cultural minority groups in everyday social practices. Peak early childhood organizations, community service agencies and government bodies involved in accreditation and professional development can make a significant contribution by collaborating with universities to conduct research to bring about innovative and equitable pedagogical practices that benefit all children and their families.

Still, there are a number of specific areas of diversity in which further study would be useful. In particular, research investigating children's voices as they negotiate aspects of identity, power relations and marginalization in everyday social practices in childhood education and community-based settings would provide significant insights into the different ways in which children locate themselves in various mainstream discourses of diversity and difference. Moreover, research that investigates how pre-service teachers negotiate and implement pedagogies of difference and diversity in their first year of practice would effectively inform undergraduate and postgraduate university courses, which specifically focus on issues of diversity and difference and on educators' work in childhood education and community-based settings. Finally, collaborative research opportunities should be promoted and encouraged between university teams, government departments responsible for children's services and education, peak early childhood organizations and resource agencies, in order to investigate the outcomes of current professional development strategies employed to enhance approaches to diversity and difference in childhood and community-based settings.

Conclusion: taking personal and professional risks for social justice

Dealing with diversity and social justice issues in the lives of children and their families, as well as making a positive contribution to this area in the community more generally, is certainly a priority area for many educators and professionals. The focus on this agenda continues to intensify in a rapidly changing world where the complexities of identities, played out on a global scale, impact severely on local communities throughout the world. Consequently, the lives of children and adults are challenged, disrupted and changed by broad social, political and economic issues that seem, for many, irrelevant and far removed from the 'world of children'. In order to make a significant difference in terms of social justice, educators, community service professionals and educational institutions need to engage more actively in taking risks in this area, challenging and disrupting the everyday relations of power that underpin the various forms of inequality that operate.

   To make a difference in social justice, we must *all* engage in taking risks around challenging inequalities; this includes disrupting the normalizing discourses around controversial issues such as sexuality (Robinson 2013). However, as Robinson (2013) argues, taking risks should be a thoughtful process involving individual agency and community responsibility in the pursuit of a different, but positive, future for ourselves, children, families and future generations. In order to be successful in this process on any level, the first risk is to deal with the contradictions around social justice that operate in everyday interactions, which continue to disrupt and undermine this work (Robinson 2013). As Foucault (1985: 8) reminds us: 'There are times in life when the question of knowing if one can think differently than one thinks, and perceive differently than one sees, is absolutely necessary if one is to go on looking and reflecting at all.'

References

ABC News (2001) Tampa enters Australian waters with 433 asylum seekers on board. Available at: www.abc.net.au/archives/80days/stories/2012/01/19/3412121.htm (accessed 12 December 2015).

Alderson, P. (2010) Young children's individual participation in matters that affect them, in N. Thomas, and B. Perey-Smith (eds) *A Handbook of Children and Young People's Participation: Perspectives from Theory and Practice*. London: Routledge.

Ali, S. (2003) *Mixed-race, Post-race. Gender, New Ethnicities and Cultural Practices*. Oxford and New York: Berg.

Allen, L. and Ingram, T. (2015) Bieber Fever: Girls, Desire and the Negotiation of Girlhood Sexualities, in E. Renold, J. Ringrose and D. R. Egan (eds) *Children, Sexuality and Sexualization*. London: Palgrave Macmillan.

Alloway, N. (1995) *Foundation Stones: The Construction of Gender in Early Childhood*. Carlton, Vic.: Curriculum Corporation.

Alloway, N. (1997) Early childhood education encounters the postmodern: what do we know? What can we count as 'true'? *Journal of Early Childhood Education*, 22(2): 1–5.

Alsop, R., Fitzsimons, A. and Lennon, K. (2002) *Theorizing Gender*. Cambridge: Polity Press.

Andreotti, V. (2011) *Actionable Postcolonial Theory in Education*. New York: Palgrave Macmillan.

Ang, I. (2014) Beyond Chinese groupism: Chinese Australians between assimilation, multiculturalism and diaspora, *Ethnic and Racial Studies*, 37(7): 1184–1196.

Appadurai, A. (2015) Disjuncture and difference in the global cultural economy, in F.J. Lechner and J. Boli (eds) *The Globalization Reader*, 5th edn. West Sussex: John Wiley & Sons Ltd.

Apple, M.W. (1999) *Power, Meaning and Identity: Essays in Critical Educational Studies*. New York: Peter Lang.

Apple, M.W. (2001) *Educating the 'Right' Way: Markets, Standards, God, and Inequality*. New York: RoutledgeFalmer.

Apple, M.W. (2012) *Education and Power*, 2nd edn. New York: Routledge.

Apple, M.W. (2013) *Knowledge, Power and Education: The Selected Works of Michael W. Apple.* New York: Routledge.

Arnaut, K. (2012) Super-diversity: elements of an emerging perspective, *Diversities*, 14(2): 1–16.

Ashcroft, B., Griffiths, G. and Tiffin, H. (2006) *The Post-colonial Studies Reader*, 2nd edn. London: Routledge.

Ashcroft, B., Griffiths, G. and Tiffin, H. (2013) *Postcolonial Studies: The Key Concepts*. Oxon: Routledge.

Asylum Seeker Resource Centre (2015) Detention and refugee statistics. Available at: www.asrc.org.au/resources/statistics/detention-and-refugee-statistics/ (accessed 11 December 2015).

Australian Bureau of Statistics (ABS) (2010) 1301.0 – yearbook chapter, 2009–10: feature article: characteristics of the population. Available at: www.abs.gov.au/AUSSTATS/abs@.nsf/Lookup/1301.0Feature+Article7012009%E2%80%9310 (accessed 10 October 2014).

Australian Bureau of Statistics (ABS) (2011) *Media Release—national: 2011 census reveals one in four Australians is born overseas.* Available at: http://www.abs.gov.au/websitedbs/censushome.nsf/home/CO-59 (accessed 13 June 2016).

Australian Bureau of Statistics (ABS) (2012a) Experience of partner violence. Available at: www.abs.gov.au/ausstats/abs@.nsf/Lookup/4906.0Chapter7002012 (accessed 20 March 2016).

Australian Bureau of Statistics (ABS) (2012b) *Cultural Diversity in Australia: Reflecting a Nation: Stories from the 2011 Census, 2012–2013.* Available at: www.abs.gov.au/ausstats/abs@.nsf/Lookup/2071.0main+features902012–2013 (accessed 10 October 2014).

Australian Bureau of Statistics (ABS) (2012c) Media release – national: census shows Asian languages on the rise in Australian households. Available at: www.abs.gov.au/websitedbs/censushome.nsf/home/CO-60 (accessed 20 March 2016).

Australian Bureau of Statistics (ABS) (2012d) Media release – national: 2011 census reveals one in four Australians is born overseas. Available at http://abs.gov.au/websitedbs/censushome.nsf/home/CO-59 (accessed 18 March 2016).

Australian Bureau of Statistics (ABS) (2014) Estimates and projections, Aboriginal and Torres Strait Islander Australians, 2001 to 2026. Available at: www.abs.gov.au/ausstats/abs@.nsf/Products/C19A0C6E4794A3FACA257CC900143A-3D?opendocument (accessed 20 March 2016).

Australian Bureau of Statistics (ABS) (2015a) Family characteristics and transitions, Australia 2012–13. Available at: www.abs.gov.au/ausstats/abs@.nsf/mf/4442.0 (accessed 21 January 2016).

Australian Bureau of Statistics (ABS) (2015b) Media release: overseas born Aussies hit a 120 year peak. Available at: www.abs.gov.au/ausstats/abs@.nsf/Latestproducts/3412.0Media%20Release12013–14?opendocument&tabname=Summary&prodno=3412.0&issue=2013–14&num=&view= (accessed 4 December 2015).

Australian Council of Social Services (ACOSS) (2014) *Poverty in Australia 2014.* Strawberry Hills: NSW. Available at: www.acoss.org.au (accessed 2 January 2015).

Australian Curriculum, Assessment and Reporting Authority (ACARA) (2012) *Australian Curriculum, Health and Physical Education: Foundation to Year 10.*

Draft for consultation. Available at: http://consultation.australiancurriculum. edu.au/Static/docs/HPE/F-10Curriculum.pdf (accessed 10 December 2015).

Australian Human Rights Commission (AHRC) (2014) *The Forgotten Children: National Enquiry into Children in Immigration Detention*. Available at: www.humanrights.gov.au/sites/default/files/document/publication/forgotten_ children_2014.pdf (accessed 24 January 2016).

Australian National Research Organisation for Women's Safety (ANNROWS) (2014) Violence against women: key statistics. Available at: www.media.aomx. com/anrows.org.au/s3fs-public/Key%20statistics%20-%20all.pdf, (accessed 16 March 2016).

Avertt, P. and Hedge, A. (2012) School social workers and early childhood student's attitudes towards gay and lesbian families, *Teaching in Higher Education*, 17(5): 537–549.

Baldassar, L. and Merla, L. (eds) (2014) *Transnational Families, Migration, and the Circulation of Care: Understanding Mobility and Absence in Family Life*. New York: Routledge.

Ball, S.J. (ed.) (1990) *Foucault and Education: Disciplines and Knowledge*. London: Routledge.

Bamblett, L. (2013) Read with me everyday: community engagement and English literacy outcomes at Erambie Mission, *Australian Aboriginal Studies*, 1: 101–109.

Barad, K. (2007) *Meeting the Universe Halfway: Quantum Physics and the Entanglement of Matter and Meaning*. Durham, NC: Duke University Press.

Baylis, J., Smith, S. and Owens, P. (2014) *The Globalization of World Politics: An Introduction to International Relations*, 6th edn. Oxford: Oxford University Press.

BBC News (2015) Donald Trump's Muslim US ban call roundly condemned. Available at: www.bbc.com/news/world-us-canada-35037701 (accessed 14 December 2015).

Beecher, B. and Jones Díaz, C. (2014) Extending literacies through partnerships with families and communities, in L. Arthur, J. Ashton and B. Beecher (eds) *Diverse Literacies in the Early Years: Implications for Practice*. Sydney: ACER.

Bell, D. and Binnie, J. (2000) *The Sexual Citizen: Queer Politics and Beyond*. Cambridge: Polity Press.

Ben-Yahuda, N. (2009) Moral panics – 36 years on, *British Journal of Criminology*, 49: 1–3.

Berlant, L. (1997) *The Queen of America Goes to Washington City: Essays on Sex and Citizenship*. Durham: Duke University Press.

Best, S. and Kellner, D. (1991) *Postmodern Theory: Critical Interrogations*. New York: Guilford Press.

Bhabha, H. (1994) *The Location of Culture*. London: Routledge.

Bhabha, H. (1998) Culture's in between, in D. Bennett (ed.) *Multicultural States. Rethinking Difference and Identity*. London: Routledge.

Bhana, D. (2013) Kiss and tell: boys, girls and sexualities in the early years, *Agenda: Empowering Women for Gender Equity*, 27(3): 57–66.

Bhana, D. (2014) *Under Pressure: The Regulation of Sexualities in South African Secondary Schools*. Braamfontein, SA: MaThoko's Books.

Bhana, D. (2016) *Childhood Sexuality and AIDS Education: The Price of Innocence*. New York: Routledge.

Bhatia, T.K and Ritchie, W.C. (eds) (2013) *The Handbook of Multilingualism and Bilingualism*, 2nd edn. Oxford: Blackwell Publishing.

Bhattacharyya, G. (2002) *Sexuality and Society. An Introduction*. London: Routledge.

Bialystok, E. (2013) The impact of bilingualism on language and literacy development, in T.K. Bhatia and W.C. Ritchie (eds) *The Handbook of Multilingualism and Bilingualism*, 2nd edn. Oxford: Blackwell Publishing.

Bialystok, E. and Calvo, A. (2013) Independent effects of bilingualism and socioeconomic status on language ability and executive functioning, *Cognition*, 130: 278–288.

Blaise, M. (2005) *Playing it Straight: Uncovering Gender Discourses in the Early Childhood Classroom*. New York: Routledge.

Blaise, M. (2009) 'What a girl wants, what a girl needs': responding to sex, gender, and sexuality in the early childhood classroom, *Journal of Research in Childhood Education*, 23(4): 450–460.

Blaise, M. (2010) Kiss and tell: gendered narratives and childhood sexuality, *Australasian Journal of Early Childhood*, Special Sexualities Issue, 35(1): 1–9.

Blaise, M. (2013) Charting new territories: re-assembling childhood sexuality in the early years classroom, *Gender and Education*, 25(7): 801–817.

Blommaert, J. (2010) *The Sociolinguistics of Globalization*. Cambridge: Cambridge University Press.

Blommaert, M. (2013) *Ethnography, Superdiversity and Linguistic Landscapes: Chronicles of Complexity*. Bristol: Multilingual Matters.

Bourdieu, P. (1986) The forms of capital, in J.G. Richardson (ed.) *Handbook of Theory and Research for the Sociology of Education*. New York: Greenwood Press.

Bourdieu, P. (1990) *The Logic of Practice*, trans. R. Nice. Cambridge: Polity Press.

Bourdieu, P. (1991a) *Outline of a Theory of Practice*, trans. R. Nice. Cambridge: Polity Press.

Bourdieu, P. (1991b) *Language and Symbolic Power*, ed. J.B. Thompson, trans. G. Raymond and M. Adamson. Cambridge: Polity Press.

Bourdieu, P. (1993) *Sociology in Question*, trans. R. Nice. London: Sage Publications.

Bourdieu, P. (1998) *The Essence of Neoliberalism*. Available at: https://mondediplo.com/1998/12/08bourdieu (accessed 18 March 2016).

Bourdieu, P. and Wacquant, L.J.D. (1992) *An Invitation to Reflexive Sociology*. Chicago, IL: University of Chicago Press.

Bourne, J. (2010) Discourses and identities in a multi-lingual primary classroom, *Oxford Review of Education*, 27(1): 103–114.

Bouvier, R. and Karlenzig, B. (2006) Accountability and Aboriginal education: dilemmas, promises and challenges, *Our Schools, Our Selves*, 15(3): 15–33.

Bowden, T. (2015) Thirty-one women killed in Australia in 15 weeks renews call for action. ABC 7.30 report. Available at: www.abc.net.au/news/2015-04-13/thirty-one-women-killed-in-australia-in-15-weeks/6390072 (accessed 16 March 2016).

Braidotti, R. (2006) *Transpositions: On Nomadic Ethics*. Cambridge: Polity Press.

Breckenridge, J. and Carmody, M. (eds) (1992) *Crimes of Violence: Australian Responses to Rape and Child Sexual Assault*. Sydney: Allen & Unwin.

Bredekamp, S. and Rosegrant, T. (eds) (1991) *Reaching Potentials: Appropriate Curriculum and Assessment of Young Children*. Washington, DC: NAEYC.

Britzman, D. P. (1997) What is this thing called love? New discourses for understanding gay and lesbian youth, in S. de Castell and M. Bryson (eds) *Radical In(ter)ventions: Identity, Politics, and Difference/s in Educational Praxis*. Albany, NY: State University of New York Press.

Britzman, D.P. (1998) *Lost Subjects, Contested Objects: Toward a Psychoanalytic Inquiry of Learning*. New York: State University of New York Press.

Britzman, D.P. (2000) Precocious education, in S. Talburt and S.R. Steinberg (eds) *Thinking Queer: Sexuality, Culture and Education*. New York: Peter Lang Publishing.

Britzman, D.P. (2003) *Practice Makes Practice: A Critical Study of Learning to Teach*, 2nd edn. New York: State University of New York Press.

Broussard, C.A., Joseph, A.L. and Thompson, M. (2012) Stressors and coping strategies used by single mothers living in poverty, *Journal of Women and Social Work*, 27(2): 190–204.

Buchori, S. and Dobinson, T. (2012) Cultural diversity in the early childhood classroom in Australia: educators' perspectives, *International Journal of Education for Diversities*, 1: 41–56.

Buckingham, D. (2013) Is there a digital generation?, in D. Buckingham and R. Willett (eds) *Digital Generations: Children, Young People and New Media*. New York: Routledge.

Bumiller, K. (2008) *In an Abusive State: How Neoliberalism Appropriated the Feminist Movement Against Sexual Violence*. London: Duke University Press.

Burr, V. (1995) *An Introduction to Social Constructionism*. London: Routledge.

Butler, J. (1990) *Gender Trouble: Feminism and the Subversion of Identity*. New York: Routledge.

Butler, J. (1993) *Bodies that Matter: On the Discursive Limits of 'Sex'*. New York: Routledge.

Butler, J. (1994) Gender as performance: an interview with Judith Butler, *Radical Philosophy*, 67: 32–39.

Butler, J. (1997) *Excitable Speech: A Politics of the Performative*. London and New York: Routledge.

Cahill, M. (2014) The colour of the dream: unmasking whiteness. *Southerly*, 74(2): 196–211. Available at: http://search.informit.com.au/documentSummary;dn=792246488096352;res=IELLCC (accessed 22 December 2015).

Cahill, B. and Theilheimer, R. (1999) Stonewall in the housekeeping area: gay and lesbian issues in the early childhood classroom, in W.J. Letts IV and J.T. Sears (eds) *Queering Elementary Education: Advancing the Dialogue about Sexualities and Schooling*. Lanham, MD: Rowan & Littlefield.

Cannella, G.S. (1997) *Deconstructing Early Childhood Education: Social Justice and Revolution*. New York: Peter Lang Publishing.

Cannella, G.S. and Diaz Soto, L. (eds) (2010) *Childhood: A Handbook*. New York: Peter Lang Publishing.

Cannella, G.S. and Viruru, R. (2004) *Childhood and Postcolonization: Power, Education, and Contemporary Practice*. New York: RoutledgeFalmer.

Carpentier, V. and Unterhater, E. (2011) Globalization, higher education and inequalities: problems and prospects, in R. King, S. Marginson and R. Naidoo (eds) *Handbook on Globalization and Higher Education*. Cheltenham: Edward Elgar.

Carrington, V. (2002) *New Times: New Families*. Dordrecht: Kluwer Academic.

Casper, V., Cuffaro, H.K., Schultz, S., Silin, J. and Wickens, E. (1998) Towards a most thorough understanding of the world: sexual orientation and early childhood education, in N. Yelland (ed.) *Gender in Early Childhood*. London: Routledge.

Cass, B. (1995) Cultural diversity and challenges in the provision of health and welfare services towards social justice: employment and community services in culturally diverse Australia, in *1995 Global Cultural Diversity Conference Proceedings, Sydney*. Sydney: Department of Immigration and Multicultural and Indigenous Affairs, Australian Government. Available at: www.immi .gov.au/multicultural/_inc/publications/confer/03/speech11a.htm (accessed 10 May 2005).

Castles, S., Cope, B., Kalantzis, M. and Morrissey, M. (1988) *Mistaken Identity: Multiculturalism and the Demise of Nationalism in Australia*. Sydney: Pluto Press.

Castles, S., Vasta, V. and Ozkul, D. (2014) A classical immigration country in transition, in J. Hollifield, P. Martin and P. Orrenius (eds) *Controlling Immigration: A Global Perspective*, 3rd edn. Stanford, CN: Stanford University Press.

Cheesman, S. (2007) Pedagogical silences in Australian early childhood social policy, *Contemporary Issues in Early Childhood*, 8(3): 244–254.

Children out of Detention (n.d.) Stats and reports. Available at: www.chilout.org/ stats_reports (accessed 24 January 2016).

Chiro, G. (2014) Cultural and linguistic diversity in Australia: navigating between the Scylla of nationhood and the Charybdis of globalization, *International Journal of Multilingualism*, 11(3): 334–346.

Claster, P.N. and Blair, S.L. (eds) (2013) *Visions of the 21st Century Family: Transforming Structures and Identities*. Bingley, UK: Emerald Group Publishing Ltd.

Cloughessy, K. and Waniganayake, M. (2014) Early childhood educators working with children who have lesbian, gay, bisexual and transgender parents: what does the literature tell us? *Early Child Development and Care*, 184(8): 1267–1280.

Cohen, S. (2011) Whose side were we on? The undeclared politics of moral panic theory, *Crime Media Culture*, 7(3): 237–243.

Collier, P. (2015) The bottom billion: why the poorest countries are failing and what can be done about it, in F.J. Lechner and J. Boli (eds) *The Globalization Reader*, 5th edn. West Sussex: John Wiley & Sons Ltd.

Collins, P.H. (1990) *Black Feminist Thought: Knowledge, Consciousness, and the Politics of Empowerment*. Boston, MA: Unwin Hyman.

Comber, B. and Kamler, B. (2004). Getting out of deficit. Pedagogies of reconnection, *Teaching Education*, 15(3): 293–310.

Connell, R.W. (1987) *Gender and Power*. Sydney: Allen & Unwin.

Conteh, J. and Brock, A. (2010) 'Safe spaces'? Sites of bilingualism for young learners in home, school and community, *International Journal of Bilingual Education and Bilingualism*, 14(3): 347–360.

Conteh, J., Martin P. and Robertson, L.H. (eds) (2007) *Multilingual Learning Stories in Schools and Communities in Britain*. Stoke-on-Trent: Trentham Books.

Cook, D.T. (2013) Editorial. Taking exception with the child consumer, *Childhood*, 20(4): 423–428.

Cooke, M. and Simpson, J. (2012) Discourses about linguistic diversity, in M. Martin-Jones, A. Blackledge and A. Creese (eds) *The Routledge Handbook of Multilingualism*. London: Routledge.

Cossman, B. (2007) *Sexual Citizens: The Legal and Cultural Regulation of Sex and Belonging*. Stanford, CN: Stanford University Press.

Couldry, N. (2010) *Why Voice Matters: Culture and Politics after Neoliberalism*. London: Sage.

Creese, A. and Blackledge, A. (2010) Translanguaging in the bilingual classroom: a pedagogy for learning and teaching? *The Modern Language Journal*, 94(1): 103–115.

Cruickshank, K. (2012) Smarter kids need to speak in many tongues: Australia is woefully behind in the teaching of a second language, *Sydney Morning Herald*, 12 November.

Crystal, D. (2010) *The Cambridge Encyclopedia of Language*. Cambridge: Cambridge University Press.

Cunningham, H. (1995) *Children and Childhood in Western Society Since 1500*. London: Longman.

Curthoys, A. (1999) An uneasy conversation: multicultural and Indigenous discourses, in G. Hage and R. Couch (eds) *The Future of Australian Multiculturalism. Reflections on the Twentieth Anniversary of Jean Martin's 'The Migrant Experience'*. Sydney: Research Institute for Humanities and Social Sciences, University of Sydney.

Dahlberg, G., Moss, P. and Pence, A. (1999) *Beyond Quality in Early Childhood Education and Care: Postmodern Perspectives*. London: Falmer Press.

Dale, A. (2015) Court bans Cronulla riot 'memorial' rally planned for this weekend. Available at: www.dailytelegraph.com.au/news/nsw/court-bans-cronulla-riot-memorial-rally-planned-for-this-weekend/story-fni0cx12–1227641206411 (accessed 11 December 2015).

Daniel, C.L. (2008) From liberal pluralism to critical multiculturalism: the need for a paradigm shift in multicultural education for social work practice in the United States, *Journal of Progressive Services*, 19(1): 19–38.

Davies, B. (1989) *Frogs and Snails and Feminist Tales: Preschool Children and Gender*. Sydney: Allen & Unwin.

Davies, B. (1993) *Shards of Glass. Children Reading and Writing beyond Gendered Identities*. Sydney: Allen & Unwin.

Davies, B. (1994) *Poststructuralist Theory and Classroom Practice*. Geelong, Victoria: Deakin University Press.

Davies, B. (1996) *Power, Knowledge and Desire: Changing School Organisation and Management Practices*. Canberra: Department of Education, Employment, Training and Youth Affairs.

Davies, B. (ed.) (2008) *Judith Butler in Conversation: Analyzing the Text and Talk of Everyday Life.* New York: Routledge.

Davies, B. (2014) *Listening to Children: Being and Becoming.* London: Routledge.

Davies, B. and Petersen, E.B. (2005) Neoliberal discourse in the academy: the forestalling of collective resistance, *Learning and Teaching in the Social Sciences (LATISS)*, 2(2): 77–97.

Davies, B. and Petersen, E.B. (2010) In/difference in the neoliberal university, *Learning and Teaching in the Social Sciences (LATISS)*, 3(2): 92–109.

Davies, C. and Robinson, K.H. (2010) Hatching babies and stork deliveries: risk and regulation in the construction of children's sexual knowledge, *Contemporary Issues in Early Childhood*, 11(3): 249–262.

Davies, C. and Robinson, K.H. (2012) Reflective practice with early and middle childhood education and care professionals. Report prepared for Child Australia.

Davies, C. and Robinson, K.H. (2013) Reconceptualising family: negotiating sexuality in a governmental climate of neoliberalism, *Contemporary Issues in Early Childhood*, 14(1): 39–53.

Davis, H. (2004) *Understanding Stuart Hall.* London: Sage Publications.

Davis, K. (2007) Locating the other: stories from practice and theory, *Childrenz Issues: Journal of the Children's Issues Centre*, 11(1): 21–25.

de Lauretis, T. (1987) *Technologies of Gender: Essays on Theory, Film, and Fiction.* Bloomington, IN: Indiana University Press.

de Lauretis, T. (1994) *The Practice of Love: Lesbian Sexuality and Perverse Desire.* Bloomington, IN: Indiana University Press.

Deleuze, G. and Guattari, F. (1987) *A Thousand Plateaus: Capitalism and Schizophrenia*, trans. B. Massumi. Minneapolis, MN: University of Minnesota Press.

DePalma, R. (2013) Choosing to lose our gender expertise: queering sex/gender in school settings, *Sex Education: Sexuality, Society and Learning*, 13(1): 1–15.

DePalma, R. and Atkinson, E. (2009) 'Permission to talk about it': LGB and straight teachers' narratives of sexualities equality, *Qualitative Inquiry*, 15(7): 876–892.

DePalma, R. and Jennett, M. (2010) Homophobia, transphobia and culture: deconstructing heteronormativity in English primary schools, *Intercultural Education*, 21(1): 15–26.

Department of Education, Employment and Workplace Relations (DEEWR) (2009) *Belonging, Being and Becoming. The Early Years Learning Framework for Australia.* Available at: www.deewr.gov.au/Earlychildhood/Policy_Agenda/Quality/Documents/Final%20EYLF%20Framework%20Report%20-%20WEB.pdf (accessed 7 May 2015).

Department of Immigration and Border Protection (DIBP) (2015) Immigration detention and community statistics summary: 30 September 2015. Available at www.border.gov.au/ReportsandPublications/Documents/statistics/immigration-detention-statistics-30-dec-2015.pdf#search=average%20period%20of%20time%20people%20are%20held%20in%20detention (accessed 20 March 2016).

Department of Immigration and Citizenship (DIC) (2010) Fact sheet 2: key facts in immigration. Available at: www.border.gov.au/about/corporate/information/fact-sheets/02key (accessed 10 December 2015).

Department of Social Services (DSS) (2011) *The People of Australia: Australia's Multicultural Policy.* Canberra: DSS.

Derman-Sparks, L. and the ABC Task Force (1989) *Anti-bias Curriculum: Tools for Empowering Young Children.* Washington, DC: National Association for the Education of Young Children.

Devine, D., Kenny, M. and Macneela, E. (2008) Naming the 'Other': children's construction and experience of racism in Irish primary schools. *Race, Ethnicity and Education,* 11(4): 369–385.

Disney, W. (1994a) *Beauty and the Beast.* Loughborough: Ladybird Books.

Disney, W. (1994b) *The Little Mermaid.* Loughborough: Ladybird Books.

Due, C. (2008) 'Who are strangers?' 'Absorbing' Sudanese refugees into a white Australia, *Australian Critical Race and Whiteness Studies Association e-journal,* 4(1): 2–13.

D'Warte, J. (2015) Reflections on language and literacy: recognizing what young people know and can do, in T. Ferfolja, C. Jones Díaz and J. Ullman (eds) *Understanding Sociological Theory and Pedagogical Practices.* Cambridge: Cambridge University Press.

Eades, D. (1995) *Aboriginal English.* Sydney: New South Wales Board of Studies.

Easteal, P. (1994) *Voices of the Survivors.* Melbourne: Spinifex.

Ecclestone, K. and Lewis, L. (2014) Interventions for resilience in educational settings: challenging policy discourses of risk and vulnerability, *Journal of Education Policy,* 29(2): 195–216.

Ehrensaft, D. (2014) From gender identity disorder to gender identity creativity: the liberation of gender non-conforming children and youth, in E.J. Meyer and A.P. Sansfaçon (eds) *Supporting Transgender and Gender Creative Youth: Schools, Families, and Communities in Action.* New York: Peter Lang.

Elam, H.J. and Elam, M. (2010) Race and racism, in M. Wetherell and C.T. Mohanty (eds) *The Sage Handbook of Identities.* London: Sage.

Elliott, M. (1992) Images of children in the media: 'soft kiddie porn', in I. Itzin (ed.) *Pornography: Women, Violence and Civil Liberties. A Radical New View.* New York: Oxford University Press.

Engels, F. (1974) *The Condition of the Working Class in England.* Moscow: Progress Publishers.

Epstein, D. (1995) 'Girls don't do bricks': gender and sexuality in the primary classroom, in J. Siraj-Blatchford and I. Siraj-Blatchford (eds) *Educating the Whole Child.* Buckingham: Open University Press.

Epstein, D. and Johnson, R. (1994) On the straight and narrow: the heterosexual presumption, homophobias and schools, in D. Epstein (ed.) *Challenging Lesbian and Gay Inequalities in Education.* Buckingham: Open University Press.

Erickson, P.A. and Murphy, L.D. (2003) *A History of Anthropological Theory,* 2nd edn. Peterborough, Ontario: Broadview Press.

Evans, D. (1993) *Sexual Citizenship: The Material Construction of Sexualities.* London: Routledge.

Falchi, T., Axelrod, Y. and Genishi, C. (2014) 'Miguel es un artista' – and Luisa is an excellent student: seeking time and space for children's multimodal practices, *Journal of Early Childhood Literacy,* 14(3): 345–366.

Fass, P. (2003) Children and globalization, *Journal of Social History*, 36(4): 963–977.

Faulkner, J. (2011) *The Importance of Being Innocent: Why We Worry about Children*. Melbourne: Cambridge University Press.

Ferfolja, T. (2014) Lesbian and gay teachers: negotiating subjectivities in Sydney schools, in M. Moreau (ed.) *Inequalities in the Teaching Profession: A Global Perspective*. Basingstoke: Palgrave Macmillan.

Ferfolja, T. and Hopkins, L. (2013) The complexities of workplace experience for lesbian and gay teachers, *Critical Studies in Education*, 54(3): 311–324.

Ferfolja, T., Jones Díaz, C. and Ullman, J. (2015) The unseen half: theories for educational practice, in T. Ferfolja, C. Jones Díaz and J. Ullman (eds) *Understanding Sociological Theory and Pedagogical Practices*. Sydney: Cambridge University Press.

Fforde, C., Bamblett, L., Lovett, R., Gorringe, S. & Fogarty, W. (2013) Discourse, deficit and identity: Aboriginality, the race paradigm and the language of representation in contemporary Australia, *Media International Australia*, 149: 162–173.

Fine, M. and McClelland, S. (2006) Sexuality education and desire: still missing discourse of desire, *Harvard Educational Review*, 76: 297–337.

Fleer, M. (2011) Technologically constructed childhoods: moving beyond a reproductive to a productive and critical view of curriculum development, *Australasian Journal of Early Childhood*, 36(1): 16–24.

Fletcher, M. and Guttmann, B. (2013) Income inequality in Australia. *Economic Round-up*, 2: 35–54. Available at: informit.com.au/documentSummary; dn=814412463302620;res=IELBUS, ISSN: 1031–8968 (accessed 3 January 2016).

Flores, G. (2014) Teachers working cooperatively with parents and caregivers when implementing LGBT themes in the elementary classroom, *American Journal of Sexuality Education*, 9(1): 114–120.

Fog Olwig, K. (2014) Migration and care: intimately related aspects of Caribbean family and kinship, in K. Bumiller (ed.) *In an Abusive State: How Neoliberalism Appropriated the Feminist Movement Against Sexual Violence*. London: Duke University Press.

Fontana, B. (2008) Hegemony and power in Gramsci, in R. Howson and K. Smith (eds) *Hegemony: Studies in Consensus and Coercion*. New York: Routledge.

Foucault, M. (1974) *The Archaeology of Knowledge*. London: Tavistock.

Foucault, M. (1977) *Discipline and Punish: The Birth of the Prison*. New York: Pantheon.

Foucault, M. (1978) *The History of Sexuality, Volume 1: An Introduction*, trans. R. Hurley. New York: Vintage Books.

Foucault, M. (1980) *Power/Knowledge*, trans. C. Gordon. New York: Pantheon Books.

Foucault, M. (1985) *The Use of Pleasure: Volume 2 of The History of Sexuality*, trans. R. Hurley. New York: Random House, Inc.

Frankenberg, R. (1993) *The Social Construction of Whiteness: White Women, Race Matters*. New York and London: Routledge.

Frankenberg, R. (1997) *Displacing Whiteness. Essays in Social and Cultural Criticism*. Durham, NC: Duke University Press.

Freud, S. (1976 [1905]) Infantile sexuality, in *Three Essays on the Theory of Sexuality*, trans. J. Strachey. New York: Basic Books.

Fung, P. (2010) Chinese machine translation, in N. Indurkhya and F.J. Damerau (eds) *Handbook of Natural Language Processing*, 3rd edn. Boca Raton, FL: Taylor & Francis.

Fuss, D. (1989) *Essentially Speaking: Feminism, Nature and Difference*. New York: Routledge.

Gandara, P. and Hopkins, M. (eds) (2010) *Forbidden Language: English Learners and Restrictive Language Policies*. New York: Teachers College Press.

García, O. (2011) *Bilingual Education in the 21st Century: A Global Perspective*. United Kingdom: Wiley Blackwell.

García, O. and Sylvan, C. (2011) Pedagogies and practices in multilingual classrooms: singularities in pluralities, *The Modern Language Journal*, 95(3): 385–400.

Gardner, S. and Martin-Jones, M. (eds) (2012) *Multilingualism, Discourse and Ethnography*. New York: Routledge.

Gee, S. and McIlveen, L. (2005) Not on our beach: Cronulla police vow to defend Australian way. *Daily Telegraph*, 9 December: 4.

Genesee, F. (1989) Early bilingual development: one language or two? *Journal of Child Language*, 16: 161–179.

Germov, J. (2004) Which class do you teach? Education and the reproduction of class, in J. Allen (ed.) *Sociology of Education: Possibilities and Practices*, 3rd edn. Southbank, Vic.: Social Science Press.

Giddens, A. (1984) *The Constitution of Society: Outline of the Theory of Structuration*. Cambridge: Polity Press.

Gilbert, A. (2014) The urban revolution, in R.N.G. Gwynne and C. Kay (eds) *Latin America Transformed: Globalization and Modernity*, 2nd edn. London: Routledge.

Gill, R. and Scharff, C. (2011) Introduction, in R. Gill and C. Scharff (eds) *New Femininities: Postfeminism, Neoliberalism and Subjectivity*. New York: Palgrave Macmillan.

Gillborn, D. (2007) Education policy as an act of white supremacy: whiteness, critical race theory and education reform, *Journal of Education Policy*, 20(4): 485–505.

Gillborn, D. and Ladson-Billings, G. (2010) Education and critical race theory, in M.W. Apple, S.T. Ball and L.A. Gandin (eds) *The Routledge International Handbook of the Sociology of Education*. Oxon: Routledge.

Giroux, H. (1988) *Schooling and the Struggle for Public Life: Critical Pedagogy in the Modern Age*. Minneapolis, MN: University of Minnesota Press.

Giroux, H. (1992) *Border Crossings: Cultural Workers and the Politics of Education*. New York: Routledge.

Giroux, H. (1995) Animating youth: the distinction of children's culture. Available at: http://gseis.ucla.edu/courses/ed253a/Giroux/Giroux2.html (accessed 8 August 2005).

Giroux, H. (1997) *Pedagogy and the Politics of Hope: Theory, Culture and Schooling*. Boulder, CO: Westview Press.

Giroux, H.A. (2011) *On Critical Pedagogy*. New York: Continuum International Publishing Company.

Giroux, H. and Pollock, G. (2011) Is Disney good for your kids? How corporate media shape youth identity in the digital age, in S. Steinberg (ed.) *Kinderculture: The Corporate Construction of Childhood*, 3rd edn. Boulder, CO: Westview Press.

Gittins, D. (1998) *The Child in Question*. London: Macmillan.

Glover, A. (1991) Young children and race: a report of a study of two and three year olds. Paper presented at the Communities Evolution and Revolution Conference, Australian Catholic University, Sydney, 11–12 October.

Gogolin, I. (2011) The challenge for superdiversity for education in Europe. *Education Enquiry*, 2(2): 239–249.

Goldsworthy, T. and Raj, M. (2014) Out of the shadows: the rise of domestic violence in Australia, *The Conversation*, 4 August. Available at: www.theconversation.com/out-of-the-shadows-the-rise-of-domestic-violence-in-australia-29280 (accessed 16 March 2016).

Goodwin, S. and Huppatz, K. (2010) *The Good Mother: Contemporary Motherhood in Australia*. Sydney: Sydney University Press.

Gorski, P.C. (2011) Unlearning deficit ideology and the scornful gaze: thoughts on authenticating the class discourse in education, *Counterpoints*, 402: 152–173. Available at: www.jstor.org/stable/42981081 (accessed 2 January 2015).

Gowlett, C. (2011) Injurious assumptions: Butler, subjectification and gen(d) erational poverty, *International Journal of Inclusive Education*, 16(9): 855–900.

Graham, S. (2012) Choosing single motherhood? Single women negotiating the nuclear family ideal, in D. Cutas and S. Chan (eds) *Families: Beyond the Nuclear Ideal*. London: Bloomsbury.

Gregory, A. and Milner, S. (2011) What is 'new' about fatherhood? The social construction of fatherhood in France and the UK, *Men and Masculinities*, 14(5): 1–19.

Greishaber, S. (1998) Constructing the gendered infant, in Yelland, N. (ed.) *Gender in Early Childhood*. London: Routledge.

Grenfell, M. (ed.) (2012) *Pierre Bourdieu: Key Concepts*, 2nd edn. London: Routledge.

Grewal, I. and Kaplan, P. (2002) *An Introduction to Women's Studies: Gender in a Transnational World*. New York: McGraw-Hill.

Greytak, E.A., Kosciw, J.G. and Díaz, E.M. (2009) *Harsh Realities: The Experiences of Transgender Youth in Our Nation's Schools*. New York: Gay Lesbian and Straight Education Network.

Grieshaber, S. (1998) Constructing the gendered infant, in N. Yelland (ed.) *Gender in Early Childhood*. London: Routledge.

Grieshaber, S. (2001) Advocacy and early childhood educators: identity and cultural conflicts, in S. Grieshaber and G. Cannella (eds) *Embracing Identities in Early Childhood Education: Diversity and Possibilities*. New York: Teachers College Press.

Grossman, A.H., D'Augelli, A.R. and Salter, N.P. (2006) Male-to-female transgender youth, *Journal of GLBT Family Studies*, 2(1): 71–92.

Guess, T.J. (2006) The social construction of whiteness: racism by intent, racism by consequence, *Critical Sociology*, 32(4): 649–673.

Guilfoyle, A., Saggers, S., Sims, M. and Hutchins, T. (2010) Culturally strong child care programs for Indigenous children, families and communities, *Australasian Journal of Early Childhood*, 35(3): 68–76.

Gunn, A. (2015) The potential of queer theorizing in early childhood education, in A.C. Gunn and Smith, L.A. (eds) *Sexual Cultures in Aotearoa New Zealand Education*. Otago, NZ: Otago University Press.

Halberstam, J. (1998) *Female Masculinities*. Durham, NC: Duke University Press.

Hall, D.E. (2004) *Subjectivity*. New York: Routledge.

Hall, S. (1992) New ethnicities, in J. Donald and A. Rattansi (eds) *'Race', Culture and Difference*. London: Sage.

Hall, S. (1996) Introduction: who needs 'identity'?, in P. Du Guy (ed.) *Questions of Cultural Identity*. London: Sage Publications.

Hall, S. (1997) The work of representation, in S. Hall (ed.) *Representation: Cultural Representation and Signifying Practices*. London: Sage, in association with the Open University.

Hall, S. (2011) The neo-liberal revolution, *Cultural Studies*, 25(6): 705–728.

Hamelink, C.J. (2015) The elusive concept of globalization, in F.J. Lechner and J. Boli (eds) *The Globalization Reader*, 5th edn. West Sussex: John Wiley & Sons Ltd.

Harding, V. (ed.) (2006) *Learn to Include*. Dulwich Hill, Australia: Learn to Include.

Harman, V. (2010) Experiences of racism and the changing nature of white privilege among lone white mothers of mixed-parentage children in the UK, *Ethnic and Racial Studies*, 33(2): 176–194.

Harraway, D. (1991) *Simians, Cyborgs, and Women: The Reinvention of Nature*. New York: Routledge.

Harrison, N. (2011) *Teaching and Learning in Aboriginal education*, 2nd edn. Australia and New Zealand: Oxford University Press.

Harvey, N. and Myint, H.H. (2014) Our language is like food: can children feed on home languages to thrive, belong and achieve in early childhood education and care? *Australasian Journal of Early Childhood*, 39(2): 42–50.

Hebbani, A. and Wills, C.H. (2012) How Muslim women in Australia navigate through media (mis)representations of hijab/burqa, *Australian Journal of Communication*, 39(1): 87–100.

Heller, M. (1996) Legitimate language in a multilingual school, *Linguistics and Education*, 8: 139–157.

Heller, M. (2012) Sociolinguistic perspectives on language and multilingualism in institutions, in S. Gardner and M. Martin-Jones (eds) *Multilingualism, Discourse and Ethnography*. New York: Routledge.

Heron, T. (2008) Globalization, neoliberalism and the exercise of human agency, *International Journal of Popular Culture Society*, 20: 85–101.

Hewitt, J.K., Campbell, P., Porpavai, K., Grover, S.R., Newman, L.K. and Warne, G.L. (2012) Hormone treatment of gender identity disorder in a cohort of children and adolescents, *Medical Journal of Australia*, 196(9): 578–581.

Hier, S.P. (2003) Risk and panic in late modernity: implications of the converging sites of social anxiety, *British Journal of Sociology*, 54(1): 3–20.

Holland, P. (2006) *Picturing Childhood: The Myth of the Child in Popular Imagery*. New York: I.B. Tauris.

Hollinsworth, D. (2006). *Race and Racism in Australia*, 3rd edn. Sydney: Social Science Press.

Hollinsworth, D. (2010) Racism and Indigenous people in Australia, *Global Dialogue*, 12(2), Summer/Autumn, Race and Racisms.

Holloway, D., Green, L. and Livingstone, S. (2013) *Zero to Eight. Young Children and their Internet Use*. London: EU Kids Online.

Hollway, W. (1984) Gender difference and the production of subjectivity, in J. Henriques, W. Hollway, C. Urwin, C. Venn and V. Walkerdine (eds) *Changing the Subject: Psychology, Social Regulation and Subjectivity*. London: Methuen.

hooks, b. (1997) Whiteness in the black imagination, in R. Frankenberg (ed.) *Displacing Whiteness: Essays in Social and Cultural Criticism*. Durham, NC: Duke University Press.

Horton, J. (2012) 'Got my shoes, got my Pokémon': everyday geographies of children's popular culture, *Geoforum*, 43: 4–13.

Hung, H.F. and Kucinskas, J. (2011) Globalization and global inequality: assessing the impact of the rise of China and India, 1980–2005, *American Journal of Sociology*, 116(5): 1478–1513.

Huppatz, K. (2015) Social class and the classroom: a reflection on the role of schooling and mothering in the production and reproduction of disadvantage and privilege, in T. Ferfolja, C. Jones Díaz and J. Ullman (eds) *Understanding Sociological Theory and Pedagogical Practices*. Sydney: Cambridge University Press.

Huuki, T. and Renold, E. (2015) Crush: mapping historical, material and affective force relations in young children's hetero-sexual playground play, *Discourse. Studies in the Cultural Politics of Education*, 1–16.

Ingraham, C. (1994) The heterosexual imaginary: feminist sociology and theories of gender, *Sociological Theory*, 12(2): 203–219.

Irvine, J. (2006) Emotional scripts of sex panics, *Sexuality Research and Social Policy*, 3(3): 82–94.

Ives, P. (2013) Global English, hegemony and education: lessons from Gramsci, *Educational Philosophy and Theory*, 41(6): 661–683.

Jabour, B. (2013) Did John Howard's Pacific Solution stop the boats, as John Howard asserts? *Guardian*, 19 July. Available at: www.theguardian.com/world/2013/jul/19/did-howard-solution-stop-boats (accessed 8 December 2015).

Jagose, A. (1996) *Queer Theory*. Melbourne: Melbourne University Press.

James, A. and Prout, A. (eds) (1990) *Constructing and Reconstructing Childhood: Contemporary Issues in the Sociological Study of Childhood*. London: Falmer Press.

James, A., Jenks, C. and Prout, A. (1998) *Theorizing Childhood*. London: Polity Press.

Jenkins, H. (ed.) (1998) *The Children's Culture Reader*. New York: New York University Press.

Jenkins, J. (2013) *English as a Lingua Franca in the International University*. London: Routledge.

Jeon, M. (2008) Korean heritage language maintenance and language ideology, *Heritage Language Journal*, 6(2): 54–71.

Jones Díaz, C. (2003) Latino/a voices in Australia: negotiating bilingual identity, *Contemporary Issues in Early Childhood*, 4(3): 314–336.

Jones Díaz, C. (2007) Intersections between language retention and identities in young bilingual children. Unpublished doctoral thesis, University of Western Sydney.

Jones Díaz, C. (2011) Children's voices: Spanish in urban multilingual and multicultural Australia, in K. Potowski and J. Rothman (eds) *Bilingual Youth: Spanish in English-speaking Societies*. Philadelphia, PA: John Benjamins Publishing Company.

Jones Díaz, C. (2014a) Literacies in childhood bilingualism: building on cultural and linguistic capital in early childhood education, in L. Arthur, J. Ashton and B. Beecher (eds) *Diverse Literacies in the Early Years: Implications for Practice*. Sydney: ACER.

Jones Díaz, C. (2014b) Institutional, material and economic constraints in languages education: unequal provision of linguistic resources in early childhood and primary settings in Australia, *International Journal of Bilingual Education and Bilingualism*, 17(3): 272–286.

Jones Díaz, C. (2015) Silences in growing up bilingual in multicultural globalized societies: negotiating languages, identity and difference in childhood, in T. Ferfolja, C. Jones Díaz and J. Ullman (eds) *Understanding Sociological Theory for Educational Practices*. Melbourne, Vic.: Cambridge University Press.

Jones Díaz, C. (2016) Growing up bilingual and negotiating identity in globalised and multicultural Australia: exploring transformations and contestations of identity and bilingualism in contexts of hybridity and diaspora, in D. Cole and C. Woodrow (eds) *Superdimensions in Globalisation and Education*. Singapore: Springer.

Jones Díaz, C. and Harvey, N. (2002) Other words, other worlds: bilingual identities and literacy, in L. Makin and C. Jones Díaz (eds) *Literacies in Early Childhood: Changing Views, Challenging Practices*. Sydney: MacLennan & Petty.

Jones Díaz, C. and Harvey, N. (2007) Other words, other worlds: bilingual identities and literacy, in L. Makin, C. Jones Díaz and C. McLaughlan (eds) *Literacies in Childhood: Challenging Views, challenging practice*, 2nd edn. Sydney: Elsevier.

Jones Díaz, C. and Walker, U. (2016) Spanish in the antipodes: diversity and hybridity of Latino/a Spanish speakers in Australia and Aotearoa-New Zealand, in P. Potowski (ed.) *Handbook of Spanish as a Minority/Heritage Language*. London: Routledge.

Jones Díaz, C., Beecher, B. and Arthur, L. (2002) Children's worlds and critical literacy, in L. Makin and C. Jones Díaz (eds) *Literacies in Early Childhood: Changing Views Challenging Practices*. Sydney: MacLennan & Petty.

Jones Díaz, C., Chodkiewicz, A. and Morgan, L. (2016, in review) Safe spaces for Aboriginal families and their children: early literacy learning, cultural representation and engagement in an Aboriginal playgroup, *Australasian Journal of Early Childhood*.

Kameniar, B.M., Imtoual, A. and Bradley, D. (2010) 'Mullin' the Yarndi' and other wicked problems at a multiracial early childhood education site in regional Australia, *Educational Policy*, 24(1): 9–27.

Kaomea, J. (2000) Pointed noses and yellow hair: deconstructing children's writing on race and ethnicity in Hawai'i, in J. Jipson and R. Johnson (eds) *Identity and Representation in Early Childhood*. New York: Peter Lang.

Kasturi, S. (2002) Constructing childhood in a corporate world: cultural studies, childhood, and Disney, in G.S. Cannella and J.L. Kincheloe (eds) *Kidworld: Childhood Studies, Global Perspectives, and Education*. New York: Peter Lang.

Katz, C. (2004) *Growing Up Global: Economic Restructuring and Children's Everyday Lives*. Minneapolis, MN: University of Minnesota Press.

Kehily, M.J. (2010) Childhood in crisis? Tracing the contours of 'crisis' and its impact upon contemporary parenting practices, *Media, Culture and Society*, 32(2): 171–185.

Kell, P. (2004) A teacher's tool kit: sociology and social theory explaining the world, in J. Allen (ed.) *Sociology of Education: Possibilities and Practices*, 3rd edn. Southbank, Vic.: Social Science Press.

Kimmel, M.S. (1994) Masculinity as homophobia: fear, shame, and silence in the construction of gender identity, in H. Brod and M. Kaufman (eds) *Theorizing Masculinities*. Thousand Oaks, CA: Sage Publications.

Kincheloe, J.L. (2002) The complex politics of McDonald's and the new childhood: colonizing Kidzworld, in G.S. Cannella and J.L. Kincheloe (eds) *Kidworld Childhood Studies, Global Perspectives and Education*. New York: Peter Lang: 75–121.

Kincheloe, J.L. and Steinberg, S.R. (1997) *Changing Multiculturalism*. Buckingham: Open University Press.

Kincheloe, J.L. and Steinberg, S.R. (1998) Addressing the crisis of whiteness. Reconfiguring white identity in a pedagogy of whiteness, in J.L. Kincheloe, S.R. Steinberg, N.M. Rodriguez and R.E. Chennault (eds) *White Reign. Deploying Whiteness in America*. London: Macmillan.

King, J.R. (1997) Keeping it quiet: gay teachers in the primary grades, in J. Tobin (ed.) *Making a Place for Pleasure in Early Childhood Education*. New Haven, CT: Yale University Press.

Kissen, R. (ed.) (2002) *Getting Ready for Benjamin. Preparing Teachers for Sexual Diversity in the Classroom*. Lanham, MD: Rowan & Littlefield.

Kitzinger, J. (1990) Who are you kidding? Children, power and the struggle against sexual abuse, in A. James and A. Prout (eds) *Constructing and Reconstructing Childhood: Contemporary Issues in the Sociological Study of Childhood*. London: Falmer Press.

Kobayashi, A. and Ray, B. (2000) Civil risk and landscapes of marginality in Canada: a pluralist approach to social justice, *Canadian Geographer*, 44(4): 401–417.

Kontopodis, M., Wulf, C. and Fichtner, B. (2011) Introduction: children, development and education – a dialogue between cultural psychological and historical anthropology, in M. Kontopodis, C. Wulf and B. Fichtner (eds) *Children,*

Development and Education: Historical, Cultural and Anthropological Perspectives. Netherlands: Springer.

Kromidas, M. (2015) 'He's cute, for her': kids' entangled pedagogies of sexuality and race in New York City, in E. Renold, J. Ringrose and D.R. Egan (eds) *Children, Sexuality and Sexualization*. Basingstoke, UK: Palgrave Macmillan: 159–173.

Krulik, N. (1997) *Anastasia*, adapted N. Krulik, illus. Thompson Brothers. New York: Golden Books.

Kumashiro, K.K. (2002) *Troubling Education: Queer Activism and Antioppressive Pedagogy*. New York: RoutledgeFalmer.

Kutner, B. (1958) Patterns of mental functioning associated with prejudice in children. *Psychological Monographs*, 72(406). Washington, DC: American Psychological Association.

Ladson-Billings, G. and Tate, W. (2006) Toward a critical race theory in education, in A. Dixson and C. Rousseau (eds) *Critical Race Theory in Education: All God's Children got a Song*. New York: Routledge.

Langer, B. (1998) Globalisation and the myth of ethnic community: Salvadoran refugees in multicultural states, in D. Bennett (ed.) *Multicultural States: Rethinking Difference and Identity*. London: Routledge.

Langley, P. (2008) *The Everyday Life of Global Finance*. Oxford: Oxford University Press.

Lanza, E. (1992) Can bilingual two-year-olds code-switch? *Journal of Child Language*, 19: 633–658.

Larbalestier, J. (1999) What is this thing called white? Reflections on 'whiteness' and multiculturalism, in G. Hage and R. Couch (eds) *The Future of Australian Multiculturalism. Reflections on the Twentieth Anniversary of Jean Martin's 'The Migrant Experience'*. Sydney: Research Institute for Humanities and Social Sciences, University of Sydney.

Lareau, A. and McNamara-Horvat, E. (1999) Moments of social inclusion and exclusion. Race, class and cultural capital in family–school relationships, *Sociology of Education*, 72(Jan.): 37–53.

Lareau, A. and Weininger, E.B. (2008) Time, work, and family life: reconceptualizing gendered time patterns through the case of children's organized activities, *Sociological Forum*, 23(3): 419–453.

Larkins, C. (2014) Enacting children's citizenship: developing understandings of how children enact themselves as citizens through actions and acts of citizenship, *Childhood*, 21(1): 7–21.

Lee, D. (2010) Gay mothers and early childhood education: standing tall. *Australasian Journal of Early Childhood*, 35(1): 16–23.

Lenz-Taguchi, H. and Palmer, A. (2013) A more 'livable' school? A diffractive analysis of the performative enactments of girls' ill-/well-being with(in) school environments, *Gender and Education*, 25(6): 671–687.

Leonardo, Z. (2010) The souls of white fold: critical pedagogy, whiteness studies and globalization discourse, *Race, Ethnicity and Education*, 5(1): 29–50.

Leonardo, Z. (2012) The race for class: reflections on a critical raceclass theory of education, *Educational Studies*, 48: 427–449.

Letts IV, W. (1999) How to make 'boys' and 'girls' in the classroom: the heteronormative nature of elementary-school science, in W. Letts IV and J.T. Sears (eds) *Queering Elementary Education: Advancing the Dialogue about Sexualities and Schooling*. Lanham, MD: Rowan & Littlefield.

Lev, A.I. (2004) *Transgender Emergence: Therapeutic Guidelines for Working with Gender Variant People and their Families*. New York: Routledge.

Levine, J. (2002) *Harmful to Minors: The Perils of Protecting Children from Sex*. Minneapolis, MN: University of Minnesota Press.

Lewin, E. (1998) *Recognizing Ourselves: Ceremonies of Lesbian and Gay Commitment*. New York: Columbia University Press.

Liddicoat, J. and Jowan Curnow, T. (2014) Students' home languages and the struggle for space in the curriculum, *International Journal of Multilingualism*, 11(3): 273–288.

Lingard, B. (2009) Testing times: the need for new intelligent accountabilities for schooling, *QTU Professional Magazine*: Available at: www.qtu.asn.au/files/9113/2780/3358/29–01–2012_1315_170.pdf (accessed 1 January 2016).

Lingard, B. (2010) Policy borrowing, policy learning: testing times in Australian schooling, *Critical Studies in Education*, 51(2): 129–147.

Livingstone, S. and Bober, M. (2013) Regulating the internet at home: contrasting the perspectives of children and parents, in D. Buckingham, and R. Willett, (eds) *Digital Generations: Children, Young People and New Media*. New York: Routledge.

Loakes, D., Moses, K., Wigglesworth, G., Simpson, J. and Billington, R. (2013) Children's language input: a study of a remote multilingual Indigenous Australian community, *Multilingua*, 32(5): 683–711.

Lofquist, D. (2011) *Same-sex Couple Households*. Washington, DC: US Department of Commerce, Economics and Statistics Administration, US Census Bureau.

Lubeck, S. (1998) Is DAP for everyone? A response, *Childhood Education*, 74(5): 299–310.

Luke, C. (1994) White women in interracial families: reflections on hybridization, feminine identities and racialized othering, *Feminist Issues*, 14(2): 49–71.

Lundeberg, M.A. (1997) You guys are overreacting: teaching prospective teachers about subtle gender bias, *Journal of Teacher Education*, 48(1): 55–61.

Macedo, D. and Bartolomé, L.L. (2014) Multiculturalism permitted in English only, *International Multilingual Research Journal*, 8(1): 24–37.

MacNaughton, G. (2000) *Rethinking Gender in Early Childhood Education*. Sydney: Allen & Unwin.

MacNaughton, G. (2001) Silences, sex-roles and subjectivities: 40 years of gender in the *Australian Journal of Early Childhood*, *Australian Journal of Early Childhood*, 26(1): 21–25.

MacNaughton, G. (2009) Deconstructing, in G. MacNaughton (ed.) *Techniques for Teaching Young Children: Choices for Theory and Practice*, 3rd edn. Frenchs Forest, Australia: Pearson.

MacNaughton, G. and Davis, K. (2001) Beyond 'othering': rethinking approaches to teaching young Anglo-Australian children about Indigenous Australians, *Contemporary Issues in Early Childhood*, 2(1): 83–93.

MacNaughton, G. and Davis, K. (2009) *'Race' and Early Childhood Education: An International Approach to Identity, Politics, and Pedagogy*. Basingstoke: Palgrave Macmillan.

Manning, K.E., Sansfaçon, A.P. and Meyer, E.J. (2014) Introduction, in E.J. Meyer, and A.P. Sansfaçon, (eds) *Supporting Transgender and Gender Creative Youth: Schools, Families, and Communities in Action*. New York: Peter Lang.

Mares, P. (2011) Fear and instrumentalism: Australian policy responses to migration from the global south, *The Round Table*, 100(415): 407–422.

Marginson, S. (1999) After globalisation: emerging politics of education, *Education Policy*, 14(1): 19–31.

Marmion, D., Obata, K. and Troy, J. (2014) *Community, Identity, Wellbeing: The Report of the Second National Indigenous Languages Survey*. Canberra: Australian Institute of Aboriginal and Torres Strait Islander Studies.

Martin, G. (2015) Stop the boats! Moral panic in Australia over asylum seekers, *Continuum*, 29(3): 304–322.

Martin-McDonald, K. and McCarthy, A. (2008) 'Making' the white terrain in Indigenous health research: literature review, *Journal of Advanced Nursing*, 61(2): 126–133.

Marx, K. (1967) *Capital. Vol. 1*. New York: International Publishers.

Maslen, G. (2011) Lost for words, *About the House Magazine*, December: 37–39.

Mau, S. (2010) *Social Transnationalism: Lifeworlds Beyond the Nation-state*. Oxon: Routledge.

May, S. (1999) Critical multiculturalism and cultural difference, in S. May (ed.) *Critical Multiculturalism: Rethinking Multicultural and Antiracist Education*. London: Falmer Press.

May, S. (2012) Language rights: promoting civic multilingualism, in M. Martin-Jones, A. Blackledge and A. Creese (eds) *The Routledge Handbook of Multilingualism*. London: Routledge.

Mayo, C. (2006) Pushing the limits of liberalism: queerness, children and the future, *Educational Theory*, 56(4): 469–487.

Mayo, E. and Nairn, A. (2009) *Consumer Kids: How Big Business is Grooming Our Children for Profit*. London: Constable.

McLaren, P. (1998) Whiteness is . . . The struggle for postcolonial hybridity, in J.L. Kincheloe, S.R. Steinberg, N.M. Rodriguez and R.E. Chennault (eds) *White Reign. Deploying Whiteness in America*. London: Macmillan.

McClelland, S.I. and Hunter, L.E. (2013) Bodies that are always out of line: a closer look at 'age appropriate sexuality', in B. Fahs, M.L. Dudy and S. Stage (eds) *The Moral Panics of Sexuality*. New York: Palgrave Macmillan.

McCleod, J. (2012) Vulnerability and the neo-liberal youth citizen: a view from Australia, *Comparative Education*, 48(1): 11–26.

McNay, L. (2000) *Gender and Agency: Reconfiguring the Subject in Feminist and Social Theory*. Cambridge: Polity Press.

McRobbie, A. and Thornton, S. (1995) Rethinking 'moral panic' for multi-mediated social worlds, *British Journal of Sociology*, 46(4): 559–574.

Meyer, E.J. and Sansfaçon, A.P. (eds) (2014) *Supporting Transgender and Gender Creative Youth: Schools, Families and Communities in Action*. New York: Peter Lang.

Milanovic, B. (2015) Global income inequality by the numbers: in history and now, in F.J. Lechner and J. Boli (eds) *The Globalization Reader*, 5th edn. West Sussex: John Wiley & Sons Ltd.

Mills, S. (2004) *Discourse*. London: Routledge.

Mitchell, L. (2010) Constructions of childhood in early childhood education policy debate in New Zealand, *Contemporary Issues in Early Childhood*, 11(4): 328–341.

Mitchel, L. (2011) Domestic violence in Australia: an overview of the issues. Available at: www.parlinfo.aph.gov.au/parlInfo/download/library/prspub/1246402/upload_binary/1246402.pdf;fileType=application%2Fpdf#search=%22library/prspub/1246402%22 (accessed 16 March 2016).

Moore, R. (2012) Whitewashing the gap: the discursive practices of whiteness, *International Journal of Critical Indigenous Studies*, 5(2): 2–12.

Moreton-Robinson, A. (ed.) (2004) *Essays in Social and Cultural Criticism: Whitening Race*. Canberra: Aboriginal Studies Press.

Moreton-Robinson, A. (2009) The discursive nature of citizenship: Indigenous sovereign rights, racism and welfare reform, *International Journal of Critical Indigenous Studies*, 2(2): 2–9.

Moreton-Robinson, A. (2011) Imagining the good indigenous citizen: race, war and the pathology of patriarchal white sovereignty, *Cultural Studies Review*, 15(2): 61–79.

Moreton-Robinson, A. and Nicoll, F. (2006) We shall fight them on the beaches: protesting cultures of white possession, *Journal of Australian Studies*, 30(89): 149–160.

Morgan, D.H.J. (1996) *Family Contentions: An Introduction to Family Studies*. Cambridge: Polity Press.

Morgan, G. (2014) Islamophobia feeds on our fear of an evil within. Available at: www.smh.com.au/comment/islamophobia-feeds-on-our-fear-of-an-evil-within-20140930-10o073.html (accessed 10 December 2014).

Morgan, G. and Poynting, S. (2012) Introduction: the transnational folk devil, in S.G. Morgan and S. Poynting (eds) *Global Islamophobia: Muslims and the Moral Panic in the West*. Surrey: Ashgate Publishing Ltd.

Morgan, L., Chodkiewicz, A. and Pennycook, A. (2015) *Developing Literacies in Informal Settings: Strengthening the Affordances of Supported Playgroups*. Sydney: University of Technology.

Moro, C. (2011) Material culture, semiotics and early childhood development, in M. Kontopodis, C. Wulf and B. Fichtner (eds) *Children, Development and Education: Cultural, Historical, Anthropological Perspectives*. Springer: Dordrecht: 57–70.

Morris, M. (2000) Dante's left foot kicks queer theory into gear, in S. Talburt and S.R. Steinberg (eds) *Thinking Queer: Sexuality, Culture, and Education*. New York: Peter Lang.

Mountz, A. (2011) Where asylum-seekers wait: feminist counter-topographies of sites between states, *Gender, Place & Culture*, 18(3): 381–399.

Moustakim, M. (2015) 'Disaffected' youth: intersections of class and ethnicity, in T. Ferfolja, C. Jones Díaz and J. Ullman (eds) *Understanding Sociological Theory and Pedagogical Practices*. Cambridge: Cambridge University Press.

Nederveen Pieterse, J. (2015) *Globalization and Culture: Global Mélange*, 3rd edn. Lanham, MD: Rowman & Littlefield.

Nettle, D. and Romaine, S. (2000) *Vanishing Voices: The Extension of the World's Languages*. Oxford: Oxford University Press.

New South Wales Board of Studies (2008) *Working with Aboriginal Communities*, rev. edn. A guide to community consultation and protocols. Sydney: Board of Studies. Available at: www.boardofstudies.nsw.edu.au (accessed 14 October 2014).

New South Wales Government, Education and Communities (2013) About racism. Available at: www.racismnoway.com.au/about-racism/timeline/index-1900s.html (accessed 17 October 2014).

Nieto, S. (2013) *Language, Culture and Teaching: Critical Perspectives*, 2nd edn. New York: Routledge.

Nudelman, M. (2015) Here's where Disney really makes money, *Business Insider: Australia*, 14 January. Available at: www.businessinsider.com/heres-where-disney-really-makes-money-2015-1 (accessed 9 January 2016).

O'Donnell, S. (2015) Black, gay in a wonderland of boogie, in D. Hodge (ed.) *Colouring the Rainbow: Blak Queer and Trans Perspectives*. Mile End, SA: Wakefield Press.

Ofcom (2012) Children and parents: media use and attitudes report. London. Available at: http://stakeholders.ofcom.org.uk/binaries/research/media literacy/oct2012/main.pdf (accessed 16 January 2016).

Office for National Statistics (ONS) (2015) *Families and Households 2015*. London: ONS. Available at: www.ons.gov.uk/ons/rel/family-demography/families-and-households/2015/stb-families-and-households.html (accessed 21 January 2016).

Olneck, M. (2000) Can multicultural education change what counts as cultural capital? *American Educational Research Journal*, 37(2): 317–348.

Osgood, J. (2010) Reconstructing professionalism in ECEC: the case for the 'critically reflective emotional professional', *Early Years*, 30(2): 119–133.

Osgood, J. (2012) *Narratives from the Nursery: Negotiating Professional Identities in Early Childhood*. London: Routledge.

Osgood, J. (2014) Playing with gender: making space for posthuman childhood(s), in J. Moyles, J. Payler and J. Georgeson (eds) *Early Years Foundations: Critical Issues*. Maidenhead: Open University Press.

Osgood, J. (2015) Reimaging gender and play, in J. Moyles (ed.) *The Excellence of Play*. Maidenhead: Open University Press.

Osgood, J. and Giugni, M. (2015) Putting posthumanist theory to work to reconfigure gender in early childhood: when theory becomes method becomes art, *Global Studies of Childhood*, 5(3): 346–360.

Osgood, J. and Robinson, K.H. (in press) Celebrating pioneering and contemporary feminist approaches to the study of gender in early childhood, in K. Smith, K. Alexander and S. Campbell (eds) *Feminism in Early Childhood*. New York: Springer.

Pacini-Ketchabaw, V. and Schecter, S. (2002). Engaging the discourse of diversity: educators' frameworks for working with linguistic and cultural difference, *Contemporary Issues in Early Childhood*, 3(3): 400–412.

Pacini-Ketchabaw, V. and Taylor, A. (2015) *Unsettling the Colonial Places and Spaces of Early Childhood Education*. New York: Routledge.

Palmer, G. (1990) Preschool children and race: an Australian study, *Australian Journal of Early Childhood*, 15(2): 3–8.

Palmer, S. (2006) *Toxic Childhood: How the Modern World is Damaging Our Children and What Can We Do About It?* London: Orion.

Papastergiadis, N. (2013) Why multiculturalism makes people so angry and sad, in H. Sykes (ed.) *Space, Place and Culture*. Melbourne: Future Leaders. Available at: www.futureleaders.com.au/index.php (accessed 15 December 2015).

Paradies, Y. (2006) Defining, conceptualizing and characterizing racism in health research, *Critical Public Health*, 16(2): 143–57.

Paradies, Y., Harris, R. and Anderson, I. (2008) The impact of racism on Indigenous health in Australia and Aotearoa: towards a research agenda. Discussion paper no. 4. Darwin: Cooperative Research Centre for Aboriginal Health.

Parish, S., Magaña, S. and Cassiman, S. (2008) It's just that much harder: multilayered hardship experiences of low-income mothers with disabilities, *Affilia*, 23: 51–65.

Parker, I. (1992) *Discourse Dynamics: Critical Analysis for Social and Individual Psychology*. London: Routledge.

Patrick, D. (2012) Indigenous contexts, in M. Martin-Jones, A. Blackledge and A. Creese (eds) *The Routledge Handbook of Multilingualism*. London: Routledge.

Pearl, E. and Lambert, W.E. (1962) The relationship of bilingualism to intelligence. *Psychological Monographs*, 76(27): 1–23.

Penn, H. (2009) *Early Childhood Education and Care: Key Lessons from Research for Policy Makers*. Brussels: European Commission. Available at: http://roar.uel.ac.uk/3362/1/ecec-report-pdf.pdf (accessed 9 January 2015).

Pennycook, A., Morgan, L., Cruickshank, K. and Jones Díaz, C. (2010–2011) Developing early literacy in informal settings: engaging disadvantaged Aboriginal and CALD families outside formal settings, ARC Linkage Grant with University of Technology, NSW FACS and NSW DEC.

Phillips, J. and Klapdor, M. (2010) Migration to Australia since federation: a guide to the statistics. Available at: www.aph.gov.au/binaries/library/pubs/bn/sp/migrationpopulation.pdf (accessed 6 December 2015).

Phillips, P. and Vandenbroek, P. (2014) Domestic, family and sexual violence in Australia: an overview of the issues. Research Paper Series, 2014–15. Available at: www.aph.gov.au/About_Parliament/Parliamentary_Departments/Parliamentary_Library/pubs/rp/rp1415/ViolenceAust (accessed 16 March 2016).

Postman, N. (1982) *The Disappearance of Childhood*. New York: Delcorte Press.

Priest, N., Walton, J., White, F., Kowal, E., Fox, B. and Paradies, Y. (2014) 'You are not born being racist, are you?' Discussing racism with primary aged children, *Race Ethnicity and Education*. Published online 4 September.

Priven, D. (2008) Grievability of first language loss: towards a reconceptualisation of European minority language education practice, *International Journal of Bilingual Education and Bilingualism*, 11(1): 95–106.

Purdie, N. (2009) A way forward for Indigenous languages. Available at: research.acer.edu.au/resdev/vol21/iss21/2/ (accessed 20 March 2016).

Qvortrup, J. (2004) The waiting child, *Childhood*, 11(3): 267–273.

Qvortrup, J. (2008) Macroanalysis of childhood, in P. Christensen and A. James (eds) *Research with Children: Perspectives and Practices*, 2nd edn. Abingdon, Oxon: Routledge: 66–86.

Reay, D. (1998) Cultural reproduction: mothers' involvement in their children's primary schooling, in M. Grenfell and D. James (eds) *Acts of Practical Theory. Bourdieu and Education*. London: Falmer Press.

Reay, D. (2010) Sociology, class and education, in M. Apple, S.J. Ball and L.A. Gandin (eds) *The Routledge International Handbook of the Sociology of Education*. London: Routledge.

Reddy, M. (1994) *Crossing the Color Line: Race, Parenting and Culture*. New Brunswick, NJ: Rutgers University Press.

Redmond, G. (2009) Children as actors: how does the child perspective literature treat agency in the context of poverty? *Social Policy and Society*, 8(4): 541–550.

Refugee Action Coalition Sydney (RAC) (2015) Refugees: the facts. Available at: www.refugeeaction.org.au/?p=3061 (accessed 8 December 2015).

Refugee Council of Australia (RCA) (2014) Myths about refugees and asylum seekers: quick mythbuster. Available at: www.refugeecouncil.org.au/fact-sheets/myths-about-refugees/quick-mythbuster/ (accessed 12 December 2015).

Refugee Council of Australia (RCA) (2015) A place to call home? The impact of Australia's refugee and asylum seeker policies on community cohesion. Available at: www.refugeecouncil.org.au/publications/reports-and-papers/ (accessed 6 December 2015).

Reid, C., Jones Díaz, C. and Alsaiari, H. (forthcoming) Cosmopolitanism, contemporary communication theory and cultural literacy in the TESOL classroom, *TESOL in Context*, Special Issue.

Renold, E. (2005) *Girls, Boys, and Junior Sexualities: Exploring Children's Gender and Sexual Relations in the Primary School*. London: Routledge.

Renold, E. (2006) 'They won't let us play . . . unless you're going out with one of them': girls, boys, and Butler's 'heterosexual matrix' in the primary years, *British Journal of Sociology of Education*, 27(4): 489–509.

Renold, E. and Mellor, D. (2013) Deleuze and Guattari in the nursery: towards an ethnographic, multi-sensory mapping of gendered bodies and becomings, in R. Coleman and J. Ringrose (eds) *Deleuze and Research Methodologies*. Edinburgh: Edinburgh University Press.

Renold, E., Ringrose, J. and Egan, D.R. (2015) Introduction, in E. Renold, J. Ringrose and D.R. Egan (eds) *Children, Sexuality and Sexualization*. Basingstoke: Palgrave Macmillan: 1–20.

Reyes, I. and Azaura, P. (2008) Emergent biliteracy in young Mexican immigrant children, *Reading Research Quarterly*, 43(4): 374–398.

Rich, A. (1980) Compulsory heterosexuality and lesbian existence, *Signs: Journal of Women in Culture and Society*, 5: 631–660.

Richardson, D. (1998) Sexuality and citizenship, *Sociology*, 32(1): 83–100.

Riley, E.A., Sitharthan, G., Clemson, L. and Diamond, M. (2011) The needs of gender-variant children and their parents: a parent survey, *International Journal of Sexual Health*, 23(3): 181–195.

Ringrose, J. and Rendd, E. (2010) Normative cruelties and gender deviants: the performative effects of bully discourses for girls and boys in school. *British Educational Research Journal*, 36 (4): 573–596.

Rizvi, F. (1993) Children and the grammar of popular racism, in C. McCarthy and W. Crichlow (eds) *Race, Identity, and Representation in Education*. New York and London: Routledge.

Robinson, K.H. (2002) Making the invisible visible: gay and lesbian issues in early childhood education, *Contemporary Issues in Early Childhood*, 3(3): 415–434.

Robinson, K.H. (2005a) Reinforcing hegemonic masculinities through sexual harassment: issues of identity, power and popularity in secondary schools, *Gender and Education*, 17(1): 19–37.

Robinson, K.H. (2005b) Childhood and sexuality: adult constructions and silenced children, in J. Mason and T. Fattore (eds) *Children Taken Seriously: In Theory, Policy and Practice*. London: Jessica Kingsley.

Robinson, K.H. (2005c) 'Queerying' gender: heteronormativity in early childhood education, *Australian Journal of Early Childhood*, 30(2): 19–28.

Robinson, K.H. (2005d) Doing anti-homophobia and anti-heterosexism in early childhood education. Moving beyond the immobilizing impacts of 'risk', 'fears' and 'silences'. Can we afford not to? *Contemporary Issues in Early Childhood Education*, 6(2): 175–188.

Robinson, K.H. (2012) Sexual harassment in schools: issues of identity and power – negotiating the complexities, contexts and contradictions of this everyday practice, in S. Saltmarsh, K.H. Robinson and C. Davies (eds) *Rethinking School Violence: Theory, Gender, Context*. London: Palgrave Macmillan.

Robinson, K.H. (2013) *Innocence, Knowledge and the Construction of Childhood: The Contradictory Nature of Sexuality and Censorship in Children's Contemporary Lives*. London: Routledge.

Robinson, K.H. and Davies, C. (2008) Docile bodies and heteronormative moral subjects: constructing the child and sexual knowledge in schools, *Sexuality and Culture*, 12(4): 221–239.

Robinson, K.H. and Davies, C. (2010) Tomboys and sissy girls: exploring girls' power, agency and female relationships in childhood through the memories of women, *Australian Journal of Early Childhood* (special edition: Childhood and Sexuality), 35(1): 24–31.

Robinson, K.H. and Davies, C. (2015) Children's gendered and sexual cultures: desiring and regulating recognition through life markers of marriage, love and relationships, in E. Renold, J. Ringrose and D.R. Egan (eds) *Children, Sexuality & Sexualization*. London: Palgrave: 174–190.

Robinson, K.H. and Ferfolja, T. (2001) 'What are we doing this for?' Dealing with lesbian and gay issues in teacher education, *British Journal of Sociology of Education*, 22(1): 121–133.

Robinson, K.H. and Jones Díaz, C. (1999) Doing theory with early childhood educators: understanding difference and diversity in personal and professional contexts. *Australian Journal of Early Childhood*, 24(4): 33–41.

Robinson, K.H. and Jones Díaz, C. (2000) *Diversity and Difference in Early Childhood: An Investigation into Centre Policies, Staff Attitudes and Practices. A Focus on Long Day Care and Preschool in the South West and*

Inner West of Sydney. Newcastle, NSW: Roger A. Baxter, OAS Engineering Pty Ltd and University of Newcastle Research Associates – TUNRA Ltd.

Robinson, K.H., Bansel, P., Denson, N., Ovenden, G. and Davies, C. (2014) *Growing Up Queer: Issues Facing Young Australians Who Are Gender Variant and Sexuality Diverse*. Melbourne: Young and Well Cooperative Research Centre.

Romaine, S. (2013) The bilingual and multilingual community, in T.K. Bhatia and W.C. Ritchie (eds) *The Handbook of Multilingualism and Bilingualism*, 2nd edn. Oxford: Blackwell Publishing.

Rose, N. (1999) *Governing the Soul: The Reshaping of the Private Self*, 2nd edn. London: Free Association Books.

Russ, R. (2014) Vanishing. *National Geographic*, July: 60–87.

Saltman, K.J. (2009) Historical and theoretical perspectives, in W. Ayers, T. Quinn and D. Stovall (eds) *Handbook of Social Justice in Education*. New York: Routledge.

Saraceno, J. (2012) Mapping whiteness and coloniality in the human service field: possibilities for a praxis of social justice in child and youth care, *International Journal of Child, Youth and Family Studies*, 2/3: 248–271.

Saunders, P. (2011) *Down and Out: Poverty and Exclusion in Australia*. Bristol: Polity Press.

Sawicki, J. (1991) *Disciplining Foucault: Feminism, Power, and the Body*. New York: Routledge.

Sawrikar, P. and Katz, I. (2008) Enhancing family and relationship service accessibility and delivery in culturally and linguistically diverse families in Australia. Australian Family Relationships Clearinghouse (AFRC) Issues, No. 3. Available at: www.aifs.gov.au/cfca/publications/enhancing-family-and-relationship-service-accessibility-and (accessed 16 March 2016).

Scarino, A. (2014) Situating the challenges in current languages in education policy in Australia – unlearning monolingualism, *International Journal of Multilingualism*, 11(3): 289–306.

Schirato, T. and Yell, S. (2000) *Communication and Cultural Literacy: An Introduction*, 2nd edn. St Leonards, NSW: Allen & Unwin.

Schwartz, P. and Cappello, D. (2001) *Ten Talks Parents Must Have with their Children about Sex and Character*. Rydalmere: Hodder Headline Australia.

Secretariat of National Aboriginal and Islander Child Care (SNAICC) (2008) *Foster their Culture: Caring for Aboriginal and Torres Strait Islander Children*. North Fitzroy, Vic.: SNAICC.

Sedgwick, E.K. (1990) *Epistemology of the Closet*. Berkeley, CA: University of California Press.

Shiells, G. (2010) Immigration history and whiteness studies: American and Australian approaches compared, *History Compass*, 8(8): 790–804.

Silin, J. (1995) *Sex, Death and the Education of Children: Our Passion for Ignorance in the Age of AIDS*. New York: Teachers College Press.

Silin, J. (1997) The pervert in the classroom, in J. Tobin (ed.) *Making a Place for Pleasure in Early Childhood Education*. New Haven, CT: Yale University Press.

Silva, E.B. and Smart, C. (1999) The 'new' practices and politics of family life, in E.B. Silva and C. Smart (eds) *The New Family?* London: Sage Publications.

Simpson, D., Lumsden, E. and McDowall Clark, R. (2015) Neoliberalism, global poverty policy and early childhood education and care: a critique of local uptake in England, *Early Years*, 35(1): 96–109.

Simpson, J., Caffery, J. and McConvell, P. (2009) *Gaps in Australia's Indigenous Language Policy: Dismantling Bilingual Education in the Northern Territory*. AIATSIS research discussion paper no. 24, Canberra: Australian Institute of Aboriginal and Torres Strait Islander Studies.

Skattebol, J., Saunders, P., Redmond, G., Bedford, M. and Cass, B. (2012) *Making a Difference: Building on Young People's Experiences of Economic Adversity*. Sydney: Social Policy Research Centre, University of New South Wales.

Sklair, L. (2015) The sociology of the global system, in F.J. Lechner and J. Boli (eds) *The Globalization Reader*, 5th edn. West Sussex: John Wiley & Sons Ltd.

Sleeter, C. (2011) An agenda to strengthen culturally responsive pedagogy, *English Teaching: Practice and Critique*, 10(2): 7–23.

Smith, E., Jones, T., Ward, R., Dixon, J., Mitchell, A. and Hillier, L. (2014) *From Blues to Rainbows. Mental Health and Wellbeing of Gender Diverse and Transgender Young People in Australia*. Melbourne: Australian Research Centre in Sex, Health, and Society.

Smock, P.J. and Greenland, F.R. (2010) Diversity in pathways to parenthood: patterns, implications, and emerging research directions, *Journal of Marriage and Family*, 72(3): 576–593.

Spender, D. (1983) *Women of Ideas (And What Men Have Done to Them)*. London: Ark Paperbacks.

Spivak, G.C. (1990) *The Post-colonial Critic: Interviews, Strategies, Dialogues*. New York: Routledge.

Spivak, G.C. (1999) *A Critique of Postcolonial Reason: Toward a History of the Vanishing Present*. Cambridge, MA: Harvard University Press.

Stark, J. (2014) Calls to help sex-change kids as demand for gender reassignment soars, *Sydney Morning Herald*, 6 July. Available from: www.smh.com.au/national/calls-to-help-sexchange-kids-as-demand-for-gender-reassignment-soars-20140705-zsvz7.html (accessed 16 February 2015).

Statistica (2016) Video game industry – statistics and facts. Available at: www.statista.com/topics/868/video-games/ (accessed 8 January 2015).

Stein, G. (2015) Nauru rape case: police 'stopped off to watch firework show' before ferrying Iranian asylum seeker to station, ABC *Lateline*. Available at: www.abc.net.au/news/2015-10-21/alleged-shortfalls-in-treatment-of-nauru-rape-victim/6872582 (accessed 8 December 2015).

Steinberg, S. (ed.) (2011) *Kinderculture: The Corporate Construction of Childhood*, 3rd edn. Boulder, CO: Westview Press.

Steinberg, S. and Kincheloe, J.L. (1997) *Kinderculture. The Corporate Construction of Childhood*. Boulder, CO: Westview Press.

Stiglitz, J.E. (2015) Globalism's discontents, in F.J. Lechner and J. Boli (eds) *The Globalization Reader*, 5th edn. West Sussex: John Wiley & Sons Ltd.

Stone Fish, L. and Harvey, R.G. (2005) *Nurturing Queer Youth*. New York: W.W. Norton & Co.

Stratton, J. and Ang, E. (1998) Multicultural imagined communities: cultural difference and national identity in the USA and Australia, in D. Bennett (ed.) *Multicultural States: Rethinking Difference and Identity*. London: Routledge.

Stryker, S. (2008) *Transgender History*. Berkeley, CA: Seal Press.

Sullivan, N. (2003) *A Critical Introduction to Queer Theory*. New York: New York University Press.

Sumner, A. (2010) *Global Poverty and the New Bottom Billion: What if Three-quarters of the World's Poor Live in the Middle-income Countries?* IDS working paper no. 349. Sussex: Institute of Development Studies.

Sumsion, J. and Wong, S. (2011) Interrogating 'belonging' in belonging, being and becoming: the early years learning framework for Australia, *Contemporary Issues in Early Childhood*, 12(1): 28–45.

Surtees, N. (2005) Teacher talk about and around sexuality in early childhood education: deciphering an unwritten code, *Contemporary Issues in Early Childhood*, 6(1): 19–29.

Surtees, N. (2006) Difference and diversity: 'talk the talk', 'walking the talk' and the spaces between, *International Journal of Equity and Innovation in Early Childhood*, 4(2): 49–65.

Surtees, N. and Gunn, A. (2010) (Re)marking heteronormativity: resisting practices in early childhood education contexts, *Australasian Journal of Early Childhood*, 35(1): 42–47.

Taylor, A. (2007) Innocent children, dangerous families and homophobic panic, in G. Morgan and S. Poynting (eds) *Outrageous: Moral Panics in Australia*. Hobart: Australian Clearing House for Youth Studies.

Taylor, A. (2010) Troubling childhood innocence: reframing the debate over the media sexualisation of children, *Australasian Journal of Early Childhood*, 35(1): 48–57.

Taylor, A. and Richardson, C. (2005) Queering home corner, *Contemporary Issues in Early Childhood*, 6(2): 163–173.

Taylor, E. (2009) The foundations of critical race theory in education: an introduction, in E. Taylor, D. Gillborn and G. Ladson-Billings (eds) *The Foundations of Critical Race Theory in Education*. New York: Routledge.

Taylor, T. (2011) Re-examining cultural contradictions: mothering ideology and the intersections of class, gender, and race, *Sociology Compass*, 5(10): 898–907.

Tazreiter, C. (2010) Local to global activism: the movement to protect the rights of refugees and asylum seekers, *Social Movement Studies*, 9(2): 201–214.

Theilheimer, R. and Cahill, B. (2001) A messy closet in the early childhood classroom, in S. Grieshaber and G.S. Cannella (eds) *Embracing Identities in Early Childhood Education: Diversity and Possibilities*. New York: Teachers College Press.

Thorne, B. (1993) *Gender Play: Boys and Girls in School*. Buckingham: Open University Press.

Thorne, B. (2005) Unpacking school lunchtime, in C.R. Cooper, C. Garcia Coll, T. Bartko *et al.* (eds) *Rethinking Diversity and Contexts as Resources for Children's Development*. Hillsdale, NJ: Lawrence Erlbaum.

Tierney, W. (2004) Globalization and educational reform: the challenges ahead, *Journal of Hispanic Higher Education*, 3(1): 5–20.

Tierney, W. (2015) Education's role in the elimination of poverty in the twenty-first century, in W. Tierney (ed.) *Rethinking Education and Poverty*. Baltimore, MD: Johns Hopkins University Press.

Tomsen, S. (2002) *Hatred, Murder and Male Honour: Anti-homophobia Homicides in New South Wales, 1980–2000*. Canberra: Australian Institute of Criminology.

Trask, B.H. (2010) *Globalization and Families: Accelerated Systemic Social Change*. New York: Springer.

Troyna, B. and Hatcher, R. (1992) *Racism in Children's Lives: A Study of Mainly White Primary Schools*. London: Routledge.

Tuffin, K. (2008) Racist discourse in New Zealand and Australia: reviewing the last 20 years, *Social and Personality Psychology Compass*, 2(2): 591–607.

United Nations Association of Australia (2015a) The global response to the refugee crisis. Available at: www.unaa.org.au/2015/09/the-global-response-to-the-refugee-crisis (accessed 4 December 2015).

United Nations Association of Australia (2015b) UNHCR: total number of Syrian refugees exceeds four million for first time. Available at: www.unhcr.org/559d67d46.html (accessed 11 December 2015).

United Nations High Commissioner of Refugees (2014) *UNHCR Statistical Yearbook 2014: Displacement Levels and Trends*. Available at: www.unhcr.org/56655f4b19.html (accessed 10 December 2015).

Uprichard, E. (2008) Children as 'being and becomings': children, childhood and temporality, *Children and Society*, 22(4): 303–313.

US Census Bureau (2010) Households and families: 2010 census briefs. Available at: www.census.gov/newsroom/releases/archives/2010_census/cb12-68.html (accessed 16 March 2016).

Usher, R. and Edwards, R. (1994) *Postmodernism and Education*. London: Routledge.

Valdés, G. (1996) *Con Respeto. Bridging the Distances between Culturally Diverse Families and Schools: An Ethnographic Portrait*. New York: Teachers College Press.

Valencia, R.R. (2010) *Dismantling Contemporary Deficit Thinking: Educational Thought and Practice*. New York: Routledge.

Vandewater, E.A., Rideout, V.J., Wartella, E.A., Xuan Huang, X., Lee, J.H. and Shim, M. (2007) Digital childhood: electronic media and technology use among infants, toddlers and pre-schoolers, *Pediatrics*, 119: 1006–1015.

Vass, G. (2010) The racialised educational landscape in Australia: listening to the whispering elephant, *Race Ethnicity and Education*, 17(2): 176–201.

Vertovec, S. (2007) Super-diversity and its implications, *Ethnic and Racial Studies*, 30(6): 1024–1054.

Vertovec, S. (2010) Towards post-multiculturalism? Changing conditions, communities and contexts of diversity, *International Social Science Journal*, 61: 83–95.

Vertovec, S. and Cohen, R. (1999) Introduction, in S. Vertovec and R. Cohen (eds) *Migration, Diasporas and Transnationalism*. Cheltenham: Edward Elgar.

Villenas, S. and Deyhle, D. (1999) Critical race theory and ethnographies. Challenging the stereotypes: Latino families, schooling, resilience and resistance, *Curriculum Inquiry*, 29(4): 413–445.

Vincent, C. (2010) The sociology of mothering, in M.W. Apple, S.J. Ball and L.A. Gandin (eds) *The Routledge International Handbook of the Sociology of Education*. New York: Routledge.

Vincent, C. and Martin, J. (2002) Class, culture and agency. Researching parental voice, *Discourse: Studies in Cultural Politics and Education*, 23(1): 109–128.

Viruru, R. and Cannella, G. (2006) A postcolonial critique of the ethnographic interview: research analyzes research, in N.K. Denzin and M.D. Giardina (eds) *Qualitative Research and the Conservative Challenge: Confronting Methodological Fundamentalism*. Walnut Creek, CA: Left Coast Press.

Volk, D. (1997) Continuities and discontinuities: teaching and learning in the home and school of a Puerto Rican five year old, in E. Gregory (ed.) *One Child, Many Worlds: Early Learning in Multicultural Communities*. London: David Fulton.

Vygotsky, L. (1978) *Mind in Society: The Development of Higher Psychological Processes*. Collection and trans. of original texts, ed. M. Cole. Cambridge, MA: Harvard University Press.

Wade, R. (2001) Showdown at the World Bank, *New Left Review* (second series), 7: 124–137.

Walkerdine, V. (1990) *School Girl Fictions*. London: Verso.

Walkerdine, V. and Bansel, P. (2010) Neoliberalism, work and subjectivity: towards a more complex account, in M. Wetherell and C. Talpade Mohanty (eds) *The Sage Handbook of Identities*. London: Sage Publications Ltd.

Wallis, A. and VanEvery, J. (2000) Sexuality in the primary school, *Sexualities*, 3(4): 409–423.

Walsh, J. (2008) Navigating globalization: immigration policy in Canada and Australia, 1945–2007, *Sociological Forum*, 23(4): 786–813.

Waters, M. (1995) *Globalization*, 2nd edn. New York: Routledge.

Watkins, M. (2015) Culture, hybridity and globalization: rethinking multicultural education in schools, in T. Ferfolja, C. Jones Díaz and J. Ullman (eds) *Understanding Sociological Theory and Pedagogical Practices*. Cambridge: Cambridge University Press.

Way, N. (1997) . . . and the poor get more numerous, *Business Review Weekly*, May.

Webb, J., Schirato, T. and Danaher, G. (2002) *Understanding Bourdieu*. Sydney: Allen & Unwin.

Weedon, C. (1997) *Feminist Practice and Poststructuralist Theory*, 2nd edn. Oxford: Blackwell.

Weeks, J. (1986) *Sexuality*. London: Routledge.

Weeks, J. (1998) The sexual citizen, *Theory, Culture and Society*, 15(3/4): 35–52.

Weeks, J., Heaphy, B. and Donovan, C. (2001) *Same Sex Intimacies: Families of Choice and Other Life Experiments*. London: Routledge.

Wells, K. (2015) *Childhood in a Global Perspective*, 2nd edn. Cambridge: Polity Press.

Wilton, T. (1996) Which one's the man? The heterosexualisation of lesbian sex, in D. Richardson (ed.) *Theorising Heterosexuality*. Buckingham: Open University Press.

Wong Fillmore, L. (1991) When learning a second language means losing the first, *Early Childhood Research Quarterly*, 6: 323–347.

Wright, T. (2011) Tell me lies: confronting the pre-school closet, *Journal of Cases in Educational Leadership*, 14(2): 1–7.

Wulf, C. (2002) *Educational Anthropology*. Münster and New York: Lit.

Wulf, C. (2011) Mimesis in early childhood: enculturation, practical knowledge and performativity, in M. Kontopodis, C. Wulf and B. Fichtner (eds) *Children, Development and Education: Cultural, Historical, Anthropological Perspectives*. Springer: Dordrecht: 89–102.

Young, R.J.C. (1990) *White Mythologies: Writing History and the West*. London: Routledge.

Young, R.J.C. (1995) *Colonial Desire. Hybridity in Theory, Culture and Race*. London: Routledge.

Young, R.J.C. (2001) *Postcolonialism: An Historical Introduction*. Oxford: Blackwell.

Zeus, L. (2015) Poverty in education and the social sciences, in W. Tierney (ed.) *Rethinking Education and Poverty*. Baltimore, MD: Johns Hopkins University Press.

Zevenbergen, R. (2007) Digital natives come to preschool: implications for early childhood practice, *Contemporary Issues in Early Childhood*, 8(1): 19–29.

Glossary

Affirmative action Policies and formal programmes developed to redress past discrimination and structural inequalities through the preferential treatment of disadvantaged groups.

Agency The power of the individual to actively participate in the construction of her/his self through the process of subjectification.

Assimilation A process by which immigrants are expected to adopt the language, culture, religion and values of the dominant group by surrendering their own language, culture and religious values.

Authoritative knowledge The privileging of certain knowledge and understandings as being representative of ultimate 'truth'.

Binary Two opposite terms defined against each other, generally representative of a hierarchical power relationship in which one is subordinated to the other – for example, the binaries of male/female, adult/child, Western/Eastern, mind/body.

Biological determinism A perspective that considers one's identity, behaviours and actions as being fundamentally determined by biology.

Capitalism An economic system that has prevailed since the Industrial Revolution in the eighteenth century, which has impacted on the structure of social relations of power operating in society. It is an economic system that is based primarily on private ownership of property and on private enterprise; it perpetuates notions of individualism, competition, supply and demand, the profit motive and neoliberalism.

Constructionism A perspective that considers identity as being historically and socially constructed across different cultures, rather than being essentialized in human biology.

Cultural capital A set of resources such as knowledge, language and literacy practices, which has value in a particular cultural field. It includes representational and symbolic knowledge systems. Like other forms of capital (for example, economic and social capital) it accumulates social power, and can be exchanged and distributed across various social fields.

Deconstruction A process of critical analysis that focuses on investigating the cultural and political meanings hidden in texts, which are representative of broader social relations of power.

Diaspora Signifies the movements of groups of people from an original 'home' to many other locations, and the networks of affiliation that are formed between these communities (Grewal and Kaplan 2002: 458).

Essentialism The perspective that characteristics of persons or groups are largely similar in all human cultures and historical periods, as they are fundamentally influenced by biological factors.

Ethnocentrism The perception that one's own culture is superior to another.

Field A social context that authorizes specific social practices, which can determine and regulate what constitutes cultural, social and economic capital.

Gender equity Aims for legal, social, political and economic equality between males and females.

Globalization Merges systems of finance, trade, labour, production, consumption, services, media, cultural practices, communication technologies and transport across multiple and global sites of economic, cultural, social and political fields.

Habitus A set of dispositions to act and think in certain ways, which is influenced by one's cultural pathways – that is, practices, habits, perceptions and attitudes generated in early childhood socialization.

Hegemony Stemming from the works of the Italian Marxist, Antonio Gramsci (1891–1937), the concept refers to the way that one powerful social group imposes its particular perspectives, beliefs, or political and economic conditions upon another.

Heteronormativity The way that everyday interactions, practices and policies construct individuals as heterosexual; this process of 'compulsory heterosexuality', as termed by Adrienne Rich (1980), is integral to the way that heterosexuality is normalized and naturalized, and non-heterosexual relationships are rendered deviant, abnormal and unnatural.

Heterosexism The belief that heterosexuals are superior to non-heterosexual identities. This perspective is demonstrated through the exclusion of non-heterosexual subjects in policies, curricula, events and activities.

Homophobia The prejudice, discrimination, harassment or acts of violence against sexual minorities, such as gays and lesbians, or those perceived by others to be gay or lesbian, based on the non-conformist ways in which they act as boys and girls, men and women. Homophobia is generally used as a term that encompasses the experiences of lesbians, but it is important to identify *lesbophobia* as it is often silenced and marginalized in this overarching term.

Hybridity A two-way borrowing and lending between cultures, which involves fusion and the creation of a new form.

Identity The social categories of the subject – that is, 'race', class, gender, sexuality, ethnicity and so on.

Ideology Stemming from the philosophy of Karl Marx, the nineteenth-century German political and economic philosopher, ideology refers to a system of beliefs or ideas perpetuated by dominant classes and imposed on less powerful people, which influences their perspectives and outlooks on the world.

Imperialism A policy of expansion where one country exerts its power and domination over another, taking over its territory, and controlling its social, political and economic life.

Individualism The perspective that the interests of the independent, unique individual ought to be paramount.

Intersectionality The importance of recognizing the multiplicity of identity – for example, the way that sexism, lesbophobia and racism intersect in the lives of lesbian women of colour.

Islamophobia A form of xenophobia (exaggerated fear of foreigners) that demonizes Muslims as terrorists, and espouses hatred and hostility towards Islam, which is often produced by the media in the form of cultural stereotypes.

Lesbophobia The prejudice, discrimination, harassment or acts of violence against lesbians, or those perceived by others to be lesbian, based on the nonconformist ways they act as girls or women.

Liberalism A political and social philosophy that stresses the rights and freedoms of the individual.

Linguicism Ideologies, structures and practices that are used to legitimate, effectuate, regulate and reproduce an unequal division of power and resources (both material and non-material) between groups that are defined on the basis of language (on the basis of the mother tongues) (Skutnabb-Kangas 1988: 42).

Linguistic capital Language resources, including speech, communication and utterances, that have the potential to accumulate social power in particular cultural fields in which they are legitimized and authorized.

Linguistic habitus Linguistic utterances, behaviours, expressions and interactions are produced in the linguistic habitus. Derived from Bourdieu's (1990; 1991), concept of habitus, this includes the dispositions, practices and perceptions in the various technologies and articulations of speech, language and communication that are adapted to and reproduced in the requirements of a given social situation.

Linguistic market The social situation or field where the value or 'price formation' of the linguistic utterance is determined by rules and regulations operating within a given situation.

Neoliberalism Involves the transformation of social relations through modes of political and economic rationality that are characterized by hyper-individualism, privatization, deregulation and withdrawal of the state from the common good. It includes political-economic practices that propose the advancement of well-being within instructional frameworks through entrepreneurial freedoms and skills characterized by free markets, free trade and private property rights. Neoliberalism operates as a global capitalist enterprise (Walkerdine and Bansel 2010) and is a worldwide phenomenon.

Oppression The exploitation, marginalization, violence, cultural imperialism and powerlessness experienced by individuals and groups.

Other This term relates to those groups that have been marginalized, silenced, denigrated or violated, and defined in opposition to, and seen as other than, the privileged and powerful groups that are identified as representing the idealized, mythical norm in society.

Postcolonial A term used to refer to the period following formal European colonization; however, it can also depict the continuing influence and power of the former colonizers over the economies and cultures of decolonized states (Grewal and Kaplan 2002).

Postmodernism A late 1960s cultural movement originally associated with the arts, architecture and music. In more recent times it has been incorporated into the humanities and social sciences, questioning the humanist focus on universalism and human progress. Grewal and Kaplan (2002: 290) indicate that, in the arts, this movement resulted in 'the rejection of the idea of newness and individual genius in favour of inquiring into methods and styles of the past'. In the humanities and social sciences, this perspective 'led to questioning the dominant narratives produced in the West and to decentering the powerful centres of knowledge and culture'.

Poststructuralism A perspective that emerged in the 1970s in response to the universal systems proposed by an earlier movement, structuralism. Structuralism, based on universalizing classifications of human society and culture, influenced the modern disciplines of social sciences (for example, sociology and anthropology) and the humanities. Poststructuralism argues that there is no one universal structural system that can apply to every place, culture and time, and that universal explanations or one dominant view leads to the suppression or invisibility of important differences (Grewal and Kaplan 2002). It questions the possibility of objectivity of authoritative knowledge, on which individual subjects construct their 'truths' about the world.

Reflexivity Individual awareness of one's own biases and prejudices, which underpin the way one operates in the world.

Social reproduction The process through which the social order and hierarchies of power are perpetuated through institutions such as the family, schools and the military.

Stereotype A set of behaviours or qualities that are believed to be fixed and unchanging, and that influence the way that one thinks about a group or person.

Subjectivity Encompasses the unconscious and conscious thoughts and emotions of the individual, or one's sense of self and how one relates to the world. In Foucauldian terms, subjectivity is constituted in discourses.

Superdiversity Captures new and increasing social formations that mark the intersections of ethnicity and cultural practices with power variables that are influenced by intensified and integrated global labour markets, free market trade agreements, technological advancement, free flow of labour movements across borders, international political instability and conflict. Diverse and fluid gendered practices, sexual diversity, religious practices and changing family structures are characteristic features of superdiverse postmulticultural societies.

Transgender An umbrella term used to describe people whose gender identity is different from the sex assigned to them at birth. An example is a child who is assigned a male sex at birth but actually feels more comfortable living as a girl and identifies as female. Sometimes trans people change their name and/or clothes, or even make changes to their bodies.

Translanguaging Encompasses the multiple linguistic repertories used in purposeful ways by bi/multilingual individuals and communities to maximize communicative potential across diverse social, cultural and linguistic contexts. It goes beyond conceptualizing the use of languages in separate contexts to include hybrid language practices where the mixing of languages is used for meaning making, strategic and communicative purposes.

Transphobia A term used to describe a range of negative feelings or behaviours towards anyone who is transgender or gender diverse, which often leads to prejudice or discriminatory actions or abuse.

Whiteness A social and historical construct that privileges white normative identities through its invisibility. It is taken for granted and evades scrutiny by remaining an unmarked identity, which is in contrast to other identities such as blackness and brownness, which are 'marked' identities. Whiteness functions through discourses of racism and cultural homogenization.

Index

Robinson, Kerry H. xi–xii
  childhood, changing worlds and
      constructions of 48, 49, 51, 54, 55, 57,
      58, 59, 62, 63, 64
  developmental theory, challenges to 130
  diversity, difference and 1, 5, 6, 7, 8, 9, 22,
      24, 25, 237, 250
  families, changing nature of 83, 87
  gender in early childhood 195, 196, 197, 199,
      206, 207
  sexuality and childhood 213, 214, 219, 220,
      221, 222, 223, 224, 225, 226, 229, 231, 233
Robinson, K.H. and Davies, C. 53, 54
  gender in early childhood 189, 196, 204,
      207, 209
  sexuality and childhood 213, 214, 219, 221,
      222–3, 226
Robinson, K.H. and Ferfolja, T. 7
Robinson, K.H. and Jones Díaz, C. 7, 8, 27, 42, 56
  critical multiculturalism 129, 138
  gender in early childhood 190, 201
  indigeneity 93, 104, 107–8
  languages, identities and 149, 153, 154
  sexuality and childhood 213, 230
Robinson, K.H., Bansel, P., Denson, N.,
    Ovenden, G. and Davies, C. 83
  gender in early childhood 191–2, 193, 199,
      200
Romaine, S. 143
romanticization of childhood 50
Rose, N. 57
Russ, R. 144

safe places
  provision of 111–12
  significance of 105–6
Saltman, K.J. 173
Saraceno, J. 131
Sarkozy, Nicolas 117
Saunders, P. 180
Sawicki, J. 15, 42, 43
Sawrikar, P. and Katz, I. 85
Scarino, A. 143, 154
Schirato, T. and Yell, S. 21
Schwartz, P. and Cappello , D. 220
science
  scientific racism 94–5
  scientific 'truths' 10–11
  social inquiry, detached and 'value free'
    science as model for 10
Secretariat of National Aboriginal and Islander
    Child Care (SNAICC) 94, 103, 142
Sedgwick, E.K. 216, 232
'self'
  construction under consumerism of 170–71
  feminist poststructuralism, childhood
    educators and 29–30

gender and, development of perspectives
    about 222
self-esteem, preoccupation with 155
self-insemination 79
sex roles, critique of socialization theory
    and 193–4
sexual citizenship 213, 214, 223–4
sexual identities
  'choice' in, notions of 215
  feminist poststructuralism and 214–15, 219
  queer theory and 215–16, 219
  sex-gender binary system, constitution
    of 192–3
  theoretical perspectives on 214–18
sexual orientation, gender performances in
    childhood and 207
sexual others, invisibility of 231–3
sexual predators, indigenous men as 97
sexual subjectivities
  intersections with 214
  socio-cultural construction of 213, 220–23
sexual violence 85–6
sexuality, childhood and 24–5, 213–36
  adulthood and childhood, oppositional
    understanding of 218
  biological determinism 216–17
  compulsory heterosexuality 231–3
  Department of Education, Employment
    and Workplace Relations (DEEWR,
    Australia) 234
  Early Years Learning Framework Australia
    (EYLFA) 234
  family life, ideal norms of 224
  feminist poststructuralism, sexual identities
    and 214–15
  gay and lesbian equity issues 231
  heteronormativity in early
    education 221–2, 226–8
  heteropolarity 220
  heterosexism in early childhood
    settings 228–31
  heterosexual desire, normalization of
    construction of 227–8
  heterosexuality, 'public' voice' and 230
  History of Sexuality (Foucault, M.) 215
  homophobia in early childhood
    settings 228–31
  innocence, sexuality, childhood and 218–20
  institutionalized heterosexuality 227
  knowledge building 222
  latent sexuality 218
  Learn to Include (Harding, V.) 235
  love, family and social relationships,
    centrality of 224
  marriage, concept of 222–3
  normative sexual subject, constitution
    of 215